JAMES HOUSTON

ALIVE TO GOD

Studies in Spirituality

presented to
James Houston

Edited by
J. I. PACKER &
LOREN WILKINSON

INTERVARSITY PRESS
DOWNERS GROVE, ILLINOIS 60515

InterVarsity Press® is the book-publishing division of InterVarsity Christian Fellowship®, a student movement active on campus at hundreds of universities, colleges and schools of nursing in the United States of America, and a member movement of the International Fellowship of Evangelical Students. For information about local and regional activities, write Public Relations Dept., InterVarsity Christian Fellowship, 6400 Schroeder Rd., P.O. Box 7895, Madison, WI 53707-7895.

ISBN 0-8308-1767-0

Computer typeset by Tyler F. Williams
Printed in the United States of America ∞

Library of Congress Cataloging-in-Publication Data

Alive to God: studies in spirituality presented to James M. Houston/
    edited by J. I. Packer and Loren Wilkinson.
        p.   cm.
    In honor of James M. Houston, on his 70th birthday.
    ISBN 0-8308-1767-0
    1. Spirituality.   2. Spirituality—History.   I. Houston, J. M.
(James Macintosh), 1922-   .   II. Packer, J. I. (James Innell)
III. Wilkinson, Loren.
BV4501.2.A334   1992
248—dc20   92-31340
                                                        CIP

17   16   15   14   13   12   11   10   9   8   7   6   5   4   3   2   1
05   04   03   02   01   00   99   98   97   96   95   94   93   92

Contents

Acknowledgments

The editors wish to thank: the staff at InterVarsity Press for their keen interest and assistance with this project; Paul Stevens, Academic Dean at Regent College, for significant help early on in the process; Tyler Williams, a recent Regent graduate, who rendered yeoman service in typesetting, layout, and other practical matters; and Dal Schindell, Director of Publications at the College, for his help in the late stages.

J. I. Packer
Loren Wilkinson

Part I
Preliminary & Perspectival

I

To James M. Houston, on His 70th Birthday

J. I. Packer & Loren Wilkinson

THIS COLLECTION OF ESSAYS IS A SEVENTIETH BIRTHDAY PRESENT to Dr. James Houston, founding principal of Regent College, Vancouver, B.C. Most of them have been written by his colleagues or former students; all of them are by persons who know him as a friend. And that is as it should be, for one of Dr. Houston's major achievements, both in his teaching and in his life, has been to deepen people's realization of what friendship can be—friendship with one another in Christ, and friendship through Christ with God the Father. Many, hearing Dr. Houston's name, will think at once of his God-given genius for friendship, both as peer and as counselor, before their mind moves on to anything else. A man, they say, is known by his friends, and the fact that these essayists are all Dr. Houston's friends surely reveals much about him, before anything further is said.[1]

Our hope is that these essays will not only honor but also in some small way delineate our friend Jim Houston. They will, we hope, do this by both their breadth and their depth.

For the first, they range across many academic disciplines—natural science, social science, history, theology, psychology, literature, education, ethics. We believe that this breadth pays fitting tribute to a man who was once an Oxford don teaching geography and afterwards became a professor first of interdisciplinary studies and then of Christian spirituality. His shift over the years from being a specialist to become a wide-ranging generalist, though a step down in the academic pecking order, was for him a step forward in the realizing of the full Christian humanism that we his friends here celebrate. No human concern is alien to Jim Houston, no field of endeavor escapes his notice, and from the beginning of Regent College's life he has been the main source and model of its integrative character.

As for depth, the common concern in all the essays is to show the deep-level links between each common discipline and life in Christ. Regent people recognize, largely because of Jim's influence, that Christians are called to live a unified life, with the triune God at the center of both our vocation and our spirituality, with all truth hailed as God's truth, and with every thought on every subject brought into captivity to Christ. Throughout his adult life Jim has combated compartmental living in the interest of his concern that Christians be "alive to God" in every sphere of thought and action. Hence the title of this book, and the glad cooperation of the 25 writers who have produced it, all of whom would affirm that because of Jim's friendship and vision they are more alive to God, one way or another, than they would have been without him.

The Man

James Houston was born in Edinburgh in 1922, but spent the first seven years of his life in Spain, where his parents worked as Exclusive Brethren missionaries. ("Exclusive" here means that they practiced church fellow-ship and communion at the Lord's Table only ever with their own kind.) Jim's colleagues at Regent have heard him speak of his father, a man of disciplined prayer and unyielding principle, but one who could not enter into the breadth and range of his son's intellectual interests and would complain that Jim seemed to be reading everything except the Bible. In fact, Jim entered fully into the family heritage of prayerful, Bible-based, Christ-centered godliness; his experience, however, of being a son to a father whom he deeply admired, yet who withheld basic approval, left him with inner wounds and frailties with which he took a long time coming to terms.

Graduation from Edinburgh University led to a job in town planning. Then a scholarship to study at Oxford came his way. Entering Brasenose College in 1945, he graduated in geography, researched in Spain for a doctorate, and became a teaching fellow of Hertford College, with prospects of becoming a professor in the English sense, that is, head of his academic department.

James Packer, who was in his second year at Oxford when Jim arrived, remembers him as already then in essence the man he has been since—quick and intuitive, with startling flashes of brilliance; warmhearted and energetic, with a gift of instant friendship and a strong instinct for pastoral care; earnest and articulate, with a flow of rhetoric that bent language in strange and memorable ways to his own purposes; and tireless as a personal evangelist, seeking to win souls. Then as now, he was all of a piece, seeing life whole, seeking God's glory in everything he did, and reaching out relationally right, left, and center with unquenchable good humor and steady joy. Then as now, he was the man of the flying idea and the dawning vision, more sensitive to sorrow and disappointment than most, but saved from self-pity by the strength of his hope in God. Academic books get bigger in successive editions as their argument is added to, and Jim Houston today is a bigger man than he was in Oxford 47 years ago. However, just as the argument of (for instance) Calvin's *Institutes* stayed the same for substance through successive enlargements from the first to the fifth edition, so Jim Houston seems, to at least one of his friends, to have grown spectacularly without changing very much at all.

Various forces were at work during Jim's years at Oxford shaping him for the future that God had planned. Certainly the most important was his marriage to Rita, another vintage Scot with a unique blend of down-to-earth insight, tender loving care, and a wit so sharp and mordant it could hurt were it not framed by so much kindness. Rita has described her relationship with Jim in terms of a hot air balloon show she once saw. The balloon soared up on the flame from its burner, and seemed to belong to the sky, but an unobtrusive rope held it firmly tied to a large Toyota on the ground. "I'm like that," said Rita to Loren Wilkinson; "I'm Jim's Toyota." None who know them both doubt the immense contribution that her godly, salty wisdom has made to all that Jim has accomplished.

A further force at work on Jim in Oxford was his broadening experience of Christian community. The narrowness of his upbringing among the Exclusive Brethren, which began to be transcended through theological coursework in Edinburgh, was finally dispelled through interdenominational fellowship, including committee work, in the Oxford Inter-Collegiate Christian Union, and church affiliation, including a venture in church planting, with Oxford's "open" Brethren. Rita tells of Jim, early in his days at Oxford, setting off on a motorbike to worship with the nearest group of "closed" (Exclusive) Brethren, some miles away. The bike broke down, so the rendezvous could not be kept, and the experience brought home to him that there were other believers in Oxford, closer at hand, with whom he might worship without displeasing God. Seeing beyond denominational differences to biblical essentials has been a mark of Jim's outlook ever since; he is the most ecumenical of evangelicals, and was later to insist on imparting his "transdenominational" stance to Regent College when others were envisaging a merely Brethren school.

It is very clear that Jim's goal, not only for himself but also for all Christians whom he nurtures, is global Christianity as such: a faith rooted in the absolutes of revelation that can address the marketplace of ideas, the kaleidoscope of cultures, and the clash of ideologies with vision, empathy and insight uncluttered by sectarian barriers. In this he may well have been reinforced by his contact as a don with C. S. Lewis, author of *Mere Christianity* and exponent of Christian fundamentals in many other works. Lewis excelled in presenting the Christian faith to the reason and imagination of the unchurched, and thus modelled the fact that the faith is best served when projected as truth and wisdom into secularity's dark jungles. Certainly, the Jim Houston of today is a mere Christianity man, whose mind homes constantly on the basics of the gospel; and it was his passion to equip lay people to speak and live the gospel in the modern secular city that eventually brought him and Rita to Vancouver to found Regent College.

Regent College

The little community that opened its doors in two hired rooms in 1970 was the kind of institution of which Jim Houston had long dreamed: a graduate school on a university campus with a solidly biblical basis of faith and a firmly evangelical faculty, with respect for, and interest in, every branch of learning and every problem that arises in developing and maintaining an authentically Christian mind. The story of Regent's start as the pioneer of a new kind of theological education, confessional more than professional and so structured as to integrate mind with heart as well as theology with other disciplines, has been told before, and the rapid growth and success of the school during its first two decades of life are familiar facts. The story is of a work of God through many gifted men and women. Essential to it, however, was and is Jim's unique combination of openness to God, breadth and depth of learning, ability to see old problems from new (and often disturbing) angles and to embody the new vision in memorable language, and willingness to make himself totally available to people—perhaps his rarest and most cherished gift of all. Regent could never have become what it is without him.

Vision for pioneering, rather than administration for maintaining, has always been Jim Houston's special strength; none need wonder, therefore, at Rita's candid appraisal: "Jim was God's man for starting the

College, but not for leading it on." When the Regent board created him chancellor (a title which he later laid aside) and took day to day leadership out of his hands, he found the transition hard; in this new role, however, he grew in his experience of God, and with that he plunged most fruitfully into study of the whole heritage of Christian spiritual life and teaching, on which his own courses of instruction at Regent and elsewhere now center. It may be that his opening up of this heritage to Protestants to whom it has been largely a closed book will prove to be Jim's greatest contribution to the life of the church. The editing of his series "Classics of Faith and Devotion," the production of his trilogy on relating to God, of which the first two items (*The Transforming Friendship* and *In Search of Happiness*) are in print already, with the third (*Desires of the Heart*) on the way, as well as his continued teaching in this field, are a legacy of enormous value. To perpetuate and extend that legacy, the Regent board, with contributions from many friends and former students, endowed Jim's professorship in 1991: following Jim's retirement, this post will be known as the James M. Houston Chair of Spiritual Theology.

But we do not look forward to your retirement, Jim, with any eagerness. We do not want to see your career close yet! Your supreme gift to us has been your bringing good news of God into our lives and the lives of very many others, and our hope is that you will be kept in health and strength to minister in this way to many more yet. Meantime, we ask you, mentor and friend as you are to so many of us, to accept these essays as a seventieth-birthday present to a scholar and teacher whom it is our delight thus to honor. Please continue to model for us what it means to be "alive to God": we need that. And we hope you will find something to enjoy in what the 25 of us have written.

Note

[1] Among the friends invited to contribute to this volume was the late Professor F. F. Bruce, who wrote: "My affection and esteem for Jim are such that in better times I'd have regarded it an honour to prepare a contribution .... As it is, however, I have just come out of the hospital ... and I don't feel equal to the task of writing a worthy contribution.... If there is to be a *tabula gratulantium*, I should be glad to have my name included." Professor Bruce died shortly after.

2

"Spiritual? Say It Isn't So!"

Carl F. H. Henry

IF IN AN EARLIER GENERATION PEOPLE SOMETIMES WERE SAID TO BE so heavenly-minded that they were of no earthly use, in our day the very opposite is more apt to be the case: they are so earthbound, it is said, that they are now alien to the spiritual world.

For all that, one reads and hears more and more about a current revival of interest in spirituality.

The Quest for Spirituality
Yet if one asks what spirituality is, one is likely to be met by a sidelong stare, as if this question would be raised only by a religious nincompoop, or could be answered by an assortment of examples without any clear definition.

To be sure, so we are told, spirituality has something to do with spirit, but just what is intended by spirit in this context is often obscure. Talk of spirituality will evoke such identifiers as the sacred, the religious, the transcendental, the charismatic, the saintly, the pious. Semantic multiplication does not stop there either. Verbally, all is fuzz.

However, spirituality is currently said to be "making a comeback." Several generations of Social Gospel activism and so-called political evangelism have failed to fulfill confident expectations of global utopia and have led instead to disillusionment with communism and socialism as political and economic ideologies. Meanwhile, experimental religion, reinforced by evangelistic crusades and television specials, has emphasized internal aspects of the religious life. To many listeners Christianity has seemed to offer a more intense subjective experience than the consciousness-exploding drug habit, since in its charismatic forms it dramatically bursts the bounds of universal linguistics and of conventional wisdom. At the very least it demands a new selfhood.

Other forms of inner religious vitality of the self-help variety have emerged here and there as ministries adjunct to churches and synagogues. People met, often in non-church contexts, to chronicle their victory over cigarette addiction, alcohol addiction and/or drug addiction. Even health-fad weight-loss programs gained an aura of religious virtue in some circles as sponsors emphasized Christian responsibility for bodily care and promoted evangelical aerobics.

Spirituality, of course, is antithetical to sensuousness and worldliness, yet the overcoming of some personal vices, commendable as it is, hardly qualifies as spirituality. One can abstain from certain personal evils yet be as unspiritual as someone who indulges in them. Spirituality has more to do with who or what one is and does than with what one isn't.

Many people today are confused over just who and what they are. During the hey-day of modernism, many persons were influenced by pantheistic or idealistic philosophies and decided that they were no longer sinners. The influx of pantheistic religions from the East carried them a step further. They decided, *mirabile dictu*, that they were secretly gods, or rather, secretly divine.

Experientially oriented religion readily confuses spirituality with the actualization of divinity supposedly lurking in one's own being and life. Divine revelation is blended into the best attainments of our human consciousness-potential. Revelation thus becomes the flip side of the inner spirit of humanity; its transcendent character and content are blurred into our own religious awareness. The historical and conceptual-propositional nature of special revelation is eclipsed; the distinctive Christian motifs are diluted instead into perspectives that the insightful self projects on the basis of one's own intimate experience with God.

Such misunderstandings actually have more in common with ancient Hinduism and Buddhism, and certain medieval mystics and their modern cultic dependencies, than with the Judeo-Christian heritage. It is one thing to recognize that God is the transcendent sovereign Creator and Preserver of a universe created *ex nihilo*, although all finite existence is confessedly now under divine wrath because of the ravages of sin, and quite another to view ultimate being as the all-inclusive Brahma or all-embracing Buddha of which we are constitutive parts. In the latter cases, in the depths of our being we are divine, finite aspects of deity, and hence not truly other than God.

Judaism in early New Testament times distinguished the earthly and merely human from the heavenly, speaking of the former as non-spiritual and the latter as spiritual. But the Greeks looked upon the eternal spiritual reality as hidden in man's psyche. By contrast, the apostle Paul emphasized the still future nature of our heavenly spiritual being, which he never confused with a conferring of divinity upon the creaturely.

Spirituality and the Spirit of God

Kittel's *Theological Dictionary of the New Testament* devotes 121 pages to the term "spirit" and related words, but anyone who thinks he can readily extract from this some clear illumination of the New Testament idea of spirituality is in for a surprise. Yet the discussion leaves no doubt that whoever does not have the Spirit of God is controlled by the spirits of this world, and that apart from the Spirit of God the heavenly things remain inaccessible to humans. The life-sustaining nurture of humanity in its created intention is supernatural and comes from God's realm, not humanity's. The key to a truly spiritual life remains the emphasis of Jesus at the outset of his public ministry, that "man does not live on bread alone, but on every word that comes from the mouth of God" (Mt 4:4).

Among the most striking aspects of the New Testament's illumination of the concept of spirituality, is its use of the word λογικός, sometimes translated "spiritual" (cf. 1Pe 2:2). The term belongs to the semantic field of λόγος, "word," and carries the sense of "rational." One finds here no implication whatever of theories that connect spirituality with the emotional and extra-rational, and regard the logical and rational as unspiritual.

Whoever infers from a reading of the New Testament that Christianity is less interested in the spirituality of humans than it is in a good and just society has, to be sure, not read very carefully. It is true that God focuses on life in community, and particularly on life in the church as a new society of faith, more than many evangelicals seem to recognize. But the main emphasis is that the regenerate church is not merely a humanitarian agency. It has a supernaturally given and supernaturally sustained life. Alongside the moral "fruit of the Spirit" intended for all believers (Gal 5:22), the diverse "spiritual gifts" found in the fellowship reflect the Spirit's presence and activity (1Co 12:11). The spiritual person is personally and individually aware that his final destiny is related to his personal decision, and is alert to the invisible immaterial realities—first and foremost deeply aware of God who is Spirit, and aware also of the existence of contingent spirits such as the unfallen angels, Satan and the demons. A truly spiritual person is not alien to such realities as a "spiritual house" and "spiritual sacrifices" (1Pe 2:5) and to "spiritual food" (1Co 10:3). To him it is the material world that is contingent; the spiritual world has ultimacy and priority.

That is not to say that anyone who discerns spirits and demons to be routinely at work, even where and when a Christian psychologist discerns none, should be hurriedly credited with spiritual insight. William Cartwright's invocation of St. Francis and St. Benedict to "bless this house . . . from all evil spiretes, Fairies, Wezeles, Bates, and Ferrytes [*sic*]" was no contribution to a biblical doctrine of the invisible spirit world. In striking contrast to the Near Eastern non-biblical religions with their multitudinous gods, and in contrast with the later Hellenic myths as well, the biblical writers show great numerical restraint in respect to the population of the spirit world; they know but one God, and one mediator between God and humanity.

Yet a Christian psychologist who thinks that we can adequately explain all the phenomena of the biblical theology and ethics without any reference whatever to demonic spirits and influences should reflect on the fact that Jesus depicted his own redemptive ministry as a conquest of Satan and of Satan's legions.

A spiritual person is no stranger to the fact that God is Spirit, and that only in spirit and in truth can he be truly and properly worshipped (Jn 4:24). Israel's neighbor-nations readily worshipped idols because of their confusion of nature and its workings with divinity. The Hebrews, by contrast, knew God to be immaterial and invisible.

The apostle Paul seems to imply that a life unfilled by the Holy Spirit is beneath the dignity of the Christian. The spiritual person is the Spirit-filled person. This essentially includes manifestation of the distinctive Christian virtues: love, joy, peace, longsuffering, kindness, goodness, faithfulness, gentleness and self-control (Gal 5:22-23). These phenomena are to flow from the believer's life as a spontaneous expression of the Spirit's presence and activity. Paul exhorts the Ephesian believers to be "filled with the Spirit" (5:18), indeed, to be continually filled and refilled.

The Imitation of Jesus Christ

For all that, the life of authentic spirituality would seem to include elements as yet unmentioned. Can a prayerless life truly be accounted a spiritual life? It is not the apostles alone who urged believers to devote abundant time to prayer, but Jesus also. Moreover, the Gospel accounts contain striking intimations that Jesus himself spent whole nights in prayer. No doubt Jesus' prayers, amid the haunting conflict of good and evil, and accompanied especially in the Garden of Gethsemane ("not what I will, but what you will," Mk 14:36) by anguished drops of blood, brought him needed strength for the extremes of torture and cruel death that awaited him on the threshold of his eternal reunion with the Father.

The Lord not only taught his disciples to pray, but he also left a pattern of petition that still richly serves his contemporary followers, even if all too often they reduce it to mere liturgical recitation.

F. W. Farrar comments in his elderly but classic *Life of Christ* that the "disciples' prayer," as it is preferably called,

> combines all that the heart of man, taught by the Spirit of God, had found most needful for the satisfaction of its truest aspirations. In the mingled love and reverence with which it teaches us to approach our Father in heaven—in the spirituality with which it leads us to seek first the kingdom of God and His righteousness,... in the manner in which it discountenances all the vain repetitions and extravagant self-tortures with which so many fanatical worshippers have believed that God could be propitiated ... it is, indeed, the pearl of prayers.[1]

Yet it is not only in respect to prayer that Jesus remains the superlative example of spirituality. In his unbroken and unreserved dedication to the will of the Father, in the active fullness of the Holy Spirit in his life, and in his constant awareness that the things of this world have even at their highest only a transitory and preparatory importance, he remains the model of Christian obedience throughout the ages. Material affluence is more a threat to spirituality than is destitution, though there is probably some truth to H. L. Mencken's comment that "poverty is a soft pedal upon all branches of a human activity, not excepting the spiritual."[2] Yet the Son of Man—born in a borrowed manger, buried in a borrowed tomb, and during his itinerant ministry often with no fixed place to lay his head—was never without access to his heavenly home.

It is on Jesus that the apostles focused supreme attention amid their determined efforts to live truly exemplary lives among the first Christians. "Follow my example, as I follow the example of Christ," Paul exhorts the Corinthians (1Co 11:1). Surely he does not have in view mechanical simulation or replication of externals. We do not fulfill his exhortation by travelling to the Holy Land and walking in the steps of the Master, or by visiting the ruins of the seven ancient churches of Asia Minor, or sharing in a summer Bible study cruise on the Mediterranean that follows the course of Paul's missionary journeys. The apostle Peter likewise did not have in view geographical considerations as much as ethical and theological concerns when he wrote that Christ "suffered for you, leaving you an example, that you should follow in his steps" (1Pe 2:21).

To be sure, in the years before the Gospels were written Paul sought so to emulate Jesus that the early Christian community would be spurred similarly in its life and walk to reflect the Risen Christ who indwelt both him and his converts. Yet nowhere does he enumerate a long specific agenda of Jesus' acts that we are to duplicate. There is moreover no self-exaltation in Paul's appeal to his own spiritual and moral example. His message is clear: it is Christ who is "head of the church" (Eph 5:23). It is "with Christ" that Paul reckons himself crucified; it is for Christ that he "considers everything a loss" (Php 3:8). It is Christ who "lives in" him (Gal 4:19), Christ who is to "dwell in your hearts" (Eph 3:17). It is to the "measure of the fullness of Christ" (Eph 4:13) that we are to aspire. We are even now to live as "risen with Christ" (Col 3:1), since "to be with Christ" is a prospect "better by far" than earthly life contains (Php 1:23).

God-Given, Not Human-Made

Theologians today do not write much about spirituality, preachers do not preach much about it, and churchgoers do not much practice it. In any case, spirituality is not something one practices as one might repeat the drilling of teeth to gain proficiency as a dentist. One does not become a professional spiritual. In that sense, it is not a matter of "having to work hard at it." It is not the nature of spirituality to be a mastered skill.

To be sure, the apostle John wrote that one who looks forward to the coming of Christ, in anticipation of that final destiny, "purifies himself, just as he is pure" (1Jn 3:3). Yet my impression is that a person never becomes habitually spiritual. Perhaps one might say, by way of under-statement, that "a little more spirituality might help," much as one speaks of another's humility (or lack of it). But would one really say of a spiritual friend that he or she is customarily spiritual?

Yet spirituality is a quality, indeed an excellence, that every believer ought to treasure and manifest. Spirituality flows spontaneously and mellifluously as an overflow of the Spirit's fullness. The Spirit's tran-scendent work in and through us will spare our neighbors from the misimpression that the deity we worship is a vague phantom too much like ourselves. We need to ask ourselves why the world around us has confused spirituality with sanctimoniousness, religiosity, and goody-goodiness. The world passes costly judgment on the church when, beholding what it misperceives to be spirituality, it privately mutters to itself, "Say it isn't so." True spirituality, however, will call forth a different reaction.

The eternal realms, not one's own resources, constitute the real supply-line for genuine spirituality. Heaven conspires with the longing heart to ready us for ultimate homecoming. Always in view is an undated invitation to dwell forever in a retirement home that is better than any this world offers, one that is unsurpassably pure. What makes heaven an exciting prospect to the spiritual Christian is that he or she has a foretaste, a sample, of the real thing. Some may think of heaven as, so to speak, a tourist stop, while regarding their present lodgings with all their material concerns as the preferred residency over which they simply cannot bring themselves mentally to hang a "for sale" sign. Spirituality, however, springs from a focusing of faith and hope on the invisible, eternal glories of the triune God in his heaven, and such focusing always makes its distinctive mark on us as we run our course here on earth.

Notes
1   F. W. Farrar, *Life of Christ* (London: Cassell, 1887) 214ff.
2   H. L. Mencken, *A Book of Prefaces* (1917; repr., Irvine, Calif.: Reprint Services Corporation, 1992) 4.3.

Part II
Biblical & Exegetical

3
The Fear of the Lord: The Foundation for a Relationship with God

Bruce K. Waltke

D<small>R. JAMES HOUSTON, REGENT COLLEGE'S DISTINGUISHED</small> founder and professor of spiritual theology, succinctly defined "the fear of the Lord" as a combination of a person's spiritual and rational responses to God's revealed will. He wrote: "'Fear of the Lord' expresses the knowledge of the will of God in that it entails both awareness of it and whole-hearted response to it."[1] He further noted in the same discussion on "living wisely before the Creator" that "fear, or reverence for God, is also associated with both distance as awe, even a holy terror, and with proximity and communion."[2] In this essay I aim to honor my dear friend and edify the church by honing the definition of the syntagms (a syntagm is a series of linguistic elements forming distinctive syntactic units)[3] that involve the Hebrew root ירא, "fear," + the direct objects "Lord" and "God," or their surrogates such as "Name," pronouns for the Deity, etc. For economy I will sometimes lump together these syntagms under the rubric "fear of the Lord." Though I did not set out to validate Dr. Houston's succinct statements about this linguistic formula, my essay in fact does so.

Expressions Involving "Fear of the Lord"[4]

One important syntagm is יִרְאַת יהוה, "the fear of the Lord," consisting of the feminine verbal noun יִרְאַת bound together with its objective genitive, יהוה. It occurs twenty-one or twenty-two times, mostly in wisdom literature: fourteen times in Proverbs,[6] thrice in Isaiah in parallel with other terms for wisdom,[7] three times in the hymns,[8] once in Chronicles in connection with Jehoshaphat's instructions to Israel's administrators,[9] and possibly, though not probably, once in Job 28:28 where many, but not the majority, of manuscripts attest it.

The Deuteronomic and Deuteronomistic literature uniformly uses a verbal form of ירא, typically the infinitive construct in Deuteronomy, with the direct object Yahweh or its surrogates, such as a pronoun or Name. This syntagm occurs thirty-three times in this literature,[10] and twenty-nine times outside of it.[11]

The so-called Holiness Code contains five occurrences of the syntagm "You will fear your God; I am Yahweh."[12]

The singular or plural verbal adjective, יְרֵא, in construct with Yahweh or its equivalents (i.e., "who fear Yahweh") occurs eighteen times.[13] H. F. Fuhs[14] arbitrarily takes the genitive in this construction as a possessive genitive (i.e., "the worshipers who belong to Yahweh," not "those who worship Yahweh"), but this is unlikely in light of the consistent use of Yahweh in the other expressions as an object of the verbal action "to fear." Also, construing it as an objective genitive is consistent with the use of the verb ירא with Yahweh as object in Ps 34:10, 86:11 and 130:4 and in other contexts pertaining to worship (e.g., Isa 63:17; Hos 10:3).

יִרְאַת אֱלֹהִים, "fear of God," or its surrogates, occurs seven times;[15] the verb ירא + אֱלֹהִים as direct object, "to fear God," twelve times;[16] and the verbal adjective of יְרֵא in construct with אֱלֹהִים, "who fear God," seven times.[17]

This data shows that this quintessential rubric, which expresses in a nutshell the basic grammar that holds the covenant community together, persists with remarkable regularity from the earliest to latest times. The English gloss, "fear the Lord," is really an inadequate rendering for this rubric because, while it denotes real fear, it fails to connote other essential nuances in the Hebrew phrase.

From Rudolf Otto's[18] description of the "holy," drawn from the history of religion, a model can be constructed that enables one both to understand and to explain the meaning of "fear of the Lord." To be sure, working as a comparative religionist, and not as an exegetical theologian, Otto[19] misconstrued the linguistic formula in the Old Testament to mean only numinous dread. Nevertheless, his descriptive study of the holy, as distinct from his dubious, conjectured history of its development, supplies insightful data from the broad field of religion for understanding the biblical expression "fear the Lord." Points of continuity between the history of religion and the religion of the Old

Testament are to be expected, but the remarkably close correlation between essential concepts in Otto's "idea of the holy" and the Old Testament "fear of the Lord" is unexpected and remarkable. Of course, "fear of the Lord" in the Old Testament also exhibits strong discontinuities with the pagan religions, because of Israel's distinctive faith. Otto's model contains three essential parts.

Rudolf Otto and the Idea of the Holy
The Distinction Between the Rational and the Non-rational
Otto commences his study by distinguishing between the rational, that which can be grasped by the mind, and the non-rational, the experience of God. The former pertains to belief, the latter to feeling; the former to universals, the latter to the moment; the former can be clearly grasped, the latter is inaccessible to our conceptual thought; the former is definable, the latter is not, though it is expressible. God in himself cannot be comprehended in merely logical statements about him; he must be experienced. Otto summarized his distinction thus:

> We began with the "rational" in the idea of God and the divine, meaning by that term that in it which is clearly to be grasped by our power of conceiving, and enters the domain of familiar and definable conceptions. We went on to maintain that beneath this sphere of clarity and lucidity lies a hidden depth, inaccessible to our conceptual thought, which we in so far call the "non-rational."[20]

The Hebrew term for the ineffable is קָדוֹשׁ, "holy," but that term does not serve Otto well because it may ambiguously also pertain to the rational, viz., to ethics, to moral purity. Therefore to express clearly the category he has in mind, Otto coins the word "numen," a term that means "holy" reality minus its rational and moral factors. This numen in connection with the human psyche can be said to be numinous. The numinous is felt as objective and outside the self. In the numinous Otto principally has in view "the creature feeling" of fear produced by the encounter with the mysterious, "the wholly other."

Although Otto merely pontificates the conjunction of "the holy" with "fear," it can be validated from the Old Testament. Fuhs noted:

> An internal association between holiness and numinous fear is documented in several passages: comparison of Ge 28:17 and Ex 3:5 [see also v. 6] shows that קָדוֹשׁ and נוֹרָא [glossed in English by "fearful," "terrible," "awesome"] are synonyms; ירא occurs in both contexts as an expression of numinous fear. Both appear in parallel in Ps 99:3; 111:9; cf. Ex 15:11; Ps 96:9; Isa 8:13; 29:23 . . . .[21]

The Dual Quality of the Numinous: Tremendum *and* Fascinans

Although the numinous is usually associated with that which is daunting, it strangely combines with it a pull of fascination. In Otto's analysis
of the *mysterium tremendum* he finds the elements of "awfulness," i.e.,
"absolute unapproachability"; of "majesty," i.e., "absolute over-
poweringness"; and of "energy" or "urgency." Concerning the first he
wrote:

> It has become a mystical awe, and set free as its accompaniment,
> reflected in self-consciousness, that "creature-feeling" that has already
> been described as the feeling of personal nothingness and submer-
> gence before the awe-inspiring object directly experienced.[22]

Concerning the last two, he said:

> Luther's *omnipotentia Dei* in his *De Servo Arbitrio* is nothing but the
> union of "majesty"—in the sense of absolute supremacy—with this
> "energy," in the sense of a force that knows not stint nor stay, which
> is urgent, active, compelling, and alive.[23]

But if the numinous repulses, inciting terror and dread on the one
hand, it also attracts, inciting love and trust on the other. Otto wrote:

> These two qualities, the daunting and the fascinating, now combine in
> a strange harmony of contrasts, and the resultant dual character of the
> numinous consciousness, to which the entire religious development
> bears witness . . . is at once the strangest and most noteworthy
> phenomenon in the whole history of religion.[24]

The numinous at one and the same time is not only something wondered
at but something that entrances, captivates, and transports with a strange
ravishment.   According to Otto: "Possession of and by the numen
becomes an end in itself; it begins to be sought for its own sake; and the
wildest and most artificial methods of asceticism are put into practice to
attain it."[25]

*The Schematization of the Numen, the Non-rational, by Ethos and
by Telos, the Rational*

As some ideas are inseparable, argued Otto, so also bi-polar religious
feelings have an inherent connection with the ethical.   Faith seeks
understanding, Anselm said. Otto observed in the history of religion:

> Almost everywhere we find the numinous attracting and appropriat-
> ing meanings derived from social and individual ideals of obligation,
> justice, and goodness. These become the "will" of the numen, and the
> numen their guardian, ordainer, and author.[26]

Otto calls this essential interconnectedness "schematization."[27] He
illustrates the notion by the essential connection of the category of
causality with its temporal "schema," the temporal sequence of two

successive events, which by being brought into connection with the category of causality is *known* and recognized as a causal relation of the two. He wrote:

> Now the relation of the rational to the non-rational element in the idea of the holy or sacred is just such a one of "schematization," and the non-rational numinous fact, schematized by the rational concepts ... yields us the complex category of "holy" itself, richly charged and complete and in its fullest meaning.[28]

The non-rational provides the warp of the holy, and the rational its weft. "We must always understand by it [the holy] the numinous completely permeated and saturated with elements signifying rationality, purpose, personality, morality," Otto summarized.[29] The sex instinct may be schematized by poetic expression, and the feelings of music by song; but these analogies fail because they are not necessary connections. "In every highly-developed religion," Otto wrote, "the appreciation of the moral obligation and duty, ranking as a claim of the deity upon man, has been developed side by side with the religious feeling itself."[30] The ethical schematizes the fearful aspect of the numinous, on the one hand, by the category of God's wrath against sin; and its attractive aspect, on the other hand, by the category of God's grace, including his goodness and love, promoting trust. According to Otto:

> The *tremendum*, the daunting and repelling moment of the numinous, is schematized by means of the rational ideas of justice, moral will, and the exclusion of what is opposed to morality; and schematized thus, it becomes the holy "wrath of God," which Scripture and Christian preaching alike proclaim. The *fascinans*, the attracting and alluring ideas of goodness, mercy and love, so schematized, becomes all that we mean by Grace.[31]

All three elements, the non-rational, the rational, and their interpenetration, make the woof of religion. They derive *a priori* from the human experience and are not *a posteriori* to it, though stimuli incite them. The rational and non-rational elements, however, though always present do not always carry the same weight. Sometimes the affectional, with its gradations of fear and trust, is dominant; sometimes, the cognitive.

With this paradigm from the history of religion in hand, we now turn to the biblical expression of our theme.

Fear of the Lord in the Old Testament
The fear of the Lord involves both the non-rational and the rational: the former, fear, love and trust; the latter, ethics, justice and uprightness. All

these elements cohere, as the following data show.

The Distinction Between Non-rational and Rational

Syntagms pertaining to "fear of the Lord" rarely refer exclusively to numinous dread, but always include it.

A veritable classroom example distinguishing between "fear" alone, signifying the inward agitation in the presence of God produced by the *mysterium tremendum*, and the syntagm "fear of the Lord," signifying also the moral dimension, is clearly seen in Ex 20:18-20:

> When the people saw the thunder and lightning and heard the trumpet and saw the mountain in smoke, *they trembled with fear* [וַיַּרְא וַיָּנֻעוּ . . .]. They stayed at a distance and said to Moses, "Speak to us yourself and we will listen. But do not have God speak to us or we will die." Moses said to the people, *"Do not fear* [אַל־תִּירָאוּ]. God has come to test you, so that *the fear of God* [יִרְאָתוֹ] will be with you to keep you from sinning."

Here יָרֵא by itself and its synonym, נוּעַ, denotes the momentary panic before the numinous presence of God, while the syntagm, "fear of God," links the numinous feeling with the ethical and enduring quality that keeps the people from sinning.

The numinous nature of Yahweh is represented by נוֹרָא, "terrible," and a wealth of verbs expressing dread.[32] To express merely the numinous with the verb יָרֵא, Hebrew sometimes uses the preposition מִן, designating movement "from" (Ps 33:8), or a compound with it, either מִלִּפְנֵי (Ecc 3:14; 8:12) or מִפְּנֵי (Ex 9:30). The preposition indicates that Yahweh is the cause or agent of the fear.[33] For example:

> Let all the earth fear [on account of] the LORD [יִירְאוּ מֵיהוה];
> let all the people of the world revere [on account of] him
> [מִמֶּנּוּ יָגוּרוּ] (Ps 33:8).

Several passages (2Sa 12:18; Jnh 1:16; Zep 3:7; Isa 57:11; 59:19; Job 37:24) superficially may seem to employ "fear of the Lord" for only numinous dread. In 2Sa 12:18, however, Samuel is added to Yahweh, throwing this verse somewhat outside of the limits of this study. Jnh 1:16 reads: וַיִּירְאוּ הָאֲנָשִׁים יִרְאָה גְדוֹלָה אֶת־יהוה, "and the men feared Yahweh exceedingly" (cf. v. 10), with reference to only the numinous. The addition of the cognate accusative construction,[34] however, breaks up the syntagm, throwing this instance also outside of this essay's frame of reference. In Zep 3:7 the aspect of real fear is prominent, but its parallel, "accept correction," shows that the rational, the moral aspect, is also present. Isa 57:11 reads:

> Whom have you so dreaded and feared [וַתִּירְאִי] . . .
> Is it not because I have long been silent
> that you do not fear me [וְאוֹתִי לֹא תִרְאִי?

The rest of the context, however, suggests that the moral element is also present with the numinous, however weakly. The next verse reads: "I will expose your righteousness and your works, and they will not benefit you." In Isa 59:19 "men will fear the name of the LORD" as he comes in awesome judgment, but he comes dressed as the righteous warrior on behalf of justice (Isa 59:11-17), suggesting that here too the formula includes a moral dimension. Job 37:24 is ambiguous in light of v. 23.

Religious emotions alone, however, seem to be in view in Ex 14:31, to be looked at below, and in Job 9:35. The fuller context of the latter reads:

If only there were someone ... to remove God's rod from me,
so that his terror would frighten me no more.
Then I would speak up without fear of him [וְלֹא אִירָאֶנּוּ],
but as it now stands with me, I cannot (Job 9:32-35).

Ex 14:31; 2Sa 12:18; Jnh 1:16; and Job 9:35 are exceptional in not clearly suggesting the rational, moral element. In light of the clear example in Ex 20:18-20 coupling the rational and non-rational in contrast to only the latter, perhaps the moral dimension ought not be eliminated in even these exceptional instances.

Some scholars wrongly contend that in the wisdom formula "fear of the Lord," the syntagm loses its emotional character.[35] This is true in Isa 29:13, an exception that in fact proves the rule. In Isaiah's apostate age "the fear of the Lord" had indeed degenerated into the purely rational, excluding the religious feeling:

These people come near to me with their mouth
and honor me with their lips,
but their hearts are far from me.
Their worship of me [יִרְאָתָם אֹתִי = "their fearing me"]
is made up only of rules taught by men.

The Lord condemns these rationalists for excluding the ineffable, the non-rational religious experience, from their theology. One may infer, therefore, that the sages who claimed divine inspiration (cf. Pr 2:6) and whose teachings providence approved by preserving them in Holy Scripture did not exclude this required element in true religion from their key religious formula.

The non-rational is also present in the syntagm "who fear the Lord." In Ps 22:24 the syntagm finds its parallel in a word signifying real fear:

You who fear the LORD [יִרְאֵי יהוה] praise him! ...
Revere him [וְגוּרוּ מִמֶּנּוּ], all you descendants of Israel.

Joüon[36] and Derousseaux[37] agree that the parallel verb גּוּר (="stand in awe") means "retreat out of fear." On the other hand, the worshiping community encountered in the psalms is also characterized by its commitment to Yahweh's covenant:

> The LORD confides in those who fear him [לִירֵאָיו],
> he makes his covenant known to them (Ps 25:14).

In true religion this awe felt in God's holy presence is just as essential as is its rational definition. Without the felt awareness of God's holiness, humans would not throw themselves through the veil of God's wrath against sin upon his merciful heart. As John Newton taught us to sing: "'Twas grace that taught my heart to fear, and grace my fears relieved."

In sum, fear of the Lord, apart from a few instances, never signifies what the English gloss might suggest, "terror" and "dread" of God alone. Rather it combines both the rational and non-rational, the ethical and the numinous, in an inseparable unity. Becker rightly asserts that numinous fear is the abiding and basic characteristic of "fear of the Lord."[38] To maintain the balance between the rational and non-rational one might employ the glosses "stand in awe" or "revere" (i.e., "awe tinged with fear"), depending on the felt degree of numinous fear and of perceived moral uprightness.

Before I conclude this section, it should be noted that this psychological attitude is intensified in Israel beyond what is found in pagan religions. Eichrodt notes two reasons for this. First, instead of yielding to the claims of the mysterious wholly other, paganisms seek to exert pressure upon it by magic. Second, instead of yielding to the one true God, they transfer and disperse their psychological energies to many deities and demons. Eichrodt said of the psychology of Old Testament believers:

> Consequently *the encounter with the one Lord of the divine realm*, in whom all the saving and destructive effects of higher powers were combined, *constituted an absolute imperilling of human existence*, against which there was no protection. The fear of God is here deepened to a basic attitude affecting the whole man.[39]

The Dual Quality of the Numinous: Tremendum *and* Fascinans

The religion of Israel, along with other religions, inherently unites the unlikely psychological bedfellows of the daunting and the attractive, of fear and love, of flight and trust, or, to paraphrase Professor Houston, of emotional distance and proximity. Israel's experience at the wondrous crossing of the Red Sea provides a textbook example:

> And when the Israelites saw the great power the LORD displayed against the Egyptians, the people *feared the LORD* [אֶת־יהוה ... וַיִּירְאוּ] *and put their trust in him* and in Moses his servant (Ex 14:31).

"The shrinking, awe and alarm of the elders in the face of the wonder-working God," says Eichrodt, "leads them to recognize Moses as his messenger and to accept in faith the liberation promised by him."[40] Their raw religious energy at the Red Sea will shortly be channeled through the Mosaic covenant given to them at Sinai (Ex 19:46).

The unified psychological poles come prominently to the fore in the surprisingly uniform Deuteronomic and Deuteronomistic expressions involving "fear of the Lord." Dt 10:12 represents the data:

And now, O Israel, what does the Lord your God ask of you but *to fear the Lord your God, ... to love him, to serve the Lord your God* [לְיִרְאָה אֶת־יהוה אֱלֹהֶיךָ ... וּלְאַהֲבָה אֹתוֹ וְלַעֲבֹד אֶת־יהוה אֱלֹהֶיךָ] with all your heart and with all your soul.

Instructively, the heart that both fears and loves God at one and the same time is not divided but unified in a single religious response to God. Elsewhere I tried to explain this curious emotional unity by claiming that both emotions are rooted in trust: faith in his threats, causing one to fear, and faith in his promises, causing one to love.[41] My rationalization, however, is debunked by Otto's study of comparative religion and such texts as Ex 14:31.

Fuhs establishes that the linguistic antonyms "fear" and "love" are in fact religious synonyms by connecting Dt 5:29 with 6:2:

According to 5:29, the people should "fear" Yahweh with their heart; according to 6:2 they should "love" him. In other words, ירא ["fear"] and אהב ["love"] belong to the terminology of the general clause in the covenant treaty and are to this extent synonymous.[42]

G. Wanke agrees that the terms are interchangeable:

The combining of two other words with ירא, namely, אהב "to love" and דבק "to cleave to," Dt 10:12, 20; 13:5, makes possible a broader understanding of the content of fearing God, esp. since what is said about ירא ["fear"]...applies to אהב ["love"] and דבק ["cling to"], and the terms are thus more or less interchangeable.[43]

Other data confirms these assessments. Dt 6:1 speaks of "this command" (singular, *contra* "These are the commands" [NIV], presumably consisting of "statutes and judgments"). The "command" is explicated in the rest of the chapter as consisting of "Love the Lord your God with all your heart, with all your soul and with all your strength" (Dt 6:5), and "Fear the Lord your God, serve him only and take your oaths in his name." According to Dt 6:2 this command (v. 1) is given so that Israel "might fear the Lord your God." The disconcerting oscillation between the psychological poles, "fear the Lord" and "love the Lord," suggests that they are interchangeable for expressing the true religious experience.

Klaus Baltzer,[44] on whose study Fuhs based his remarks on Dt 5:29 and

6:2, has shown from his comparison of the covenants in the Old Testament with ancient Near East vassal treaties that the command "to love God" is the central command, the substance, of the covenant (cf. Dt 6:5). In Jos 24, however, "fear the Lord" expresses its substance. In this account Joshua renews in Canaan the covenant between Yahweh and Israel that Moses mediated in Sinai and renewed at Moab. The substance of the covenant in its finally renewed form is "fear the Lord," not "love the Lord." The substance begins with "And now" [וְעַתָּה] (v. 14):

> Now fear the LORD and serve him with all faithfulness. Throw away the gods your forefathers worshiped beyond the River and in Egypt, and serve the LORD.

The positive aspect of the covenant formula is "fear the Lord" and its negative aspect "throw away the gods." Baltzer wrote:

> This relationship is defined both positively and negatively in a series of imperatives:

וְעַתָּה יְראוּ אֶת־יהוה

וְעִבְדוּ אֹתוֹ   בְּתָמִים וּבֶאֱמֶת

וְהָסִירוּ אֶת־אֱלֹהִים   אֲשֶׁר עָבְדוּ אֲבוֹתֵיכֶם

וְעִבְדוּ אֶת־יהוה

> The point is absolute loyalty toward Yahweh. This loyalty presupposes the rejection of the service (i.e., the cult) of "foreign gods."[45]

"Fear of the Lord" here encapsulates Israel's religion and as such entails the emotional opposites of fear, namely, "love" and "trust." Actually, as Derousseaux noted, ירא, "fear," goes beyond עבד, "serve," and אהב, "love," which may express merely earthly loyalty, by incorporating also acknowledgment of Yahweh's absolute sovereignty.[46]

In that light the syntagm "who fear Yahweh" in the Psalter and in other contexts of worship such as Mal 3:20 [Eng. 4:2] designates true worshipers who loyally love God and fear him.

In Israel this religious experience, call it "worship" if you will, surpassed the pagan religious experience because it was focused on the one, true, living, and holy God, not on a pantheon of warring deities displaying the same vices as depraved humans.

The religious experience involving both fear and love of God, which is at the heart of the covenant relationship, cannot be taught through the sheer dint of a teacher's will, any more than any other spiritual response can be communicated through human willpower. It must be awakened by the Spirit in the heart of the elect people (cf. 1Co 2:9-16). It can be commanded, however, for this affective aspect in religion depends on the will of the audience. Humans suppress the fear of the Lord, whose awesome majesty is clearly displayed in creation. The Lord chided Israel for quenching this instinct:

"Should you not fear me?" declares the LORD.
"Should you not tremble in my presence?
I made the sand a boundary for the sea,
an everlasting barrier it cannot cross.
The waves may roll, but they cannot prevail;
they may roar, but they cannot cross it.
But these people have stubborn and rebellious hearts;
they have turned aside and gone away.
They do not say to themselves,
'Let us fear the LORD our God [נִירָא נָא אֶת־יהוה אֱלֹהֵינוּ]...'" (Jer 5:22-24a).
Humans need to contemplate God's revelations of himself, not hide themselves among the trees so as not to encounter him and hear his voice.

Before leaving this section, note that through the rational, moral dimension the emotions of love and trust are intensified in Israel's religion beyond anything found in pagan religions. Yahweh graciously committed himself to his people as the sovereign, covenant-keeping God. The pagan deities, by contrast, were capricious and themselves subordinate to chance. Eichrodt says:

> The confident trust which constantly prevails as the basic note in Israel's fear of God has no parallel in the other religions of the ancient Near East. The will of these nature gods is too little reliable and too ambiguous for men to be able to credit them with a coherent total purpose; and they are themselves too strongly exposed to the evil power of the demons for their promises to be able to banish anxiety.[47]

The Schematization of the Numen, the Non-rational, by Ethos and by Telos, the Rational

God's will, his law if you please, schematizes Israel's religious, non-natural emotions of fearing and loving God. This revealed schematization gave Israel's religion its distinctive character and set it above all paganism: "See," says Moses, "I have taught you decrees and laws as the LORD my God commanded me .... Observe them carefully, for this will show your wisdom and understanding to the nations, who will hear about all these decrees and say, 'Surely this great nation is a wise and understanding people'" (Dt 4:5-6). Whereas pagans responded with myth and ritual, magical words accompanying voodoo rites, to manipulate their deities to perform their will, God's covenant demanded that Israel submit to his will. Any attempt to manipulate God and human destiny by observing superstitious practices and/or the occult repulses God. Instead, he demands ethical behavior: "Do my will and you will live, and not die."

God revealed his will in two ways: to all humans through conscience, and to his covenant people in particular through special revelations (e.g., the Mosaic law, the teaching of the sages, the prophetic oracles, and meditation upon inspired hymns). "Fear of אֱלֹהִים ['God']," the name associated with his transcendence, is often connnected with general revelation, and "fear of יהוה ['the Lord']," his covenantal name, with particular revelation. No ironclad distinction, however, can be made between "fear of God" and "fear of the Lord" because some literary strata prefer one name over the other and because the line between them, consisting of the emotional, the rational, and their interpretation of one another, becomes attenuated. Both expressions entail the avoidance of evil (cf. Job 1:1; 8:2-3; 28:28 with Ps 34:12-15; Pr 3:7; 16:6). These elements are, as Eichrodt said, "an indispensable virtue of the judge [Ex 18:21], and part of the necessary equipment of the king [2Sa 23:3; Isa 11:2]."[48] Nevertheless, sometimes there is some difference. "Fear of God," in contrast to "fear of the Lord," may refer, as Whybray put it, "to a standard of moral conduct known and accepted by men in general."[49]

Let us look first then at "fear of God" used in this distinctive sense, and then at "fear of the Lord."

As is well known, two rival explanations are given on how finite humans know as much as they do and how they acquire knowledge so quickly. Most continental European philosophers take the view that some knowledge is innate, but English scholars in the tradition of Locke, Berkeley and Hume hold that the mind is *tabula rasa* at birth and knowledge is acquired only empirically. Studies in linguistics during the past several decades, most notably those by Noam Chomsky,[50] have broken the impasse by showing that knowledge of linguistic universals is so deeply ingrained in the human consciousness that they can only be explained as inherited, not as learned. Chomsky wrote:

In short, the structure of particular languages may very well be largely determined by factors over which the individual has no conscious control and concerning which society may have little choice or freedom. On the basis of the best information now available, it seems reasonable to suppose that a child cannot help constructing a particular sort of transformational grammar to account for the data presented to him. ... Thus it may well be that the general features of language structure reflect, not so much the course of one's experience, but rather the general character of one's capacity to acquire knowledge—in the traditional sense, one's innate ideas and innate principles.[51]

So also humans inherently share unvarying rules of moral intuition, but in their spiritually fallen condition they more or less suppress this critical faculty (Ro 1:18; 2:12-16). Alister E. McGrath, in his recent article on "Doctrine and Ethics," seems to contradict himself. On the one hand, he says: "Works such as Jeffrey Stout's *Ethics after Babel* destroyed the credibility of the idea of a 'universal morality.'"[52] Later, however, he writes: "[The doctrine of original sin] allows us to understand that human beings are fallen, with an alarming degree of ability to do evil while knowing that it is evil." Western culture today is in a state of moral chaos because it has self-consciously rejected its innate "fear of God" and its inherited "fear of the Lord" and chosen instead spiritual darkness, including the so-called New Age movement which distorts the distinction between truth and error.

Abraham distrusted the moral atmosphere of Abimelech's court because he thought it suppressed this innate moral sense. In his apology to Abimelech, the pagan king of Gerar, who confessed to God that he had "a clear conscience" [בְּתָם־לְבָבִי] (Ge 20:5), the patriarch explained his distrust: "I said to myself, 'There is surely no fear of God [אֵין־יִרְאַת אֱלֹהִים] in this place, and they will kill me because of my wife'" (Ge 20:11). The Egyptian midwives, in contrast to their Pharaoh, also did not suppress their intuitive sense of right and wrong. When the Pharaoh commanded them to kill the Israelite male babies they refused, "because they [the midwives] feared God [וַתִּירֶאןָ ... אֶת־אֱלֹהִים]" (Ex 1:17).

"Fear of the Lord" includes this general knowledge and more. In much of the Old Testament, especially Deuteronomy and the Deuteronomistic literature, it refers to the covenant the Lord made with Israel through his mediator Moses. The stipulations of this covenant include both moral and cultic regulations. The use of the formula in 2Ki 17:32-39 shows that the latter is in view; its use in Dt 4:10, 17:19, and 31:12-13 points to the former.

Becker distinguished three main meanings for what he summarized as "fear of God": *cultic* (fear of God as worship), *moral* (fear of God as upright behavior), and *legal* (fear of God as observance of the law). He assigned to the first the bulk of the Old Testament passages, including Deuteronomic and Deuteronomistic literature; to the second, such passages as Ge 20:11 and Ex 1:17, 21 discussed above, along with references in the wisdom literature and elsewhere; and to the third, passages in the Psalms where "fear of the Lord" becomes a synonym for the law (Ps 19:10; 111:10; 112:1; 119:38, 63; 128:1, 4). But these distinctions are too rigid and often debatable. Blocher is certainly right when he criticizes this rigid categorization: "Becker's distinctions may be too clear-cut, especially as they are based on current, but questionable, source-criticism hypotheses."[53] Derousseaux[54] rightly replaces "cultic fear" with "covenant-fear" (*crainte d'alliance*) mostly in Deuteronomy, for he too thinks Becker's distinctions too clear-cut. In the wisdom literature, especially in Ecclesiastes and Job, "fear of God" may refer to the moral laws of general revelation, but in Proverbs, especially in chapters 1–9, "the fear of the Lord" denotes the sage's "teachings." "My son," he says, "if you accept my words...you will find the fear of the LORD" (Pr 2:15). In these chapters he labels his teachings as "laws" and "commandments" (cf. 1:8; 3:1; etc.).

Before concluding this section we need to remind ourselves that here numinous fear and law combine themselves. Ps 119:120 and 119:161 clearly exhibit this phenomenon, using a different Hebrew verb or ירא with the preposition מִן.[55] Dt 28:58, however, does weave fear of the Lord together with the law:

> If you do not carefully follow all the words of this law, which are written in this book, and do not revere this glorious and awesome name—the LORD your God—the LORD will send fearful plagues on you and your descendants, harsh and prolonged disasters, and severe and lingering illnesses.

The rational element can be taught and learned, and so commanded: "Come, my children, listen to me; I will teach you the fear of the LORD" (Ps 34:10), whereupon the sage-king gives his own moral instructions. Before the instruction, however, he impressed upon his audience God's greatness in saving him. Indeed, both the emotional and rational aspects of the fear of the Lord can be demanded: the former, as noted above, because humans can repent, stop quenching their innate religious instincts, and contemplate God's revelations of himself; the latter, because they can direct their wills to cognitively grasp the revealed content.

Conclusion
Syntagms involving the verbal root ירא, "fear," with God or equivalents as its direct object, denote a rich and complex thought that epitomizes Israel's religion. At one and the same time it signifies non-rational, numinous fear combined with love and trust, both of which are schematized by moral uprightness. In some texts the non-rational predominates, in others the rational; but "awe" of God characterizes its core. This root of religious experience is organized by God's will, revealed through conscience and usually overlaid with special revelation.

In sum, "fear of the Lord/God" entails two axes, each with its own poles. We can depict the rich and complex nature of "fear of the Lord" by this diagram:

General Revelation

rational axis

Fear ——————————————————————— Love
  non-rational axis

Special Revelation

On the non-rational axis the poles are "fear" and "love," and on the rational axis, general revelation and special revelation. Both elements are normally present on the horizontal axis, but in varying degrees. The vertical axis may become attenuated with little difference between its poles,[56] though sometimes general revelation is clearly in view with "fear of God" and special revelation with "fear of the Lord." Both axes are normally present in varying degrees, though in a few texts the rational axis is not apparent. Specific nuances of the syntagms involving "fear of the Lord" in the biblical texts must be plotted in relation to these poles. Sometimes fear is subordinated to love and vice versa; sometimes the affective emotions are subordinated to cognitive understanding and vice versa.

Stimuli inciting "fear of the Lord" have not been investigated here. Suffice it to note that God's marvelous revelations in creation, in sacred history, and in Scripture are sufficient reasons "to fear him" in the fullest sense of that word. The problem is not the lack of the numinous—it is everywhere; nor the lack of moral consciousness—it is inherent in human nature. Rather, people make their hearts stubborn and rebellious against God (cf. Jer 5:20-25). In short, God demands both the affective and the cognitive aspects of fear, for both depend on the human will. One cannot be indifferent to "fear of the Lord"; it is a matter of life and death. "Such fear," says Professor Houston, "brings blessing in every sphere of life."[57]

Notes

[1] James M. Houston, *I Believe in the Creator* (Grand Rapids: Eerdmans, 1980) 188.

[2] Ibid., 189.

[3] Bruce K. Waltke & M. O'Connor, *Introduction to Biblical Hebrew Syntax* (Winona Lake, Ind.: Eisenbrauns, 1990) 52.

[4] All Scriptural citations in this essay refer to the Hebrew text. The English reference may differ by one verse.

[5] Waltke & O'Connor, *Syntax*, 146.

[6] Pr 1:7, 29; 2:5; 8:13; 9:10; 10:27; 14:26, 27; 15:16, 33; 16:6; 19:23; 22:4; 23:17.

7   Isa 11:2, 3; 33:6.

8   Ps 19:10; 111:10; 34:11, a thanksgiving song with wisdom instruction.

9   2Ch 19:9.

10 Dt 4:10; 5:29 (26); 6:2, 13, 24; 8:6; 10:12, 20; 13:5; 14:23; 17:19; 28:58; 31:12, 13; Jos 4:24; 24:14; Jdg 6:10; 1Sa 12:14, 24; 1Ki 8:40, 43 parallel 2Ch 6:31, 33;   2Ki 17:7, 25, 28, 32, 33, 34, 36, 39, 41 (cf. vv. 35, 37, 38 where the syntagm refers to other gods); Ne 1:11 is an echo of Deuteronomistic literature.

11 1Sa 12:18, 24; 2Sa 6:9 parallel to 1Ch 13:12; 1Ki 18:3, 12; 2Ki 4:1; Isa 25:3; 57:11; 59:19; Jer 5:24; 10:7; 26:19; 32:39; Hos 10:3; Zep 3:7; Mal 2:5; 3:5 (with reference to יהוה צְבָאוֹת'); Ps 34:10; 67:8; 72:5 (text?); 86:11; 112:1; 119:63; Job 1:9; Pr 3:7; 14:21; Neh 1:11; 2Ch 6:31.

12 Lev 19:14, 32: 25:17, 36, 43.

13 Isa 3:10; 50:10; Ps 15:4; 22:24; 25:10, 12; 61:6; 115:11, 13; 118:4; 128:1, 4; 135:20; 145:19; Mal 3:16, 20; Pr 14:2; 31:30.

14 H. F. Fuhs, "ירא," *TDOT* 6.308-309.

15 Ge 20:11; Ex 20:20; 2Sa 23:3; Neh 5:9, 15; יִרְאַת שַׁדַּי, "fear of Shaddai," in Job 6:14; יִרְאַת אֲדֹנָי, "fear of the Lord" (not Yahweh), in Job 28:28.

16 Ge 42:18; Ex 1:17, 21; Dt 25:18; Jnh 1:9 ("the God of heaven"); Ps 55:20; Job 9:35; 37:24; Ecc 5:6; 12:13; 8:12; Neh 7:2.

17 Ge 22:12; Ex 18:21; Ps 66:16; Job 1:1, 8; Ecc 7:18; 8:12.

18 Rudolf Otto, *The Idea of the Holy* (tr. John W. Harvey; Oxford: Oxford University Press, 1923; paperback 1958).

19 Ibid., 109-10.

20 Ibid., 58.

21 Fuhs, "ירא," 6.300.

22 Otto, *Idea*, 17.

23 Ibid., 23-24.

24 Ibid., 31.

25 Ibid., 33.

26 Ibid., 110.

27 Ibid., 45-49.

28 Ibid., 45.

29 Ibid., 109.

30 Ibid., 51.

31 Ibid., 140.

32 Fuhs, "ירא," 6.239-94.

33 Waltke & O'Connor, *Syntax*, 213.

34 Ibid., 167.

35 Günther Wanke, "φοβέω," *TDNT* 9.201-202.

36 Paul Joüon, "Crainte et peur en hebreu biblique," *Bib* 6 (1925) 176.

37 Louis Derousseaux, *La crainte de Dieu dans l'Ancien Testament. Lectio divina* 63 (Paris: Cerf) 74.

38 Joachim Becker, *Gottesfurcht im Alten Testament, Analecta Biblica* (Rome: Pontifical Biblical Institute, 1965) 80-82.

39 Walter Eichrodt, *Theology of the Old Testament* (tr. J. A. Baker II; Philadelphia: Westminster, 1967) 270.

40 Ibid., 274.

41 Bruce K. Waltke, "Evangelical Spirituality: A Biblical Scholar's Perspective," *JETS* 31 (1988) 14.

42 Fuhs, "ירא," 6.307.

43 Wanke, "φοβέω," 9.201.

44 Klaus Baltzer, *The Covenant Formulary in Old Testament, Jewish, and Early Christian Writings* (tr. David E. Green; Oxford: Basil Blackwell, 1971).

45 Ibid., 21.

46 Derousseaux, *La crainte*, 220, 256.

[47] Eichrodt, *Theology*, 272.

[48] Ibid., 273.

[49] R. N. Whybray, *Wisdom in Proverbs: The Concept of Wisdom in Proverbs 1-9* (London: SCM, 1965) 96.

[50] Noam Chomsky, *Aspects of Theory of Syntax* (Cambridge, Mass.: M.I.T. Press, 1965) 33-59. See now Paul Johnson, *The Intellectuals* (London: Weidenfeld and Nicolson, 1989) 338. Johnson mistakenly cites Chomsky's *Syntactic Structures*.

[51] Chomsky, *Aspects*, 59.

[52] Alister E. McGrath, "Doctrine and Ethics," *JETS* 34 (1991) 147.

[53] Henri Blocher, "The Fear of the Lord as the 'Principle' of Wisdom," *TynBul* 28 (1977) 8.

[54] Derousseaux, *La crainte*, 10 n. 23, 100-101.

[55] Ibid., 9.

[56] H. A. Brongers, "La crainte du Seigneur (Jir at Jhwh, Jir at 'Elohim)," *Oudtestamentische Studien* 5 (1948) 163.

[57] Houston, *I Believe*, 189.

4
Piety in the Pentateuch

David W. Baker

THE ADMONITION TO "PRACTICE WHAT YOU PREACH" INDICATES one bifurcation in life, that between what we say should be done (what we preach) and what we in fact do (what we practice). This distinction appears not only in human manners, but also in literature, a point relevant to studying the biblical text. Legal or *prescriptive* texts tells us what should be done, while *descriptive* or historical literature records what is actually performed.

The Pentateuch, the five books of Moses, consists of prose almost exclusively, with both of these major subgenres present. The historical, descriptive material details how people actually lived in relationship with their fellows and with God. The prescriptive material explains how people should live within these same relationships. Comparing the approach of the two genres to the same theme in the Pentateuch can be instructive. For example, one can investigate the behavior expected within the family structure as reflected in prescriptive texts, and then compare that to actual families, all too often dysfunctional, as they appear in the descriptive texts.

This paper investigates desired and actual modes of relationship between individuals and their God found in the Pentateuch. In what shapes and guises does personal piety show itself in these foundational documents of Judaeo-Christian faith, and how does this compare with what we should be doing or do in fact practice ourselves?

The Hebrew-Jewish name for the Pentateuch, the *Torah*, usually translated "Law," indicates Israel's perception of the dominant literary form within the document. Numerous verses within the Pentateuch which provide guidance for personal and corporate behavior to some extent justify this identification. The literary structure of the Pentateuch, however, seems to indicate that description, the encounters of human beings with God in their personal history, is an even more prominent element of the books. Laws are indeed there, ranging from the universal Ten Commandments in Exodus 20 and Deuteronomy 5 to the much more particular instructions to Moses and his representatives on how they are to build the tabernacle and its components in Exodus 25–29. These laws, however, are invariably set within the framework of historical narrative.

This is clear in the case of the Ten Commandments, for example, in comparison to similar legal, or more specifically covenantal, material in other literatures from the ancient Near East. The latter provide only the bare legal documents themselves, while historical narrative frames the former at both ends. Exodus 1–19 describes God bringing the Israelites to Mount Sinai and giving the law (20–23). They respond to and ratify the covenant in chapter 24. Law finds its meaning and place in society through narrative.

This distinction between description and prescription, and the apparent priority of the former over the latter, has theological as well as literary implications. God is not simply an impersonal Lawgiver. He is not the celestial Watchmaker organizing his universe through physical and judicial laws only to abandon it and allow it to run on its own. Rather, he is a God moving and acting in and through history. He meets and interacts with his creation in the everyday events of their existence in a much more intimate, immanent way than simply as a distant, transcendent Creator. God thus is real to his people not only through decree but through dialogue; he not only commands, but he personally communicates.

Prescriptions for Piety

People living in relationship, whether with a small group such as a family or with a larger unit such as a clan or nation, need direction about how these relationships may or may not take place. Life in community demands some kind of control or guidelines, whether in a formal, written document or orally within a family as part of the socialization process. In the Pentateuch, Israel receives instruction on how to be and live as the people of God, relating not only to each other, but also to God himself.

God revealed the laws in Exodus, Leviticus and Numbers at Mount Sinai through his servant Moses, according to the Old Testament narrative. While intended as corporate guidelines for a new nation, they do touch on individuals and their personal piety. An example is the regulations for the various types of offering prescribed in Leviticus 1–7. The laws are general rather than specific ("When any of you," Lev 1:2), but personal involvement is required in several instances. The offerer must personally lay his hand upon the head of the animal which he brings for the "peace" or well-being offering and for the sin offering (Lev 3:2, 8, 13; 4:4, 15, 24, 29, 33). The person identifies with the animal, showing actual involvement with the sacrifice. No longer is this some impersonal ritual, happening "out there" somewhere; now it is one involving identification. An offerer's personally bringing the sacrifice to the altar (Lev 7:30) accentuates this same involvement.

These directions for worship and service of God are notably universal in application. They pertain exclusively neither to the religious elite nor to the Israelite masses. All are expected to participate, not only in the specific sacrifices mentioned in Leviticus 1–7, but in all aspects of learning to fear God (Dt 31:11-12). Not only Israelite adults, but their children, and even non-Israelite residents of the land (cf. Nu 9:14) are expected to take their share in the nation's religious life. The people's leaders are not above religious obligation (the king, Dt 17:19; cf. Lev 4:22-26; the priest, Dt 18:13; cf. Lev 4:3-12; 21), nor are the poor excluded due to their lack of means. Options are provided for sacrifices of differing values (Lev 1:3, 10, 14; 5:7, 11) so that all may participate.

The purpose of the nation's religious devotion was to show forth and maintain an exclusive, monogamous relationship with Yahweh, her God, who married Israel at Mount Sinai (see Hos 1). The Israelites must keep themselves distinct from their neighbors (Lev 20:22, 24, 26; Dt 14:1-2) because they belong to God alone. It is in order to maintain this exclusivity, and to prevent any possible spiritual adultery, that Yahweh directs Israel to do away with the practices of the original inhabitants of the Promised Land (Dt 12:2).

Religious practice was not limited in Israel to cultic activity, but permeated all aspects of society. Interpersonal relations fall within the scope of one's existence under God's covenant (Ex 20:12-17; Dt 5:16-21), as do all events of life, from birth (Lev 12) to death (Lev 21:1-11). Israel must live as a "kingdom of priests" (Ex 19:6), allowing no spiritual schizophrenia to disjoin sacred and profane. Since they are God's people, with Yahweh as their king, all areas of their life are sacred, a truth which will be made apparent in the final Day of the Lord (Zec 14:20-21).

These aspects of being the people of God, as mandated in the prescriptive texts, were not onerous burdens, a connotation too often associated with the word "law." The sacred festivals were not burdensome either, but rather provided the people with occasions for rejoicing (Dt 16:11).

Even the sacrifices were to be accompanied with joy (Dt 12:7, 12), which was both the attitude in which they should be performed (Dt 28:47) and the result that would follow from performing them.

Piety in Practice

In Israel, as in our own lives, the expectations laid down and the reality of response often did not correspond. The Old Testament prophets repeatedly called upon the people, reminding them of the covenant to which they and their forefathers had agreed, but which they were now blatantly ignoring. The lives of the giants of Old Testament faith are instructive in the way that they responded in devotion to God, especially when we see this in light of the Old Testament laws. In the Genesis narratives, the lives of the patriarchs reflect their understanding of their calling long before God spelled out the Mosaic covenantal obligations. Two men in particular, Abraham and Joseph, stand as strong examples of a deep, fervent devotion to God and his service, even though the specific forms and modes of this service had not yet, apparently, been explicitly delineated for them to follow.

Even prior to their time, we see a desire to worship God on the part of humankind's second generation. Cain and Abel both brought gifts which were a result of their own labors in order to honor Yahweh (Ge 4:3-4). While this whole passage continues to perplex exegetes due to a number of interpretational issues, it does indicate an early impulse toward worship. Other early instances of people seeking a personal relationship with God, whatever the exact nature of that relationship might be, include those who "call on the name of Yahweh" (Ge 4:26; cf. 26:25) and some who "walk with God" (Ge 5:22; cf. 24:40). Noah in particular was singled out from among his sinful and corrupt generation as one of the latter (Ge 6:9). He is also the first who is said to have built an altar for sacrifice (Ge 8:20), though an altar might be implicit in the tale of Cain's and Abel's offerings (Ge 4:1-5). These examples make clear that a personal desire to worship precedes any formal, established protocol of worship.

It is only when we reach Abraham that the author fleshes out the character of his subject. There are several different, and at times conflicting, aspects of Abraham's character portrayed. Like Noah, he took part in altar building, and did so on numerous occasions (Ge 12:7, 8; 13:18; 22:9) in various locations throughout the land promised to him by God (Ge 12:1). This was apparently a way of personally laying some kind of claim to the land which God had promised would be his. As with Noah, God looked with favor upon Abraham, and God gave him a unique promise of land, descendants and blessing (Ge 12:1-3; 15:13-16; 17:1-8), a promise which was passed on as an inheritance to his descendants (Ge 16:10; 21:23; 28:20; 35:11-12; 48:4).

Abraham was not consistently a giant of the faith, however, in spite of acknowledgments that faith was one of his strong characteristics (Ge 15:6; cf. Ro 4; Gal 3:6; Jas 2:23). He did not at first trust God to fulfill his promise of descendants through his wife Sarah, but took it upon himself to sire an heir through Hagar (Ge 16:2-4; cf. 17:17; 18:12, 15). Nor did he trust God to protect him from foreign rulers who might covet his beautiful wife. He therefore twice passed her off as his sister (Ge 12:10-20; 20; cf. 26:6-11). We watch his faith in the power and providence of God grow, however, within the brief span of the narrative concerning him. By the time we reach Genesis 22, the man who feared lest God not be able to provide him a natural heir (cf. Ge 15:1-3) was ready and willing to slaughter his only son whom God had given in fulfillment of his promise (vv. 8-10). This is an encouraging example, showing that weakness of faith is not the end. Faith that wavers at first may nevertheless be a beginning for a deepening and ripening relationship with God. If God acknowledges the faith of such a weak person as Abraham initially was, this should give each of us hope in our own human frailty.

Joseph also develops interestingly in the way he relates to people and to God. While having a special place, even as a lad, in the heart of his father (Ge 37:3) and possibly of his God also (Ge 37:5-6, 9, although mention of God as the source of the dreams is noticeably absent), the way he announced his special destiny to his older brothers seems less than exemplary (Ge 37:1-20). A deepened spirituality soon became evident, however, in both his words and his actions. Although living in a hostile environment, ignominiously sold into slavery far away from home and separated, as one might think, from family religious influences, he maintained his personal integrity in the face of strong pressure. When his master's wife attempted to seduce and even rape him, Joseph resisted the temptation and fled from it (Ge 39:6-12). The response he gave to her seductive request shows his personal piety and integrity. Not only would an act of adultery have damaged Joseph's relationship with his master, had the latter found out about the affair, but it would have been a sin against God (v. 9). Joseph was convinced that he lived in the presence of his God even though he was in a foreign country where Yahweh was not even recognized. His personal piety was able to sustain him in the face of overwhelming sensual pressures.

Joseph also recognized the power of God in an area in which Yahweh was not known as a famous practitioner, namely the interpretation of dreams (40–41). The Egyptians had trained personnel who involved themselves professionally in this type of task, while Joseph was simply a prisoner. He had a close enough relationship with his God, however, to recognize that, although it is not God's primary role, he could interpret dreams. Joseph provided an interpretation to Pharaoh and his officials, acknowledging, however, that this ability came from the power of God rather than his own resources (Ge 40:8; 41:16, 25). He had such a relationship with God, even when geographically removed from fellow worshipers, that he could lay claim to God's omniscient wisdom and omnipotent power in moments of need (v. 32).

Joseph's closeness to his God also altered his perspective on the treachery which his brothers inflicted upon him when they sold him into slavery (Ge 37:18-36). He tells his brothers, "You sold me here; for God sent me before you to preserve life" (Ge 45:5, NRSV). He recognized God's providence and sovereignty even in this act which caused him such pain. He perceived that the pain was used for preservation.

Constraints of space do not permit me to examine further aspects of personal and corporate piety, though they abound among both the famous and the nameless in the Pentateuch. I limit myself now to noting that we catch a glimpse of the closeness of God's people to him by noting how they named their children. Hebrew names are often phrases or even sentences which themselves can be translated. Their meaning is at times explicitly commented upon in the text. For example, the place called Bethel is so named because Jacob, having received a revelation from God there, recognizes that it is in truth a "house of God [בֵּית־אֵל]" (Ge 28:19; cf. 16:13, 14). Even though often simply noted without comment, personal names with such a theophoric element, involving the use of the word "God" (אֵל), are not rare in the Pentateuch. They include Mehujael and Methushael (Ge 4:18), Mahalalel (Ge 5:12), Ishmael (Ge 16:11), Eldaah (Ge 25:4), Israel (Ge 38:28), Jahleel (Ge 46:14; Nu 26:26), Malkiel (Ge 46:17; Nu 26:45), Jahziel (Ge 46:24; cf. Jahzeel, Nu 26:48), Uzziel (Ex 6:18), Mishael and Elzaphan (Ex 8:22), Elisheba and Elazar (Ex 6:23), Elkanah (Ex 6:24), Putiel (Ex 6:25), Elizur (Nu 1:5), Eliab (Nu 1:9), Elishama (Nu 1:10), Eliasaph (Nu 1:14), Elizaphan (Nu 3:30), and Eldad (Nu 11:26; cf. Elidad, Nu 34:21). Numerous other names indicate awareness of divine activity, though without specifically mentioning God, but they will not be noted here. Even the names listed indicate that there was a piety among the worshippers of God which they chose to reflect in this way. Their naming habits bear a witness which is not only synchronic, showing their grateful appreciation of God at this juncture in their life, but is also diachronic, passing this appreciation on through the name to a future generation.

Holistic Piety

Contemporary society in North America views religion as something which, if acknowledged at all, should be only a private matter. It most certainly does not have anything to do with one's public life. Israel recognized that this schizophrenic approach to reality is not valid. For Israel, religion was not a private, unimportant aspect of one's existence, but rather an organizing principle for all of life. Living in a theocratic state, Israelites recognized no clear distinctions between religious and civil, between secular and sacred, between what fell within the purview of God and what was to be the concern of humanity. All the earth is the Lord's, as Israel's creation theology stated (Ge 1), not only because he made it, but because he still is active in providing for it and maintaining it; and all life is the Lord's, for the same reason.

This understanding of the position of God in national and individual life is reflected both in Israel's prescriptive legal documents, and also in the descriptions of life as they actually lived it, which their historical literature records. God and his will are foundational for all aspects of life. This fact is reflected not only in worship and obedience, where it might be expected, but also in private matters as intimate as naming a child. Surely this holistic approach to life in all of its relational and spiritual aspects was healthy not only for individuals within the nation, but also for the nation as a whole. Being born into a society which expects and mandates a certain relationship with God and one's fellows provided an anchor and foundation for existence. On the other hand, the required practice of a genuine, personal relationship with God, a piety maintained by each member of the family of Israel, strengthened the corporate bonds of the nation itself and of the nation with God. This triangle of "individual-nation-God" is one which, if all of the interrelationships within it are carefully nurtured, stands as a model for the whole world.

5
When the Spirit Came Mightily: The Spirituality of Israel's Charismatic Leaders

Carl Edwin Armerding

A SURPRISING FEATURE OF MODERN LIFE IS THE DOMINANCE OF "spirituality" in current culture. In an age that prides itself on rationalism, post-Enlightenment categories have not merely infiltrated the city, but thrown open the gates. From the popular press to the university bookstore, the language of spirituality is all the rage. Contemporary culture, generated by pop stars as well as literary critics, frequently celebrates the life of the spirit over the life of the mind.

But what do we mean by spirituality? Our times are long on discussion but short on definition. Much modern spirituality is no more than a vague feeling that the emotions or the soul must break free of rational categories. Modern cults and a variety of self-help seminars, drawing on Eastern religions and a return to animism, together with a dash of contemporary psychology, only muddy the waters. So, prior to setting out on a journey through Old Testament spirituality, I will attempt a working definition.

Spirituality Defined
Spirituality is that which has to do with the spirit. First, of course, this means the human spirit, which in biblical terms is that part of a unified anthropology which corresponds to, and draws from, the Spirit that is in, or is, God. Concomitant, then, to such a conception is an understanding of the role of the Divine Spirit, which in Old Testament terms

animates, or gives life to, humanity (together with "all creatures great and small") (Ps 104:39; Ecc 12:7). Of course, Old Testament thought knows nothing of the separation of "spirit" and "flesh," in the sense of the dualism held to in medieval spirituality. Nor would the Old Testament writers be comfortable with a conflict between "spirit" and "mind." God *is* spirit, as our Lord affirmed (Jn 4:24), and as such can come into the natural (flesh) realm to bring about supernatural birth (Jn 3:6), or to renew the mind (Eph 4:23ff.), but neither testament would be comfortable with a division of human personality into separate spheres of "flesh" and "spirit" or "mind" and "spirit."

To speak, then, of "spirituality" in a biblical sense is to speak of the vital connection between the creature and the Creator, where the mind of the Spirit meets the mind of the believer, shaping the believer's will and producing a response of love and devotion. It is to enter the realm where the creature is not only made alive by the Creator, but is responsive to the Creator, and thus able to relate to him. If in the Old Testament the spirit is the vital principle of "life" or "life-force" that comes from God, then "spirituality" is the creature's response to God, from whom that life-force has come, and upon whom it is dependent.

It is customary to look for Old Testament spirituality in the psalms of David, or amongst Moses and the prophets, whose language of redemption, and experience of communion with God, is so foundational to the history of salvation. Equally popular has been the search for Old Testament spirituality in the Song of Songs, with its history of mystical interpretation. Even the wisdom teachers, with their intensely pragmatic approach to life, are known for their commitment to the "fear of Yahweh."

But Old Testament spirituality is nowhere more interesting, and perhaps nowhere less understood, than amongst Israel's charismatic leaders, the judges who ruled over the tempestuous period of settlement and conquest. The more interesting because, for many a reader, spirituality seems strangely absent. And yet, in the varied expressions of charismatic enduement so characteristic of the book of Judges, the text goes out of its way to mark the explicit connection between the Spirit of God and the spirit of the judge.

It is that connection which I would like to examine in this brief paper, presented in honor of my longtime colleague and friend Jim Houston. Charismatic spirituality remains a minefield, not least because of the many and varied claims put forward in the name of contemporary charismatic experience. Whether, and how, Old Testament charismatic spirituality fits with contemporary charismatic life in the late twentieth century must be left to the reader's judgment, but there can be little doubt that God came mightily, and in what we might call an unorthodox manner, on the strange and memorable figures who populate the book of Judges. The study that follows will consider those experiences of "divine encounter" as a basis for charismatic spirituality in Israel, under three headings: *What kind of persons had charismatic spiritual encounters?* (preparation for charismatic spiritual encounter), *What happened to people in charismatic spiritual encounters?* (the nature of charismatic spiritual encounter), and *What sort of piety resulted from charismatic spiritual encounters?* (the results of charismatic spiritual encounter). The paper will conclude with a brief summary of the lessons to be learned. Basic models will be drawn from the books of Judges and 1 Samuel, with supplementary evidence sought wherever it is to be found.

What Kind of Persons Had Charismatic Spiritual Encounters? (Preparation for Divine Encounter)

Popular theories of spirituality generally hold to the belief that spiritual encounters come to individuals who already have some bent toward God. In contrast, the period of charismatic spirituality, represented by the judges, was a time marked by little or no such human initiative. The theological framework of Judges (2:10-19) depicts a nation with a penchant for forgetting the ways of the Lord, and what break there is in this pattern reflects communal desperation in the face of cruel enemies. Moving from the theological framework of Judges to the individual "hero accounts," we find equally slender evidence for the seeking, spiritual personality. Throughout the book, and on into the companion period in early monarchy days, the narrative seems dominated by characters (Gideon, Jephthah, Samson, Saul) who did not take initiatives toward God. In other words, they were creatures of their time, and shared the common habit of forgetting Yahweh's covenant. Even where more seemingly sensitive personalities arise (e.g., Samuel and David), the initiative seems still to be in divine hands.

Charismatic spirituality, then, is marked by divine initiative, in response to nothing more than God's sovereign commitment to maintain his covenant faithfulness toward a nation which, when conditions were sufficiently bad, had the sense to cry out in distress. This is especially interesting in light of the intense individualism of the period. The age of the judges, often called "the Heroic Age of Israel," was a time when the hero figure dominated both history and narrative. Given the narrator's interest in individual exploits, and the fascinating personalities whose exploits are recorded, we should have expected at least a few true saints, if not *before* their "conversion," certainly *afterward.* Augustine of Hippo may have been a bit of a playboy prior to his encounter with God, but certainly afterward he reflected classical categories of spirituality in what was to become the medieval pattern (consciousness of sin and deep repentance, asceticism, preoccupation with God, a life of prayer and meditation, service to the church, etc.). Amongst the "charismatic" figures, the closest to this pattern is David, yet though a deeply reflective figure, David is hardly marked by the withdrawal kind of asceticism that was the hallmark of a later spirituality.

Granted, however, that these charismatic figures had significant encounters with God, and are therefore an important part of Old Testament spirituality, what preparation is discernible in the fragmentary records we have of their lives prior to the encounters? It might be useful to look at the judges in order and ask this question.

Othniel (Jdg 3:7-11). When compared with some of his successors, Othniel appears a model of domestic fidelity and filial devotion, but on the subject of his preparation for divine encounter the text is silent. Of courage he has no lack, whether before becoming a judge (Jos 15:16-17/Jdg 1:12-13) or after (Jdg 3:10-11). But concerning his encounter with God, the text is characteristically laconic, "he [the LORD] raised up for them a deliverer ... who saved them." There follows also the formulaic "The Spirit of the LORD came upon him, so that he became Israel's judge and went to war . . . ." Whether Othniel was spiritually inclined or just another war hero, we cannot tell. The salient fact in the narrative is the divine initiative. Beyond that, all information is lacking.

Ehud (Jdg 3:12-30). A narrative with far more epic features follows the Othniel cycle, but any search for a "divine spark" in the hero is equally futile. Ehud was left-handed, crafty, cunning, articulate and convincing. But did he ever long after God, or withdraw to a quiet place to pray? We have no way of knowing. No mention is made of the divine Spirit, and no word informs the reader that Ehud loved God, or ever sought him for the necessary equipping for leadership. It just happened: that is all we can say.

Shamgar (Jdg 3:31). He was a strange and shadowy figure; nothing is known of Shamgar's spiritual life or even whether he personally encountered God.

Deborah and Barak (Jdg 4-5). Deborah was a prophetess, whose role was to sit (NIV: hold court) under a palm tree and sort out competing claims amongst disputant Israelites. Her co-judge, Barak, was a classic military leader, though the story turns on his reluctance to lead and subsequent humiliation in favor of a woman. In neither is there any hint of classical piety, though Deborah typically sounds a Yahwistic battle cry (4:14), and both figures are represented as singers of the triumphant Yahwistic battle hymn (Jdg 5). In addition to there being no evident preparation, there is little to suggest a direct spiritual encounter.

Gideon (Jdg 7-8). Gideon is surely one of the most tragic figures in biblical history, reaching the heights of Israelite heroic glory only to usher in the sad depths of internecine strife which marked the brief reign of his son, the "anti-judge" Abimelech.

Again, the initiative we see is Yahweh's. We are told much more about God's encounter with Gideon than with his predecessors. An angel of Yahweh is involved (Jdg 6:11ff.; see below), with a divine announcement, "The LORD is with you, mighty warrior," following which the reluctant and fearful Gideon is given a sign vision. Although the encounter culminates in an act of brave defiance of Baal, and a series of divine-human dialogues, there is little evidence that Gideon was a man consumed with any passion for God, or bent toward spiritual things. God's coming to Gideon seems designed simply to overpower his reluctance and fear, so as to make him, for a time, a significant man of God.

Jephthah (Jdg 11-12). Far more interesting is Jephthah, for if there was any hint of spiritual sensitivity in such as Othniel, Deborah or Gideon, such is wholly lacking in Jephthah. The story is entirely "secular" in its assumptions about Jephthah's origins and propensities, and even the formulaic commitment of Yahweh to his covenant as a basis for deliverance is shrouded in the mysterious description of divine ambivalence which precedes the Jephthah cycle (cf. Jdg 10:6-16).

Jephthah, nevertheless, is marked out by the text as another of those on whom "the Spirit of the LORD came" (Jdg 11:29). At that point, he had successfully wrested leadership of the Transjordanian coalition from the reluctant elders of Gilead and confronted the king of the Ammonites with a powerful apologetic speech on the rightness of his claim. Yahweh is invoked in the argument, but there is nothing else to indicate a propensity toward divine things.

Samson (Jdg 13-16). Of all the judges, the most curious and enigmatic is Samson. Although clearly a part of the "Judges cycles," his story has features which set it sharply apart from the others, to the point where many scholars have assumed a separate original source.[1] Because both the language of prayer and the language of divine encounter are a rich part of the story (or stories), the reader is all the more intrigued by the question of preparation and initiative.

As with a number of biblical figures (Jacob, Moses, Samuel, Jeremiah, John the Baptist, Jesus, Timothy), the events of Samson's spiritual encounter begin long before he himself has had opportunity to determine his own direction. Judges 13 describes the angelic visit to Manoah's wife, and the order for the boy to be subject to a kind of Naziritic vow (cf. Nu 6).

From that beginning, the text jumps (6:24ff.) to a summary description of the boy Samson's early years, with the intriguing comment, "He grew and Yahweh blessed him, and the Spirit of Yahweh began to stir him while he was in Maheneh Dan, between Zorah and Eshtaol." Would that we knew more about that stirring, and the beginnings of what was to be a life full of fury and passion, both for God and against humankind. But, as with the early years of our Lord, there is little detail. What we do know, and it is consistent with the other accounts in Judges, is that the initiative came from God, not Samson. From Samson's later life, we are forced to conclude that he, of all the judges, conforms least to conventional stereotypes of the "spiritual" person. And yet, for intensity of feeling, involvement with the Spirit, and explicit prayer, there is no figure in holy writ whose depth of passion and range of spiritual encounter exceed those of Samson. Again, however, the initiative lies with God.

Samuel (1Sa 1—16). Amongst the charismatic leaders of Israel, none stands taller than Samuel, the last and greatest of the judges. Born as an answer to prayer, dedicated to Yahweh's service from birth, and educated at the temple in Shiloh, Samuel should naturally have absorbed a disposition toward the numinous. On the other side of the equation, however, we must consider that Samuel's family home was marked by domestic strife, and the temple to which he was sent had become a center of religious decline and unchecked immorality. That Samuel himself, as a boy, was able to rise above all this is evidence, according to the text, not of Samuel's predisposition toward God, but of Yahweh's sovereign choice of Samuel. Again, the picture of divine initiative dominates the scene.

The story is, of course, well known. The boy Samuel is thrice confronted by the divine word in the middle of the night, and only after repeated promptings do both Samuel and the aged Eli recognize the voice of God. The text (1Sa 3:7) explicitly states the reason for Samuel's spiritual insensitivity: "Now Samuel did not yet know the LORD: the word of the LORD had not yet been revealed to him." Nothing could be clearer. The later Samuel will become a towering transitional figure as the nation moves toward monarchy, and be a regular recipient of divine revelation. But evidence of a "spiritually inclined personality" is as lacking in the later period as in the beginning.

Saul (1Sa). 1 Samuel 9 presents Saul as a winsome young man, sensitive to his father's possible worry (v. 5), and with commendable humility (v. 21), but when confronted with prophetic revelation concerning his own role, he seems not to know what to do with it. Soon, in accordance with Samuel's prediction, "the Spirit of God came upon him in power" (10:10) with accompanying outbursts of prophecy, all of which surprised the onlookers who asked, "What is this that has happened to the son of Kish? Is Saul also among the prophets?" (v. 11). By now Saul must have realized he was the target of divine encounter, but when the moment comes for him to be discovered and anointed, he is off hiding among the baggage (10:22).

Saul is one of the great charismatic heroes of ancient history, the more tragic because of his fatal flaws. But when it comes to "seeking God," there is little evidence that he ever really did. Throughout Saul's life, Samuel is always the guardian of the religious interest, and when Saul does attempt a foray into spiritual territory, he usually fails. In the end, following two clear acts of covenant disobedience, the same Spirit of Yahweh which captured him now abandons him (1Sa 16:14), by which time Saul is on his way toward becoming a compulsive manic-depressive.

What must be remembered, however, is that not only did Saul encounter God, but Yahweh's Spirit "came mightily upon him." The verb used (see below) captures the essence of charismatic spirituality, and is repeatedly applied to Samson and Saul. By this measurement, Samson and Saul represent the apex of charismatic spirituality, but again, divine initiative, not human personality, is the determining factor.

David (1Sa 16—1Ki 2). Finally, with David, we come to a heroic, charismatic figure of significant spiritual stature. If a major point of the Saul narrative in 1 Samuel 9 is to stress physical attractiveness, possibly in contrast to David's "spiritual" appeal, certainly the narrative of 1 Samuel 16 provides the counterpoint.

David, from the beginning, is the ideal person, the one God was seeking, whose qualities could be seen only by him who "looks at the heart" (1Sa 16:7). Noticeable, however, is the fact that the initiative, as usual, comes from outside the individual. God is the ultimate inspiration, Samuel is the seeking and anointing agent, and only after the anointing does David encounter the Spirit (1Sa 16:13). David may have been far closer to what we, and God, might consider a person sensitive to divine things, but it was God who sought and filled David, and not David who sought God.

Summary

The saintly personality, and common ideas of spirituality that are derived from the saintly character, have left the Western world with the idea that saints are born, not made. The period of charismatic spirituality, even when David is included, gives the lie to this axiom. The writer of Hebrews, who knew better, listed among the heroes of faith "Gideon, Barak, Samson, Jephthah, David, and Samuel," along with the prophets and assorted martyrs (Heb 11:32). None of these, though touched deeply by the divine Spirit, came anywhere near the medieval ideal of asceticism and reflective tranquillity which continues to dominate popular notions about spirituality. In addition to feats of spiritual valor (see Heb 11:33f), this collection of saints included takers of petty vengeance (Gideon), crafty deceivers (Ehud), makers of rash vows (Jephthah), womanizers (Samson) and adulterers (David). But each in turn also knew God, and God knew them, despite the sense one gets from the narrative that most of them would never have gone looking for God had he not stopped them in their tracks.

Charismatic spirituality, then, appears here as a spirituality marked by divine initiative, and largely manifested in persons with no obvious inclination toward spiritual things. God's covenant promises to Abraham are the basis for his specific activity within the period of charismatic leadership, but how and why the particular individual hero is chosen is nowhere stated. We are left with the ancient question, "Who has known the ways of the Lord, and who has been his counsellor?"

What Happened to People in Charismatic Spiritual Encounters? (The Nature of Divine Encounter)

In Old Testament charismatic spirituality, encounters with God follow a logical, and possibly theological, order. First, spiritual encounters of this kind often, though not always, begin with a revelatory word to or about the individual, in which God's arresting intention is made clear. Only then does the individual have an encounter with God, characteristically described as a meeting with God's Spirit.

Word as Preparation for the Spirit

The charismatic figures we are considering fall into three categories, based on what kind of revelatory preparation preceded their own personal encounter with the Spirit, as follows: Those with no clear revelatory pre-history; those who are the subject of, or recipient of, prophetic utterance; and those to whom the word comes through angelic visitation.

First, charismatics whose stories contain no evidence of revelatory phenomena include Othniel, Ehud, Shamgar and Jephthah. Two of these four, Othniel and Jephthah, are explicitly stated to have encountered the Spirit.

Second, charismatics who were the subject of, or recipient of, prophetic utterance form a significant category, though the experiences differ widely among themselves. Deborah (Jdg 4) is herself a prophetess, and though she fits clearly the pattern of charismatic spirituality, nothing is said about any subsequent encounters with God. In the associated narrative, Barak is called and commanded by God, through Deborah the prophet of Yahweh (Jdg 4:6), but again we know little of the rest of his spiritual history. The Gideon story is accompanied by a brief introductory prophetic narrative (Jdg 6:7-10), but nothing in the narrative indicates any direct encounter between the prophet and Gideon. The angelic visitation is the key to Gideon's spiritual history.

With Samuel, we find a classic prophetic call (1Sa 3), comparable in form to the call of Moses and the Father's acknowledging of Jesus at his baptism. Samuel, like Deborah, continues to prophesy, presumably in an ecstatic prophetic style (1Sa 19:18-24), though there is no further evidence of charismatic encounter with the Spirit.

Both Saul and David, following the introduction of kingship, are called, anointed, and introduced by prophetic utterance. Both will be models of charismatic spiritual encounter, manifesting gifts associated with charismatic spirituality. Each of them, however, is chosen by God through the prophet Samuel, for a particular covenantal task, for which the gifting will be an affirmation or an enabling (cf. 1Sa 10:9-11; 1Sa 19:17-24 and 1Sa 16:13). Word, again, precedes Spirit.

Third, we find two charismatics, Gideon and Samson, whose encounters with their empowering God are preceded by or associated with angelic visitation. In the case of Gideon, the visitation is personal (Jdg 6:11-23) and functions very much like the prophetic calls of Moses, Saul, and others. The angel, in fact, turns out to be Yahweh himself in some incarnational form (Jdg 6:14), and the message revealed through the angelic visitation is not unlike the more direct divine-human dialogue common to Old Testament figures.

In the case of Samson, the angel visits his mother and father (Jdg 13), revealing Samson's manner of life (Nazirite) and the purpose for which he will later be gifted, i.e., the beginning of God's vengeance on the Philistines (Jdg 13:5). One is reminded of the angelic visitation to the parents of John the Baptist.

Encounters with the Spirit

Following consequentially, and usually chronologically, comes the individual divine encounter, but even here no universal rules can be discerned.[2] We have already seen that when the Spirit is given, he[3] comes sovereignly, to individuals whose preparation is known only to God. Is there anything we can say about the encounter itself?

Taking the references from Judges and 1 Samuel to God's Spirit coming upon an individual,[4] we find little evidence to describe the encounter itself. Apart from the effects, the terminology used may be our only clue to what happened. Three verbal expressions describe the various encounters. Because we are here at the very heart of charismatic spirituality, I want to examine this usage in some detail.

Beginning with what may be considered the mildest expression, we find the five-times-repeated reference "the Spirit came upon X" (וַתְּהִי עָלָיו אֶל/עַל). This is said of Othniel at his inauguration to judgeship (Jdg 3:10), of Jephthah after his speech and before he mustered the troops (Jdg 11:29), of Saul in the case of an "evil spirit" possessing him (1Sa 19:9), of the messengers of Saul when they broke into unsought prophetic utterance (1Sa 19:20), and finally of Saul himself under the same circumstances (1Sa 19:23).[5] The connotation is surely one of an external force, or personality, possessing or controlling the individual so endued.

Moving to a slightly stronger verb, which incorporates one of the richest metaphorical expressions in the Bible, we discover in Jdg 6:34 that Gideon is "clothed" (לָבְשָׁה) with the Spirit.[6] Throughout Scripture, clothing—its material (garments of skin, fine linen, a robe, an ephod or a tunic, sackcloth, camel's hair, etc.), its colors (purple, scarlet, white, blue), its condition (clean or filthy garments, soft raiment, dipped in blood, white and clean), or even its existence or lack of same (clothed as opposed to naked)—has great significance for understanding a situation.

The figure is extended even further when clothing is used as a metaphor for a spiritual quality. We read of priests clothed with salvation (2Ch 6:41), Job clothed with worms and scabs (Job 7:5), enemies of God clothed with shame (Job 8:22, etc.), a worshipper clothed with joy (Ps 30:11), enemies clothed with shame and disgrace (Ps 35:26), pastures clothed with flocks (Ps 65:12), Yahweh clothed in majesty and strength (Ps 93:1, etc.), a scoffer clothing himself with cursing (Ps 109:18), a godly wife clothed with strength and honor (Pr 31:25), the righteous clothed with garments of salvation (Isa 61:10), evil men at the end of time clothed with terror or doom (Eze 7:18,27), princes clothed with trembling (Eze 26:16), Lebanon clothed with gloom (Eze 31:15). Turning to the New Testament we discover the same rich imagery. Paul's vivid figures include the departed believer being "clothed in immortality" (1Co 15:54) and "clothed with our heavenly dwelling" (2Co 5:2), as well as believers "clothing yourselves with Christ" (Ro 13:14; Gal 3:27) and "putting on" the new person (Eph 4:24).[7] Peter speaks of clothing in ethical terms ("clothed with humility," 1Pe 5:5), and the Apocalypse imagines figures clothed with the sun (Rev 12:1) or a cloud (Rev 10:1), and multitudes of the redeemed clothed in white robes and fine linen.

But Luke contains the most interesting and informative figure for comparison purposes, when our Lord himself tells the disciples to "stay in the city until you have been clothed with power from on high" (Lk 24:49).[8] The figure expresses almost exactly the sense conveyed by the three references in Judges and the Chronicles: the Spirit is given, like a garment, not merely covering spiritual nakedness, but in a sense creating the new personality who emerges from the spiritual encounter with God.

A third, and perhaps yet stronger verb, is found in the expression translated "and the Spirit came mightily upon *X*" (וַתִּצְלַח).[9] The normal sense of the verb צלה is "to prosper greatly." As a metaphor to describe the prospering of the Spirit, the verb is employed only in Judges and 1 Samuel, and then only of three great charismatic figures, Samson, Saul and David.

Of Samson, the expression is first used when he comes face to face with a hostile young lion, approaching the vineyards of Timnah (Jdg 14:6). Next, in the moment of his angry response to the perfidy of his bride and her townsmen, the Spirit again "came mightily upon" Samson (Jdg 14:19). And, finally, having agreed to let the men of Judah bind him with new ropes, as Samson was about to be handed over to the Philistines, suddenly "the Spirit of the LORD came upon him in power" (Jdg 15:14). Earlier, the Spirit had "begun to move" Samson; now in each case a threat had arisen to his mission, and God's Spirit supernaturally endued him with the needed equipment. "Success" or "prosperity" in overcoming the threat was required, and Samson's "spirituality" was appropriate to the occasion.

For Saul, the situation is not dissimilar. His encounter with God through Samuel will need a sign to confirm it, both in Saul's own eyes and in the eyes of Israel. The sign is prophecy, as promised in 1Sa 10:6 and fulfilled in 1Sa 10:10, and the source of the gift in each instance is the coming of the Spirit "with power" (וַתִּצְלַח). A third time the narrative invokes the same strong expression (1Sa 11:6) to describe the spiritual source of Saul's righteous anger, which led to his affirmation as the military leader of Jabesh Gilead, and thus of all Israel. The charismatic spirituality of Saul, like that of Samson, is a spirituality of power.

The final figure of whom this verb is used is David. Following, and consequent upon, his anointing by Samuel ("from that day on"; 1Sa 16:13), the Spirit of Yahweh "came mightily upon David." David does not require the sign of prophecy, as he is already affirmed by certain heroic qualities (cf. 1Sa 16:18; 17:34-5) and will soon be affirmed by military prowess (1Sa 17), all of which are, for the reader, a consequence of his encounter with the Spirit ("from that day on...in power"; 1Sa 16:13). This is classic charismatic spirituality.

What Kind of Piety Resulted from Charismatic Spiritual Encounters? (The Effects of Divine Encounter)

Classics of spiritual life through the ages, as typified by *The Confessions* of Augustine, paint a picture of spiritual growth following spiritual awakening. We have noted above the classic elements: a life of intensified prayer, heightened ethical sensitivity, zeal for God's work, and often a commitment to institutional service within the church. Having looked at the pattern of Old Testament charismatic spirituality, we now ask if there is evidence of a clear pattern of such effects.

Charismatic Spirituality and Prayer

Traditional language of prayer is often wanting in narrative portions of the Old Testament, being replaced with the phenomenon of a running dialogue with God. Gideon, from his encounter with Yahweh (Jdg 6) through his victory over Midian (Jdg 7), seems to live in the direct presence of God, though significantly, from the beginning of chapter eight onward, there is no reference to the Spirit or to dialogue with God.

If Gideon's life began with prayer and then declined, Samson's may be just the opposite. Initially, Samson seemed to lack an awareness of what God was doing through him (Jdg 14:4), but this insensitivity was later reversed. Two incidents stand as markers in the narrative. Jdg 15:18-19 pictures Samson, at the moment of his greatest victory, crying out to the Lord for survival, and being heard. Then, after the tragedy with Delilah and his subsequent imprisonment, Samson's life is ended in communion with God (Jdg 16:28), his final prayer dominated, as earlier, by the theme of divine vengeance upon the Philistines.

Samuel and David could be cited also, for both had regular and consistent communion with God. But Gideon and Samson may be the more interesting examples, precisely because they do not fit the pattern of spirituality in other ways.

Charismatic Spirituality and Ethical Behavior

Changed behavior of all kinds is a mark of the spiritual life, but heightened ethical sensitivities stand out. Is there, then, any evidence of heightened ethical behavior on the part of the classic charismatics?

The answer is difficult to come by, and made more so because the period of charismatic spirituality must be judged by its own standards.

Societal standards from what is called a "Heroic Age"[10] would hardly have been acceptable even a few hundred years later, much less now. But, even granting the differences, there is little we can say about the relationship between spiritual encounters and ethics. Most of those touched by God's Spirit seem creatures of their age and time.

Charismatic Spirituality and Zeal for God's Work

Here is where charismatic encounter left its mark. These encounters with the Spirit were given as God's means to deliver his covenant people; zeal for national restoration followed. Othniel "went to war" (Jdg 3:16), Gideon "blew a trumpet" (Jdg 6:34), Jephthah "crossed Gilead and Manasseh" (Jdg 11:29), and Saul cut oxen into pieces to send throughout Israel (1Sa 11:6ff.). Each was an act of mustering the people to accomplish Yahweh's redemptive purpose of Holy War. Zeal for Yahweh, and the call back to covenant integrity, became the hallmark of charismatic spirituality.

Old Testament Charismatic Spirituality and New Testament Models

The book of Luke-Acts provides the New Testament narrative equivalent to the Old Testament record of charismatic spirituality, while 1 Corinthians provides the doctrinal base. Encounter spirituality, and the gifting that follows, sets the ethos of the church in both books. Charismatic spiritual life, dominated as it is by personalities and bold action rather than rational structures, is not always smooth, but the mighty working of the Spirit, as in the Old Testament, attests to the presence of God and gives life to the community. Strong, charismatic figures, filled with the Spirit, boldly challenge the accepted order, with victory upon victory for the covenant people. Peter, Stephen, Barnabas and Paul stand in the tradition of Jesus Christ himself as, filled with the Spirit, they witness to the power of God in the New Covenant.

Summary

We are left with some clear principles. First, biblical spirituality, at least of the charismatic model, though dominated by strong personalities, is not dependent upon a spiritual personality. The initiative comes from God, and seems to depend much more on his sovereign purposes than on an individual with a bent toward divine things.

Second, the charismatic spirituality of the Old Testament is closely tied to divine revelation and its salvific purpose. God, whose Spirit was the key to charismatic spirituality, usually indicated through a vision or a revelation what his purpose would be in the spiritual encounter to follow. The actual encounter was both a sign gift to confirm the revelation and a supernatural enduement to accomplish the task.

Third, charismatic spirituality, at least for some, did heighten an awareness of God. The immediacy of divine-human communication is a mark of the period, and those who have encountered God by his Spirit communicate freely with him.

Fourth, while charismatic spirituality may not have radically reshaped the ethics of the recipient, there is no question that the one so endued had a fresh zeal for God. With the power to perform, and revelation pointing to the goal, the gifted individual seemed also strangely warmed and motivated to serve. Charismatic spirituality, then, is spirituality zealous for God's work.

Finally, charismatic spirituality was largely independent of official religious institutions. Old Testament charismatic spirituality arose in an age of individualism. The priesthood, which should have been flourishing, was largely absent or in decline. Classical prophets, successors to the earlier charismatics, would arise much later. Thus, charismatic spirituality is essentially an "outsider" form of spirituality. That it baffled as well as fascinated the godly in its own day is evident from its treatment by the editors of Joshua—2 Kings. Not surprisingly, the same perplexing anomalies emerge in our own struggle to evaluate contemporary spiritual encounters in the tradition of Gideon, Jephthah, Samson and Saul, wherever and however they may be manifested.

Notes

1   See the standard introductory material for chapters 13-16 of the book of Judges.
2   As in the Acts of the Apostles, where references to the Holy Spirit "falling" or "filling" are sporadic and occasional, leaving the reader unable to discern a clear pattern of cause and effect.
3   By using the personal pronoun, I may be accused of reading New Testament trinitarian categories back into the Old Testament. It is not clear, apart from such, how one can adequately account for the personal nature of the encounter, for the "Spirit" which comes is evidently God himself, in a form (spirit) which is appropriate to the encounter.
4   Othniel (Jdg 3:10); Gideon (6:34); Jephthah (11:29); Samson (13:25; 14:6; 14:19; 15:14); Saul (1Sa 10:6; 10:10; 11:6); David (16:13); the messengers of Saul (19:20); Saul (19:23). Outside these two books, similar expressions are found concerning Bezalel (Ex 31:3; 35:31); Balaam (Nu 24:2); Azariah ben Oded (2Ch 15:1); Zechariah ben Jehoiada (2Ch 24:20); the Branch (Isa 11:2); the Messianic Figure (Isa 61:1); Ezekiel (Eze 11:5); Micah (Mic 3:8).
5   Apart from these references, only in Nu 24:2 (Balaam), 2Ch 15:1 (Azariah), and 2Ch 20:14 (Jahaziel) do we find the same combination.
6   Apart from Gideon, only Amasai, chief of David's Thirty (1Ch 12:18 [Heb. 19]) and Zechariah ben Jehoiada (2Ch 24:20) are thus described. Brief mention should be made of Amasai, an otherwise unknown "Chief of the Thirty," who is "clothed with" the Spirit, in consequence of which he utters a few lines of inspired heroic poetry. The incident is dated by scholars to David's outlaw period, and Amasai's spiritual encounter is fully consistent with the charismatic spirituality of the period in question.
7   These, and other New Testament references, draw on a variety of Greek verbs, especially

ἐνδύω. The reader should consult both Hebrew and Greek concordances for the rich vocabulary involved.

[8] NIV: AV here employs an equivalent (be endued with power) rather than the literal "be clothed with" (ἐνδύω).

[9] AV translates the verb, in this context, with both "came mightily upon" and "came upon." NIV attempts a consistent "came . . . in power."

[10] See my dissertation, *The Heroic Ages of Israel and Greece* (Ann Arbor, Mich.: University Microfilms, 1968).

6

How Did Jesus Pray?
The Spirituality of Jesus in the
Apostolic Church[1]

Markus Bockmuehl

TODAY, THE TERM "SPIRITUALITY" HAS BECOME SOMETHING OF A buzzword. While one can encounter it in the whole gamut of orthodox Christian denominations, it seems to be equally popular in the New Age movement. Even in a business world keen to emulate the success of Japanese labor practices one can hear talk of "corporate spirituality." Given this wide range of usage, one wonders what useful meaning this term might have in the Christian context, where it is employed to describe a certain character or quality of the regenerate life.

The *Oxford English Dictionary* offers little help: none of its six suggested categories of meaning sufficiently approximates the modern usage. Even the archaic term "ghostliness" (used in the days when people spoke of the "Holy Ghost") would seem to come nearer the mark, as do the French *spiritualité* and Italian *spiritualitá*, both of which can denote the Christian spiritual life.

Among the saner pronouncements on this subject is that of David Fyffe, writing over seventy years ago in Hastings' *Encyclopædia of Religion and Ethics* (vol. II, p. 808). Noting the great variety of meanings assigned to the term "spirituality," including evangelical Christianity's tendency to reserve it for "the warmer religious emotions," he underscores that "it has its proper and peculiar application as the distinguishing quality of NT believers." The spiritual person (i.e., πνευματικός), according to the New Testament, manifests the Holy Spirit as the vital and determining principle of his or her life. Hence "the NT usage [of this term] does not permit us to apply the epithet to anyone who has been moved in some vague way by holy impulses, for a definite and well-marked character is indicated by this description." Christian spirituality is the quality of a life that manifests the Spirit of Christ.

Central to the experience of the early Christians was an ongoing relationship with the exalted Jesus. This relationship is predominantly described by two interlocking groups of metaphors, one relating to participation in Christ, the other to imitation of him. The former affirms the present and continuing reality of salvation and is expressed (i) in status imagery like the body of Christ (Ro 12; 1 Co 12), the vine and its branches (Jn 15), and the treasure or citizenship in heaven (Mt 6; Php 3; Col 3; Eph 2; Heb 12); and (ii) in the narrative metaphor of the believer's participation in the death and resurrection of Christ, both initially at baptism (Ro 6; Col 2) and continually in the afflictions and aspirations of the Christian life (e.g., 2Co 4:7-12; Col 1:24; Heb 13:12f; 1Pe 4:13; cf. Mk 8:34; 10:39 par.).

The image of participation naturally gives rise to that of imitation, which was a practice deeply engrained in the Jewish understanding of the teacher-disciple relationship.[2] Paul, the former Pharisee, repeatedly encourages his churches to "become imitators of me as I am of Christ" (1Co 11:1 and passim). For a believer to be "in Christ" means to follow his teaching and example. Both these aspects of imitation are already present in Jesus' own teaching, and are actively encouraged in the Apostolic churches.

Perhaps the single most important expression of both participation in Christ and imitation of Christ is prayer. Prayer conveys most profoundly the openness, trust and dependence in the depth of our being which characterize a true relationship with God.

Proceeding from these observations, the present article examines the New Testament's account of the prayer life of Jesus as an important facet of early Christian spirituality. It is dedicated to James M. Houston in gratitude and personal indebtedness for his untiring ministry of teaching, writing, and spiritual direction.

The material itself suggests an approach in three stages, reflecting the interpretation of Jesus' prayer life in the Synoptic Gospels, in the Gospel of John, and in the remainder of the New Testament.[3]

The Synoptic Gospels
Jesus' Experience of Prayer
The public ministry of Jesus begins with his baptism by John. As a

symbol of personal and national repentance and restoration, it was evidently an experience of great spiritual significance for Jesus, primarily in view of the accompanying vision of the Spirit of God descending like a dove while a heavenly voice declared his Messianic status as the specially favored "Son of God" (Mk 1:9-11 par.). This vision appears in turn to have precipitated the episode of temptation in the wilderness. The source of the "temptation," which in Matthew and Luke takes the form of an identity crisis over his newly affirmed "Son of God" title (Mt 4:3, 6 par.), is none other than Satan. Although not explicitly concerned with prayer, these first two scenes of baptism and temptation are in fact highly suggestive of the basic orientation which characterizes Jesus' spiritual life, for they show his whole purpose and identity to be centered on his divine commissioning and relationship to God as Son. In the narrative of the Gospels, three crises precipitate a testing of this identity: the temptation in the wilderness, the questioning of his disciples at Caesarea Philippi, and the prayer at Gethsemane.

Perhaps more than any other part of the New Testament, the stories of Jesus manifest a dramatic, sometimes breathtaking spirituality of close familial intimacy with God and an externalized, cosmic conflict with evil. Satan and his demons are the chief opponents of Jesus and the imminent kingdom of God (in addition to the healing miracles, see Mk 4:15, 8:33 par.; Lk 13:16; 22:3, 31); his message and ministry have come to topple them from power (see esp. Lk 10:18, Mk 3:27 par.).

Jesus appears to have nurtured his close relationship with God above all in frequent, extended periods of solitary prayer. Although he often stresses the importance of faith for healing and deliverance (and rebukes the disciples for their lack of it), he clearly also believed that the most difficult obstacles were only to be overcome by the kind of faith that is nurtured in persistent personal prayer (Mk 9:29 par.). That is where he sought and found the strength to carry on his own ministry. Above all else, Jesus' confident spirituality is rooted and anchored in the security of his communion with the heavenly Father (which in Luke begins as early as his childhood, 2:49).

Among the Synoptic Gospels it is Luke above all who develops the theme of Jesus' prayer life. Jesus is praying when he receives his post-baptismal vision (3:21). He prepares for the selection of the Twelve by spending a night in prayer (6:12; cf. 5:16), and he thanks God for the successful mission of the Seventy (10:21-22). Both his question to the disciples at Caesarea Philippi (9:18) and his transfiguration (9:28-36) appear in the context of prayer. Luke makes prayer the repeated subject of Jesus' teaching (chap. 11, 18) and he alone reports on Jesus' intercession for the disciples (22:31-32).[4]

Nevertheless, it is rare for Synoptic miracle stories *explicitly* to represent Jesus at prayer.[5] Exorcisms in particular are never said to be accompanied by prayer; possibly this is due to the image of Jesus as the one who, fortified by the assurance of his sonship, appears in the role of the "stronger man" to assault and defeat Beelzebul (Mk 3:27; cf. Lk 11:22).

In the Synoptic Gospels generally, Jesus repeatedly withdraws from friend and foe alike to a lonely place at night or before daybreak (e.g., Mk 1:35, 45 par.). The location can be a mountain (Lk 6:12, 9:28), and is finally a quiet spot in the garden of Gethsemane, just beneath the city in the Kidron valley (Mk 14:32-42 par.). But Jesus also assumed that the Temple is a place of prayer (Lk 18:10; Mk 11:17 par.). He undoubtedly prayed there himself, as indeed he appears to have joined in the customary forms of prayer associated with the annual festivals in Jerusalem, including the Passover celebration which concluded with the singing of the second half of the *Hallel* (i.e., Ps 116—18: cf. Mk 14:26 par.). Jesus would have participated in the daily recitation of the *Shema* ("Hear O Israel," Dt 6:4-5: note Mk 12:29-30) and possibly early versions of the *Amidah* (Eighteen Benedictions) or the *Kaddish*, synagogal prayers whose concerns are also present in his own teaching.[6]

From the centrality of this relationship arose his deep conviction that all the circumstances of life, history and even nature were subject to the unstoppable advance of the kingdom of God. This, clearly, is the consistent attitude in his personal encounters, where the call of God puts all human loyalties in their place (Mt 8:21-22 etc.). People came to recognize the extraordinary power and authority which emanated from Jesus' prayer life (Mt 8:8-9 par.; 19:13).

Jesus not only claimed this closeness with God for himself. By his example and teaching, especially in parables, he encouraged his followers to adopt the same sense of conscious expectancy and awareness of God's presence and care for them. Jesus simply took for granted *that* his disciples would pray (Mk 11:25 par.) and was more concerned with *how* they prayed: boldly, expectantly, with undaunted persistence and faith (Mt 7:7 par.); privately and in secret (Mt 6:6); as to a *loving* Father and a *righteous* Judge who will surely act (cf. Lk 11:11-13; 18:1-8); not in meaningless, unthinking words (Mt 6:7); not expecting God's mercy unless they themselves were merciful (Mt 6:14-15 par.). Humility and childlike candor are needed in approaching God (Lk 18.9-14, 15-17). Prayer protects against worry (Mt 6:11, 25-33; cf. Php 4:7) and losing heart (Lk 18:1). It is a safe haven in the time of trial (Mt 6:13; 26:41), and corporate prayer in particular is sure to be heard (Mt 18:19-20). In view of the massive kingdom harvest, the disciples are to ask God for workers (Lk 10:2 par.), which is in effect to ask him for the human resources needed that the kingdom may come.[7]

Although the Synoptic Gospels do not offer much explicit evidence, what little we do know suggests that Jesus himself practiced these same principles of prayer.

Jesus' Prayers

Six actual prayers are recorded and merit our attention; an additional one in Lk 22:31-32 is merely reported and will be considered in conjunction with John 17 below.

First there is Jesus' thanksgiving for revelation in Mt 11:25-26 and Lk 10:21. In Luke, not implausibly, the setting for this prayer is the Lord's joyful response to the successful mission of the Seventy:

> At that same time Jesus, full of joy through the Holy Spirit, said, "I praise you, Father, Lord of heaven and earth, because you have hidden these things from the wise and learned, and revealed them to little children. Yes, Father, for this was your good pleasure."

The defeat of Satan and the demons in his name (Lk 10:17-18) causes Jesus to rejoice. He celebrates the mysterious work of God who has chosen to manifest the arrival of his kingdom not to the theologians and the establishment, but to the simple people ("infants") who have become his disciples. Here, then, is a spontaneous, Spirit-filled expression of gratitude for God's work, which springs from Jesus' childlike, trusting identification with the Father's intentions: "Yes, Father, for this was your good pleasure."

By far the most important passage is Lk 11:1-13, which contains the Lord's Prayer. This prayer, whether in its Lucan or Matthean version, strikingly encapsulates Jesus' own attitude to prayer and to God; Tertullian, indeed, was probably not amiss to regard it as the very epitome of the gospel (*On Prayer*, 1).

In Matthew, the longer and more familiar version of the Lord's Prayer is presented as part of the Sermon on the Mount. It is one of very few passages in which Jesus speaks of corporate prayer (but cf. Mt 18:19-20). In the Matthean context its unique form and brevity agree well with the Gospel's criticism of both spiritual ostentation in the synagogue and meaningless wordiness among Gentiles (Mt 6:5-15).

Luke, by contrast, has this text as the first of two passages specifically on prayer (18:1-8 being the second). His version is usually thought to be closer to the original, although Matthew's prayer shows signs of having been used liturgically in Aramaic.[8] Significantly for our purposes, the disciples' request, "Lord, teach us to pray" (Lk 11:1), arises *from their observation of Jesus at prayer.* Even allowing that part of their motive was the desire not to be outdone by John's disciples (11:1), they clearly admire and want to imitate their Master in this regard.

For Luke, the prayer simply begins with "Father," i.e., "Abba" in Aramaic. This word, which was a child's familiar address to a father or older man (although expressing a greater sense of respect and loyalty than "Daddy"[9]), was apparently Jesus' characteristic form of address to God.[10] Even the early Gentile church regarded this Aramaic term as so significant as to continue its use in Greek (Mk 14:36; Ro 8:15; Gal 4:6). Clearly it was thought to symbolize Jesus' own characteristically close relationship with the Father, in which Christians now participate. The loving fatherhood of God evokes and undergirds the trust by which we can pray.

In substance, these verses display the manifest conviction that true prayer intends first and foremost to affirm the Father's will: it wants to contribute to his eternal glory by magnifying him in the world. There is no hint here of asking God to change his intended course of action, or of bending his will in keeping with our plans and desires. That kind of prayer implies a view of God which is far too small and petty-minded. Instead, our will and our needs are conceived as an integral (and significant) part of the larger concern for God's kingdom on earth. When our will is transformed into God's will, God is glorified in providing the answer to our needs. Rabban Gamaliel III said: "Do his will as your will, that he may do your will as his will" (*m. 'Abot* 2.4).

The Lord's Prayer, then, has as its definitive concern the believer's trusting affirmation of the will of God. We cannot in fact genuinely pray for the hallowing of God's name, the coming of his kingdom and the accomplishing of his will without undergoing a profound realignment of our will with his. All three Synoptic Gospels (as well as the church fathers) see Gethsemane as the place where Jesus most graphically demonstrated this.

Nevertheless, it would be a serious misunderstanding of Jesus' prayer to suppose that this affirmation of God's will implies a kind of spiritual sublimation of human needs and desires. Personal petitions do form an important part of this prayer. They are best understood as the translation into the concrete personal realm of the first three requests. May God's name be hallowed, his will be done and his kingdom come—by his providing our material sustenance day by day, forgiving our sins in the context of human reconciliation, and protecting us from the trial by which the evil one wants to make us deny God's providential fatherhood and bully us into allegiance.[11] And thus, in fact, the Lord's Prayer comes full circle: as Jesus' own ministry makes clear, God's name is honored and his kingdom comes precisely where his people are delivered from evil and their material and spiritual sustenance is supplied (see esp. Mt 10:7-8 par.; 12:28 par.). Petition, then, has its rightful place in prayer: not as a plea that God may change his course of action, but as the concrete shape *on earth as it is in heaven* of "Hallowed be your name, your kingdom come."

The third recorded prayer of Jesus is set in the garden of Gethsemane. After the Last Supper he left the city with his disciples for the Mount of Olives, but they appear to have stopped in an olive grove or garden in the valley, just across the Kidron. Jesus went aside by himself to pray, in Mark's version (14:36): "*Abba*, Father, . . . everything is possible for you. Take this cup from me. Yet not what I will, but what you will." Evident internal strife marks this final time alone with God (Mt 26:38 par.; cf. Jn 12:27). Along with the discovery of Judas' betrayal, the events of the preceding days have made it quite clear that this must be the end. Jesus had realized and affirmed God's will for him at least since Caesarea Philippi (cf. Mk 8:31 par.), but here he comes closer than at any other time to a plea that God may change his purpose. This shows Jesus at his most human, the Jesus whom the writer to the Hebrews upholds as the high priest subject to weakness (4:14-5:10, esp 5:7).

Even here, however, with a painfully burning request in view, Jesus is portrayed as drawing on the wellspring of unquestioned trust in the Father's providence. In spite of palpably desperate circumstances, his *cri de cœur* begins with *Abba*—Mark's account contains the only explicit use of this term in the Gospels. His task is harsh, but it is still the assignment of the same Father, whose character and therefore whose will he knows to be unchangingly providential, merciful, all-powerful. This conviction allows him to affirm God's will as his—without thereby stifling his natural human desire of going only to the brim of the bitter cup, not having to drink it down to the dregs. The Lord's Prayer here becomes the prayer of Jesus in a very personal way. With his trust in man betrayed and all certainty eclipsed, Jesus' faith remains founded on the bedrock of the fatherhood of God. Because God is Father, "your will be done" still means "your kingdom come." Even when it seems all but impossible to pronounce them, those words remain a prayer for salvation.

Job, in a somewhat different spirit, may have said, "Though he slay me, yet will I trust in him" (Job 13:15, AV). Jesus' prayer, however, shows not righteous tenacity so much as a humble, obedient hope in the unchanging goodness of the Father's will.[12]

The seven last words of Jesus are reported differently in the four

Gospels; only the Synoptic Gospels have Jesus praying on the cross. Of the three traditional prayers, two appear only in Luke and one only in Mark and Matthew.

Jesus, being nailed to the cross, asks: "Father, forgive them; for they do not know what they are doing" (Lk 23:34).[13] At least three significant observations can be made about this prayer. First, along with the promise to the repentant criminal, Jesus' prayer provides a kind of confirmation of the atoning and redemptive significance of his martyrdom on the cross (which in Luke otherwise appears only in 22:20 and 24:46-47). Second, it beautifully illustrates the attitude of meekness, mercy and fortitude for which the passion of Jesus was prominently remembered in the early church (see esp. 1Pe 2:21-25). And third, at the same time this request strikingly embodies his own (and early Christian) radical teaching about love and prayer for one's enemies (Lk 6:27-36 par.; Ro 12:14; 1Co 4:12).

Jesus' final prayer of desperation, hauntingly recorded in its original form[14] in Mt 27:46 (cf. Mk 15:34), is a clear echo of Ps 22:1: "My God, my God, why have you forsaken me?" It is hard to exaggerate the literary and theological impact of this prayer; its dramatic significance in Mark and Matthew is heightened all the more in that for them these are Jesus' only words spoken from the cross. On the most obvious and literal level, this is the last outcry of a broken man, crushed in spirit as he feels abandoned by humans and God. The bystanders, in a stroke of tragic irony, mistake Jesus' Hebrew address to God (*Eli, Eli*; Mark has Aramaic *Eloi, Eloi*) as a call for the expected end-time return of Elijah (*Eliyahu*). They are thus completely blind to the remarkable transparency of these words. Here is a man, alone and in terrible agony in his dying moments, casting his desperate plight before a silent God.

And yet: these very words explicitly recall Psalm 22, the quintessential prayer of the suffering innocent. Here is the bitterly forthright lament of the righteous believer who, bereft of every human consolation, holds on to the only certainty that remains: God's unchanging character as the Holy One who did not put to shame the trust of those who have gone before. What is more, lament (vv. 1-21a) before long turns into thanksgiving and praise for deliverance obtained (vv. 21b-31), even in the face of imminent death (v. 29).

Whether the whole of Psalm 22 resonates in Jesus' words is unclear; the passion narratives, at any rate, clearly assign it pride of place in their interpretation of his experience (cf. also vv. 7-8 with Mk 15:29 par. and Lk 23:35; v. 18 with Mk 15:24 par.). Here is Jesus the righteous, shaken but unblemished, faithful to the last.

Jesus' final utterance, recorded simply as a loud cry in Matthew and Mark, is also rendered as a prayer in Luke: "Father, into your hands I commit my spirit" (23:46). Explicitly or implicitly, the bearing of this prayer from Ps 31:5 typifies the death of Jesus in all the Gospels (cf. also Jn 19:30). Having drunk the bitter cup, true to his call even when this exacted the ultimate price, Jesus expires. For his enemies, this is the perfunctory but welcome seal of his failure; for the evangelists, here is his cosmic, crowning act of submission to the one who, nevertheless, is *Father.*

These prayers of Gethsemane and the cross had a profound impact on Christian spirituality in the New Testament and beyond. It seems that Luke consciously formulated the prayers of the church in Acts to reflect the prayers of Jesus.[15]

More particularly, the Lord's struggle at Gethsemane became a natural illustration of the Lord's Prayer for the church fathers,[16] while the tradition of his prayers on the cross fed directly into Christian reflection on martyrdom. Echoes of Luke's account of the prayers on the cross are found on the lips of the first Christian martyr,[17] and the attitude they exemplify is explicitly commended in 1Pe 2:23: even in the midst of abuse and suffering, Christ "entrusted himself to him who judges justly" (cf. Lk 23:46).

Martyrdom, it seems, came to be closely associated with participation in the suffering of Jesus. Thus we hear of the apostles, "suffering disgrace for the Name" (Ac 5:41), filling up what is "still lacking in regard to Christ's afflictions" (Col 1:24; cf. 2Co 4:10-11). Ignatius of Antioch looks forward to becoming "an imitator of the sufferings of my God" (Ign. *Rom.* 6:3); Polycarp rejoices that he may "share in the cup of Christ" (*Mart. Pol.* 14.2). Christ, indeed, suffers in the martyrs to manifest his glory (*Passion of Perpetua* 6.2; Eusebius, *Ecclesiastical History* 5.1.23). In the light of this, the traditions about Jesus' prayer life were obviously of broad exemplary importance for the spirituality of the early church.

The Gospel of John

As in other respects, the Fourth Gospel differs markedly from the Synoptics in its view of Jesus' prayer life. A baptismal vision is reported of John the Baptist rather than of Jesus (1:32); there is no temptation narrative, no teaching specifically on prayer, and no prayer on the cross. On the other hand, the Synoptic Gospels' description of Jesus' relationship to God as Father is now translated into a glorified relationship of the Son who is one with the Father (10:30). Jesus here is the Word become flesh (1:14); he has life in himself, authority to judge, and his voice raises the dead (5:26-29; 6:39f; cf. 11:43-44). Anyone who knows him knows the Father, and he and the Father make their dwelling with those who love them (14:7, 21, 23). Jesus speaks for the Father (12:50); whatever he says and does he has first seen or heard from him (3:11, 32; 5:19, 30; 8:26, 38, 40; 15:15). Jesus withdraws to the mountain by himself (6:15), but we do not explicitly hear of him spending long hours at prayer. John's picture of Jesus does not present his prayer life as a model to be followed in our approach to God, but instead regards spiritual and mystical union with Christ as being in itself the way to the Father (14:6; 15:1-17). The disciples are to pray in his name (14:13-14), but they are nowhere encouraged to pray *like* him.

Aside from the grace before the miracle of the loaves and fishes (6:11), Jesus' first prayer occurs at the tomb of Lazarus (11:41-42). This, however, is the utterance of the Son who is one with the Father, and is hardly a prayer to be emulated by his disciples:

> Father, I thank you that you have heard me. I knew that you always hear me, but I said this for the benefit of the people standing here, that they may believe that you sent me.

The same spirit of oneness with the Father occurs in chapter 12, a parallel to the Gethsemane prayer set here at the beginning of the passion narrative. Jesus, clearly troubled by the events that lie ahead, considers the prayer "Father, save me from this hour"—but only to move beyond it and pray instead for the glorification of God's name, which of course is why he has come (12:27-28, 30):

> "Now my heart is troubled, and what shall I say? 'Father, save me from this hour'? No, it was for this very reason I came to this hour. Father, glorify your name." Then a voice came from heaven, "I have glorified it, and will glorify it again." . . . Jesus said, "This voice was for your benefit, not mine."

The Johannine Jesus, though resolute in going to the cross, nevertheless shares the anxiety described in the Synoptic Gethsemane accounts. Here as there, however, the will of the Father is the higher concern. The Son for John is at one with the Father and faithfully seeks to glorify him; immediate confirmation of this is given from heaven.

One final text is of eminent significance in understanding the prayer life of Jesus in its impact on the early church: John 17 presents the most extensive prayer text of any of the Gospels. For several centuries this has been known as Jesus' "high priestly prayer," since one of its main themes is Jesus' representation of his disciples before God. A term like "testamentary prayer" may, however, be more descriptive.[18]

The prayer begins with Jesus asking to be glorified so that he may in turn glorify the Father (17:1-5). This theme is clearly a continuation of the previous prayer in 12:28, here applied to his imminent crucifixion and exaltation in the "hour" that has now "come." Indeed the whole passage can be read as an elaboration of the request "Glorify your name," clearly in close connection with the Synoptic Gethsemane prayer "your will be done." In other words, Jesus here prays for the glorification of the Father by his completion of the intended design, including the return to his eternal glory.

A crucial part of Jesus', and thereby the Father's, glorification is the protection and sanctification of those who have been entrusted to him, who do not belong to the world but are sent into it. In a sense Jesus cannot be fully glorified if any of his people are lost, since he is glorified in them (17:10) and has given them the glory he received from the Father (17:22). This is in order that they may be completely one, may see Jesus' glory and be fully united with him (17:21-26). Thus the world will be able to know plainly both Jesus' and God's love for his people (17:23).

Two important conclusions follow for the understanding of Jesus' spirituality in the Gospel of John. The first was intimated earlier: unlike the Synoptic Gospels, the Fourth Gospel presents Jesus' prayer life not primarily as an example to imitate, but as indicative of the Son's mystical union with the Father, in which believers come to *participate.*

Second, more than any other text in the Gospels, John 17 highlights Jesus' role in effective *intercession* for his disciples as they continue their lives in the world. The opposition of the evil one continues after Jesus' victory on the cross; and the world, for which Jesus emphatically does *not* pray (v. 9), is Satan's domain (cf. 12:31; also 1Jn 5:19). Nevertheless, believers now have a powerful advocate with the Father whose intercession is sure to be heard, so that the adversary cannot prevail.[19]

At this point it is worth briefly retracing our steps to the Synoptic Gospels, where Jesus' intercession is not a major theme. True, there are several sayings of the form "If anyone is ashamed of me . . . /denies me before others, I also will deny before my Father in heaven" (Mk 8:38 par. Lk 9:26; Mt 10:33 par. Lk 12:9; cf. Rev 3:5). This implies that, at least in regard to the final judgment, Jesus' advocacy is of crucial importance. Nevertheless, Luke 22:31-32 is the only explicit Synoptic reference to Jesus' intercession on behalf of others:[20]

> Simon, Simon, listen! Satan has asked to sift you as wheat. But I have prayed for you, Simon, that your faith may not fail. And when you have turned back, strengthen your brothers.

Faced by the impending tribulation of his arrest and the likely scattering of his followers, Jesus perceives Satan's antagonism to this small band of disciples and confidently entrusts Peter's (and through him the disciples') continuing faithfulness to God. Jesus once again is stronger than Satan; his prayer therefore must be superior to that of the adversary (who, it appears, must also *request* to "sift" the disciples; cf. Job 1-2). Like John 17, these verses occur in the context of the passion narrative, quite possibly pointing to the Lord's continuing post-resurrection role of intercession with the Father.

Through Jesus' intercession, then, believers are assured of their participation in the love of God and the union of the Father and the Son: "I in them and you in me. May they be brought to complete unity to let the world know that you sent me and have loved them even as you have loved me" (Jn 17:23).

This theme is one which also comes to prominence in Romans, Hebrews, and 1 John.

The Rest of the New Testament

Although there are a large number of potentially relevant texts about the exalted Christ or the activity of the Spirit, I want here to concentrate specifically on a few New Testament passages which allude directly to Jesus praying. This will serve further to indicate the influence of the spirituality of Jesus in the early church.

Romans 8 celebrates the believers' liberation from sin and death by "the Spirit of life in Christ Jesus" and their adoption as children of God. Throughout the passage, "Christ" and "Spirit" are interchangeable: as "Christ is in you," so the Spirit dwells in you (vv. 9-11). This Spirit of Christ comes to the aid of Christians who in their weakness and longing for their future glory may not know how to pray as they ought; so the Spirit, who is intimately known by God, "intercedes for us with groans that words cannot express" (vv. 26-27). It is the same Spirit who was earlier said to confirm and bear witness to our adoption as children of God who may boldly address him with the prayer of Jesus, "*Abba!*" (vv. 15-16; cf. Gal 4:6). The identification is completed in v. 34, where the same Christ Jesus who died and was raised is now at the right hand of God and intercedes for us. For Paul, then, Christians' imitation of Jesus' own prayer goes hand in hand with participation in the benefits of his heavenly intercession for them. His position at the right hand of God is here not simply an expression of his exalted power, but enables him uniquely to win the Father's favor on behalf of his people, the church. It is through him, and presumably by the power of his intercession, that Christians have inalienable access to the love of God in Christ (vv. 31-39; cf. Eph 3:12 etc.).

Jesus' prayer is not the explicit subject of attention elsewhere in Paul's writings. Nevertheless, other texts about Christ's being at the right hand of God (Col 3:1; cf. Eph 1:20; 1Pe 3:22) are at least compatible with, if not indeed suggestive of, the theme of his intercession for believers.[21] Similarly, what Paul says about sharing in the sufferings of Christ (e.g., in 2Co 4:10-11, Php 3:10, Col 1:24; cf. 1Pe 4:13) is quite plausibly of a piece with the "Gethsemane spirituality" we discussed earlier. The related (but more general) theme of Christ's self-humbling obedience even to the point of death on a cross is specifically endorsed as the paradigm of Christian conduct in the well-known christological passage Php 2:5-11.

Some of the most evocative language about Jesus' prayer life occurs in the anonymous letter to the Hebrews. Here the primary emphasis of the theme of Christ's sitting at God's right hand is to distinguish him from angels and lesser beings (1:13 etc.). Such "high" christology notwithstanding, in chapter 5:7-9 the author wields powerful words about the humanity of Jesus, highlighting what appears to be the struggle at Gethsemane:

> During the days of Jesus' life on earth, he offered up prayers and petitions with loud cries and tears to the one who could save him from death, and he was heard because of his reverent submission. Although he was a son, he learned obedience from what he suffered and, once made perfect, he became the source of eternal salvation for all who obey him and was designated by God to be a high priest in the order of Melchizedek.

Taking the humanity of Jesus seriously, Hebrews regards Jesus' anxious Gethsemane prayer and his attitude of submission as both exemplary (cf. Heb 12:2) *and* contributing to the redemption in which Christians participate. Because Jesus experienced weakness and testing as we do, he can sympathize and deal gently with us (cf. 4:15).

But conversely, Hebrews goes on to say, Jesus has "gone through the heavens" (4:14) and entered behind the curtain of the heavenly Holy of Holies (6:19-20; 9:25) as sinless, eternal high priest on our behalf. As such he is the guarantee of our salvation and our effective intercessor: "Therefore he is able to save completely those who come to God through him, because he always lives to intercede for them" (7:25). Once again it is clear how both the motif of exemplary submission at Gethsemane and that of intercession for his disciples are taken up from the traditions about the prayer of Jesus.

We come then, finally, to 1Jn 2:1-2, where Jesus once again appears as our heavenly advocate:

> My dear children, I write this to you so that you will not sin. But if anybody does sin, we have one who speaks to the Father in our defense—Jesus Christ, the Righteous One. He is the atoning sacrifice

for our sins, and not only for ours but also for the sins of the whole world.

In many ways the first Letter of John closely reflects the theology of the Fourth Gospel. But unlike John 17, and more as in Hebrews, the subject of Christ's intercession here is not general protection but specifically atonement for sin: it is his sacrifice which intervenes with the Father for the sin of the believer. This sacrificial atonement not only represents a once-and-for-all forgiveness, but in the person of Christ our advocate (παράκλητος) it is still continually present before the Father to cleanse us from every sin (cf. v. 7).

Conclusion

The prayer life of Jesus profoundly influenced early Christian spirituality. He taught and practiced the habit of frequent times alone with God. He encouraged his disciples to pray as he did: boldly, trustingly, persistently, and yet always having God's greater glory as his chief concern. Next to the Lord's Prayer, which majors on this theme and came to be said thrice daily (e.g., *Did.* 8.3), the most influential prayers of Jesus were those of his passion, chiefly at Gethsemane and on the cross. His spirit of guileless submission, even in the midst of profound anxiety, became a pattern of the Christian life in times of adversity or persecution. Similarly, Jesus' earthly and exalted intercession for the disciples, mentioned in the Synoptics and profiled in John and several epistles, became a powerful source of encouragement to the early Christians. It greatly bolstered their assurance of the Father's undivided love and favor to know that by his Spirit Christ himself, their friend, high priest, and advocate, was always praying with them and on their behalf.[22] His intercession meant that true Christian prayer, in James Houston's words, was addressed "*to* the Father, *through* the Son, *by* the Holy Spirit."[23]

Notes

[1] The author is grateful for comments on this essay received from Mr. Paul Spilsbury of Queens' College, Cambridge.

[2] Cf. e.g., Sir 6:34-36; *m. 'Abot* 1:4; 5:15, 18; 6:6; and see H.L. Strack & G. Stemberger, *Introduction to the Talmud and Midrash* (tr. M. Bockmuehl; Edinburgh: T&T Clark, 1991) 14ff.

[3] Although redactional questions will be addressed as they present themselves, it is not my purpose to distinguish sharply between the prayers of the historical Jesus and their reformulation by the Gospel writers. Instead, I want here to concentrate on the theological *uses* made of these traditions in the New Testament church.

[4] These texts have been most fully treated by Ludger Feldkämper, *Der betende Jesus als Heilsmittler nach Lukas* (St. Augustin: Steyler Verlag, 1978).

[5] Probably only Mk 7:34; and see below on Jn 11:41-42. Mk 6:41//Mt 14:19//Lk 9:16 and Mk 8:6//Mt 15:36 may have more to say about his (Jewish) custom of grace before meals: see

further Mk 14:22 par.; Lk 24:30, etc. Note also the apparent (and unusual) blessing *of the loaves* in Lk 9:16.

6   The theological content of these prayers (but not, it seems, the form and setting) is reflected in the Lord's Prayer. See esp. Asher Finkel, "The Prayer of Jesus in Matthew," *Standing Before God: Studies on Prayer in Scriptures and in Tradition with Essays in Honor of John M. Oesterreicher* (ed. A. Finkel & L. Frizzell; New York: Ktav, 1981) 131-169; and e.g., Joseph Heinemann, "The Background of Jesus' Prayer in the Jewish Liturgical Tradition," *The Lord's Prayer and Jewish Liturgy* (ed. J. J. Petuchowski; London: Burns & Oates, 1978) 81-89.

7   These qualities of prayer in the Gospels are attractively summarized by the mainly devotional study of J. G. S. S. Thomson, *The Praying Christ: A Study of Jesus' Doctrine and Practice of Prayer* (Grand Rapids: Eerdmans, 1959) 12-22: importunity, tenacity, humility, charity, simplicity, intensity, unity, expectancy.

8   Cf. e.g., Joachim Jeremias, *New Testament Theology* (tr. J. Bowden; London: SCM, 1971) 196; Finkel, "Prayer," 143 and passim.

9   For this correction of the view of Joachim Jeremias (e.g., in "Abba," *The Prayers of Jesus*, SBT 2/6 [London: SCM, 1967] 11-65), see James Barr, "'Abba Isn't 'Daddy,'" *JTS* 39 (1988) 28-47.

10   It may best reflect the complex evidence to say that Jesus' use of "Abba" was not a unique, but nevertheless an unusual and *distinctive* mark of his relationship with God. This is the line taken by James Dunn, who writes, "By 'distinctive' I mean both characteristic of Jesus and sufficiently unusual among his contemporaries to mark him out, but not necessarily set him in a class apart" (*Jesus and the Spirit* [London: SCM, 1975] 366 n.71). For first-century parallels of divine sonship, including Honi the Circle-Drawer and his grandson Hanan, see e.g., *m. Ta'an.* 3:8 and *b. Ta'an.* 23b (conveniently discussed e.g., in Geza Vermes, *Jesus the Jew* [2nd ed.; London: SCM, 1983] 70, 211).

11   "Lead us not into temptation" means "Bring us not to the point where we succumb under trial": cf. 11QPsa 24:11, and esp. *b. Ber.* 60b, used in the morning service of the synagogue: "And do not bring us into the power [lit. hands] of sin, transgression, iniquity, temptation, or disgrace." Cf. *Authorized Daily Prayer Book* (ed. S. Singer; London: Eyre & Spottiswoode, 1962) 8.

12   For a closer Old Testament parallel see perhaps La 3:22, read in the context of 3:1-20.

13   Although this prayer is absent from a significant part of the earliest manuscript evidence, the clear trend in the majority of the tradition is towards its inclusion in the canonical text. Its content makes a later invention seem unlikely, while an anti-Jewish motivation might well be thought to account for its excision in part of the tradition.

14   I.e., Hebrew address and Aramaic question: see Joachim Jeremias, "Ἠλ(ε)ίας," *TDNT* 2.935 n.62.

15   This is argued in detail by Feldkämper, *Der betende Jesus*, 306-332.

16   See e.g., Tertullian, *On Prayer*, 4; Cyprian, *On the Lord's Prayer*, 14.

17   Acts 7:59-60, there addressed to Jesus; cf. later e.g., Eusebius, *Eccl. Hist.* 5.2.5.

18   Thus e.g., M. M. B. Turner, "Prayer in the Gospels and Acts," in *Teach Us to Pray: Prayer in the Bible and the World* (ed. D. A. Carson; Exeter: Paternoster; Grand Rapids: Baker/World Evangelical Fellowship, 1990) 77.

19   Cf. further 15:7, 15: Jesus is sure to procure an answer to the prayers of his friends, those who abide in him.

20   On a more general note, compare also the interceding guardian angels of Mt 18:10. This theme occurs previously in Tob 12:12, 15, while 2 Macc 15:14-16 records a vision of Jeremiah's intercession for the people of God. Along with Mt 18:10, these two texts from the Apocrypha were of pivotal importance in the patristic doctrine of the intercession of angels and saints (e.g., Origen, *On Prayer*, 1.10.2—11.5; cf. 3.31.5).

21   Also cf. possibly the language about Christ's ability to keep his people from falling etc.: Jude 24; cf. Heb 2:18; Ro 14:4; 2 Ti 1:12.

22   Thus also Origen, *On Prayer*, 1.10.2: to pray aright is to share in the prayer of God's Logos who prays for and alongside those whose mediator, high priest and advocate he is; cf.

similarly Cyprian, *On the Lord's Prayer*, 30. Origen considered that, since it is inappropriate to pray to someone who prays himself, one ought not to pray simply to Jesus; but that, on the other hand, prayer should not be addressed to God except *through* Jesus (*On Prayer*, 1.15.2 and passim; this point assumes additional poignancy in replying to the Jews: *Against Celsus* 3.34; 5.5; 8.13). See further Wilhelm Gessel, *Die Theologie des Gebetes nach "De Oratione" von Origenes* (Munich: Schöningh, 1975) 204-206, 236-238.

[23] James Houston, *The Transforming Friendship* (Oxford: Lion, 1989) 7 and passim (ital. mine).

7

The Judgment of the Nations: Matthew 25:31-46

W. J. Dumbrell

T HIS ESSAY IS GRATEFULLY DEDICATED TO JIM HOUSTON, WHO continues to show us all what Christian spirituality really means.

The Son of Man Will Judge

Mt 25:31-46, the parable of the sheep and goats, completes the ministry of Jesus with a dramatic flourish. It stands as the climax to the eschatological discourse of Matthew 24—25 and occurs immediately before the passion narrative. It is a judgment scene, set forth by Jesus seated on a mountain, the typical location of the important pronouncements in the First Gospel. In this eschatological address, of comparable length to the Sermon on the Mount with which Matthew's Jesus began his public ministry, Jesus concludes the mission to Israel with which the First Gospel has been chiefly concerned.

A judgment scene of this character is common enough in apocalyptic writings. This one is remarkable for its very high Christology. Jesus as the Son of Man, the title of self-choice, preeminently attaching to his public ministry, is the ubiquitous recipient of all good deeds ever done throughout the world by his watchful servants. Thus the true meaning of faithful service, the theme of the address as a whole, is revealed in this final speech.[1]

The address is directed to the disciples as Jesus sits on the Mount of Olives, the mountain of eschatological expectation (Zec 14:4) over against Jerusalem, but it is intended for the world. The great turning point in Jesus' ministry has come, for Jesus has left the Temple for the last time, betokening in this way the final rejection of national Israel. So his pronouncement that the house of Israel (now "theirs" only, Mt 23:38) is left to them desolate is immediately and dramatically followed by his departure from the Temple which was the sign of Israel's special election. The destruction of the Temple will complete this national rejection, and the destruction of Temple and city will be an anticipation of the general judgment when the erstwhile sons of the kingdom will be plunged into outer darkness. From now on national Israel is no longer the people of God. The national house has been forfeited and wider issues are now to be discussed.[2]

Nothing in the material of Matthew 24, the address which takes its rise from the disciples' question (24:3) prompted by Jesus' prediction of the destruction of the Temple, takes us beyond the fall of Jerusalem in AD 70, and thus beyond the final desolation of the nation brought about by its rejection of its Messiah. The judgment upon Jerusalem in AD 70 will be the historical indication that the Son of Man reigning in heaven (v. 30) is coming in judgment against apostate Israel. The destruction of Jerusalem, terrible as it will be, will be a grim witness to the heavenly exaltation of the Son of Man.

Mt 25:31-46 completes the major discourse of chapters 24—25 and is the last section of the last of five formal discourses in Matthew, each one of which contains a reference to judgment in its concluding section (7:24-27, which concludes with four warnings and a judgment, 10:40-42, 13:49, 18:35). The whole of Matthew 24—25 (which concludes, like the first address, Matthew 5—7, with four warnings and a judgment) can well be divided into three large sections, 24:4-35; 24:36—25:30; 25:31-46. The first section informs the reader of the end of the age in the shape of the fall of Jerusalem and what can be considered as a sign of it; it also foretells persecution, false prophecy, apostasy; it exhorts the disciples to faith and perseverance; it emphasizes the proximity and certainty of the Lord's coming. In the second section no new information is given. Only the fact of the impending disaster is stressed, with or without illustrations. This prospect is repeated again and again. The coming of the Son of Man will be sudden, or, rather, unexpected. And so there is a summons to vigilance and to a responsible life-style, to an existence that fulfills faithfully the entrusted task. The exhortations make use of the motive of judgment, the prospect of reward and punishment according to conduct. The third section, Mt 25:31-46, develops this judgment idea into a very lively scene, a universal and final event that is dominated by the Son of Man. There is no longer any exhortation and the disciples are no longer summoned. It is purely informational as is the first section.

Mt 25:31-46 climaxes the ministry of Jesus with its scenario, as the judgment at the eschaton announces the advent, in effect, of the Day of the Lord. By the time of the exile, the Day of the Lord had become the Day on which God would judge Israel and the whole world. Beyond the judgment of this Day there awaited for the people of God a new age of peace and blessedness. The essential apocalyptic claim was that the Day of the Lord would come and on that Day God himself would be enthroned as King. The Day would usher in the new era on earth, for God himself would directly intervene within the course of world history to sum it up.

Mt 25:31-46, often termed parabolic, is really not a parable though there is a simile within it about sheep and goats (vv. 32-33). Some have described it as a "mashal" in the broader sense of figurative speech. Whatever the genre of the address, at the conclusion of the ministry this is the message for the Israel of his generation that Jesus wishes to be imprinted upon their minds as he leaves. The judgment is described in picture language without actual images. The Son of Man, presented in general terms in the Synoptics as the figure associated with divine judgment,[3] and thus concerned with the redemption and vindication of Israel, now returns as Son of God, surrounded by his glory, the array of deity. We have just seen the presentation of the Son of Man coming on clouds of heaven with the destruction of Jerusalem in view (Mt 24), and we are reminded that the fall of Jerusalem was a direct anticipation of the final end. Since the final end of history is the event to which the whole of world history has pointed, the emphasized note of glory in the passage, i.e., the revelation of the divine splendor, is appropriately emphasized; this is the great spectacle, the final grand denouement at the end of the age, the glorious return of Christ for judgment. The whole heavenly complement of angels is involved, and the world gathers before the returning Son of Man. The talents parable has shown us what this judgment involves. For the rejected it will mean the final estrangement from God and dwelling in outer darkness.

The expressions which characterize the advent of the Son of Man, "in his glory," "all the angels with him," "the throne of his glory," are typical apocalyptic features associated elsewhere with the Son of Man.[4] The session of the Son of Man on the royal throne then occurs, and there is telescoped into this presentation the Da 7:9-14 roles of the Ancient of Days and one "like a Son of Man." Son of Man is the title of humility in the Gospels, but now its bearer reappears at the end of the age, invested with all the dignity of deity. All nations are then gathered together, sheep and goats, and the scattered flock of God is brought together in this unfolding of messianic triumph (cf. Jn 10:16; 11:52).

The passive "gathered" implies a divine action, carried out here, we imagine, by the angels (cf. Mk 13:27; Mt 24:31). The erstwhile earthly Son of Man who had nowhere to lay down his head and who had given his life as a ransom for many now returns at the consummation of the age as the Judge of all, seated on the divine judgment throne. The idea of a transition to kingship has been expressed by the mention of the "throne of his glory."

The Judge is possessed of all wisdom, all authority, all power and all justice. It is not a trial that is described, simply a judgment; no defense is now possible, for life itself has provided the formal arraignment. The time for decision is now over; the decisions by which destinies have already been shaped have been made. It remains but for the Judge to indicate the eternal consequences. All that now awaits is the handing down of the sentence. The righteous, the sheep on the right hand, in whom is found the true spirit of obedience, namely self-forgetfulness in fulfillment of the love command, receive their sentence first; the goats on the left hand are to witness the honors conferred by the Judge of all before their own condemnation. No imagination, insight or recognition is necessary on the hearers' or readers' part, and there is no real application.[5]

The kingship of the Son of Man here means that the situation of Da 7:13-14 has been implemented: dominion has been given to the Son of Man, and the vindication of the saints now proceeds as a consequence. The transition of thought from Son of Man to King here is a natural one.[6] This person judging is Israel's Messiah, and messianic titles abound: Son of Man, King, Son of God (implied in "my Father"). For Jesus, the term Son of Man had been a redefinition of the messianic office in a way appropriate to his public ministry. In the light of this end-time full disclosure of what he really is, the title of humiliation, Son of Man, may now be jettisoned for acceptance of full Messiahship as reigning King, not only of Israel but also of the universe as a whole. King, Judge and Redeemer meet in the person of the one enthroned.

The blessedness stood prepared before the foundation of the world, for the kingdom of God is clearly the goal of history, not an afterthought. The inheritance is not now the limited Promised Land of the Old Testament, but the kingdom itself, the rule beneficent by the Messiah under God over all creation.

All the Nations

But who precisely are being judged? Who are πάντα τὰ ἔθνη, "all the nations" (v. 32)? Is this all peoples, all nations excluding Jews, or simply all the Gentiles, excluding Jews and Christians? Are they the leadership within the Christian community, where the least of the brethren are the Christian missionaries or members of the suffering community? The interpretation of the parable is usually made to turn on the identification of πάντα τὰ ἔθνη (v. 32). The Old Testament can speak in the widest terms under πάντα τὰ ἔθνη of all humankind, particularly in judgment texts.[7] Have all the nations now been evangelized so that the conditions of the commission of Mt 28:19-20 have been fulfilled and disciples of all nations have been made?[8] And is it professed disciples only who are being judged, or all the members of the nations to which they belong?

Normally in the Old Testament גּוֹיִם (LXX ἔθνη), "nations," denotes the human groups, the nations other than Israel. Israel, as the people of God, was normally designated עַם (LXX λαός), "people." The position, however, in Matthew has been the subject of much discussion. Ten cases of ἔθνη in Matthew clearly refer to Gentiles alone.[9] There are four cases in Matthew where the word ἔθνη can mean other than Gentiles; these are as follows. (1) Mt 21:43: "The kingdom of God will be taken away from you and given to a people [ἔθνει] who will produce its fruit." Here ἔθνος represents the new people of God including Jews. (2) Mt 24:7 describes war between nations, "nation against nation." It is likely that ἔθνος in this very general reference does include the Jewish nation. (3) The universality of the gospel preaching at Mt 24:14 indicates an activity in all nations, including Jews. (4) Finally πάντα τὰ ἔθνη at Mt 28:19, which commits the disciples to a worldwide mission, must include Jews.

The dividing line in the use of ἔθνος in Matthew has been the theological rejection of Israel by Jesus at Mt 21:43. Before that Matthew carefully observes the Jewish distinction between גּוֹי and עַם. After that the Jews have put themselves on a level of parity with the world at large and are included from that point on in the world groupings. Since Mt 25:32 speaks about πάντα τὰ ἔθνη being involved in the final judgment, this seems a further universal reference. Jews with Gentiles are gathered here: all humankind is being judged.

May we notice the simple uncomplicated works of love in Mt 25:31-46, the little ministries in life that are now seen to have had so much significance? Jesus tears asunder here every false covering under which men claim to be spiritual when they omit the common calls on mercy and kindness. The list of six are given as examples, but the list is not intended to be comprehensive. Food and drink as basic head the list, clothing then is next and finally hospitality and visiting troubled people. These are basic mundane services, but all are works of love, done not by the healers and miracle workers and evangelists, but by the little people. The sixth work, visitation of prisoners, does not occur in comparable Jewish lists of good works.[10] The importance of these works of love is witnessed to by the fact that they are referred to four times in the passage (vv. 35-36, 37-39, 42-43, 44).

Jesus' Brothers

The second critical point in the exegesis of the section is, who are the brothers of Jesus, even these least (v. 40)? Are they the lost sheep of the house of Israel? Are they more narrowly Jesus' followers, the believers, irrespective of what nation they might have belonged to? Does the passage then deal with acts of charity at all, or does it deal with rewards and punishments meted out to Gentiles who accepted or rejected Christian missionaries? Or are they non-Christian Gentiles who have had no knowledge of Jesus and who cannot be judged on the same basis as Jews or Christians?

The common interpretation until recent times was that they are the needy and the least of people everywhere to whom concerned *agape* has been shown. This line of exegesis held that the Lord would return at the end of time to judge all humankind, Gentiles, Jews and Christians, on the basis of their conduct, with no distinction whatsoever.

Strong reasons have been advanced against the above traditional view for identifying the needy brethren as the disciples or the church, particularly on the redactionist view that the passage reflects the later church situation. The expressions "least of these brothers of mine" (v. 40) combines two terms that Matthew uses for disciples. The disciples are called Jesus' "brothers" (Mt 12:48-50; 28:10), and children (or disciples?) are called "little ones" (18:6, 10, 14) employing the positive degree of the word of which "least" (25:40, 45) is the superlative. Further in the closely parallel 10:40, 42 the little one to whom a cup of cold water is given and with whom Jesus identifies himself is clearly a disciple. But despite the close parallel between 10:40-42 and 25:31-46 there is a significant difference between the sheep in Matthew 25 and those who give a cup of cold water in 10:42. The sheep in Matthew 25 do not know that those for whom they care are disciples, but the giver of the cup of cold water in 10:42 does know. Nothing otherwise indicates in this most general assembly at the end-time that the reference is only to disciples or Christians, and the word (brothers) is not used in v. 45, where it ought to have stood if the notion was important.[11]

We submit that Jesus associates himself here with all the marginalized, the hopeless, the helpless, the unclean whose position on the social ladder no one is prepared to share. They are overlooked and ostracized and possess no significance, prestige or power. The sheep were not responding to the oppressed because they were disciples but because they were human beings in need. That is why they inherited eternal life. The upshot seems to be that all people in or out of the church are responsible for all people, since the Son of Man is confronted anonymously in the poor, the hungry and the imprisoned. The religious requirement has been absorbed into the moral since in Mt 25:31-46 the benefactors are not conscious of having met the need of religious persons. The blessed did not know until the final judgment that they were to be rewarded, and they were not conscious of having served the One who could bless or punish. They have fulfilled the admonition of Mt 6:3 that the right hand should not know what the left hand is doing.

Judgment According to Works
So a kingdom has been prepared for the righteous from the beginning of the world, but for the devil and his angels, fire. But it has been observed that there is surprisingly little that is distinctively Christian in this pericope. The righteous are invited to enter the kingdom because they have shown themselves worthy by their good deeds. There is also no reference to a saving faith. No horrendous crimes are related, no murder or adultery or blasphemy or idolatry; nor have heroic virtues been commended. No other good deeds are weighed in the balance. The goats on the left hand, who are surprised at their exclusion, had simply neglected to do the mysteriously significant good deeds, and it is that which damns. They thought that they had made the required religious responses or had not yet been called upon to make them. They had failed to understand what full religious responsibility really entailed.

Apart from the major consideration later to be raised, there are two elements supporting the universalist view that the deeds performed have been acts of charity as such extended towards the needy as such. Firstly, Da 7:9-14, which is presupposed as fulfilled by this scenario here, envisages an analogous rule by the Son of Man/King over all nations with a universal judgment having been called. Second, since this is clearly the last judgment, the mandate of Mt 28:19-20 whereby the world is to be evangelized must be regarded as having been fulfilled. The evangelized world, therefore, with the progress of the gospel having been concluded, now awaits the final verdict to be passed on individuals. If both of these considerations may be applied, together with the use of "all nations" which speaks for universality, the restriction to Christians or Christian missionaries is unjustified.

But it is argued that the traditional interpretation of this section makes Jesus committed to a doctrine of works righteousness. Since that cannot be allowed, the poor and the sick and the needy have to be the lowly and oppressed Christian community. Those who argue this way would then treat the passage not as a direct admonition to good works as such but as a call for their ongoing demonstration, to promote an assurance of election and salvation.

We need however, to reconsider the context from its basic Jewish point of view, since Jesus is speaking as a Jew to fellow Jews. The context is a private audience between Jesus and the disciples, and this is the last rabbinic-type instruction by Jesus to them before the crucifixion. Thus the view of the judgment is particularly Jewish. As for the Jewishness of the scene and in regard to the doctrine of the last judgment in Judaism, G. F. Moore claimed that "Jewish eschatology is the ultimate step in the individualization of religion ... [because] every man is finally judged individually and saved or damned by his own deeds."[12] The expectation of final universal judgment became an established constituent of the Jewish worldview from the second century BC. Stemming from the old prophetic belief in the Day of Yahweh, when the God of Israel would save his people and punish their enemies, the concept of judgment had steadily widened in scope and acquired a more transcendental form, so that this final vindication of divine sovereignty became associated with both the notion of the resurrection of the dead and the catastrophic end of the existing world order. The universality of this judgment is graphically depicted in Jubilees 5:13-14, where judgment is ordained for every creature. Nothing in heaven above or Sheol beneath can escape it. The essential theme is that of Yahweh's ultimate vindication of his sovereignty over those who have opposed him and of the retribution which he exacts for their pride and enmity. 4 Ezra 7:32-8 gives the most impressive account of final judgment, while Matthew shows this universality at 10:5b-6, 23:15. So far as the basis for judgment is concerned, 1 Enoch mentions that at the judgment good deeds are weighed against bad (104:3; 61:8). 4 Ezra says that each human must answer for himself or herself before the divine tribunal (7:104-5). The task of judgment is to reveal and establish the sovereignty of God and his right action, as much as it is to vindicate the righteousness of his people.

Equally, from a Christian perspective, the liberation and the vindication of the poor is one of the covenantal signs of the inbreaking of the kingdom of God. Love of one's neighbor and Christian work for justice and equity in human arrangements are a testimony to Christian faith and to one's hope for the promised kingdom. Christians seek justice because they recognize that where justice happens, the hungry are fed and the poor have the good news preached to them, and the rule of God can be perceived. In basic Christian terms, a call for works of righteousness is not a call for works righteousness.[13]

Good Works and Covenant Status

It is, to be sure, often suggested that the traditional interpretation of this section makes the neighbor an instrument for the service of God and "leads to blatant works righteousness."[14] This, it is claimed, is a surrender of the central evangelical point in the pericope. Is it really true, then, that the traditional interpretation which we commend is an attack upon the concept of justification by faith? Here we must remind ourselves of the Jewish context of the last judgment in which this parable was uttered. The covenant pattern of salvation involved covenant acceptance, covenant maintenance and then acceptance by final judgment.[15] For Judaism at the time of Jesus, entry into the covenant was based on the grace and mercy of God. The covenant was a relationship initiated and arranged by God with Israel. Those born in Israel were in the covenant already; proselytes were brought into the covenant. In Judaism the condition of remaining in the covenant was the production of good deeds; though these did not earn salvation. Obedience for Judaism was a status-maintaining activity. Obedience did not need to be perfect, for God had arranged a system of atonement for failures. Ultimately it was the intention to obey which was decisive. Judaism generally assumed that people were capable of keeping the law. Grace followed by obedience met the covenantal directions.

The belief that God would judge people according to their works was a common property not only of Judaism but also of Paul. Judgment according to works is plainly and frequently attested in the New Testament,[16] and the notion of a judgment according to works is one of Paul's foundational doctrines. Paul is clear that certain acts and attitudes will prevent believers from entering the kingdom of God (1Co 6:9; Gal 5:21; Eph 5:5).[17] In Gal 5:19-21 works of the flesh are characteristic of people who do not live according to the Spirit, and Paul there gives an example of the sorts of things done characteristically by unbelievers. Evil deeds speak for covenant exclusion, and their doers do not belong to the Spirit's rule. The ungodly will not enter the kingdom of heaven, and this ungodliness is shown by formed character. It is not that certain deeds exclude but that such deeds mold the character which excludes. People's characters and the actions they produce are indications of whether they are inheritors of the kingdom, for the behavior of believers must be consistent with their status. Works should be understood as evidence of whether a person belonged to the righteous or to the wicked. So for New

Testament Christianity the intention of the heart was more important than an individual deed. Christians in Christ Jesus are created for good works (Eph 2:10); good works are the fruit, i.e., the character, produced by the Spirit.

The warnings issued by Paul in regard to performance of good works appear to be modeled on the rabbinic lists for inheriting the age to come. So in Paul, as in Judaism, works are not the criterion of the possession of an inheritance but evidence of a personal standing within the covenant, in Christian terms a standing in Christ. In Ro 2:1-11, where the coming of the Day of the Lord ushers in universal judgment, Paul is not arguing from Jewish presuppositions but from shared Jewish and Christian presuppositions. Nor is he speaking hypothetically. Paul is appealing to a specifically Christian doctrine of judgment based on a gospel which has previously been discussed. Paul has not unthinkingly taken over any Jewish doctrines, for he notes (v. 5) that God's righteous judgment will thereby be revealed; what is clear to faith now will be made plain to all. God is a righteous Judge who has no favorites and the judgment according to works is a proof of this. Jew and Gentile alike will stand or fall on the basis of their deeds. Paul is also attacking here the view that membership in the nation of Israel was the guarantee of life in the world to come.

Jewish literature did not normally depict judgment according to works as the calculation or weighing of individual deeds. Paul in Ro 2:1-11 rules out merit by speaking (v. 7) of those who seek, not earn, glory, honor and immortality.[18] By contrast v. 8 describes the selfish motives of those who resist the truth of the gospel. In the summary vv. 9-11 the believer and the unbeliever are described respectively as "every one who does evil" and "every one who does good." Just as justification is offered to all, so all will be judged. Paul is also aware that the covenant relationship must constantly be affirmed and maintained, and he knows of no gift of God which does not also convey the obligation and the capacity to serve.

Justification and Final Judgment

Thus the problem of the relationship between justification and final judgment, raised by the traditional interpretation of Mt 25:31-46, is only a problem when justification is seen in once and for all forensic terms.[19] The Pauline warnings to those who fail to give evidence of the reality of justification are real. There will be one final judgment at which all these issues will be resolved (Ro 2:5, 16; 1Co 3:13; 2Co 5:10). Eternal life is a privilege to be gained by righteous living (Ro 2:6-8; 6:22; 1Co 9:23-27; Gal

6:8-10). Justification for Paul is finally an eschatological idea, not merely the wiping of the slate clean at a point in present time. God has already in justification by faith pronounced the eschatological verdict over the person of faith. While occasional failures do not jeopardize Christian security which is lost only if one's standing in Christ is lost, Paul is more concerned about the general directions of life and less about individual acts. He does not regard his converts as perfect but only as persons in whom sin is no longer the dominating factor, and the word "blameless" which expresses the Pauline hopes for believers at the parousia does not denote sinlessness, but wholehearted consecration (1Co 1:8). Those who profess to be Christians will be tested on the judgment day. God alone can judge, for God alone knows the true worth of each human being.

We may apply the Mt 25:31-46 passage in Christian terms as follows. The essence of Christian spirituality is the manifestation of the love of God shed abroad in our hearts (Ro 5:5). Christ works in us to will and to do mostly the small things in life, the feeding of the hungry, the succoring of the poor, the visiting of the sick. While we appear in all areas to be working out our own salvation with fear and trembling, it is Christ who works in us to exhibit the compassion of the Son of Man to the disadvantaged and the poor and the troubled especially. He will acknowledge what he has been doing in us when the last day arrives.

What a pathetic little assemblage it was that sat with the Son of Man on the Mount of Olives! How little to show for a ministry of three years, and what unpromising material was Jesus working with! Yet the destiny of each of them depended upon their attitude to that Son of Man who sat there in apparent insignificance on that spring day in or about AD 30 when Pontius Pilate was procurator of Judaea. The Son of Man was on his way to die as the suffering Servant of God, for Israel and then for the world beyond. But the vista in this pericope is that one day the Son of Man will stand at the right hand of God with all the expectations of Da 7:14 having been fulfilled. Matthew wants his readers to understand that Jesus who died has risen in glory, and now there only awaits the celebration of his triumph by all at the end of the age.

Notes

[1] R. Pregeant, *Christology Beyond Dogma* (Missoula, Mont.: Scholars Press, 1978) 116.
[2] F.W. Burnett, *The Testament of Jesus-Sophia: A Redaction Critical Study of the Eschatological Discourse in Matthew* (Lanham, Md.: University of America Press, 1981) 125-132.
[3] R. Maddox, "The Function of the Son of Man According to the Synoptic Gospels," *NTS* 15 (1968/9) 45-74.
[4] D. R. Catchpole, "The Poor on Earth and the Son of Man in Heaven: A Reappraisal of Matthew 25:31-46," *BJRL* 61 (1979) 380.
[5] L. Cope, "Matthew xxv 31-46: Sheep and Goats Reinterpreted," *NT* 11 (1969) 34.

[6] R. H. Stein, *An Introduction to the Parables of Jesus* (Philadelphia: Westminster, 1981) 132.

[7] Ps 67; 117; 148:11, where all people are to praise Yahweh. Ps 98 and 99 depict the universal operation of the kingdom of God over all peoples, Isa 66:18 is a judgment context involving all people.

[8] V. Furnish, *The Love Command* (Philadelphia: Fortress, 1972) 83.

[9] Mt 4:15; 5:47; 6:7; 6:32; 10:5; 10:8; 12:18-21 (twice); 18:17; 20:19. So J. P. Meier, "Nations or Gentiles in Matthew 28:19," *CBQ* 39 (1977) 94-102.

[10] For comparable Jewish lists see J. Friedrich, *Gott im Bruder* (Stuttgart: Calwer, 1977) 165-176.

[11] For a thorough examination of the point involved here see Catchpole, "The Poor on Earth," 392-395.

[12] G. F. Moore, *Judaism in the First Centuries of the Christian Era—The Age of the Tannaim* (Cambridge, Mass.: Harvard University Press, 1932) 2.94-95.

[13] L. Klein, "Who Are the Least of the Brethren," *Dialog* 21 (1982) 140.

[14] Ibid., 139.

[15] E. P. Sanders, *Paul and Palestinian Judaism: A Comparison of Patterns of Religion* (Philadelphia: Fortress, 1977) 422.

[16] 1Co 3:8-15; 2Co 5:10; Eph 6:8; Col 3:23-25; cf. Mt 12:36ff., 16:27; Jn 5:28ff.; Rev 20:13, 22:12.

[17] S. H. Travis, *Christ and the Judgement of God* (Basingstoke, U.K.: Marshall Pickering, 1986) 56-64.

[18] Klyne R. Snodgrass, "Justification by Grace—to the Doers: An Analysis of the Place of Romans 2 in the Theology of Paul," *NTS* 32 (1986) 81.

[19] Travis, *Christ*, 61.

8

Poems for People Under Pressure: The Apocalypse of John and the Contemplative Life

R. Paul Stevens

THE APOCALYPSE OF JOHN (THE REVELATION) USHERS US INTO a world of dragons, beasts, angels, cosmic catastrophes and martyrs chanting hymns. We are swept from one riveting vision to the next as we are transported from heaven to earth and back again, in an upstairs-downstairs drama. Bowls of judgment are poured out on the earth while cringing multitudes call on hills to cover them from the wrath of the Lamb. There is a final battle, a wedding supper, and an exquisite garden city. It is not hard to see why the Apocalypse and contemplation are seldom linked in Christian spirituality.

Contemplation denotes the kind of prayer in which the mind "does not function discursively but is arrested in a simple attention and one-pointedness."[1] The goal of such contemplation, as expounded by classical authors like John Cassian, John of the Cross, Teresa of Avila, and Francis of Sales, is union with God, sometimes described as the spiritual marriage. While there is no general agreement on how far the senses and rational thought may be involved in the contemplative experience, it is agreed that contemplation has to do with dwelling in the presence of God. But can we experience God first-hand while being inundated with visions of complex creatures, cosmic convulsions, a stylized presentation of Jesus that defies literal interpretation (Rev 1:12-18), and ghastly, though victorious, battles against a demonized culture and world system? Certainly not, if contemplation is defined as it is by John of the Cross as a way of total negation through which one transcends objects of attention in a kind of living death to this finite realm of existence.[2] "The poor man," says John of the Cross, "who is naked of desires and whims will be clothed by God with His purity, satisfaction, and will" (Maxim, 91). How could this square with John's Apocalypse?

Contemplation is usually conceived as requiring withdrawal from culture and politics and dehabituation from the media, including Christian media. Contemplation thus makes us think of stillness. Apocalypse, however, makes us think of earth-shattering thunder and blinding light. Contemplation is closet-work; apocalypse is cosmos-work. Contemplation is located in the desert, while apocalypse rubs our nose in the earthiness of the marketplace, and compels us to explore the spirituality of buying and selling (13:17), casting votes (13:7), and turning on the television (13:15). So the Apocalypse of John and contemplation seem to be an incompatible couple.

The marriage of this odd-couple is complicated by the fact that apocalypse is a lost literary genre to the modern Western Christian. Apocalypse was to the first century what science fiction is to the twentieth. Imagine trying to explain science fiction to a first-century tentmaker in Ephesus, or apocalypse to a modern cab-driver in Boston or Toronto. Comparisons may, however, be made. The Revelation of John can be compared with a dissolve-fade slide show (the Lion dissolves into a Lamb standing as though slain), a drama (organized in overlapping sequences of seven seals, trumpets and bowls, with the major pastoral messages offered at the moments of maximum dramatic intensity), or a symphony (it contains more songs than all the rest of the New Testament). But none of these comparisons does justice to this unique form of literature that flourished between 200 BC and AD 100. While there is no general agreement on the exact nature of an apocalypse,[3] the Apocalypse Group of the Society of Biblical Literature has crafted a useful definition:

> "Apocalypse" is a genre of revelatory literature with a narrative framework, in which a revelation is mediated by an otherworldly being to a human recipient, disclosing a transcendent reality which is both temporal, insofar as it envisages eschatological salvation, and spatial insofar as it involves another, supernatural world.[4]

Unquestionably John is an apocalyptist. But is he a contemplative?

The Desert Experience of John
Each time John is "in the Spirit" he is transported to a location conducive

to a direct awareness of God: *on Patmos* (1:10)—in exile waiting like Ezekiel for God to act; *in heaven* (4:2)—in a transcendent order of reality like Paul in the third heaven; *in the desert* (17:3)—stripped of the stimulation of culture like John the Baptist; and *on a mountain great and high* (21:10)—in a place of revelation like Peter, James and John on the Mount of Transfiguration. John received the vision while an exile for Jesus on the island of Patmos, in the Spirit on the Lord's Day (1:9-10). He was exactly where the contemplative way places a person: in the desert, dehabituated from Christian service, alone with God in the Spirit and experiencing the *kairos* time of Christian sabbath.

While "desert" has only a secondary place in the Apocalypse it is presented with a unique twist. In chapter 12 the radiant woman gives birth to the Christ-child, and this woman, who, according to one interpretation, represents the believing messianic community (which now includes John's readers), is whisked off to the desert to be protected from the Dragon's onslaught for a period of distress (12:6). Mounce shows that John's readers would have read the word "desert" as signifying not a demon-infested wasteland but a place of spiritual refuge.⁵ Kiddle⁶ argues that the desert experience of the Christ-bearing community describes a state of spiritual detachment from normal civilized life. Either way John's vision is encouraging his readers with the thought that God would meet them protectively *where they were.* The desert is the experience of ordinary believers in the thick of life in a pagan empire. This is especially apparent in chapter 17, where the Spirit opens John's eyes to the great Harlot-*cum*-Babylon who represents the reality of the surrounding pagan culture, social, intellectual, commercial, and intellectual,⁷ all articulated by the Beast and the Dragon. John views the world system as colonized by Satan, and therefore his desert experiences direct his attention (and ours) to the spiritual realities of life *in the world.*

John presents a thoroughly "lay" spirituality, intended for ordinary Christians compelled to worship Caesar in Pergamum⁸ and Christian bronze workers in Thyatira struggling with the orgies and idol feasts of the pagan guilds to which they were forced to belong (3:20). Lay spirituality must deal not only with church life (Rev 2–3) but with power, politics, economics, marketing, and social responsibilities in secular or religious society. This John does. The stillness he seeks is not human-made quietude but that of the word spoken by God himself in Ps 46:10 in the context of our conflict-ridden life in this world. There the world's Maker and Lord commands all the powers of evil: "Be still, and know that I am God." Thus desert-stillness and contemplative-stillness are discovered right in the center of life rather than at its circumference.

John accomplishes this discovery by pulling back the curtain of "normal" perception to let us see a transcendent reality that is actually present in our everyday existence. The Lamb has triumphed even though the Harlot appears to reign supreme. Heaven, for John, is not up there, or to come later, but it bursts into the here and now. He shows us how the world looks to a person in the Spirit. The "otherworldly" atmosphere of the vision is precisely what makes it so relevant when the church is facing persecution from a hostile culture or is being seduced by a friendly culture. It tells us that behind either hostility or seduction is a sinister personage called the Beast that is really Satan's puppet. Behind that is the plan and purpose of God, who is already overruling (13:7; 17:17) and will eventually be seen to rule everything (19:1).

The Revelation is much more than a book of predictions. Rather than tell us what will take place, it gets right inside history to see what H. H. Rowley described as a "unique divine initiative at the end of history . . . when God would act in a way as solely his own as his act of creation had been."[9] The world, according to John the apocalyptist, is both more tragic and more hopeful than is immediately apparent. "Apocalyptic," James Moffatt concludes, "always spread its gorgeous pinions in the dusk of the national fortunes, but it strained to the near dawn of relief."[10] Without this contemplative perspective, believers in the seven churches of Asia would be drowning in a sea of godless political authority, diabolical supernaturalism, debased mysticism and paganized culture. But how will throwing poems to such drowning people save them? What has the exotic imagery of the Apocalypse to do with the contemplative hunger to know God directly and personally?

The Convergence of Apocalyptic and Contemplation

A justifiable and useful distinction can be made between meditation and contemplation: meditation is the act of turning our attention from the things of the world to the things of God, but contemplation involves turning our attention from the things of God to attend to God himself. It is this writer's conviction that the apocalyptic form of the Revelation is a vital path that can lead twentieth-century Christians to attend to God himself.

First, both the Revelation and contemplation are concerned *to cultivate direct experience of God* and not merely to talk about him. This is the highest ministry of words. Christians frequently undervalue words, considering words as mere representations, conveying information that can be processed and digitized in order to reduce the knowledge of God to doctrine over which we have rational control. But poets and apocalyptists use words and word-pictures to empower us to experience the God whose presence cannot be controlled. They view each word as a logos, a literary creation that brings into being, albeit in a limited way, the reality it signifies. Robert Siegel, a poet-novelist, agrees with Tolkien's line: "We make by the same law by which we're made."[11]

The Revelation was intended to be read aloud (1:3) and inwardly digested through listening in the heart,[12] not to be studied and analyzed. It has what Swete calls an auditory[13] logic through which John invites his reader-hearers to share his contemplation through their own heart's responsiveness: "He who has an ear, let him hear what the Spirit says to the churches" (2:7, 11, 17, 29; 3:6, 13, 22). The Revelation is fundamentally aural and dramatic in character. Speaking to this, one scholar observed that "a written text was essentially a transcription which, like modern musical notation, became an intelligible message only when it was performed *orally* to others or to oneself."[14] When read aloud the Revelation would have the effect of a symphony performed, which is real when heard rather than seen.

The Revelation is intended to foster first-hand experience of God. John engineers this not by describing the spiritual life but by evoking it through visions. He empowers us to attend to God by envisioning a God who attends to us; God keeps a half-hour silence in heaven to receive the prayers of the saints (8:1-4). As a further link with the focus of contemplation on union with God, John envisions the consummation of the spiritual life and human history as a marriage (19:7-9; 21:2), a marriage so glorious that all direct experiences of God in this life are by comparison mere betrothal exchanges and assurances. Both the Apocalypse and contemplation converge on the supremacy of knowing God over merely knowing about him.

Second, both the Apocalypse of John and the act of contemplation *call for a life of radical discipleship.* One either worships Jesus by laying down one's life for him, or one destroys oneself by worshipping the Beast. So while John transmits the heavenly call to "come out of her [Babylon], my people, so that you will not share in her sins" (18:4), these people must be rescued while *in* Babylon. For until they are martyred there is nowhere else they can serve God. John invites his friends to find God in the center of life, not in its circumference. This is precisely one of the distinguishing marks of a *Christian* apocalypse. As Mounce says:

> Revelation differs from standard apocalyptic in its view of history .... For the apocalyptists the present age is evil and without meaning. It is only a passing interlude on the way to that all-important final period preceding the end. In contrast, the book of Revelation takes as

its starting point the redemptive activity of God in history.[15]

Neither contemplation nor the Apocalypse of John has room for nominal Christianity. Both presuppose that those who meet God directly will become God-intoxicated persons. The Revelation has more color than any other book of the New Testament—jasper, carnelian, emerald, sapphire—but discipleship is presented in stark black and white. Eugene Peterson says, "Apocalypse is arson—it secretly sets a fire in the imagination that boils the fat out of an obese culture-religion and renders a clear gospel love, a pure gospel hope, a purged gospel faith."[16]

Third, both the Apocalypse of John and contemplation *move us beyond normal rational understanding.* In his careful article on "contemplation," Neville Ward notes that meditation on the truth of Christ has an important role to play in keeping contemplation from drifting into non-Christian experience.[17] It is important to note that the appeal of the Revelation is neither mindless nor careless about truth. For example, John has deliberately crafted his message around the exodus symbols and the liberation theme[18] to impress us with the truth that God has chosen to side with people who are suffering oppression and seduction. Seduced people are persecuted people, and John knows they will need an empowering vision of our all-powerful God and the coming Kingdom to be more than survivors. Revelation is a pastoral letter written to believers who need to understand that God is embracing their present and personal history triumphantly. As Eugene Boring suggests:

> Revelation is the prophetic/pastoral response to two questions, which are the same question: the question of God ("Who, if anyone, rules this world?") and the question of history ("What, if any, is the meaning of the tragic events which comprise our history?").[19]

Using a number of existing traditional elements, both canonical and noncanonical, John has crafted a document that functions "as a kind of pictorial narrative theodicy which acknowledged the legitimacy of the question . . . 'If there is a good God who is in control of things, why doesn't he do something about present evil?' The apocalyptists' response: 'He will, for history is a unified story which is not over yet.'"[20] John operates not by teaching and instructing, but by envisioning and empowering. But there is more to the Apocalypse than a guided visual meditation on the truth of God and his coming Kingdom in Jesus.

Contemplation involves the hunger to move beyond the mere progression of logical ideas and words, to the experience of attending to God himself. The Revelation accomplishes this partly by foiling our attempts to understand as mere doctrine the second coming of Christ and the realities associated with it. Sometimes Revelation challenges and offends our rationality. For example, among the disturbing features of this book are the following: the overlapping sequences of judgments (6—19) defy consistent interpretation as a series of twenty-one events in linear time; the book successfully eludes every attempt to be mined as a book of predictions; as in Job, Satan, in this book, has access to heaven (12:7); the earthly career of Jesus appears to be completely discounted (12:5); it is uncertain when, in the scheme of things, Jesus comes, as he always seems to be "coming" (11:15; 19:7); when Jesus does come more definitively he presides at a funeral wake (19:11-21); the only Christians on earth are martyrs; Satan's work is far from over even though Jesus has already accomplished his saving work; our final destiny is not in heaven but in a new heaven and a new earth; the new heaven and new earth appear to be incomplete, with work, healing and human creativity still continuing (21:24; 22:2). All of this is upsetting to the exegete and theologian but thrilling to the contemplative. Revelation is not irrational but supra-rational; it dethrones, but does not destroy, reason and therefore satisfies the spiritual hunger to move beyond mind-control to the simple awareness of God as King.

The Apocalyptic Contemplative
Having explored the convergence of the Apocalypse of John and the contemplative experience, we can anticipate some of the fruits of this unlikely marriage.

First, *we will pray imaginatively.* Revelation is to the second coming of Jesus what the Ignatian exercises are to the first coming of Jesus: both involve an imaginative presentation of the affective and spiritual meaning of the coming of Jesus in a way designed to evoke a deep and personal encounter with the Lord himself. This cannot be done without some use of our imagination. Cheryl Forbes says, "We cannot have faith [belief in what is unseen] unless we have imagination; imagination is the vehicle through which faith is expressed."[21] Our prayers are often fitful and half-hearted because we cannot "see" the One to whom we pray, and we cannot envision what we are praying about.

Since the Renaissance, the Industrial Revolution and the advent of the high-tech society, our lives have been de-imaged and stripped of imagination. But imagination relates to our essential dignity as made in the "image" of God (Ge 1:27), a visual and social metaphor of God himself. Human beings are God's imagination incarnated, icons of God, just as Christ was his word incarnated. God expressed his glory in creation not primarily through propositions but through persons with imaginations. Mystery can be understood only through imagination. Jesus, who is

God's perfect image, used metaphors and images to express the deepest truths about God, himself and the kingdom.

Fiorenza suggests that "the strength of Revelation's language and images lies not in the theological argumentation or historical information but in their evocative power inviting imaginative participation."[22] With marvellous reserve John indicates the throne of God and the effects of God's presence without actually describing, or attempting to describe, the indescribable; thereby he enlarges our faith without seducing us into idolatry (4:1-5). "Come Lord Jesus" (22:20) is the epicenter of prayer in this book, but the prayer is evoked not by persuasion or instruction but by an imaginative presentation of all the realities associated with the second coming of Jesus. James Moffatt describes John's visions as "poetic coefficients rather than logical definitions of the author's faith."[23] Eugene Peterson develops the same idea: "The Revelation is, in large part, a provisioning of the imagination to take seriously the dangers at the same time it receives exuberantly the securities, and so stand in the midst of and against evil."[24] The repeated exhortation, "He who has an ear, hear," is a call to converse with God imaginatively.

Second, *we will live the metaphors and symbols of the Christian life.* The word "symbol" derives from a Greek word that means "to draw together." By using symbols, John leads his readers to a new level of understanding and meaning: the spiritual and the divine. He is cultivating kingdom-consciousness, a worldview that will empower us to live triumphantly in this world even when we appear to be losing battles. John does this through symbols. The Lamb, Dragon, Harlot, Babylon, pregnant woman, witness, and martyr are like the symbolic language of Orthodox icons. Speaking of the symbolism of the icons, Baggley says:

> The icons are not simply illustrations of Biblical themes or stories; rather they are an embodiment of a long tradition of meditation on these themes and incidents and their significance for man's soul.... So we who approach icons must be aware of the variety of levels of truth and significance which have been brought together in any one iconographic theme or individual icon.[25]

Similarly, John's Apocalypse is the fruit of inspired meditation on hundreds of symbolic Old Testament ideas, words, places and people in the light of Christ's first and second coming, though without a single quotation. Swete suggests that Revelation is a "Christian rereading of the whole Jewish heritage."[26] But John's interest in a metaphorical interpretation of the Old Testament is pastoral, not merely intellectual.

This pastoral interest is especially apparent in his choice of the martyr as the central metaphor of the spiritual life. In the twenty-two chapters of the Revelation we do not meet a single living Christian left on earth; all the Christians one meets in vision after vision are martyrs. The Greek word "witness" (μάρτυς) is here invested with its second meaning: the Christian is simply one who gives up his life in order to find another life in Jesus. It is irrelevant whether one does this on the installment plan stage by stage or in one extravagant act. The challenge of living this metaphor is simple: either overcome with Jesus, or be overcome by the Red Dragon, Beast, Harlot and Babylon. Overcomers are not super-saints, but mere Christians.[27]   Both apocalyptic and contemplation dissolve nominal Christianity in the furnace of transformation. But how can one live the martyr metaphor?

A Celtic text—an Irish homily of the seventh century—takes up the idea that martyrdom was the normal spiritual commitment of the early Christians and expresses some of the options in terms of a society less hostile though more seductive: *Red* martyrdom consists in death for Jesus' sake. *Green* martyrdom consists of fasting and labor through which the believer flees from his evil desires and lives a life of repentance. *White* martyrdom consists of abandoning everything one loves for the sake of God.[28] Eugene Peterson shows us that by cultivating the praying imagination, John helps us *see* enough to live the martyr metaphor, whether red, green or white:

> The contribution of the Revelation to the work of witness is not instruction, telling us how to make a coherent apology of the faith, but imagination, strengthening the spirit with images that keep us "steadfast, immovable, always abounding in the work of the Lord" (1Co 15:58). Instruction in witness is important, but courage is critical, for it take place in the pitched battle.[29]

Third, *we will worship God in the complexity of life in the world.* Martyr-candidates are invited to look into heaven (4:1) and to join the concentric circles of heavenly creatures enthralled with the glory of God. Before one encounters eschatological drama, one is invited to worship the God who is both Creator and Redeemer.[30] In the last two chapters, where Christ makes all things new, John envisions an endless environment of worship in which the greatest gift is to see God's face (22:4). God is beautiful. So worship is the dominating atmosphere of the Revelation. Every chapter directs us Godward instead of toward the pretentious and false worship of the Emperor.[31] John's business as a pastor is to keep his people dealing with God, and worship does this better than anything.

Indeed, in this book *everyone* worships. Unless we worship God we shall inevitably worship the evil trinity: the Beast, the Harlot and the False Prophet, joining those who choose to be sent to hell singing pseudo-hymns: "Who is like the beast?" According to John it is impossible not to worship. Behind this choice for John's addressees is the imperial cult which had worship centers located in each of the seven cities/towns in Asia where churches had been planted.[32] Whether to worship Christ or Caesar amounts to choosing between the Lamb and the Harlot.

Faced with the temptations of idolatry and apostasy we must worship God (22:9). The best time and place to do this is in the thick of life, not in our leisure-time. Eugene Peterson sums up the crucial relation of worship to the challenges of everyday life in these words:

> Failure in worship consigns us to a life of spasms and jerks, at the mercy of every advertisement, every seduction, every siren. Without worship we live manipulated and manipulating lives. We move in either frightened panic or deluded lethargy as we are, in turn, alarmed by spectres and soothed by placebos.[33]

Finally, *we will live with kingdom consciousness.* Speaking for a generation without hope, Lesslie Newbigin says, "We are without conviction about any worthwhile end to which the travail of history might lead .... The gospel is vastly more than an offer to men who care to accept it of a meaning for their personal lives. It is the declaration of God's cosmic purpose by which the whole public history of mankind is sustained and overruled, and by which men without exception will be judged."[34] Unfortunately, evidences of hopelessness are not restricted to those without faith in Jesus. Among Christians one finds both short- and long-range despair about the world (with a prayer for a speedy evacuation) as well as pathetic need to squeeze everything one can get out of this life, as if there were no other life and no other world. John invites a different approach.

In the Revelation we are invited to live with an open heaven. If we "see" heaven, we will see earth the way it really is. Kingdom-consciousness is another way of speaking of this: living hopefully within the tension of the "here" and "not-yet-but-coming" kingdom of Jesus. This heavenly-mindedness is conspicuously lacking in Western Christianity today. Muggeridge speaks prophetically in words which fall on largely deafened ears: "The only ultimate disaster that can befall us, I have come to realize, is to feel ourselves to be at home here on earth."[35] C. S. Lewis made a similar judgment:

> The Christians who did most for the present world were just those who thought most about the next .... It is since Christians have largely

ceased to think of the other world that they have become so ineffective in this. Aim at heaven and you will get earth "thrown in": aim at earth and you will get neither.[36]

Kingdom-consciousness delivers us from false messianism (that our witness, work, social action, pastoral service and compassionate ministry will save society) and from false pessimism (that our work in this world has to be successful and "religious" to be meaningful). Like all contemplatives, apocalyptic Christians will seem a little bit irrelevant to the worldlings around.

The Apocalypse of John and the contemplative life belong together. The Revelation insists that being aware of God (the goal of contemplation) is indissolubly linked with the prayer, "Come, Lord Jesus" (the burden of the Apocalypse). Final and full God-consciousness comes with kingdom-consciousness. To pray "Come, Lord Jesus" (22:20) is not to ask to be evacuated from this life, but rather to pray imaginatively, to live the martyr metaphor, to worship while working in Babylon and to cultivate kingdom-consciousness until Christ introduces us to a better world by his second coming, whether that is sooner or later. The apocalyptic contemplative prays "Come, Lord Jesus," and therefore lives in the light of heaven's triumphant cry: "The kingdom of the world has become the kingdom of our Lord and of his Christ, and he will reign for ever and ever" (11:15). "Come, Lord Jesus" is simultaneously the deepest prayer of both the apocalyptic Christian and the contemplative one.

Notes

[1] J. Neville Ward, "Contemplation," in *The Westminster Dictionary of Christian Spirituality* (ed. Gordon S. Wakefield; Philadelphia: Westminster, 1983) 95.

[2] Evelyn Toft, "Some Contexts for the Ascetical Language of John of the Cross," *Mystics Quarterly* 17 (1991) 28-29.

[3] David Hellholm, "The Problem of Apocalyptic Genre and the Apocalypse of John," *Semeia* 36 (1986) 36-64; David Aune, "The Apocalypse of John and the Problem of Genre," *Semeia* 36 (1986) 65-96.

[4] John J. Collins, *The Apocalyptic Imagination: An Introduction to the Jewish Matrix of Christianity* (New York: Crossroad, 1987) 4.

[5] Robert H. Mounce, *The Book of Revelation*, NICNT (Grand Rapids: Eerdmans, 1977) 239.

[6] Martin Kiddle, *The Revelation of St. John*, MNTC (London: Hodder & Stoughton, 1940) 229.

[7] Merrill C. Tenney, *Interpreting Revelation* (Grand Rapids: Eerdmans, 1980) 82.

[8] Paul Barnett, "Revelation in Its Roman Setting," *Reformed Theological Review* 50 (1991) 59-62.

[9] H. H. Rowley, *The Relevance of Apocalyptic: A Study of Jewish and Christian Apocalypses from Daniel to the Revelation* (Greenwood, S.C.: Attic Press, 1980) 170.

[10] James Moffatt, "The Revelation of St. John the Divine," *Expositor's Greek Testament* (ed. W. Robertson Nicoll; Grand Rapids: Eerdmans, 1956) 5.295.

[11] Harold Fickett, "A Conversation with Poet/Novelist Robert Siegel," *Christianity Today* (21 November 1980) 37.

[12] David Barr, "The Apocalypse of John as Oral Enactment," *Interpretation* 40 (1986) 243-246.

[13] John Swete, *Revelation* (Philadelphia: Trinity, 1990) 17.

[14] P. Saenger, "Silent Reading: Its Impact on Late Medieval Script and Society," *Viator: Medieval and Renaissance Studies* 13 (1982) 371.

[15] Mounce, *Book of Revelation*, 24.

[16] Eugene H. Peterson, "The Apocalyptic Pastor," *The Reformed Journal* 38 (1988) 17.

[17] Ward, "Contemplation," 96.

[18] Stephen Hre Kio, "The Exodus Symbol of Liberation in the Apocalypse and Its Relevance for Some Aspects of Translation," *Bible Translator* 40 (1989) 120-135.

[19] Eugene M. Boring, "The Theology of Revelation: The Lord Our God the Almighty Reigns," *Interpretation* 40 (1986) 257.

[20] Ibid., 260.

[21] Cheryl Forbes, *Imagination: Embracing a Theology of Wonder* (Portland: Multnomah Press, 1986) 46.

[22] E. S. Fiorenza, *Invitation to the Book of Revelation* (Garden City, N.Y.: Doubleday, 1981) 18.

[23] Moffatt, "Revelation," 301.

[24] Eugene H. Peterson, *Reversed Thunder: The Revelation of John and the Praying Imagination* (San Francisco: Harper & Row, 1988) 111.

[25] John Baggley, *Doors of Perception: Icons and their Spiritual Significance* (Crestwood, N.Y.: St. Vladimir's Seminary Press, 1988) 52.

[26] Swete, *Revelation*, 40.

[27] James E. Rosscup, "The Overcomer of the Apocalypse," *Grace Theological Journal* 3 (1982) 261-286.

[28] Timothy Ware, *The Orthodox Church* (Harmondsworth, U.K.: Penguin, 1983) 23.

[29] Peterson, *Reversed Thunder*, 112.

[30] David Peterson, "Worship in the Revelation of John," *Reformed Theological Review* 47 (1988) 75.

[31] Barnett, "Revelation in Its Roman Setting," 63-68; Paul Barnett, "Polemical Parallelism: Some Further Reflections on the Apocalypse," *JSNT* 35 (1989) 112.

[32] Barnett, "Revelation in Its Roman Setting," 61.

[33] Peterson, *Reversed Thunder*, 60.

[34] Lesslie Newbigin, *Honest Religion for Secular Man* (London: SCM, 1969) 46.

[35] Malcolm Muggeridge, *Jesus Rediscovered* (London: Collins, 1969) 17-18.

[36] C. S. Lewis, *Christian Behaviour* (London: Geoffrey Bles, 1943) 51.

9
Some Reflections on Pauline Spirituality

Gordon D. Fee

Ｉ**T IS A SPECIAL PRIVILEGE FOR ME TO OFFER THE FOLLOWING**
reflections in honor of my esteemed colleague Jim Houston, whose life
and teaching have been a constant reminder to us all that discipleship
means to love God with one's whole being, not simply with one's head,
as so often happens among theological academics. The subject of these
reflections is one that is close to my own heart as well, since I am one
Paulinist who thinks that the apostle has been poorly served in the
church on this score. Paul is basically viewed and studied as either a
theologian or a missionary evangelist, which of course are parts of the
whole; but any careful reading of his letters will reveal that spirituality
is crucial to his own life in Christ, as well as being the ultimate urgency
of his ministry to others. Such a bold statement, of course, needs
justification, which is what the following reflections are all about.

A Linguistic Note
Failure to recognize the central role of spirituality in Paul stems at least
in part from the use of the English word "spiritual" to translate the
adjective πνευματικός in the Pauline letters.[1] This lower-case translation
tends to obscure the fact that for Paul πνευματικός is primarily an
adjective for the Spirit, referring to that which belongs to, or pertains to,
the Spirit.[2]

Indeed, almost every non-Pauline understanding of the term "spiritual" can be traced to an inadequate English translation. Thus "spiritual" has been understood to mean religious (as over against either
secular or mundane),[3] non-material/corporeal,[4] mystical,[5] pertaining to

the interior life of the believer,[6] or, in its worst moments, elitist (a spiritual Christian over against an everyday or carnal one).[7] But in fact not one of these meanings can be found either in Greek literature[8] or in Paul. For Paul "spiritual" in every case has some reference to the Spirit of God. Thus, for example, in Ro 1:11 he wants to impart some "spiritual gift" (= "gift of the Spirit"); in Col 1:9 he prays that they will be filled with all "spiritual wisdom and insight" (= "wisdom and insight from the Spirit"); in Col 3:16/Eph 5:19 the "spiritual songs" are "songs inspired by the Spirit"; and the "spiritual blessings" of Eph 1:3 are "blessings that come from life in the Spirit."

Even more significant are those places where Paul refers to believers as πνευματικόι, where he clearly intends "people of the Spirit." The key Pauline passage in this regard is 1Co 2:6–3:1, which has had an unfortunate history of misinterpretation in the church.[9] Paul's point in context is a clear one. He is in the middle of an argument over against the Corinthians, who are into "wisdom," which they apparently consider to be their special gift of the Spirit, but which instead was full of all the overtones this word had in the Greek world. Against their "wisdom" Paul has argued in 1:18–2:5 that true wisdom, God's wisdom, stands in radical contradiction to that of the world, since it takes the form of a crucified Messiah, abject foolishness and weakness to merely human wisdom.

In 2:6-16, and with biting irony for those who think of themselves as "πνευματικόι" (Spirit people), Paul argues that in their by-passing the cross for "wisdom" they have taken their place with the world, which in its wisdom "crucified the author of life"(!). With that he sets out in the starkest form possible the absolute contrast between believers and non-believers, those who have gone the way of God's wisdom and those who have not. The key to all of this is the Spirit, whom believers— including the Corinthians—have received. That the "foolishness of the cross" is God's wisdom has been revealed by the Spirit (v. 10); for only the Spirit of God knows the mind of God and has revealed it to us (v. 11). In receiving the Spirit, he goes on in v. 12, we did not receive that which makes us think like the world, but the Spirit of God himself, by whose presence in our lives we understand what God has graciously done in our behalf. Therefore (v. 13) what things we speak (about Christ crucified; cf. v. 2) are not in keeping with human wisdom but are taught us by the Spirit, which means that we explain "spiritual things" (i.e., "the things freely given us by the Spirit of God," v. 12) by "spiritual means" (i.e., "by means of the words taught by the Spirit").[10]

In contrast to us, who by the Spirit understand what God has been about in the cross, Paul continues in v. 14, there is the " ψυχικός person" (the person who is merely human, without the Spirit of God). Such a person does not receive the things of the Spirit of God—indeed, cannot know them—precisely because such things are discerned only by "spiritual" means (that is, by means of the Spirit). The one who is spiritual (the Spirit person), on the other hand, discerns all things (v. 15), precisely because by the Spirit we have received the mind of Christ (v. 16).

Then, with full irony, in 3:1-4 Paul presses his advantage. Even though they think of themselves—and in reality are—Spirit people, their thinking and behavior is that of non-Spirit people, so he has had to treat them accordingly—as mere babies. As long as there is quarreling and strife going on among them, Paul asks, are they not acting like mere human beings, that is, precisely like people who do not have the Spirit? The point of Paul's argument, of course, is "Stop it." My point is that for Paul what distinguishes believer from non-believer is the Spirit, pure and simple. God's people have the Spirit, and are by that very fact "spiritual" (= Spirit people), while others are not, nor can they be "spiritual" in any meaningful (for Paul) sense of that word, precisely because they lack the one thing necessary for "spiritual" life, the Spirit of the living God.

Paul uses πνευματικόι similarly in Gal 6:1. In a long argument (5:13—6:10) that Spirit people behave differently from those who are either in the flesh or under law, Paul concedes that even people of the Spirit from time to time may be "overtaken in a transgression" (6:1). Therefore, the rest of the believing community, as Spirit people, should restore such a one with the gentleness/meekness that is theirs by the Spirit.[11]

All of this to say, then, that for Paul "spirituality" is nothing more nor less than life in the Spirit, to which theme we now turn for a brief overview. Then we will look finally at what this meant for Paul's "spiritual" life, as we most commonly use this term, to refer to the life of prayer and devotion.

Life in the Spirit
Any careful reading of Paul's letters makes it abundantly clear that the Spirit is the key element, the *sine qua non*, of all Christian life and experience. To put that in theological perspective, it needs to be noted that, contrary to historic Protestantism, "justification by faith" is not the central theme of Pauline theology.[12] That is but one metaphor among many, and therefore much too narrow a view to capture the many-splendored richness of God's eschatological salvation that has been effected in Christ. For Paul the theme "salvation in Christ" dominates everything, from beginning to end. And for him "salvation

in Christ" is the activity of the triune God. God the Father, the subject of the saving verbs, has fore-ordained and initiated salvation for his people; God the Son, through his death on the cross, has effected it, and thereby accomplished for his people adoption, justification, redemption, sanctification, reconciliation, and propitiation, to name the primary metaphors. But it is God the Spirit who has effectively appropriated God's salvation in Christ in the life of the believer and of the believing community. Without the latter, the former simply does not happen.

Thus Gal 4:4-6: at the historically propitious moment God sent forth his Son to redeem, so that we might receive the full rights of sonship; and because "sonship" is what he had in mind he sent forth the Spirit of his Son into our hearts, who cries out "Abba, Father" to God. Similarly Tit 3:5-7: on the basis of sheer mercy, God saved us, through the washing of renewal and regeneration that come from the Spirit, whom he lavishly poured out on us through Christ, having justified us by the grace of Christ. And so it goes everywhere. Christ's saving act becomes an experienced reality through the gift of the Spirit of God, God's own personal presence in our human lives. Without the Spirit of God, one simply is not a part of the people of God.

So much is this so—that is, that Christian conversion is an experienced realization of God's own presence by his Spirit—that Paul writing to the Galatians appeals to this singular reality as the certain evidence that they do not need to succumb to Jewish boundary markers (Gal 3:2-5).[13] He wants to learn only one thing from them (v. 2), whether they received the Spirit by "works of law" or by "the hearing of faith." Since he has them on this one, he goes on to ask whether having begun by Spirit they intend now to come to completion by "flesh" (= circumcision). "Have you experienced[14] so much in vain?" he asks (v. 4). Finally, in v. 5 he appeals to their present experience of the Spirit: "He who supplies you with the Spirit and works miracles in your midst, does he do this by works of law or by the hearing of faith?"[15] The Spirit is the absolute key to everything, and the certain evidence that justification is by faith, not by doing works of law.

Not only so, but the whole of ongoing Christian life, both individual and corporate, is to be lived out in terms of the Spirit. The primary imperative for Paul, therefore, is "walk by the Spirit" (Gal 5:16); God's people are "led by the Spirit" (v. 18); their ethical life is described as bearing the fruit of the Spirit (vv. 22-23); and because, following the crucifixion of the flesh, they now live by means of the Spirit, they must behave in keeping with the Spirit (v. 25); they thereby sow and reap for and by the

Spirit (6:8).

This, then, is what it means to be "spiritual" from Paul's point of view; it means to be a Spirit person, one whose whole life is full of, and lived out by, the power of the Spirit.

The Spirit and "Spiritual" Life

But if what we have described above is how Paul basically understood "spirituality," it needs to be added that for him such Spirit-uality was also continuously "spiritual" in the sense of the word more common to us, that is, in a life of prayer and devotion. And it is this aspect of life in the Spirit that gets short shrift in traditional Protestant theology, which tends to regard Paul basically as a thinker or a doer, rather than as a pray-er and a passionate lover of God.[16]

It is doubtful, of course, whether Paul would have easily recognized himself in our descriptions, nor would he have easily accommodated himself to our dichotomies. The gospel of Christ, which was the passion of his life, was not an abstraction to be thought about, but a reality to be proclaimed, experienced, and lived out, as one awaited its final consummation at the coming of our Lord. And it was to be lived out before God, and for one another.

Through Christ and the Spirit, God was now understood as a Father, and his people as brothers and sisters in the divine household, heirs of his glory because fellow-heirs with the eternal Son. Thus Paul's primary metaphors for the church (family, temple, body) all evoke images of the most intimate kind of bonding between believers and their Lord and with one another. This is the "participation in the Spirit" (or "fellowship of the Spirit") for which he prays in 2Co 13:13 and to which he appeals in Php 2:1. When Paul could not be with a congregation in person, he understood himself to be present with them in the Spirit when they gathered together with the power and presence of the Lord Jesus (1Co 5:3-5; cf. Col 2:5) and read his letter.[17]

Such a bonding in the Spirit between the believer and his or her Lord and within the community led naturally to a life of continual prayer. Thus the apostle not only repeatedly prays for his brothers and sisters in Christ in his letters, but also regularly reports on such prayer, while frequently calling on his readers to pray for him and others as well. My interest in this dimension of Paul's life in the Spirit, however, is not simply with the fact that he prayed continuously, but with the nature and form of that praying, because here, it seems to me, we get in touch with the real Paul in ways that conventional biblical theology seldom does, thereby missing a great deal.

Prayer as Rejoicing, Thanksgiving, Petition

In a series of concluding exhortations in his earliest letter, Paul urges the Thessalonians to "be joyful always, pray continuously, give thanks in all circumstances" (1Th 5:16); for, he adds, this is what God himself wills for them as they live out the life of Christ in Thessalonica. Most likely Paul is not talking about joy or thanksgiving in general; rather he is urging upon them life in the Spirit as a life of prayer. And prayer for him will naturally take the form of joy, praise, and thanksgiving, as well as petition.

Paul himself was as good as his imperative. Not too many months before this letter Paul and Silas were doing this very thing in the local jail in Philippi ("praying and singing hymns to God"; Ac 16:25—in this case loudly enough for the rest of the jail to hear). So also earlier in this same letter (1 Thessalonians), Paul spoke thus of the return of Timothy: "How can we *thank* God enough for you in return for all the *joy* we have *in the presence of our God* because of you? Night and day we *pray* most earnestly that we may see you again ...." (3:9-10). Some twelve years or so later, one finds this same collocation in his letter to Philippi (1:3-4, "I *thank* my God every time I remember you. In all my prayers for all of you, I *always pray with joy* because of your partnership in the gospel").

Continual prayer marked the apostle's life; but prayer was not simply petition for his congregations. First of all, prayer for them meant to be in remembrance of them; and remembrance of them was for him a cause of joy and thanksgiving. Thus he begins nearly every letter, frequently expressed in terms of "thanking God for [all of] you"—including the Corinthians, so many of whom stood over against him, as well as the Philippians and Thessalonians, his joy and crown. Thanksgiving had to do with people, not things or events; and the reason he could thank God for them all was precisely that they were all God's people, not his.

Two things about such continual thanksgiving and Paul's life in the Spirit need further theological reflection:

First, a life of continual thanksgiving—primarily in prayer, but to others for their generosity as well—is one of the certain signs of spiritual health (= a healthy life in the Spirit). It reflects a life that evidences the only proper posture before God—humility[18]—a life that is constantly aware of God's mercies, of living on the beneficiary side of life. Genuine thanksgiving stems from a grateful heart that has experienced truly what Paul asked the Corinthians rhetorically, "What have you that you have not received?" One can count on it as axiomatic—the diminution of thanksgiving in one's life is invariably accompanied by a concomitant increase of self-reliance and self-confidence. Gratitude is evidence of living under grace. Thus triumphalism is out, because life in the Spirit presupposes a life of prayer, which assumes a posture of humility before God and overflows with thanksgiving.

Second, that Paul's thanksgivings are most often expressed for people, not for things or events, is also evidence of spiritual health. Here is the key to genuinely sound relationships within the community of faith—to recognize others as gifts, as belonging first of all to God, no matter how nettlesome some of his gifts might seem to be to us. Thanking God for his people does not eliminate correcting or challenging them; Paul will still do that. But thanking God for them offers the possibility of reducing one's own self-importance in relationship to others. Here again, Paul models a kind of spirituality that we could well emulate. Whereas he came out fighting for the truth of the gospel—and his apostleship as it related to the gospel—Paul had the wonderful capacity to take himself as a person with hardly any seriousness at all (as Php 1:12-26 offers marvelous evidence). When one lives as a truly free person before God, others have little or no control over one's life. And it is exactly that freedom that allows Paul always to give thanks to God for others who are his fellow-heirs in Christ (whether his converts or not, as in Colossians).

Because prayer begins as remembrance, evoking joy and thanksgiving in the Spirit, Paul therefore cannot help but petition God on their behalf as well. What is striking is the content of these petitions, which tend to take two expressions: a concern for their growth in the Lord, and a concern for the growth of the gospel. The latter concern, which sometimes includes a concern for deliverance from peril, is always front and center when he requests prayer *from them* in his behalf.[19] But in prayer *for them*, it is always that they might become Spirit people more and more, in terms of their own growth in grace. Thus in Col 1:9-11 he prays that they may know more of the Spirit's insight and wisdom, so that they might live worthy of Christ and be pleasing to him. To which he appends four participles that further define such a life: bearing fruit in every good work, growing in their knowledge of God (that is, coming to know his character the more), being strengthened by the power of the Spirit for endurance and patience, and joyfully giving thanks to the Father who has qualified them for their ultimate inheritance. One wonders whether it is possible to pray more significantly than this!

Thus prayer as rejoicing, thanksgiving, and petition marked Paul's own spirituality (life in the Spirit in terms of personal devotion), and was what he urged, and prayed, for his congregations. Paul was a pray-er *before* he was a doer or a thinker.

Prayer in the Spirit

One final matter central to prayer and Spirit needs to be noted, what Paul calls "prayer in the Spirit." Here is an especially sensitive area in Pauline spirituality that needs to be faced squarely both by New Testament scholarship and by the church at large, and not tip-toed around because of generations of theological uneasiness or prejudice.

In Eph 6:18, in the context of spiritual warfare ("our struggle is not against flesh and blood, but against the rulers," etc.), Paul urges this congregation to "pray in the Spirit." Since this is the same language Paul uses about his own prayer habits in 1Co 14:13-16, one may legitimately assume that in using this language, at least one form such prayer would take would be praying "in a tongue." The argument in 1Co 14:1-19 gives clear evidence for the fact that praying in the Spirit, in tongues, held a significant place in Paul's own prayer life. Four texts are significant for our understanding this dimension of Pauline spirituality, three of which come from the argument in 1 Corinthians 14.

(1) 1Co 14:2. It is clear from the outset—and from the argument throughout—that Paul is trying to curb the practice (apparently highly regarded by the Corinthians themselves) of praying out in tongues without interpretation in the gathered community.[20] The concern of the argument throughout, as vv. 18-19 make certain, is what happens in the *community* at worship; and for Paul intelligibility is the key to edification when the church assembles. This is why Paul can offer such positive words about "tongues," while at the same time trying to curb it in the community, at least without interpretation. Thus in trying to stifle it as a community activity, he is careful not to quash it as a form of personal spirituality, precisely because it held a significant role in his own spiritual life.

The first word about "tongues" in this passage (14:2) is therefore both a positive one and one that sets what else he has to say in perspective. Here we learn two things about his understanding of this phenomenon. First, the person who "speaks in tongues" does not speak to people but to God. That is, such "speech" is obviously prayer speech. This is further confirmed by the explicit collocation of the verb "pray" with "in tongues" in v. 14, as well as by the implication in v. 28, let such a person "speak to himself [= privately] and God."

Second, such speech to God is not understood by the "mind" of the one praying. Rather "no one understands, but one by the Spirit speaks mysteries." For many in the West, of course, this is to damn Paul—and others who so speak to God—because only what passes through the cortex of the brain is allowed value in the age of enlightenment. Such "enlightenment," however, is simply the ultimate form of rationalism, where value is to be found only in what is "rational" (= having to do with the thinking processes) and where almost no value at all is given to the non-rational (indeed, it is often perceived as irrational).

But Paul and the early church had not been tampered with by the mind-set of rationalism, and he found great value in prayer that was from the heart, from within, but which did not necessarily need approval from the mind to be uttered before God. Indeed, in v. 4 Paul insists that such prayer is edifying to the one who so prays.

(2) 1Co 14:14-17. In this passage we are given yet further insight into prayer in the Spirit. By prayer and singing "with my spirit," Paul almost certainly means that the Holy Spirit prays through his own spirit.[21] Both the context and the explicit language of v. 14 demand that "praying in tongues" is what is in view. Two further matters are noteworthy.

First, Paul insists that he will do both, that is, he will pray and sing both with his understanding and in the Spirit, where his own understanding is not "fruitful." Whatever else, therefore, "prayer in the Spirit" is neither the most important nor the only kind of praying Paul will do. But it is obviously for him a part of the whole. What he disallows is such praying in the public assembly without interpretation, because it edifies only the speaker, not the others.

Second, vv. 16-17 indicate that such prayer in the Spirit may take the form of "blessing God" and "thanksgiving," which we have noted above is a key element in Paul's understanding of prayer.

(3) 1Co 14:18-19. Here is an unfortunately much-abused text, which in fact lifts the curtain just a little, so that we may look in on Paul's own personal life of prayer. It is purely prejudicial, and an assertion that should be forever laid to rest, that Paul is here "damning tongues with faint praise." How he could have known he prayed in tongues more than all of them is an irrelevancy. What is relevant is that Paul could make such an assertion to a community that so highly prized this gift as evidence of "heavenly spirituality." Had he not been able to justify the assertion, the entire argument comes aground. Probably to *their* own great surprise, he prizes their prize as well—but as having to do with "praying to himself" (v. 28, = in private), not in the congregation. In church he will only pray "with his mind," since congregational utterances, whatever form they take (i.e., to God or to others), must be intelligible so that the whole community can be edified. Otherwise, why gather; why not simply pray and sing only in private with no public expression of corporate worship? Thus this passage tells us that Paul can make a distinction between private and public prayer, and that in his own

private prayer, he prayed in the Spirit more than all of them.

(4) Ro 8:26-27. Here is another much discussed text, especially as to whether or not it refers to "speaking in tongues."[22] Against such lie the facts (a) that Paul does not explicitly speak about "tongues," and (b) that the words στεναγμοῖς ἀλαλήτοις, "with groans that words cannot express," should properly mean "without words" or "unexpressed."

On the other hand, the parallels with 1 Corinthians 14 are equally striking: (a) as in 1Co 14:2 and 14-16, the Spirit prays (in this case, intercedes) through the believer; and (b) the believer who so prays by the Spirit does not necessarily understand what the Spirit is saying. Despite the words στεναγμοῖς ἀλαλήτοις, it is difficult to imagine this passage as arguing that there is no articulation in prayer; therefore, Paul probably means not so much that the words "cannot even be spoken," but that even though spoken they are inarticulate in the sense of not being understood by the speaker.

In any case, even if not referring directly to tongues as such, here is yet another text, appearing at a crucial point in an argument, which gives certain evidence for a kind of praying in the Spirit that is not "praying with the mind."

All together these texts indicate that Pauline "spirituality" included, as an integral part, prayer that was Spirit-inspired and Spirit-uttered, which included both praise/thanksgiving to God and intercession (presumably on behalf of others as well as for oneself). This is not the only form of prayer for Paul, but it formed a significant part of prayer for him. All of which is but one more indication that for him, "spirituality," even in our sense of that term, was primarily "Spirit-uality."

A Concluding Postscript

Because of the way this paper is set up, it may appear as if my intent were to press for "tongues" as a necessary part of biblical spirituality. But such is not the case. I really intend these primarily as reflections. My first interest is with Paul himself. As one who has lived with the apostle through his letters over many years, I am convinced that his spiritual life, as much as can be seen through the thin curtains that tend to keep it hidden from us, is every bit as significant for our understanding of the man and his theology as is his "theology" itself and his apostolic ministry as an apostle to the Gentiles.

By this final section, however, I do intend that we cease looking at Paul only through the bifocals of our own Enlightenment-conditioned culture, and let him be his own person in the first-century church. What seems clear to me is that Paul simply cannot be understood apart from the central role the Spirit played in his own spiritual life, in his ministry, and in the life of his churches. To look at his "Spirit-uality" in this way not only will help us to appreciate biblical spirituality a bit more, but will, I hope, help us also to listen to Paul a bit more carefully—even a bit differently—as we try to hear him theologically.

I trust that such reflections, even if not fully agreed with, are in some measure in keeping with the concerns of my dear brother in Christ in whose honor they have been put to paper.

Notes

[1] Even more unjustifiable is the translation of 1Co in the NIV, "he utters mysteries with his spirit" (where Paul clearly intends "he utters mysteries by the Spirit") or of 2Ti 1:7 in the RSV and NIV, "For God did not give us a spirit of timidity, but a spirit of power, of love and of self-discipline" (where the context demands something like the GNB: "For the Spirit that God has given us does not make us timid; instead, his Spirit fills us with power, love, and self-control").

[2] The word is almost an exclusively Pauline word in the New Testament, occurring 24 or 26 times in his letters, 15 times in 1 Corinthians alone. The adverb πνευματικός, which occurs in 1Co 2:14, also refers to the Spirit, meaning "discerned by means of the Spirit" (see G. D. Fee, *The First Epistle to the Corinthians* [Grand Rapids: Eerdmans, 1987] 116-17).

[3] The closest Paul comes to this concept is in Ro 15:27 and 1Co 9:11, where he speaks of the reciprocity between Christian service or ministry and receiving material benefits. He describes the former as "sharing/sowing τὰ πνευματικά [spiritual things]," but even here this choice of words has not to do with "spiritual" and "material," but with "the things of the Spirit" and material support.

[4] This is often perceived to be the meaning of "spiritual body" in 1Co 15:44-46. But this contrast in particular is not between material and non-material, but between two *bodies*, one that belongs to our earthly existence, called ψυχικόν (= natural, of this present existence), the other that belongs to the heavenly sphere, the realm of the Spirit. It is still a "body," but is fitted for heavenly existence. Probably the best translation, therefore, is "supernatural" (as over against "natural"), or "heavenly" (as over against "earthly"). But it is not non-corporeal; it is a *body*, after all.

[5] This meaning is especially read into the so-called "spiritual food and drink" problem of 1Co 10:3-4. But Paul's usage here has been called forth by the problem in Corinth itself, where they not only think of themselves as "spiritual" (almost certainly in a kind of triumphalist way over against Paul and his weaknesses) but as secured by the sacraments, which they apparently took to be evidence of their higher "spirituality." So Paul takes them on: the Israelites had their own form of "spiritual" food and drink, but it did most of them no good, since God was not pleased with them and overthrew them in the desert. Thus even here, in an indirect way to be sure, the adjective ultimately refers to the Spirit.

[6] Theoretically this could be a possible meaning of the word, since Paul does use πνεῦμα a few times to refer to the interior expression of the human personality (cf. Ro 8:16, "the Spirit bears witness with our spirit"; 2Co 2:13, "I had no rest in my spirit"). But in fact in none of the 24 occurrences of πνευματικός does it refer to that which belongs to, or pertains to, the human spirit.

[7] This usage is the result of both bad translations and unfortunate exegesis of 1Co 2:6—3:1. See the discussion below.

[8] The closest thing to it is an obscure passage in Philo (*Rev. Div. Her.* 2.4.2); a bit later than Paul, Plutarch appears to use it to refer to the non-material side of human existence, but even this passage is disputed.

[9] See n. 7 above. Almost every elitist, or deeper life, brand of Christianity has found

justification for its perspective in this passage, quite missing Paul's concern.

[10] On the meaning of this complex verse, see Fee, *1 Corinthians*, 114-15.

[11] Not "in a spirit of gentleness" (RSV) nor "gently" (NIV). The noun "gentleness" is precisely that noted in v. 23 as a fruit of the Spirit. Thus it is not "a spirit of" but "the Spirit who gives."

[12] This theme in fact is only found in three of Paul's letters (Gal, Ro, Php), and always in contexts where he is fighting against the imposition of Jewish "law," in the form of circumcision, upon his Gentile converts. This is not to downplay this metaphor, but simply to note that it is but one among several, all stemming from different ways of describing human fallenness (slavery to sin, hence "redemption"; under God's wrath, hence "propitiation"; alienated from God, hence "reconciliation"; etc.).

[13] The issue in Galatians is not first of all justification by faith (i.e., entrance requirements), but whether Gentiles who have already been justified by faith in Christ and given the Spirit must also submit to Jewish boundary markers (as Ge 17:1-14 makes so clear). For arguments presenting this perspective see T. David Gordon, "The Problem in Galatia," *Interpretation* 4 (1987); and J. D. Dunn, "The Theology of Galatians," *Society of Biblical Literature Seminar Papers* (Atlanta: Scholars Press, 1988) 1-16.

[14] The English versions have tended to translate ἐπάθετε, "suffered," in this passage (but see NEB, NRSV, Weymouth), on the legitimate linguistic grounds that this is the only meaning of the verb found elsewhere in Paul. But in fact the first meaning of the verb in Greek is simply "to experience." Since (1) there is not a hint elsewhere in this letter of "suffering" on the part of the Galatians, and (2) the context seems to cry out for the basic meaning of the verb here, this would seem to be Paul's clear intent. He is appealing to their having experienced so much of the Spirit's presence and activity in their midst.

[15] One can only wonder in passing how such an argument would work in contemporary Christian churches!

[16] The problem for us, of course, is that what we call "spirituality" is not something Paul wears on his sleeve. His letters are too *ad hoc*, too much aimed at correction or instruction, for him to reflect on his own personal piety. What we do learn comes to us from incidental moments, most often in passing, when he momentarily lifts the curtain of his private life. But such moments do occur, and since they are seldom the point of anything (thus not easily viewed as skewed by some other agenda), we need therefore to take them all the more seriously as reflecting the real life of the apostle as he himself lived in the Spirit.

[17] On this text as having to do with Paul's real presence by the Spirit and not simply "with you in mind" see Fee, *1 Corinthians*, 204-6.

[18] In some expressions of the charismatic movement 1Th 4:18 has been used in a way that seemed to come very close to arrogance; continual praise was seen as a way of getting even more from God, as though God could be manipulated by our "praise" and "gratitude."

[19] There is no content given in 1Th 5:25; but see 2Th 3:1-2 and Php 1:19.

[20] Very likely in this case he is also trying to curb its less than orderly expression, especially if, as 14:23 suggests and 14:27 implies, many of them were speaking out in tongues at the same time.

[21] Hence my suggested translation, "my S/spirit prays." See *1 Corinthians*, 669-70.

[22] See the debate aroused by Käsemann's espousal of this text as referring directly to the same glossolalic phenomenon as in 1 Co 14. For views that differ from what is suggested here, see the commentaries by Cranfield, Morris and Dunn.

Part III
Theological & Historical

10
Pride, Humility, and God

John Stott

To have enjoyed the friendship of Jim and Rita Houston for the best part of twenty-five years is to have been much enriched by it. I shall always be grateful for Jim's summons to us to develop an appropriate spirituality at the end of the twentieth century, in protest against its secularizing tendencies; for the risk he has been willing to take in inviting us to explore the spirituality of Christian traditions other than our own; and for Rita's no-nonsense determination to keep his feet on *terra firma,* lest his spirit should soar out of touch with the real world.

A neglected but indispensable ingredient of Christian spirituality is humility. As Richard Baxter put it, "humility is not a mere ornament of a Christian, but an essential part of the new creature."[1] Indeed, perhaps at no point does the gospel come into more violent collision with the world than in its insistence on humility as the paramount virtue. The wisdom of the world despises humility. Western culture has been greatly influenced, often unconsciously, by the power-philosophy of Nietzsche, who envisaged the emergence of "a daring and ruler race." His hero was the *Übermensch,* tough, brash, masculine and overbearing, who would become a "lord of the earth." But if the ideal of Nietzsche was the superman, the ideal of Jesus was the little child. There is no possibility of finding a compromise between these alternative models; we are obliged to choose.

Pride, then, is more than the first of the seven deadly sins; it is itself the essence of all sin. For it is the stubborn refusal to let God be God, with the corresponding ambition to take his place. It is the attempt to dethrone God and enthrone ourselves. Sin is self-deification. But God says that, since he is God and he alone, he will not share his glory with any other (e.g., Isa 42:8; 48:11).

Humility, then, is not a synonym for hypocrisy, pretending to be other than we are. The real hypocrisy is pride, the pretense that we can manage without God or rival God. Humility is honesty, acknowledging the truth about ourselves, that as creatures we depend on our Creator's power and as sinners on our Savior's grace. Only God depends for himself on himself. His eternal self-dependence is the ultimate reality in which humility rejoices and against which pride rebels.

So it is that God works, and announces his intention to work, in order that people will come to acknowledge that he is God. The most notable examples in Scripture relate to Israel's two redemptions from captivity, the exodus from Egypt and the restoration from Babylon. As Moses chronicles the former and Ezekiel the latter, both issue warnings of judgment and promises of salvation, and in doing so both disclose the purpose (and therefore the consequence) of God's activity: "Then you [my people] and they [the nations] will know that I am the LORD." This refrain occurs regularly throughout Exodus 6—10 and Ezekiel 6—36.

That is to say: when God rescues his people out of their Egyptian slavery by "mighty acts of judgment" (Ex 6:7, i.e., the plagues), not only will they know that he is Yahweh, their Savior, but the Egyptians will know it too, and will know that there is no one like him (e.g., Ex 7:5; 8:10; 9:14). In the same way, when God's judgment falls, first on his own people on account of their rebellion, leading to their dispersion, and then on the surrounding nations, leading to Israel's restoration, both Israel and the nations will know that he is God. Indeed, he will act not for their sake, but for the sake of his holy name (Eze 36:22-23).

Of course, whenever human beings act in order to draw attention to themselves and to impress people with who they are, their behavior is regarded as exhibitionist and reprehensible. How then, it is asked, can we possibly accept that God acts in order to gain recognition for himself? Our answer begins with the reminder that it is always perilous to argue by analogy, and doubly so when the analogy assumes that God (infinite and all-holy) can be compared with human beings (finite and fallen). For example, "jealousy," "wrath" and "vengeance," which in human beings are condemned as sinful, are nevertheless attributed to God in Scripture because he is God and because in him these reactions to evil are perfect, free from all taint of evil themselves.

Similarly, it is because Yahweh is the only God and Savior, and there is no other, that he desires—even requires—every knee to bow to him (Isa 45:22-23). Worship is due to him; it is not due to us.

It is also because he and he alone is God, that pride (the attempt to dethrone him) is such a heinous offense, and that humility (doing obeisance before his throne) is essentially good and beautiful. Hence too the biblical epigram, which occurs in many different contexts, enunciated first in the Old Testament and endorsed in the New, that God "abases the proud and exalts the humble." This fundamental divine principle runs clean counter to conventional wisdom, which insists that in order to succeed we have to exalt ourselves, whereas if we humble ourselves, we are sure to fail. But Jesus calls us to a radical re-evaluation, as a result of which we live by his values and repudiate the self-centered values of the world.

Scripture goes on to indicate that God's basic principle—exalting the humble and humbling the exalted—applies equally to world history and to salvation history.

World History

The ancient Greeks had a saying that "those whom the gods would destroy they first make mad," their particular madness being *hubris,* a combination of arrogance and insolence. The biblical equivalent is that "pride goes before destruction, a haughty spirit before a fall" (Pr 16:18), and Scripture provides numerous illustrations of this principle.

Since God alone is able truthfully to declare "I am the LORD, and there is no other" (Isa 45:6,18), it is intolerable that any nations or individuals should presume to make these words their own, as Assyria did (Zep 2:15) and later Babylon (Isa 47:8, 10). Any human claim to be God constitutes such an offense against reality, indeed such a monumental lie, that God in his truth cannot condone it or even allow it to remain unchallenged. "I the Lord bring down the tall tree," he says, "and make the low tree grow tall" (Eze 17:24; cf. Isa 10:33). It reminds me of what Australians say in their desire for a classless society and their dislike of people who threaten it by their vanity: they talk of the need to "lop tall poppies."

Israel and Judah were tiny kingdoms squashed between the successive empires of Assyria, Babylonia and Persia to the northeast and of Egypt to the southwest. Their history consisted of constant invasions by these superpowers, which overran and subjugated their territory. They were pawns on a huge imperial chess board, pygmy buffer states between rival giants. God used these pagan nations to punish and discipline his people, the prophets explained. But when they became proud of their success, he discarded them like worn-out tools.

First came Assyria, the "rod of God's anger" (Isa 10:5), the instrument of his judgment on Israel. But when Assyria started boasting of its wisdom and power, God said: "I will punish the king of Assyria for the willful pride of his heart and the haughty look in his eyes" (Isa 10:12).

Next, God raised up the Babylonians to overthrow Assyria, and to replace them as his sword for judging his own people. But soon he had to say of them: "I will put an end to the arrogance of the haughty and will humble the pride of the ruthless" (Isa 13:11).

Much the same pattern was repeated in relation to the Egyptian empire, situated to Israel's south and personified in Pharaoh: "I am against you, Pharaoh king of Egypt, you great monster lying among your streams. You say, 'The Nile is mine; I made it for myself.' But I will put hooks in your jaws.... I will pull you out from among your streams .... I will leave you in the desert.... I will give you as food to the beasts of the earth and the birds of the air" (Eze 29:3-5). For the Babylonians would invade their land and "shatter the pride of Egypt" (Eze 32:12).

The same prophetic insight which condemned the oppressive super-powers for their arrogant imperialism and their boastful self-sufficiency, without any recognition of the sovereignty of Yahweh, also exposed the pride of the little nations with which Israel and Judah were surrounded—Syria, Ammon, Moab, Edom, Philistia, Tyre and Sidon. Three examples will be sufficient. Isaiah and Jeremiah wrote of "Moab's pride, her overweening pride and conceit, her pride and arrogance and the haughtiness of her heart" (Jer 48:29; cf. Isa 16:6), and Isaiah predicted that God would "bring down their pride" (Isa 25:10-11).

The heartland of Edom was rugged and mountainous, and its almost impregnable fortresses had made it self-confident. So God's word came to it through Jeremiah: "The terror you inspire and the pride of your heart have deceived you, you who live in the clefts of the rocks, who occupy the heights of the hill. Though you build your nest as high as the eagle's, from there I will bring you down" (Jer 49:16).

The pride of Tyre and Sidon was in their ocean-going ships, in their maritime commerce, and in the great affluence which their mercantile enterprise had brought them (Eze 28:5). But these things had given them a false sense of security. Their prosperity was not destined to last. For the Lord Almighty had planned "to bring low the pride of all glory and to humble all who are renowned on the earth" (Isa 23:9).

Usually it was the nations—both large and small—which were condemned for their arrogance. In two notable instances, however, the nation was personified, and it was the ruler or king who was indicted. In both cases, moreover, he was represented as making a blatant claim to divine status and honor, and doing so in terms reminiscent of Satan's original rebellion against God. The king of Babylon was thus accused: "You said in your heart, 'I will ascend to heaven; I will raise my throne above the stars of God; ... I will ascend above the tops of the clouds; I will make myself like the Most High'" (Isa 14:13-14). But he who thus exalted himself was abased. The king of Tyre was charged with a similar offense: "In the pride of your heart you say, 'I am a god; I sit on the throne of a god ....' But you are a man and not a god" (Eze 28:1-10). The essence of pride is thus seen to be the determined occupation of the throne which belongs to God alone.

If these appear to have been national personifications, some named persons, dictators conspicuous for their tyrannical rule, were also condemned and deposed. In the Old Testament the most striking example is Nebuchadnezzar. Soliloquizing on the flat roof of his Babylonian palace, he asked himself: "Is not this the great Babylon I have built as the royal residence, by my mighty power and for the glory of my majesty?" He claimed for himself the kingdom, the power and the glory, which Jesus ascribed to God, and thus directed the doxology to himself instead (Da 4:29-30; Mt 6:13 margin). It is no surprise to read that, before he had finished speaking, God's judgment fell upon him. He was deprived of both his authority and his sanity. Only when he acknowledged the Most High as the sovereign Lord were his kingdom and his reason simultaneously restored to him. For "those who walk in pride he [God] is able to humble" (Da 4:31-37).

The New Testament equivalent to this incident seems to be the death under divine judgment of Herod Agrippa I (AD 41-44), who resembled his grandfather Herod the Great in both the extent of his kingdom and the tyranny of his reign. Anxious to establish his throne by currying favor with the Jews, he launched an entirely unwarranted campaign of persecution against the church in Jerusalem. He first had the apostle James, John's brother, beheaded, and then, seeing that this pleased the Jews, he had Peter arrested and imprisoned, intending after the Passover to subject him to a public trial and execution (Ac 12:1-4). Not only was Peter miraculously rescued, however, on the night before the trial, but a little later in Caesarea Herod himself was struck down. Both Luke and Josephus tell the story, though each with different details which supplement the other account. Both refer to the royal robes which Herod was wearing, Josephus adding that his outer garment was "made wholly of silver and of a contexture truly wonderful." Both also say that, whether because of his address or because of his shining vesture or both, the crowd hailed him as a god. And both add that because he accepted their impious flattery, and thereby glorified himself instead of God, he became afflicted by an internal disease and died (Ac 12:19b-24; Josephus, *Antiquities,* 19.8.2).[2]

Once again we are given a graphic example of how those who exalt themselves are brought low, and tyrants are toppled from their thrones. They domineer society for a while, and ruthlessly crush all opposition. They suppress everything beautiful, good and true until, it seems, truth is swallowed up by falsehood, justice by oppression and freedom by despotism. They swagger about, self-important and self-confident, and surround themselves with such protective power that their position appears impregnable. But sooner or later their fall is inevitable. Believers appeal to God saying: "Surely you place them on slippery ground; you cast them down to ruin. How suddenly are they destroyed, completely swept away by terrors!" (Ps 73:18-19). Again, "the wicked plot against the righteous and gnash their teeth at them; but the Lord laughs at the wicked, for he knows their day is coming .... I have seen a wicked and ruthless man flourishing like a green tree in its native soil, but he soon passed away and was no more; though I looked for him, he could not be found" (Ps 37:12-13, 35-36).

It has been the same throughout the history of the world. All tyranny is dreadful while it lasts; but it does not last. Wickedness flourishes for a while, but then withers. Evil empires rise, but then fall. Hitler boasted that his Third Reich would continue for a thousand years; it lasted exactly twelve years, three months and two days. Idi Amin maintained himself in power by a reign of terror, but after seven years Uganda was rid of him. Military juntas have seized power in many Latin American countries, but in the end oligarchies have yielded to the forces of democracy. As I write, the world is watching with astonishment the dismantling of the Soviet Communist Party and the KGB. And now we wait confidently for the downfall of Saddam Hussein, for sooner or later God always humbles the proud and brings down the mighty from their thrones.

And if not all proud persons and groups are humbled during their life-time, they will certainly be brought low on the day of judgment. For on that day all veils of illusion and masks of unreality will be stripped from us, and we will all see and be seen clearly. Idols will be exposed in their falsehood, and the living God will be revealed in his truth. In that blinding moment of reality all people of all times and places will acknowledge that God is God, and human arrogance will be seen for the empty puff of vanity that it is. For "the arrogance of man will be brought low, and the pride of men humbled; the Lord alone will be exalted in that day" (Isa 2:17; cf. 10, 11 and Rev 6:15-16).

Salvation History

Within the general history of the world, over which the sovereign Lord presides, whether people acknowledge him or not, he has been working out a particular history of salvation. It began with the covenant he made with Abraham and renewed with Israel, and which culminated in Christ and the new community of Christ. In world history, as God of the creation, he has been active in the life of the nations; in salvation history, as God of the covenant, he has been specially active in the life of his people Israel.

In both histories the same double epigram has operated, that God humbles those who exalt themselves and exalts those who humble themselves. In world history, however, the negative aspect has prevailed: God has brought low the pride of those who have refused to acknowledge him as God. In salvation history, by contrast, the epigram's positive aspect has predominated: God has delighted to exalt those who have humbled themselves before him. Indeed, he has disclosed himself in these terms:

Who is like the LORD our God,
    the One who sits enthroned on high,
who stoops down to look
    on the heavens and the earth?
He raises the poor from the dust
    and lifts the needy from the ash heap;
he seats them with princes,
    with the princes of their people (Ps 113:5-8).

In other words, this is the kind of God he is. At the same time, and in consequence, he tells us the kind of people he wants us to be. He wants us "to walk humbly" with our God (Mic 6:8). Humility is to be an essential characteristic of his redeemed people.

Before we are ready, however, to reflect on the humility God expects in his people, we need to consider his own humility of mind and action. We are told that Christ Jesus, who shared eternally in the very nature of God, did not regard this equality with God as a prize or privilege to be selfishly enjoyed, but "made himself nothing" (NIV) by taking the very nature of a servant. Then, having thus "emptied himself" (RSV) of his glory, he "humbled himself" to serve. He fed the hungry and healed the sick. He fraternized with the dropouts of Palestinian society. He even donned a slave's apron and washed his apostles' feet. And the final stage of his self-humiliation was to become obedient to death, even to death by crucifixion. Therefore, because he had thus humbled himself to the depths, God exalted him to the heights, giving him the highest rank, in order that every knee should bow to him and every tongue confess him Lord (Php 2:6-11). In this way the divine epigram was perfectly exemplified in the incarnation, death and exaltation of the Son of God. He who by nature was highly exalted humbled himself, and he who humbled himself was highly exalted.

The same principle was displayed in the way the incarnation took place, in the choice of an unknown peasant girl to be the mother of God's Son. In conscious allusion to Hannah's hymn after the birth of Samuel ("the Lord . . . humbles and he exalts, he raises the poor from the dust and lifts the needy from the ash heap, he seats them with princes and has them inherit a throne of honor," 1Sa 2:7-8), Mary sings that "he has been mindful of the humble state of his servant," "has scattered those who are proud . . ." and "has brought down rulers from their thrones but has lifted up the humble" (Lk 1:46-52).

Doctrine and ethics, Christian belief and Christian behavior, have never been more strongly welded together than in this emphasis on humility. The essence of the good news is that God the Son humbled himself to the cross for us, and the essence of the good life is that we must humble ourselves in the service of others. In fact, we are told, the very same humble mind which characterized Christ is now to characterize us. We are to renounce selfish ambition and conceit, and "in humility consider others better than" ourselves (Php 2:3-11).

Personal History
In his public teaching ministry Jesus commended humility as the preeminent characteristic of the citizens of God's kingdom, and went on to describe it as the humility of a child. "He called a little child and had him stand among them. And he said: 'I tell you the truth, unless you change and become like little children, you will never enter the kingdom of heaven. Therefore, whoever humbles himself like this child is the greatest in the kingdom of heaven'" (Mt 18:2-4). That is, not only is greatness in the kingdom measured by humility, but even entry into the kingdom is impossible without it.

Many people are puzzled by this teaching, since children are seldom humble in either character or conduct. Jesus must therefore have been alluding to their humility of status, not behavior. Children are rightly called "dependents." They depend on their parents for everything. For what they know they depend on what they have been taught, and for what they have they depend on what they have been given. These two areas are, in fact, the very ones Jesus specifies when he develops the model of a child's humility.

In our thinking we are to be adults not children, putting our God-given intellectual powers to their fullest use (1Co 14:20). Nevertheless, in the process of learning we are to be like children. Jesus thanked his Father that he had "hidden these things from the wise and learned" and had instead "revealed them to little children" (Mt 11:25). What he was rejecting was not, of course, wisdom and learning in themselves, but rather pride of intellect and trust in autonomous reason. Similarly, what he was advocating was neither ignorance nor irrationality, but rather humility before God's self-revelation in Christ. Christian humility begins with an open-minded readiness to listen to God and submit to his revelation. "If anyone ... does not agree to the sound instruction of our Lord Jesus Christ and to godly teaching, he is conceited and understands nothing" (1Ti 6:3-4: "I call him a pompous ignoramus" NEB). By contrast, the person who is "humble and contrite in spirit" is one who "trembles" at God's word (Isa 66:2; cf. Ezr 9:4; 2Ki 22:19; Da 10:12).

Childlike humility is to be expressed not only in an open mind (the way we learn what is taught us), but also in an open hand (the way we receive what is offered us). Jesus stressed this in relation to the kingdom: "I tell you the truth, anyone who will not receive the kingdom of God like a little child will never enter it" (Mk 10:15). In other words, the kingdom (a synonym for salvation) is a free gift to be received; no merit can earn it, or even contribute to it.

The humility of dependence is thus seen to lie at the root of our evangelical faith. What God has said through Christ and done through Christ, that is, the fullness of his word and deed, his revelation and redemption, both of which were finished in Christ, are now offered to us freely, and are to be received humbly as by a little child.

In fact, at every stage of our Christian development, and in every sphere of our Christian discipleship, pride is our greatest enemy and humility our greatest friend. This is so, for example, in justification (how we can be accepted by God), sanctification (how we can grow in holiness) and ministry (how we can serve God and others).

The central gospel truth of justification by grace through faith without works was not a Pauline innovation, for Jesus himself had taught it plainly in his parable of the Pharisee and the tax collector. He depicted the Pharisee as relying for his acceptance on his fasting, tithing and righteous living. The tax collector, however, "would not even look up to heaven, but beat his breast and said, 'God, have mercy on me, a sinner.'" This man, rather than the other, Jesus concluded, "went home justified before God." "For" (here comes the double epigram) "everyone who exalts himself will be humbled, and he who humbles himself will be exalted" (Lk 18:9-14). Thus merit and mercy are the only possible alternatives as objects of our faith. But to trust in our own merit is to court rejection; to trust in God's mercy is to find acceptance.

Nothing keeps more people out of God's kingdom than pride. The gospel begins by insisting that we deserve nothing at his hand except judgment, and that self-salvation is therefore impossible. The "scandal" (i.e., stumbling block) of the cross is precisely that it undermines our self-righteousness and deprives us of all grounds for boasting. It tells us that we have no merit to plead, no gift to offer, no excuse to make. Our proud human heart would do almost anything to retain at least a modicum of self-respect, but the gospel brings us the ultimate humiliation of being declared bankrupt and stripped naked.

The same double epigram, which Jesus applied to justification, James went on to apply to sanctification, although in slightly different words: "God opposes the proud but gives grace to the humble" (Jas 4:6, quoting Pr 3:34). Again, "Humble yourselves before the Lord, and he will lift you up" (Jas 4:10). The context of this summons is the temptation to be a friend of the world and so an enemy of God. James is clear that God's grace is amply sufficient to enable us to live a godly life and to keep ourselves "from being polluted by the world" (Jas 1:27). But God gives his grace only to the humble, who admit their dependence on it. If, therefore, we hope for his grace to lift us up to holiness, we must "humble ourselves before the Lord" (Jas 4:10).

The apostle Peter quotes the same proverb (3:34; Jas 4:6), but applies it to service rather than sanctification (1Pe 5:5). He goes on to write of "God's mighty hand," the symbol of his power in creating the universe (e.g., Isa 48:13), redeeming Israel from her Egyptian bondage (e.g., Ex 13:9) and raising Jesus from the dead (Eph 1:19-23). We must humble ourselves "under God's mighty hand," Peter says (1Pe 5:6). We have all had the experience of dropping something, which then rolled under a piece of furniture, so that when we stooped to pick it up, we were unable to do so because it was not there. Just so, if we want to be exalted by God's mighty hand, and used in his service, we must first humble ourselves under it. "One of our most heinous and palpable sins is *pride*," wrote Richard Baxter. "O what a constant companion, what a tyrannical commander, what a sly, subtle and insinuating enemy is this sin of pride!"[3] Again, a proud preacher of humility is "at least a self-condemning man."[4]

In all three examples—justification, sanctification and ministry—the same principle applies. "God opposes the proud, but gives grace to the humble." "Those who exalt themselves will be humbled, and those who humble themselves will be exalted." The mighty hand of God can lift us up, to acceptance, holiness and usefulness, but only if we abase ourselves under it. In brief, the only way up is down.

Chrysostom is one of the church fathers who regularly referred in his homilies to the beauty of a humble spirit and the ugliness of pride. "Nothing is like humility," he said: "this is mother, and root and nurse, and foundation, and bond of all good things: without this we are abominable, and execrable, and polluted."[5] Chrysostom also supplied the remedy for pride in a couple of terse sentences. "How ... can a man extinguish pride? By knowing God. For ... if we know him, all pride is banished."[6] With this we are back where we began. Pride is primarily an offense against God, a rejection of his sovereignty, a trespass into forbidden territory. Only when God is given the honor due to him does human arrogance wither away and die.

Michael Ramsey went further. In one of his ordination charges given while Archbishop of Canterbury, he offered some wise and practical advice on how to grow in humility, with which we may fully close:

First, thank God, often and always .... Thank God, carefully and wonderingly, for your continuing privileges and for every experience of his goodness. Thankfulness is a soil in which pride does not easily grow. Secondly, take care about confession of your sins .... Be sure to criticize yourself in God's presence: that is your self-examination. And put yourself under the divine criticism: that is your confession .... Thirdly, be ready to accept humiliations. They can hurt terribly, but they help you to be humble. There can be the trivial humiliations. Accept them. There can be the bigger humiliations .... All these can be so many chances to be a little nearer to our humble and crucified Lord .... Fourthly, do not worry about status .... there is only one status that our Lord bids us be concerned with, and that is the status of proximity to himself .... Fifthly, use your sense of humor. Laugh about things, laugh at the absurdities of life, laugh about yourself, and about your own absurdity. We are all of us infinitesimally small and ludicrous creatures within God's universe. You have to be serious, but never be solemn, because if you are solemn about anything there is the risk of becoming solemn about yourself.[7]

Notes

[1] Richard Baxter, *The Reformed Pastor* (1656; repr.; 2d ed.; London: Epworth, 1950) 99.
[2] Compare the blasphemy and death of Antiochus Epiphanes (2Macc 9;5ff.).
[3] Baxter, *Reformed Pastor*, 95.
[4] Ibid., 100.
[5] Chrysostom, *The Acts, Nicene and Post-Nicene Fathers* 30 (ed. P. Schaff, 1st series; repr.; Grand Rapids: Eerdmans, 1980) 11.192.
[6] Chrysostom, *2 Thessalonians*, ibid., 13.379.
[7] Michael Ramsey, *The Christian Priest Today* (London: SPCK, 1972) 79-81.

II

The Spiritual Relevance of Angels

Thomas F. Torrance

NOWHERE IN THE HOLY SCRIPTURES IS SPECIAL ATTENTION given to angels as such, but incidental references to them abound in both the Old and the New Testaments in connection with the announcement of a heavenly message or the heralding of a divine act of salvation. We are told nothing about the essential being and nature of angels beyond the fact that they are spiritual creatures of a celestial order, but we are told something of what they do in the spiritual interrelations between heaven and earth, and between God, who is beyond the heaven of heavens, and humanity. They belong to the realm of all created realities in heaven and earth, visible and invisible (Col 1:16-20). The worship of angels is forbidden as an intrusion beyond the boundaries of what is divinely revealed.[1] Angels have no religious significance, no revelatory content and no independent function of their own: they are marginal figures acting under the commission of God on the boundary between heaven and earth. However, we are commanded to give heed to their ministry for they are sent by God as heavenly messengers (מַלְאָכִים, ἄγγελοι) on terrestrial errands, so that in giving heed to them we give heed to God himself.[2] What may we say, then, in the light of the many biblical allusions to angels about their relevance for Christian spirituality?

·

Angels in the Bible
In the Old Testament the term angel (מַלְאָךְ) is sometimes applied in the general sense of messenger to envoys, prophets and priests,[3] but it is usually restricted throughout the Bible to heavenly beings sent directly from God as the heralds of his presence and the bearers of a specific

message in connection with his saving purpose. The distinctive thing about angels is that they become present, speak and act not on their own but only in virtue of an immediate relation to God whose face they see and reflect *velut in speculo* (as Calvin expressed it).[4] They veil his majesty from human vision, yet in such a way that God himself is pleased to be present, speak and act through them.[5]

This is particularly the case in respect of the appearance of what is frequently called "the angel of the LORD."[6] It is illuminating that the place where he appears, as in the encounter between Joshua and the angelic Captain of the Lord's host, is recognized as "holy ground" in the same way as the ground on which Moses encountered Yahweh at the burning bush (Ex 3:2; Ac 7:30, 35; cf. Ac 7:53). The angel of the Lord acts and speaks in precisely the same way in which God himself acts and speaks, and sometimes is even identified with God (e.g., Ge 31:11, 13; Ex 3:2, 6). Karl Barth has expressed this well with his usual theological precision: "When an angel is present, although he is not God, it is *eo ipso* the case that God is present. When an angel says anything, although he is not God, it is God who speaks. When an angel acts, for all the infinite distance between God and heaven or God and the angel, it is God who acts."[7] Thus as so often in the Old Testament, "this angelophany shows itself to be really a theophany."[8]

As uniquely related to the direct action of God in this way angels are to be regarded, not as personified concepts, symbolical agencies or ethereal figures that merely appear in dreams and visions, but as real existent beings of an incomprehensible nature which eludes us.[9] They appear from time to time fleetingly on the edge of our earthly existence, and are, as it were, both tangential to the being of God and tangential to human being. They have their existence in standing before the throne of God and functioning in the relation between God and humanity as God's commissioned witnesses and representatives in the history of salvation. They tell us that something being done on earth is the counterpart of what is done in heaven, but are not themselves the operative nexus between the two things. They are a window opening into the invisible heavenly background of God's revealing and saving acts reaching from the establishment of God's covenant of grace with the people of Israel to its messianic fulfillment in the incarnation of his beloved Son as Jesus Christ.

What angels are in themselves baffles our understanding. As Gregory the Theologian once said, our minds go into a spin at trying to find the right way in which to speak of the elusive nature of angels.[10] They are neither corporeal nor incorporeal in our sense even if they sometimes appear in human form, for, as Calvin pointed out, in depicting them the Scripture "matches the measure of our comprehension."[11] They just are what they are as angelic beings existing before God and reflecting his light, hymning the majesty of the Godhead and contemplating his eternal glory. It is as such that angels are sent by God to fulfill a spiritual ministry as his heavenly messengers and joyful ministrants to us on earth. "Are not all angels ministering spirits [λειτουργικὰ πνεύματα] sent to serve those who will inherit salvation?" (Heb 1:14).

Angels as God's Messengers

Central to the ministry of angels is their activity as bearers of a message from God, which they deliver in such a pure way that it is the echo of God's own voice which sounds through their words, and in such a distinctive way that what they say is utterly different from anything that human beings can dream up for themselves and say to one another. Angels never draw attention to themselves but refer to the Word of God beyond themselves altogether; for they are sent to transmit that Word, and serve it at the point where the heavenly realm impinges upon the earthly realm and an opening is made for communication between God and humanity.[12] Of paradigmatic significance here is the biblical account of Jacob's dream at Bethel of a ladder set up between earth and heaven on which the angels of God were ascending and descending, and of our Lord's reference to that in his words to Nathaniel, "I tell you the truth, you shall see heaven open, and the angels of God ascending and descending on the Son of Man" (Jn 1:51; cf. Ge 28:12). The angels are in no sense mediators between God and humanity. They themselves are not the ladder erected between earth and heaven but only the messengers ascending and descending upon it, thus functioning incidentally yet significantly at the point where God's very own Word breaks through to humanity and finally becomes incarnate in Jesus Christ the Savior of the world.

Angels are not sent to indwell us like the Holy Spirit,[13] and we are not united to them as we are united to Christ through his Spirit, but they are present and active in our midst as God's agents fulfilling his behests. That is surely how we are to assess the marginal presence of angels at decisive points in the gospel story: the appearance of the angel of the Lord to Zechariah the father of John the Baptist, the forerunner of the messianic kingdom (Lk 1:11-25), the mission of Gabriel to Joseph and to the Virgin Mary to announce the advent of the Messiah (Mt 1:20-25; Lk 1:26-38; cf. Mt 2:13, 19; Lk 2:21), the chorus of angels heard by the shepherds in the fields around Bethlehem (Lk 2:9-15), the presence of angels strengthening Jesus at his temptation in the wilderness and at his agony in the garden of Gethsemane (Mt 4:11; Lk 22:43; cf. Mt 26:53), the appearance of angels at the empty tomb telling the women of the resurrection of Jesus (Mt 28:2, 5-7; Lk 24:4-8; Jn 20:12), and again at Jesus' ascension into heaven when the two angels dressed in white robes told the disciples that this same Jesus would come again in the way in which they had seen him go into heaven (Ac 1:10-11). We are also told that angels will accompany the Son of Man at his parousia (Mt 16:27, 25:31; 1Th 4:10; 2Th 1:7; cf. Mt 13:41, 49; 24:31). Jesus Christ, God become human, is the one Mediator between God and humanity, but angels of light are sent to surround, serve and attest with their radiant presence the incarnate economy of his saving parousia in space and time; they joyfully join with Christ in the salvation of the lost and herald his triumph over all the forces of death and darkness (Lk 15:7; Mt 13:39-50; 24:31; 25:31; Rev 4—19).

Angels and Biblical Understanding

This spiritual ministry of angels as heavenly messengers still remains valid for us, for they are sent to minister to us also who are to be inheritors of salvation. Throughout the whole history of salvation they served the covenant community at the boundary, so to speak, of its pilgrim existence, witnessing to the mystery of divine revelation and signaling the advent of salvation promised by God, when he would deliver his people from the harsh restriction of oppression and captivity and bring them into a "large place," thereby making space in their life for communion with himself.[14] Angels themselves are not restricted or hemmed in by space and time as we are,[15] but they direct us at the boundary of our earthly existence within space and time and at the frontiers of human knowledge to listen to the voice of God from beyond and to distinguish it from all earthly voices. They bear witness to the heavenly world that confronts us in the Bible, where we grasp something of its content only as we become open to what is far beyond ourselves. The accompanying presence of the holy angels in the mediation of divine revelation through the prophets and apostles helps us to approach the *Holy* Bible in a correspondingly *holy* way, reverencing the mystery and sanctity of divine revelation, and to learn to interpret the Scriptures in an appropriately *open* way in accordance with their divine origin from far beyond ourselves.

To give due attention in this way to the angelic witness that surrounds, serves and attests divine revelation does not lead to a spiritualistic or subjectivist interpretation of the Scriptures, for there is a powerful ontological ingredient in the ministry of angels which has the opposite effect. Existing and ministering as real spiritual beings on the boundaries of space and time, the angels echo the spoken voice of God beyond the voices of the cosmos and thus direct our attention in interpreting the Scriptures to the objective reality of the mighty living Word of God that reaches us in space and time from beyond space and time. The appearance of angels is fleeting, but the word of angels is steadfast, for where angels bear witness, God bears witness to himself, and where God bears witness to himself there he sends his angels as ministering spirits to serve his will for the sake of those who are to inherit salvation.

The spiritual ministry of angels has thus an important epistemological and hermeneutical function, for the witness they bear at the limits of our existence in space and time summons us to engage in a correspondingly spiritual or angelic way of handling the Bible. Thus we are not to subject the Word of God that sounds through to us in the Bible to the distinctions, limitations and necessities of our finite forms of thought and speech, but on the contrary are to allow the Word of God constantly to renew and reshape our forms of thought and speech in dynamic conformity with its spiritual content and nature. In virtue of their divine inspiration the Holy Scriptures are tuned in to transcendent truth beyond themselves, so that the statements they employ have an essentially open-ended character, which means that they are to be interpreted in the light of the divine realities and events to which they refer and not the other way round. It belongs to the witness of angels constantly to keep before us that vertical perspective of the written Word of God, so that our handling of it may be ever open to the direct revealing and saving intervention of God in person. If the heavens are opened as the angels ascend and descend upon the Son of Man who is the incarnate Word of God, we must surely approach and interpret the written Word of God in a similar manner, for in their own appointed way the Holy Scriptures constitute the ladder of communication between earth and heaven on which there constantly ascend and descend the heavenly messengers sent to help us lift up our hearts and minds to God in spiritual communion with him. The awesome personal presence of God thus mediated to us through the Bible makes it for us none other than the very house of God and the gate of heaven (Ge 28:16-17).

Angels as Worshippers
Inseparably intertwined with this ministry of angels in their ascent and descent as heavenly messengers is the doxological function they have in antiphonic echoing in the worship of God's people on earth the paeans and chants of the countless host of those who worship and glorify God

in heaven. We have already taken as a primary cue for understanding the ministry of angels the question asked in the Epistle to the Hebrews: "Are not all angels ministering spirits [λειτουργικὰ πνεύματα] sent to serve those who will inherit salvation?" (Heb 1:14). While the language used there certainly speaks of the ministry of angels as a "liturgy of service," that can hardly be dissociated from the role exercised by angels in divine worship: "Let all God's angels worship him" (Heb 1:6; cf. Dt 32:43). At any rate, angels certainly function as *liturgical spirits* in their divine mission to serve the lordship and priesthood of the ascended Christ Jesus by surrounding his throne with hymns of praise and reflecting his heavenly glory.[16]

Luke tells us that the birth of Jesus at Bethlehem was heralded by the appearance of an angel of the Lord who was joined by a "great company of the heavenly host . . . praising God and saying, 'Glory to God in the highest, and on earth peace to men on whom his favor rests'" (Lk 2:13-14). And John records in several chapters of the Apocalypse snatches of the heavenly liturgy hymned by angels and their fellow servants that are echoed in the eucharistic liturgy of the church on earth:[17] "Holy, holy, holy, is the Lord God Almighty, who was, and is, and is to come" .... "You are worthy, our Lord and God, to receive glory and honor and power, for you created all things, and by your will they were created and have their being" (Rev 4:8, 11). That is followed by exultant glorifying of the Lamb of God who has triumphantly broken open the sealed scroll of human destiny, thereby liberating from the shackles of guilt those for whom he was slain. A new song is sung: "You are worthy to take the scroll and to open its seals, because you were slain, and with your blood you purchased men for God from every tribe and language and people and nation. You have made them to be a kingdom and priests to serve our God, and they will reign on the earth" (Rev 4:9-10). Then John writes that he heard around the throne and the royal entourage of living creatures and elders the voices of many angels, numbering myriads of myriads and thousands of thousands,[18] saying with a loud voice: "Worthy is the Lamb, who was slain, to receive power and wealth and wisdom and strength and honor and glory and praise! . . . To him who sits on the throne and to the Lamb be praise and honor and glory and power for ever and ever!" (Rev 5:9-13).

Angels and Christian Worship
This doxological service of angels is clearly not restricted to what goes on in heaven but bears directly on the on-going worship of the church on earth. This worship takes place in eager expectation of the advent of

Christ, when there will be a new heaven and a new earth, for the first heaven and the first earth will pass away. Thus in John's apocalyptic visions the New Jerusalem within which the choral liturgy of angels unceasingly resounds is seen coming down from God out of heaven, and a great voice out of heaven is heard saying, "Now the dwelling of God is with men, and he will live with them. They will be his people, and God himself will be with them and be their God" (Rev 21:3). It is in eschatological anticipation of that transforming conjunction of heaven and earth that the triumphant doxology reverberating around the throne of God breaks into the worship of the church on earth and makes it participate in the worship of the church in heaven. That is what happens, Paul tells us, through the inaudible intercession of the Holy Spirit, who echoes within the prayers of the church on earth the redeeming and triumphant intercession of Christ (Ro 8:15-17, 26, 34). Because that relation crosses the boundaries between earth and heaven, time and eternity, it is not something that can be expressed in the straightforward language of space and time, though it may be expressed, at least in part, in the fragmented forms of apocalyptic disclosure. Just as Jesus Christ alone mediates between God and humanity, yet not without the adjunct ministry of angels, so it is the Holy Spirit alone who gives us union and communion with Christ in all our worship of God, yet not without the incidental but significant accompaniment of angels whose spiritual activity is transparent to and blends with the activity of the Holy Spirit.

The relevance of this angelic ministry to Christian spirituality is nowhere more evident than in the *trisagion* of Isa 6:3, "Holy, holy, holy is the LORD Almighty, the whole earth is full of his glory," and of Rev 4:8, "Holy, holy, holy is the Lord God Almighty who was, and is, and is to come," which bears witness to the triunity of God and is unceasingly echoed in the liturgy of the church on earth. In Isaiah's vision of the Lord sitting upon a throne high and lifted up, with his train filling the temple, the *trisagion* is chanted antiphonally by the seraphim or "burning ones" who reflect the consuming holiness of God, cleansed by which sinful human lips may also participate in divine worship. The teaching of the epistle to the Hebrews similarly speaks of angels as "flames of fire" and of God himself as "a consuming fire" in line with the imagery of the Old Testament.[19] Similar language is used in the book of Revelation of the flaming spirits before the throne of God where cherubim-like creatures unceasingly sing the three-fold sanctus in giving "glory, honor and thanks to him who is sits on the throne and lives for ever and ever," and prostrate themselves before him in worship (Rev 4:5-11). These angel spirits in different forms, after the manner of the cherubim in the biblical Holy of Holies who overshadowed the mercy seat with their wings (Ex 25:20), exercise their ministry in shielding human worshippers from the blazing majesty of God and in restraining them from intruding unworthily into his all-holy presence.[20]

The sharp relevance of this angelic ministry to Christian spirituality is evident in the rebuke it implies for any idea of uncontrolled experimenting in the worship of God and for any over-familiarity in addressing the Lord Jesus Christ, both of which are only too common today. To trespass upon the majesty of the Lord God is to sin against his Holy Spirit, for it is by the Spirit that we have access through the Son to the Father. Before the transcendent holiness of the Triune God, Father, Son and Holy Spirit, and before the ineffable mystery of atonement through the blood of Christ the incarnate Son of God, we cannot but fall down on our knees in utter awe and adoration, in unrestrained wonder and praise. It is surely thus that the liturgy of the church on earth corresponds to the liturgy of the general assembly and church of the firstborn in heaven (Heb 12:23). "Thee, mighty God, heavenly King, we magnify and praise. With angels and archangels and with all the company of heaven, we worship and adore Thy glorious name, evermore praising Thee and saying: Holy, Holy, Lord God of Hosts, heaven and earth and full of thy glory; Glory be to Thee, O Lord Most High." "Amen. Blessing and glory, and wisdom and thanksgiving, and honour, and power, and might be unto our God for ever and ever. Amen."[21]

The fact that the doxological *trisagion* occupies a supreme place in the Old Testament and the New Testament accounts of the choral liturgy that unceasingly reverberates in the vaults of heaven, together with the fact that the great apocalyptic hymn of the end-time is called "the song of Moses the servant of God and the song of the Lamb" (Rev 15:3), tells us that Jewish and Christian elements do and must blend together in the ultimate worship of the redeemed people of God. Just as in Christ Jesus Gentile believers like wild olive branches are grafted onto the trunk of Israel and are supported by its roots, thus constituting with it one good olive tree (Ro 11:24), and just as the Christian church is incorporated into the commonwealth of Israel to form one body reconciled to God and to one another in God's household, Jews and Gentiles thus having access together through Christ in one Spirit to the Father, so the divine worship of Jews and Christians becomes integrated as Jews and Christians draw near to God and are built together upon the foundation of the apostles and prophets for an habitation of God through the Spirit (Eph 2:12-22). This was already clearly implied in the words of Jesus to the woman of

Samaria as they are recorded by John: "You Samaritans worship what you do not know; we worship what we do know, for salvation is from the Jews. Yet a time is coming and has now come when the true worshipers will worship the Father in spirit and truth, for they are the kind of worshipers the Father seeks. God is spirit and his worshipers must worship in spirit and in truth" (Jn 4:22-24).

It was just such a blend that developed in the musical liturgy of Byzantium, in which the traditional eucharistic chant of the Orthodox church incorporated powerful elements gleaned from the Jewish tradition in antiphonic reciting of the ancient psalms and in the Passover liturgy of redemption that had long been cultivated in the Jerusalem Temple and the homes of Israel.[22] This remarkable combination of Jewish and Christian elements in the church's worship of God is quite as relevant and important for us today as it ever was. We Gentile Christians constantly stray in our culture-conditioned interpretation of the gospel by putting a Gentile mask over the face of Jesus and thereby hindering our Jewish friends from recognizing in him their own messianic King. We for our part, however, need Jewish eyes to enable us properly to understand the gospel by reading aright the New Testament, which is, in itself, as Jewish as the Old Testament, and by interpreting these Christian Scriptures within the matrix of God's unique self-revelation through Israel. Likewise we Gentile Christians are constantly tempted to intrude into our worship of God distorting elements from our own cultural and ethnic developments, whether in the West or in the East, which have the effect of detaching it from the great dramatic events in the history of God's revealing and saving acts in Israel enacted for the blessing of all humankind. Hence we need to learn again and again how to draw near to God in solidarity with the Jews, the one people especially elected and divinely shaped through its long historical ordeal in covenant relation with the Lord to be the unique depository of the oracles of God. To the Jews belongs the sonship, the glory, the covenants, the giving of the law, the worship and the promises made to the patriarchs, and of them according to the flesh is the Christ who is over all, God blessed for ever. Apart from Jesus the Jew, the Son of David, born of the Virgin Mary, we Gentiles, as Paul told us, have no hope and are without God in the world (cf. Ro 3:2, 9:4-5; Eph 2:12). The necessary Jewishness of Christian faith and praise must never be played down.

The current corruption of Gentile Christian worship may be illustrated from what happened to European art after the Renaissance. In the era of Impressionism the phenomenal surface of painting became abstracted from its integrating geometric frame so that it tended to lose its objective meaning and became fuzzy, and that in turn gave rise to Expressionism whereby its significance was sought in the fact of its reflecting the romantic or realist perceptions of the painter himself. All the time, however, a steady disintegration of form was taking place, so that interest turned to abstract art; but no abstract patterns imposed upon a fragmented pictorial surface were able to hold the phenomenalist particulars together in a meaningful whole.[23] Something similar took place in the so-called quest for the historical Jesus, in which appeared the steady bankruptcy of the historico-critical method due to its detaching of empirical data from their own intrinsic intelligibility; it is also now taking place particularly in Protestant worship, as it becomes detached from the liturgical frame grounded in the great dramatic events of salvation history, and slips into self-expressionism and subjectivism. This process has long been evident in many of our modern hymns, which are more concerned with what goes on in the human soul than with the living God, so that they are often no longer forms of musical prayer offered to the Lord, but forms of ego-centered spiritual poetry or romantic musing on inward religious experience.

What does the ministry of angels have to say to this kind of inverted spirituality, however sincere it may be? Just as angels do not draw attention to themselves but point away to the Lord who has sent them as his messengers and witnesses, so their function among us is to direct our attention away from ourselves to glorify God alone in the highest. The result of this ministry is evident in, for instance, the composition of the ancient canticle, *Gloria in Excelsis*, chanted in extension of the praise of the angelic multitude that was overheard by the shepherds in the fields: "Glory to God in the highest, and in earth peace, goodwill towards men. We praise thee, we bless thee, we worship thee, we glorify thee, we give thanks to thee for thy great glory, O Lord God, heavenly King, God the Father Almighty." It belongs to the liturgical service of angels to open the eyes of our faith to the invisible heavenly realm that overarches the worship of God's people on earth so that their offering of thanksgiving, praise and prayer may be tuned into and blend with the ceaseless hymning of the heavenly choirs that surround the throne of God the Father Almighty, Maker of all things visible and invisible. This was the point of Richard Baxter's hymn:

Ye holy angels bright,
Who wait at God's right hand,
Or through the realms of light
Fly at your Lord's command,
Assist our song,

Or else the theme
Too high doth seem,
For mortal tongue.[24]

The liturgy evoked in the church on earth is thus linked in the communion of the Spirit to the liturgy of the church in heaven in such a way that what is offered on earth is called into counterpoint, as it were, to the *canto firmo* of the holy ones in heaven. As such, however, the liturgical pattern that arises in the church's worship is determined and shaped by the pattern that the revealing and saving acts of God took in the history of his covenanted relationship with Israel and brought to fulfillment in the incarnate life, death and resurrection of the Lord Jesus Christ as the Savior of the world. In apocalyptic language this is the pattern of worship exhibited in "the Song of Moses and of the Lamb"; and in angelic language it is the pattern of both Jewish devotion exhibited by the ministry of Michael, meaning "Who is like God?" (Da 8:14; 9:21; Lk 1:19, 26; Jude 9; Rev 12:7), and the pattern of evangelical worship exhibited by the ministry of Gabriel, meaning "the mighty man of God" (Da 8:16; 9:21; Lk 1:19, 26). If the former is traditionally held to stand guard over the messianic expectations of the people of Israel, the latter is traditionally held to stand guard over the fulfillment of those expectations in the Incarnation. Hence it is right that the first strophe of the historic *Gloria in Excelsis* is augmented by a second strophe: "O Lord, the only-begotten Son, Jesus Christ: O Lord God, Lamb of God, Son of the Father, who takest away the sins of the world, receive our prayer. Thou who sittest at the right hand of the Father, have mercy upon us. For thou only art holy; thou only art the Lord; thou only, O Christ, with the Holy Spirit, art the Most High, in the glory of God the Father. Amen."

Where has this understanding of doxological worship been expressed more beautifully or with fuller theological perception than in the *Te Deum?*

We praise thee, O God; we acknowledge thee to be the Lord.
All the earth doth worship thee, the Father everlasting.
To thee all angels cry aloud, the heavens and all the powers therein.
To thee cherubim and seraphim continually do cry,
Holy, Holy, Holy, Lord God of hosts;
Heaven and earth are full of the majesty of thy glory.
The glorious company of the apostles praise thee.
The goodly fellowship of the prophets praise thee.
The noble army of martyrs praise thee.
The holy church throughout all the world doth acknowledge thee,

The Father of an infinite majesty;
Thine honourable, true, and only Son;
Also the Holy Ghost the Comforter.
Thou art the King of Glory, O Christ;
Thou art the everlasting Son of the Father.
When thou tookest upon thee to deliver man, thou didst not abhor the
      Virgin's womb.
When thou hadst overcome the sharpness of death, thou didst open
      the kingdom of heaven to all believers.
Thou sittest at the right hand of God, in the glory of the Father.
We believe that thou shalt come to be our Judge.
We therefore pray thee, help thy servants, whom thou hast redeemed
      with his most precious blood.
Make them to be numbered with thy saints, in glory everlasting.

Angels and Providence
There is a further aspect of the ministry of angels to which reference
must be made, namely their role in the providential and eschatological
activity of God in the history of his human children and indeed of
creation as a whole. As the Apocalypse tells us, the Lamb of God is in the
midst of the throne, from first to last triumphant over all the forces of
darkness (Rev 5:6). It is the Lord Jesus Christ himself who rules over all
things through the power of his cross and resurrection, but angels are
given a subordinate function to fulfill in the great apocalyptic strife
between the Lamb of God and Satan, between the kingdom of God and
all the bestial powers of darkness. Angels are found in the very heart of
redemptive history as it presses victoriously forward to its final consummation when the Savior will come again in radiant glory to judge both
the quick and the dead, and to make all things new.

As we have seen, what the Bible tells us about the existence and nature
of angels has to do only with the incidental service which they are sent
to exercise at the point where heaven touches earth and earth is open to
the touch of heaven, in the saving economy of God's creative and critical
interrelations with humankind. As heavenly messengers angels cannot
be conceived by us in terms of human or earthly corporeality, or as
subject like us to the limits and laws of space and time in our world.
Unlike God they have no creative or redemptive power, but by their
concomitant presence and operation they are meant to indicate to us that
salvation events are due entirely to God's gracious intervention on our
behalf, and are not to be put down to chance or necessity, nor to be
explained in terms of physical laws, even if those laws are open-structured

as indeed relativity and quantum theory now regard them. Thus the all-important relation between the forgiveness of our sins and the atoning death of Christ on the cross, or between our new birth and the resurrection of Jesus from the dead, may not be accounted for by the kind of logico-causal nexus that obtains between intra-mundane events in our finite and fallen world, but only by the inexplicable power of the immediate presence and operation of God himself.

It was by the Holy Spirit that Jesus was conceived by the Virgin Mary (Mt 1:20; Lk 1:35); by the Spirit (or finger) of God that he cast out demons, thereby showing that the kingdom of God had come (Mt 12:28; Lk 11:20); through the eternal Spirit that he offered himself up in atoning sacrifice for our sins (Heb 9:14); and through the Holy Spirit that he was raised from the dead (Ro 1:4). It is precisely in virtue of the same power of the Spirit that we are purged from our sins by the blood of Christ: Calvary and Pentecost belong inseparably together. It is an essentially divine and spiritual nexus that operates in all God's mighty acts of creation and redemption, and in judgment too. All the works of God are characterized by an infinite flexibility and differentiality which cannot be caught in the mesh of our conceptual connections and constructs, for they manifest an entirely different kind of force from anything we know or can imagine in this world: it is none other than the inherent transcendent power of God's own eternal being, the power of God who *is* Spirit (Jn 4:24).

It is the part of angels, in their divine mission, to bear witness to the distinctive nature of God's power and to the unfettered freedom of God in all his interaction with us in space and time.[25] This is the same freedom with which he brought the vast universe into being out of nothing, and with which he became human in Jesus Christ in space and time without ceasing to be the God he eternally is. It is in fact the unlimited freedom of the love of God which God himself is, it is the ultimate power of all order, and the final judgment of all disorder. This baffling incomprehensible nexus of divine events is so utterly inexpressible in the grammar of human thought and speech that the Holy Scriptures in the Old and New Testaments alike resort to the strange broken forms of what is called apocalyptic to indicate it. The visionary sections of Daniel and Revelation are the classic examples. That mode of divine self-disclosure does not take place, however, without the witness of angels who forbid us to interpret these unique apocalyptic visions in any literal or linear way, while nevertheless bidding us take them seriously as pointing to what really happens when God himself penetrates into the chaotic violence of our alienated and guilt-laden existence in order to judge and redeem humankind by the power of the Lamb and his atoning sacrifice on the cross.[26]

Angels and the Future

The witness of angels to this humanly unaccountable character of divine activity is relevant to our understanding of both salvation and judgment, and of the interaction of God with the world not only in the past or present but also in the future.[27] Our clue to the unfolding pattern of God's activity must certainly be taken from the whole history of salvation, but above all from the incarnate form that activity has taken once for all in the birth, life, death and resurrection of Jesus Christ, whereby in our stead and for our sake, he has penetrated the strongholds of guilt and death and hell, and vanquished the power of the devil and all his demonic minions. This is just what we find in the book of Revelation, in the eschatological account it presents of what takes place behind the scenes in the interaction of the kingdom of God with the cosmic powers and forces that seek to dominate the history of human-kind and the future course of the created order. At its heart the spotlight of revelation is focused upon the life and mission of the church in history, interpreted according to the pattern of the incarnate life and ministry of Jesus, and the proleptic unfolding of its cosmic impact in the final events of judgment, resurrection and the renewing of heaven and earth. Here the eschatological thrust of the gospel of the Incarnation, as it penetrates into the very center of world history and presses toward the final day of reckoning, is presented in terms of the evangelical humili-ation and exaltation, the veiling and unveiling, of the Lamb of God in the heart of human affairs, as a sort of extended Christology or soteriology projected into the historical process. But all through that account the witness of angels provides us with the perspective in which to recognize the redemptive purpose and pattern of the mystery of God.[28]

By virtue of the angels' presence the eyes and ears of faith penetrate through the opaque apocalyptic imagery to discern the invisible and inaudible heavenly background to all that happens on earth. The herald angels testify to the triumph of the kingdom of Christ over all the forces of evil and darkness and enable us here and now to glimpse the silver lining behind the fearful wrath of history. Angels in different forms participate at every stage in the unfolding of the apocalyptic drama,[29] bearing witness to the fact that God himself is at work judging evil and making all things serve his creative and redemptive purpose.[30] At the same time they link earth to heaven in such a way that they both present the prayers of the martyrs and saints like incense before the throne of God, and make the triumphant songs of the heavenly host of the redeemed resonate in the worship of the church on earth. This is what happens when we sing the hymn of Horatius Bonar, "Glory Be to God the Father":

"Glory, blessing, praise eternal!"
Thus the choir of angels sings;
"Honour, riches, power, dominion!"
Thus its praise creation brings;
Glory, glory, glory, glory,
Glory to the King of Kings.[31]

Angels and Mission

The mingling together of providence and mission in which angels are charged with their spiritual ministry operates not only on the vast scale of the cosmic panorama, but in relation to the lives of individuals as well. Their providential service was clearly indicated in the Old Testament account of the angel of the Lord who was sent on special errands to particular people like Gideon or Manoah or Daniel. This was usually in connection with the deliverance of the people of God from the alien oppression, for "the angel of the LORD encamps around those who fear him, and he delivers them" (Ps 34:7).[32] The bearing of that service on mission was strikingly indicated in the call of Isaiah of Jerusalem as one of the seraphim touched his lips with a burning coal taken from the altar: "Then I heard the voice of the Lord saying, 'Whom shall I send? And who will go for us?' And I said, 'Here am I. Send me!'" (Isa 6:8). In the New Testament, apart from the presence of angels at crucial points in the gospel story which we need not recall again, reference may be made to the visit of an angel to Cornelius the Roman centurion in Caesarea who announced to him that his prayers and alms had ascended as a memorial before God (Ac 10:1-8).[33] This is an event with distinctly missionary as well as liturgical significance, which makes it clear that angels may be sent by God to bear a message to people beyond the bounds of the church. Thus Peter learned, as he said to Cornelius, that "God does not show favoritism but accepts men from every nation who fear him and do what is right" (Ac 10:34-35).

I recall very vividly an incident of this kind in the missionary life of my father in Sichuan. One day he received a letter from a Chinese who had never heard of the gospel, but who recounted that all his life he had been seeking for eternal life, and had made long pilgrimages to various shrines and temples in pursuit of his quest. One night after many years he dreamed that in his travels along a mountain road he came to a great stone arch with the words chiseled on it "The Way to Eternal Life." As he made to go through the arch he was confronted by a man in white garments who asked what he wanted, and when he spoke of his search for eternal life, he was told to enter, but in his excitement he woke up. As soon as morning arrived he went to tell a friend about his dream, and on his way encountered a stranger in the village who thrust into his hand a piece of paper bearing the very words of his dream, "The Way to Eternal Life." It was a tract written by my father about Jesus as the Way, the Truth and the Life apart from whom there is no way to the Father (Jn 14:6). It had my father's name and address printed at the bottom. God had sent his angel to that Chinese pilgrim to show him the way to the Lord Jesus Christ, the one Mediator between God and humanity, whom to know and believe is to have eternal life.[34] Thus divine providence and evangelical mission came together.

In the fulfillment of God's supreme purpose, angels are surely still active in their missionary as well as their providential service. Disregard of the ministry of angels will certainly lead to a serious deficiency in Christian spirituality, bringing many forms of shallowness and instability in its train. That modern eyes should be opened to the ministry of angels is very much to be desired.

Notes

[1] Col 2:18; Rev 19:10, 22:8ff. See also Dt 6:15, and Mt 4:19, 22:8ff. See John Calvin, *Institutes*, 1.14.3ff.,10.

[2] Consult the illuminating discussion by Karl Barth on the limits of angelology, *Church Dogmatics* (Edinburgh: T & T Clark, 1960) 3.3.369ff.; and on the service of angels as witnesses, 459ff., 477ff. Cf. "ἄγγελος," *TDNT* 1.83-87.

[3] 2Ch 36:15; Isa 44:26; Hag 1:13; Mal 2:7; Ecc 5:6; cf. Mal 3:1.

[4] Calvin, *Institutes*, 1.14.5. The phrase means "as in a mirror," and echoes 1Co 13:12.

[5] Thus Ex 33:14-15: "My Presence will go with you ..." "if your Presence does not go with us, do not send us up from here." According to A. B. Davidson, "The angel of his face (presence) is not an angel who sees his face or stands before it, but one in whom his face (presence) is reflected and seen." James Hastings, *A Dictionary of the Bible* (Edinburgh: T & T Clark, 1963) 1.24.

[6] מַלְאַךְ יהוה, ἄγγελος κυρίου, see for example Ge 22:11, 15; 31:11ff.; Ex 3:2; Jdg 2:1; Mt 1:20; 2:9; Ac 5:19, 12:7, 27:23, etc. Cf. Barth, *Church Dogmatics*, 486ff.

[7] Ibid., 484.

[8] Ibid., 456. Cf. 486: "To deny the angels is to deny God himself."

[9] In a charming little book Billy Graham speaks of angels as "God's secret agents," not "spiritual will-o'-the wisps"! *Angels, God's Secret Agents* (Waco, Tex.: Word, 1986) 15, 26.

[10] Gregory Nazianzen, *Second Theological Oration*, 31.

[11] Calvin, *Institutes*, 1.14.8.

[12] Cf. the biblical concept of revelation expressed by the Hebrew גָּלָה or the Greek ἀποκαλύπτω which implies an uncovering or unveiling both of God and humanity.

[13] Cf. Graham, *Angels*, 33.

[14] Recall the basic meaning of the Hebrew notion of salvation (יָשַׁע) as deliverance from

the limitations and restrictions of oppression and distress into conditions of freedom and openness. See Georg Fohrer, "σῴζω, σωτηρία," *TDNT* 7.970-978; and also Christoph Barth, *Die Errettung vom Tode in den individuellen Klage-und Dankliedern des Alten Testaments* (Switzerland: Zellikon Evangelischer, 1947) 127. Cf. further the characteristic reference of the psalmist to this concept of deliverance, 18:19; 31:8;118:3.

¹⁵ With respect to mundane time and space angels appear to be timeless and spaceless (cf. the presence of the angel Gabriel to Daniel and then to the Virgin Mary). Mt 22:30 indicates that angels are not involved, as we are, in the spatio-temporal processes of becoming. How, where and when they exist is entirely bound up with their mission between heaven and earth, eternity and time. The "time" as well as the "place" of their existence is governed and limited by the eternity and omnipresence of God (cf. Mt 24:36; Mk 12:25).

¹⁶ Cf. Graham, *Angels*, 52: "God's glory will not be denied, and every heavenly being gives silent or vocal testimony to the splendor of God."

¹⁷ For an account of the Apocalypse as the earliest source-book of the Christian liturgy, see my essay "Liturgy and Apocalypse," *Church Service Society Annual* 24 (Edinburgh, May 1954) 3-18.

¹⁸ As Barth rightly remarks, *Church Dogmatics*, 456, "these are not statistical but hyperbolical statements."

¹⁹ Heb 1:7, 12.29, citing from Ps 104:4. Cf. 2Esdras 8:22; and see also Ge 3:24 and Ex 3:2.

²⁰ Cf. the concern of Athanasius for a godly and reverent approach to the Holy Trinity which will not transgress the limits between the finite reason and the ineffable nature of God: "Thus far human knowledge goes. Here the cherubim spread the covering of their wings." *Letters to Serapion on the Holy Spirit*, 1.17.

²¹ From the liturgy of Holy Communion for the General Assembly of the Church of Scotland, *Ordinal and Service Book* (3rd ed.; Edinburgh: St Andrews Press, 1962) 7, 11.

²² Consult the Ben Shahn edition of *The Haggadah* (Eng. trans.; intro. and notes Cecil Roth; Boston: Little, Brown, 1965). See especially the *Peri pascha* of Melito of Sardis, the *Epistolae festales* of Athanasius and the *De adoratione et cultu in spiritu et veritate* of Cyril of Alexandria.

²³ Cf. the illuminating account of this given by Erich Kahler, *The Disintegration of Form in the Arts* (New York: G. Braziller, 1968).

²⁴ *Church Hymnal* (3rd ed.; Oxford: Oxford University Press, 1973) § 363.

²⁵ Cf. the wholly supernatural action of the angel sent twice by the Lord to deliver Peter from imprisonment (Ac 5:19ff., 12:7ff.).

²⁶ For what follows consult again my essay "Liturgy and Apocalypse," 3-18; and see my sermonic exposition of the book of Revelation in *The Apocalypse Today* (Grand Rapids: Eerdmans, 1960).

²⁷ Cf. our Lord's parabolic account of the great harvest at the end of the world when it will be the task of angels to separate the tares from the wheat, and of the judgment that will follow (Mt 23:24-50). See further "the little apocalypse" (Mt 24—25; Mk 13).

²⁸ Relate Jn 19:28-30 to Rev 10:7; cf. Lk 18:31, 22:37.

²⁹ The "angels" of the seven churches to which divine approbation and rebuke are addressed in Revelation 2—3 appear to be church leaders or bishops acting as messengers of God sent by him to preside over the churches, or possibly the "guardian angels" (cf. Mt 18:10) of the churches who see the face of the Lord, the Alpha and the Omega, the First and the Last, and reflect his judgments.

³⁰ Refer to Barth's long discussion, "The Ambassadors of God and their Opponents," *Church Dogmatics*, 477-531.

³¹ *The Church Hymnal*, § 354.

³² Cf. Ge 32:2, where מַחֲנָיִם means "camps." See also Ps 91:11-12, "For he will command his angels concerning you, to guard you in all your ways; they will lift you up in their hands, so that you will not strike your foot against a stone," which is cited in Mt 4:6, Lk 4:10ff.

³³ It may be recalled that in the Old Testament Apocrypha the angel Raphael is said to have the function of bringing "the memorial of prayer before the Holy One" (Tobit 12:12, 15; cf.

Rev 8:5).

[34] See Graham, *Angels*, 15, where he relays his wife's account of a not dissimilar incident, this time of the providential deliverance of a woman attacked by a tiger in China.

12

Contemplating the Trinitarian Mystery of Christ

James B. Torrance

D R. JAMES DENNEY, THE BELOVED SCOTTISH THEOLOGIAN AND New Testament scholar, used to say that in the ideal church all our theologians would be evangelists and our evangelists theologians. He was echoing the language of Plato's *Republic,* where Plato said that in the ideal state all politicians would be philosophers and philosophers politicians! We might add that in such a church all our theologians would also be men and women of prayer.

James Houston stands in that noble tradition of Scottish thinkers who have had not only a great desire to reflect theologically on the nature of the Christian gospel, but a passion to communicate it to others. Our lifelong friendship began as undergraduates together in Edinburgh University in the psychology classroom, where we had to observe one another and carry out tests for laboratory purposes! I soon came to see in him not only an able, mature scholar, but a man of prayer, consumed by missionary zeal to share with others the treasures he discovered in the Scriptures—with a vivid awareness of the place of Christ and the Spirit in the Christian life. I shall long remember how almost thirty years ago he came to me in Edinburgh when he was teaching geography in Oxford to expound his vision of a college where lay people from many professions and walks of life could come together in a context of worship and academic study and take degrees in theology to equip them for their witness in their different spheres. That of course was the vision which blossomed into Regent College. I can think of no one better equipped to fulfill there his task of being professor of Spiritual Theology in Regent's ecumenical context of worship, evangelism, missionary concern and academic scholarship.

The Trinitarian Viewpoint

Dr. Houston has grasped clearly the trinitarian nature of Christian spirituality[1] in a day when much religion in the West is in practice deeply subjective and individualistic, indeed narcissistic, preoccupied with self-expression, self-fulfillment, self-realization, and self-esteem, leading at times to a neo-gnosticism where the self is equated with God. The authentic work of the Holy Spirit is to lift us out of all such inverted preoccupation with the self to find the true fulfillment of our humanity in Christ, in the loving heart of the Father. The triune God of grace who has his own true being-in-communion has created us in his image in order that we might find our true being-in-communion with him and one another. The ministry of Christ and the Spirit is to lift us up into this life of communion as members of the body of Christ, participating together in the very triune life of God. Bishop Lesslie Newbigin has commented that when the average Christian in Europe or North America hears the name of God, he or she does not think of the Trinity. After many years of missionary work among Eastern religions, he returned to find that much of the worship in the West is *in practice*, if not in theory, *unitarian*. The "religion" of so many people today is moulded by concepts of God which obscure the joyful witness of the Bible to the triune God of grace. God is conceived of too often as the remote sovereign Individual Monad "out there," the law-giver, the contract-God who needs to be, or can be, conditioned into being gracious by devout religious behavior or by this or that religious act, be it even repentance or prayer. The Reformers were concerned to sweep away these views of God, but in spite of the Reformation, such concepts are alive and highly influential in our day. This is why theologians like Karl Barth, Rahner, Moltmann, Jüngel, Zizioulas, T. Smail and others have in their different ways labored to call the church back to the centrality of the doctrine of the Trinity, not only for a more biblical doctrine of God, but also for a better understanding of worship, as well as for a better concept of the human person and of true community.[2]

Among the Christian churches there are many different forms of worship, Reformed, Lutheran, Presbyterian, Episcopalian, Methodist, Baptist, Pentecostal, Roman Catholic, Eastern Orthodox. Within our different churches there are wide varieties, deriving from different traditions, some more liturgical than others. Today many churches and groups are experimenting with different forms of worship to find relevant ways of communicating the gospel in the context of a changing, increasingly secular world or in response to the challenge of feminism. The question therefore arises with considerable urgency, what is authentic Christian worship whatever form it takes? More specifically, what is the place of Christ and the Holy Spirit in Christian worship?

Two Views of Worship

As we reflect on the wide variety of contemporary forms of worship, it seems to me that we can discern two very different views.[3]

The first view—probably the commonest and most widespread—is that worship is something which *we* do, mainly in church on Sunday. We go to church, we sing our psalms and hymns to God, we intercede for the world, we listen to the sermon (too often simply an exhortation), we offer our time and talents to God. No doubt we need God's grace to help us to do it; we do it because Jesus taught us to do it and left us an example as to how to do it. *But worship is what WE do.* In theological language, the only priesthood is our priesthood, the only offering our offering, the only intercessions our intercessions.

Indeed this view of worship is in practice unitarian, has no real doctrine of the Mediator or sole priesthood of Christ, is human-centered, with no proper doctrine of the Holy Spirit, is often non-sacramental, and can easily engender weariness. We sit in the pew watching the minister "doing his thing" and exhorting us "to do our thing," and go home thinking we have done our duty for another week! This kind of "do-it-yourself-with-the-help-of-the-minister" worship is what our forebears would have called "legal worship" as opposed to "evangelical" worship—what the ancient church would have described as "Arian" or "Pelagian," and not truly catholic. It is certainly not trinitarian.

The second view of worship, the view for which the Reformers contended, is that worship is rather the gift of participating through the Spirit in the (incarnate) Son's communication with the Father—the gift of participating, in union with Christ, in what *he* has done for us once and for all by his self-offering to the Father in his life and death on the cross, and in what *he* is continuing to do for us in the presence of the Father, and in *his* mission from the Father to the world. The bread we break, is it not our sharing in the body of Christ? The cup of blessing which we bless, is it not our sharing in the blood of Christ? Our sonship and communion with the Father, are they not our sharing by the Spirit of adoption in Christ's sonship and communion with the Father? Our intercessions and mission to the world, are they not participation in the mission and intercessions of him who is "the apostle and high priest whom we confess" (Heb 3:1)? Is this not the meaning of life "in the Spirit"?

This second view is trinitarian and incarnational, taking seriously New Testament teaching about the sole priesthood and headship of Christ, his self-offering for us to the Father, and our life in union with Christ through the Spirit, with a vision of the church as the body of Christ. It is fundamentally "sacramental"—but in a way which enshrines the gospel of grace, that our Father in the gift of his Son and the gift of the Spirit gives us what he demands—the worship of our hearts and minds—lifting us up out of ourselves to participate in the very life of the Godhead. This is the heart of our theology of the Eucharist—of "holy communion."

The second view is both catholic and evangelical. Whereas the first view can be divisive, in that every church and denomination "does its own thing" and worships God in its own way, the second is unifying, in that it recognizes that there is only one way to come to the Father, namely through Christ in the communion of the Spirit and in the communion of the saints, whatever outward form our worship may take. If the first way can engender weariness, this second way, the way of grace, releases joy and ecstasy, for with inward peace we are lifted up by the Spirit into the presence of the Father, into a world of praise and adoration and fellowship in Christ.

It might be argued that the distinction between these two views is drawn too sharply. Is there not a middle position, as in fact probably most of our good church people suppose? I think this is true, but it is in fact a modification of the first view. It might be stated this way. *Yes, worship is what we do*—but *we* worship God, Father, Son and Holy Spirit, *we* pray to Christ as God, *we* invoke the Holy Spirit, *we* respond to the preaching of the Word, *we* intercede for the world and *we* offer our money, time and service to God.

This view might be defended on the ground of "the priesthood of all believers" and as being trinitarian, but it falls short of the New Testament understanding of participation through the Spirit in what *Christ* has done and is doing for us in our humanity, in his communion with the Father and his mission from the Father to the world. It is a do-it-yourself-in-response-to-Christ worship, and is to this extent a modification of the first view, but with more Christian content. Its weakness is that it falls short of an adequate understanding of the role of Christ and of the Spirit in our worship of the Father. It lacks appreciation of the sole priesthood of Christ as the *leitourgos,* the leader of our worship, as set forth in the epistle to the Hebrews (8:1, 2). It fails to see that *the real Agent in the worship is Christ,* drawing us by the Spirit into his life of communion with the Father.

This highlights for us the fact that in our understanding of the Trinity in Christian worship, the triune God is not only the *object* of our worship, but paradoxically by grace, this God is the *agent!* That is seen when we consider the place of Christ in worship. In the New Testament, two things are held together. *God* comes to us as person in Christ, and therefore *we pray to Christ as God*. But on the other hand, Jesus as the Word made flesh is our brother, a weak, suffering, tempted, struggling person, *praying for us and with us to the Father*, and uniting us with himself now as our risen and ascended Lord in his communion with the Father and his intercessions for the world. It is because of this that not only is the triune God the *object* of our worship, but our worship is the gift of participating through the Spirit in Christ's own fellowship with the Father. The Christ to whom we pray himself lived a life of prayer, and draws us into his life of prayer, putting his word "Father" onto our lips so that our life might become, in the words of the title of Henry Scougal's devotional classic, "the life of God in the soul of man." By sharing in Jesus' present life of communion with the Father in the Spirit, we are given to participate in the eternal Son's eternal communion with the Father. In Pauline terms, the Father "sent the Spirit of his Son into our hearts, the Spirit who calls out [and we with him] '*Abba*, Father'" (Gal 4:6).

If this account of "two views of worship" in our church today is accurate, we must ask why we have drifted away from the trinitarian view of the great Greek Fathers like Irenaeus, Athanasius, Cyril, and the Cappadocian divines, the view for which the Reformers contended, into this human-centered "unitarian" alternative. Is not the dominance of "the first view of worship" one supreme reason that the doctrine of the Trinity has receded?

Life in Christ

What we have said about the two views of worship can be said about mission, evangelism and the social witness of the church. There are two very different views of each of these. But are these activities primarily ours? Do we engage in them simply because Jesus commanded us to do them and left us an example as to how to do them? Then, no doubt, we would need God's grace to enable *us* to do them. Then God's grace would be conceived of in semi-Pelagian terms as simply "enabling grace," "infused" grace, an "invisible" thing we need, an efficacious impersonal cause (like gasoline to drive our cars!) that is there to make programs work. But in reality, are not mission, evangelism and social action also, like worship, activities in which we are called through the personal activity of the Holy Spirit to participate in Christ's ministry—in the work of the triune God as he establishes his kingdom? In the Bible, grace is always conceived of in personal terms. In grace, the triune God personally stands in for us, gives himself to us and draws us into his inner life. In worship and intercession, Jesus "our great high priest" in our humanity faces the Father with the concerns of the world and all humanity on his heart. In grace, he stands in for us, the One on behalf of the many, and calls us by grace to share in his ministry of intercession as a royal priesthood (1Pe 2:9). In mission and compassionate service, he faces the world in our humanity with the concerns of his Father (and our Father) on his heart, the apostle as well as the high priest of our profession. Again, in grace he stands in for us, sent by the Father to usher in the kingdom, and anoints us by the Spirit to share his mission to all nations. "And surely I am with you always." In both worship and mission, he baptizes us by the Spirit into his body that we might participate as members of his body in his ministry. "Therefore, holy brothers [and sisters] who share in the heavenly calling, fix your thoughts on Jesus, the apostle and high priest whom we confess" (Heb 3:1).

In our Western pragmatic society, where we are so concerned about questions of "know-how" and "techniques" for mission, evangelism, church growth, and fund-raising, we need to heed Bonhoeffer's plea that we give priority to the "who question" over the "how question" if we would understand the Bible and the biblical meaning of grace. Who is the Father to whom we pray in the name of Christ? Who is the Christ in whose mission we go forth to all nations? Who is the Holy Spirit who draws us into a life of wonderful communion? Only as we know who this triune God of grace is, and what he has done once and for all and is continuing to do for us and with us and in us, can we truly know how to serve him.

God's grace is free grace—unconditionally free. But it is also costly grace. We are summoned unconditionally to live a life of costly service, in prayer, mission, and evangelism, to offer ourselves in total obedience (Ro 12:1). How does our ministry relate to Christ's ministry, his once and for all ministry and his continuing ministry? Perhaps the apostle Paul gives us the clue in Gal 2:20: "I no longer live, but Christ lives in me. The life I live in the body, I live by faith in [and by the faithfulness of] the Son of God who loved me and gave himself for me." Is this not "life in Christ," participating by the Spirit in the life and ministry of Christ? Can we not also say, *We* pray, and yet it is not so much we who pray, but Christ and the Holy Spirit who pray for us and with us and in us (Ro 8:26, 27,

34)? Again, we evangelize and seek to carry the gospel of the kingdom to all nations, and yet it is not so much we who do it, but Christ working in us and through us, baptizing people by the Spirit into his kingdom. We exhort people to be reconciled to God and to one another, but it is God in Christ who has by grace reconciled the world to himself in his own person once and for all (Eph 2:8-18), who exercises his continuing reconciling ministry in us and through us today (2Co 5:18-21). Again, in social concern we seek to give all their humanity, for to hold out Christ to the world in evangelical concern is not only to hold out personal salvation, but to offer authentic humanity to all. But again Christ is the Agent. He has assumed our humanity, sanctified it, realized true humanity for us in his vicarious humanity, and now as the Risen Lord, the Last Adam, he realizes it in us and through us as we give ourselves in compassionate caring concern for all his creatures. What was lost in Adam is restored in Christ and through Christ—full humanity, nothing less.

The Trinitarian Mystery of Christ

Here we see something of the meaning of the New Testament word "mystery," the trinitarian "mystery" of Christ's person and reconciling work, not only in the Pauline epistles, but in our understanding of the Gospels. "The secret of the kingdom of God has been given to you" (Mk 4:11). The prime task of Christian theology is to probe this mystery in the light of revelation, if we would understand aright the nature of Christian worship, mission and evangelism in their unity as different ways of participating in the triune life and ministry of the God of grace in his purposes for the world, and if we would avoid the dualism between theory and practice, academic scholarship and worship, theology and evangelism which has so often characterized and impoverished post-Enlightenment Christianity.[4]

In the New Testament the word μυστήριον, "mystery," is used in four main ways. First of all it refers to the hidden trinitarian purposes of God for all nations in creation and in the election of Israel, the "hidden secret" now revealed in Christ and fulfilled in his reconciling ministry. So Paul writes, "The commission God gave me to present to you the word of God in its fullness—the mystery that has been kept hidden for ages and generations, but is now disclosed to the saints. To them God has chosen to make known among the Gentiles the glorious riches of this mystery, which is Christ in you, the hope of glory" (Col 1:25-27). What is this hidden secret? It is the purpose of the triune God of grace in creating Jews and Gentiles, both men and women, to share his life of loving communion. He does not abandon this purpose, but fulfills it in the election of Israel so that in the fullness of time in Christ, all nations might be called to participate in his triune life by being reconciled to him and to one another. "I will be your God and you will be my people." This is the secret of Paul's apostleship, to make known to the nations (Gentiles) this mystery, this gospel of reconciliation, which was revealed to him on the Damascus road (Col 1:19, 2:2, 4:3; Eph 1:9, 3:2-13, 16-21; Ro 16:25-27). The Father revealed his loving purposes in his Son, and calls the church to participate in their fulfillment by life in the Spirit. The doctrine of the Trinity is, so to speak, the grammar of God's mission to the world, as well as the grammar of worship and prayer.

Second, the word "mystery" is used to speak of the Incarnation itself, that God in revealing his divinity to us conceals it in the frail humanity of Jesus, where it is seen by the eye of faith. The hidden mystery is God as human in Jesus Christ. So in 1Ti 3:16, "Beyond all question, the mystery of godliness is great: He appeared in a body, was vindicated by the Spirit, was seen by angels, was preached among the nations, was believed on in the world, was taken up in glory." The God who reveals himself hides himself in a human body, speaks in parables in human language (Mt 11:22; Mk 4:11; Jn 8:43), and dies on a cross (1Co 1:21-25). Only through the Holy Spirit can we discern this mystery (Jn 3:3-21; 1Co 12:3) and see the glory of God in the face of Jesus Christ.

Third, "mystery" is used to speak of our relationship with Christ in his body, the relationship between Christ the head and the members. In being called to know this mystery we are called to participate in it, to find the fulfillment of our destiny in the purposes of God as members of his body where we are brought into union with one another. So the apostle speaks of the relationship between husband and wife as one participatory union. "This is a profound mystery—but I am talking about Christ and the church" (Eph 5:22-33). Christ takes up our relationships, sanctifies them and makes us one in his Body, in union with him. Our mutual loving of one another, as in our love for God, is participatory loving. As the Son indwells the Father, and we dwell in him, so we indwell one another in "perichoretic unity," setting forth the *perichoresis* (mutual indwelling) which is in the triune God. This is the real secret of κοινωνία, "fellowship" (cf. Jn 15:8-17; and our Lord's high priestly prayer in chapter 17).

Fourth, the word "mystery" refers to the eschatological fulfillment of the triune purposes of God in bringing his children to glory in the resurrection and in the kingdom of God—"Christ in you, the hope of glory" (Col 1:27; 1Co 15:51)—when "the mystery of God will be accomplished" (Rev 10:7).

It is in contemplation of the "hidden mystery" revealed in Christ, and in our reflection on the significance of this for our understanding of worship, mission and the whole of the Christian life, that there unfold the great doctrines of the Trinity, creation, the election of Israel, the Incarnation, the vicarious humanity of Christ, atonement, participation, life in the Spirit, church and sacraments, and our eschatological hope in the kingdom of God.

At the center of the New Testament stands, not our experience, however important that may be, but a unique, absolute relationship between Jesus and the Father, in a life lived in the Spirit, and in that Father-Son relationship we see the disclosure of that communion which is in God himself, and into which we are now drawn by the Holy Spirit. The nature of true ἀγάπη, communion, is defined by that relationship in which we see disclosed, not only the triune God himself, but the inner purpose of creation that we too in the image of the triune God should find our true being-in-communion. Jesus said: "All things have been committed to me by my Father. No one knows the Son except the Father, and no one knows the Father except the Son and those to whom the Son chooses to reveal him" (Mt 11:27). There is given to us in Christ this unique, absolute relationship in which Jesus lives a life of intimate communion with the Father, in his life of worship, mission and service, in which we are called to participate by our life in the Spirit. *He is the Agent* ("Christ in you, the hope of glory"), as he establishes the Father's kingdom and fulfills the trinitarian purposes of God for this world and for all nations.

Trinitarian Contemplation of Christ

In our contemplation of Christ and the mystery of the kingdom of God, as we follow each stage in the life of Christ in the gospel, it is fruitful to focus on four things:

(1) The mystery of the presence of the triune God in Christ, as he represents God to humanity and humanity to God.

(2) The mystery of incarnation, deity veiled in humanity (God as human), revealed only to the eye of faith.

(3) The mystery of "the wonderful exchange," of God as human in Christ in our place, standing in for us, taking what is ours, to give us what is his. This is the mystery of "Christ for us."

(4) The mystery of the relationship into which Christ draws us by the Spirit, to participate in his sonship and communion with the Father, and in his mission from the Father to the world. This is the mystery of "Christ in us."

This four-fold contemplation reveals the trinitarian purposes of God in Christ and illumines every stage in the gospel, Jesus' birth of Mary, his baptism in Jordan, his temptation, his ministry and prayer life, the transfiguration on Mt. Tabor, his passion and death, his resurrection and continuing ministry as the high priest and apostle whom we confess. Here we see the heart of a theology of worship and mission.

The story of the birth of Jesus is the story of the Eternal Son "who is in the bosom of the Father [*in sinu patris*]" taking our humanity in the womb of Mary, that he might share with us his sonship and lift us up into the life of God. As Irenaeus puts it: "He takes what is ours to give us what is his." He who is the eternal Son of the Father by nature becomes "Son of Man" that we might become the sons and daughters of God by grace. This is the "wonderful exchange" (*mirifica commutatio*, Calvin calls it) that is consummated in his taking our place on the cross, taking our enmity and death to himself, to give us his love and life in exchange (2Co 5:18-21).

It has been the mistake of much Western theology, Catholic and Protestant, to limit "substitution" to Christ's death on the cross, to the issue of salvation from sin. The idea has a much wider significance, embracing indeed his whole ministry for us. For example, it is at the heart of our understanding of prayer and the priesthood of Christ. Christ takes our selfish feeble prayers, sanctifies them, and presents them to the Father and in turn puts in his prayer "*Abba*, Father" onto our lips. He stands in for us, intercedes for us and with us and in us, precisely when we do not know how to pray as we ought (Ro 8:26, 34; Heb, passim). We have an Advocate with the Father. Substitution, standing in for us, taking what is ours to give us what is his, characterizes every stage of Christ's ministry from the Incarnation to the parousia. Christ's work, as the Scottish theologian John McLeod Campbell used to say, has a retrospective *and* a prospective aspect. Retrospectively, he deals with our past sin, guilt, condemnation, death, wiping out our sins once and for all, carrying our old humanity to the grave. Prospectively his mission from the Father is "to bring many sons to glory," to lift us up into his life of eternal sonship and communion with the Father in the Spirit. These two are never divorced in the New Testament. Jesus rises from the dead to enter into his new ministry of being "the leader of our worship" (λειτουργός), a high priest "forever," "who ever lives to intercede for us." This ministry will be an eternal ministry, continuing when his ministry of saving us from sin and death will have ended (1Co 15:24). We shall worship the Father through the Son in the Spirit for all eternity. This will be our eternal joy. He is the eternal Mediator of an eternal covenant. In the words of another great Scottish theologian of the thirteenth century, John Duns Scotus, our privilege and high destiny is to be forever *con-diligentes Deo*—"co-lovers with God," participating in the life of mutual love between the Father and the Son, in the life of the man Jesus who is the one true *con-diligens* with the Father.

Trinitarian Participation with Christ

Participation is a key concept in the New Testament. It is in Greek the word κοινωνία, meaning fellowship, communion, sharing, having all in common with one whom we love. There is κοινωνία in the triune God, between Jesus and the Father, and between Christ and the members of his body. This must be carefully distinguished from the Platonic concept of participation, *methexis*, seen in Plato's doctrine of the Forms. For Plato any particular, sensible object is what it is by "participation" in some "form," as we predicate, e.g., Truth, Beauty, Goodness of any particular person or thing. In Platonism the important thing is not the particular thing or person, but the Universal, the Idea. Indeed we do not know particulars as particulars, but only as they participate in Universals. This particular oak tree is an oak in that it participates in the form of an oak. But in the New Testament understanding of participation as κοινωνία, we commune with someone whom we love personally, with the Father, with Jesus Christ, with one another in the Spirit, sharing all, having all "in common." We can see the importance of this distinction in mystical theology in different understandings of the "imitation of Christ." In the Platonic tradition Christ is seen as the ideal Man, the ideal embodiment of Truth and Beauty and Goodness. Then the imitation of Christ (as in aesthetic worship) is motivated by our desire to embody in our spirituality a like Truth and Beauty and Goodness. This is the concept of eros expounded in Plato's dialogue *The Symposium*—the desire for Beauty and Justice and Goodness which motivates the good life. But then our interest would be not so much in Jesus for his own sake, but in the ideals he embodies as our Exemplar. But in the New Testament understanding our relationship with Christ is one of ἀγάπη. We love him for his own sake, and participate in his life and ministry in fellowship with him, and hence in conformity to *him*, not just to his ideals.

Correspondingly, there are two views of "contemplation." The one contemplates the Ideal, abstracted from all particulars, where the soul seeks the beatific vision of Eternal Goodness, in the tradition of Plato's dialogue *Phaedo*, abstracted even from life in the body. This can be a flight from reality. The other is that of this essay where we contemplate the trinitarian mystery of the Person of Christ in loving communion with him in all the historical particularity of his incarnation, death, resurrection and continuing mediatorial ministry, in our desire "to know Christ and the power of his resurrection and the fellowship of sharing in his sufferings" (Php 3:10). It is intensely particular, personal and historical, not a flight from the world but a sharing in his concern for the world.

In similar fashion, we have to distinguish a Platonic from a biblical view of "the one and the many." In the Platonic doctrine of the Forms (as in Hindu mysticism), the interest is in the One, the Universal, the Ideal, but not in the many particulars, the phenomena which participate in the One. But in the Bible, both in the Old Testament interpretation of the election of Israel to be a royal priesthood, the one on behalf of the many, and in the New Testament understanding of Christ as our high priest, giving himself as "a ransom for many," we have a totally different notion (as in Mk 10:45 or Ro 5). Christ is the One for the many, where the many find their fulfillment in loving communion with the One, where Christ's atoning work is for each one of the many and is personalized by the ministry of the Holy Spirit for each person whom he loves in fulfillment of the trinitarian purposes of God. It is in this biblical sense that we speak of "the all-inclusive vicarious humanity of Christ" and his concern for all and see in him our humanity renewed, made righteous, sanctified, offered without spot and wrinkle to the Father, hidden with Christ in God, waiting to be revealed at the last day. It is in that humanity realized for us in Christ, in his priesthood and apostolic ministry, that we are called to participate in a life of worship, prayer, communion and missionary service. It is in his "transforming friendship" that we find eternal joy.

Notes

[1] See his beautiful book *The Transforming Friendship: A Guide to Prayer* (Oxford: Lion, 1989).

[2] The British Council of Churches in 1983 appointed a "Study Commission on Trinitarian Doctrine Today" with representatives from all main British churches, and in 1989 published the results in two booklets, *The Forgotten Trinity* A third volume of essays under the same title will appear shortly. They constitute a unanimous ecumenical call to our churches to return to the triune God of grace and to recover a New Testament understanding of the uniqueness of Christ and the Spirit.

[3] See my article, "The Vicarious Humanity of Christ," in *The Incarnation, Ecumenical Studies in the Nicene-Constantinopolitan Creed, AD 381* (ed. T. F. Torrance; Edinburgh: Handsel, 1981); "The Place of Jesus Christ in Worship," in *Theological Foundations for Ministry* (ed. Ray S. Anderson; Grand Rapids: Eerdmans, 1979). Cp. J. G. S. S. Thomsan, *The Praying Christ* (Grand Rapids: Eerdmans, 1959); also the third volume of *The Forgotten Trinity*

[4] Cf. Lesslie Newbigin, *Foolishness to the Greeks: The Gospel and Western Culture* (London: SPCK, 1986); *The Gospel in a Pluralist Society* (London: SPCK, 1989); *The Open Secret* (London: SPCK, 1978).

13
Proving the Spirit of Christ: Walter Hilton's Acid Test

David L. Jeffrey

I T IS NOT NECESSARILY A COMFORT TO KNOW IT, BUT OUR CONTEM-
porary spiritual culture, polluted as it is by flamboyant hypocrisy,
pastoral malpractice, and spectacular travesties of responsible leadership, is not for all that uniquely odious in the history of the church.
There have been many rivals. Ecclesiastical dereliction at Rome in the
fourteenth and fifteenth centuries, in England in the same period, and
again in the eighteenth century, to take just three of many possible
examples, offered contradictions of the spirit of Christ in the visible
leadership of the church more revolting (and fit for pages of *National
Enquirer* reportage, had such been available) than any of the tragic
embarrassments and degradations of our own time. Yet comparison
with one or another of these dark chapters can prove of more benefit
than any mere "misery-likes-company" condolence to which weary
temptation might incline us. For in those times, as now, the spiritually
discerning counsel of God's faithful servants, called forth from them by
the abuses they faced, provided invaluable insights for their and our
shared and continuing spiritual battle.

English spiritual and theological writing of the fourteenth century in
particular confirms that the initial effect of such self-inflicted wound-
ing upon the church can parallel the obvious reactions in the world at
large—a loss of confidence and disinclination to trust "spiritual" authorities, degenerating at its worst to profound cynicism and disrespect
for all Christian institutions and their various appeals. In this respect,
students of literature may recall that Langland's *Piers Plowman* and
Chaucer's *Canterbury Tales* represent for the age of Wyclif almost

universal reactions to vocational betrayal and pastoral double-standards (including egregious moral and sexual abuse by church leaders). But more far-reaching than such public revulsion, and potentially more devastating, is the spread, consequent upon these lapses, of widespread spiritual haze, blurred focus and confused categories in those who desire to remain faithful, what fourteenth-century English spiritual writer Walter Hilton called a "be-clouding" of the image of Jesus in the church.

When a "steady beholding of Jesus" is circumstantially so occluded in the spiritual life of individual believers, Hilton writes, we are in danger of losing that which alone can authentically define us as a church. For what causes the church to be itself is its shared, active memory of what God has declared about his holiness in Jesus. What makes it possible for us to recognize each other as brothers and sisters is the living likeness of Jesus in our dealings with others. Yet if we have let other "images"— other representations of "Christian" life advertised by some who pass for prophets and Christian leaders—become directly or indirectly the occasion of a clouded view of Jesus, then we have wittingly or unwittingly victimized ourselves through a kind of second-hand idolatry. Accordingly, Hilton argues in his *Ladder of Perfection*, if we want to deal with the deeper consequences of betrayals of Jesus in the public witness of the church, we will have to begin with reformation in our own spiritual discernment. For spiritual discernment, one of the essential attributes of Christian maturity at any time, is crucial to spiritual survival when wolves in sheep's clothing seem to be met at almost every turn.

Self-Examination

We might expect Hilton to adduce notorious examples of miscreance in the church, even for the purposes of identifying characteristics of spiritual deceivers, or "counterfeit lights" as he calls them, in his own age. He does not do this. Rather, consistently with the whole point of his teaching, he goes directly to the question of self-examination, or "examination of conscience" in the individual believer. This is in fact the prime concern of all his writing.[1] If each believer grows in honest self-knowledge before God, he argues, predators will not be able to masquerade successfully as shepherds:

> I believe that a soul that has truly recognized its own murkiness is not vulnerable to a counterfeit light. That is, when a person truly and unstintingly sets himself to forsake the love of the world, and is enabled by grace to come to spiritual consciousness and self-knowledge, governing himself meekly in that experience, he shall not be deceived by errors, heresies, or fantasies (p. 117).

Spiritual self-knowledge, we see, is the necessary condition of spiritual discernment.

Hilton was an Augustinian canon, a member of the order which produced also Thomas à Kempis and Martin Luther. As a canon, he had dealings not only with members of his religious community, but also with tradesmen, provisioners, and government officials in the world at large. He wrote for and counseled both those with a special religious vocation and those whose primary calling was to secular work.[2] As a result of his broad contact with both worlds, he had doubtless acquired much experience in the study of human nature and motivation. He indicates that he had come to appreciate well the maxim of Augustine that if one wishes to know what sort of person one is dealing with, one has only to discover what it is that person most loves, and how he or she expresses that love. All the rest will then fall into place.[3] But he applies this rule of thumb to self-examination, speaking of "many people" and "such a person" in such a way as to allow his reader to draw the appropriate inferences without over-reaction or defensiveness. "Many people," he writes, do all the right things, "but only as a matter of rational choice and directed will, having no love or spiritual delight in them" (p. 43). This he calls virtuous "performance"—good in so far as it produces good, but not necessarily of value to the performer. We all know people like this, he suggests, and may properly admire them, but at the same time we can see that their virtuous deeds lack the higher good of being done out of an overmastering love of Jesus, as a reflex or axiom of love and gratitude. The overmastering impulse of "real affection" transforms the spirit in which we serve, making each action another means toward our contemplation of Jesus, our spirit-absorbed "looking at Him." And that is what we need.

Hilton observes that there are three means that Christians typically employ in "offering themselves to contemplation," or, indeed, to effective spiritual self-examination. "These are: the reading of Holy Scripture and the teaching of godly authors; spiritual meditation; and effectual fervent prayer" (p. 44).

Hilton concentrates particularly on the believer's responsibility to practice meditation. It is in disciplined meditation, he observes, that we can take a thoughtful inventory of our own sins and shortcomings, including our "false humility and inordinate worry about the flesh and the world." This practice of self-examination teaches us to be honest with ourselves about who we are. "Know this well," he cautions,

> ... until your heart is substantially cleansed from sin—through the
> application of stable truth with respect to your own life on the one

hand, and a diligent beholding of Christ's life on the other—you may
not have a spiritual knowing of God perfectly. Consider well the
gospel where he says: "Blessed are the pure in heart, for they shall see
God" (Mt 5:8).

In meditation likewise we can assess our need of specific Christian
virtues, and reflect on how best to pray for and work toward realization
of such necessary virtues as "meekness, mildness, patience, righteousness
of heart, spiritual strength, temperance, purity, peace, sobriety, faith,
hope, and charity." It is the first and the last of this list, meekness and
charitable love, which in fact he regards as most crucial to our growth in
spiritual self-knowledge and its concomitant, spiritual discernment. For
it is the presence—or absence—of meekness and charitable love which
most surely distinguishes integrity of heart from hypocrisy. Hilton's
examples are practical:

> . . . a true preacher of God's word, rich in charitable love and in
> meekness, called of God and received by his holy church, shall have a
> special reward, a crown for his preaching. And hypocrites and charla-
> tans, who have neither meekness nor charity and are sent neither by
> God nor his holy church, when they preach they have their reward
> here.

Love and Meekness

Hilton uses the word "charity" or "charitable love" in precisely the sense
of Augustine's *caritas* and Paul's ἀγάπη, "love," as reflected in the AV
translation of 1 Corinthians 13. What he speaks about is selfless as distinct
from self-serving love, born of motivation which is unambiguously
self-transcending. This, on sound biblical evidence, he shows to be the
kind of love to which each of us is called by our Lord and which is to
mark us as his servants. For our part, therefore, we should on principle
"love and honor all persons in our hearts, and approve and receive all
their deeds that have the appearance of goodness, even though it is
possible that some of the doers may in God's sight be badly motivated"
(p. 86). But "this does not apply," he adds quickly, "in the case of those
who are openly heretical or evil. These types we should flee, eschewing
their presence or association," if their motivations—that is, their evidently self-serving rather than self-sacrificing affections—have been
clearly demonstrated. Leaning on 1Co 13:1-3, he writes:

> If someone who is a kind of living curse builds a church or feeds a poor
> man, you may appropriately deem it as nothing, for spiritually speak-
> ing, so it is. And if an open heretic and charlatan, rebel to the church,
> should preach and teach—even if he converts a hundred thousand

souls—you may believe that the deeds do him no spiritual good. For such men are plainly out of charity, without which anything we may do is nothing.

The test we apply to others is thus the test we must apply in the meekness of daily self-examination to ourselves. Indeed it is an axiom of this test that it cannot be used with accuracy or effectiveness outwardly if it is not being applied first and foremost to ourselves. The presence of charitable love (it is a gift, as Hilton has already made clear, not the achievement of our effort) will not be discerned in any except that person who is "perfectly meek." He or she alone experiences self-transcending love, and therefore is alone able to speak of it truthfully.

Meekness, in this sense, is the virtue most basic to Christian discernment. For example, we will want to concur with Hilton that "to reprove a sinner for his sin with the purpose of his amending while yet there is time, that is a deed of charity. But to hate the sinner instead of the sin, that is against charitable love." But he immediately then adds a weighty *caveat*: "One who is himself truly meek can distinguish one from the other, and nobody else can. One could, in fact, have all the intelligence of the philosophers and not manage this distinction.... Even a man who has clerical training and a theological education and yet is not genuinely meek will err and stumble here, confusing the one with the other" (p. 87). For meekness, like charity, is not something which can "be learned from the knowledge of men." It too is a gift of God's grace, earnestly to be sought for by one who is possessed by charitable love and who thus yearns for the spirit of Christ. And what is meekness? In Hilton's succinct definition, "he is truly meek who truthfully knows and is conscious of himself as he truly is" (p. 88). Meekness is to accept the truth about oneself without cavil—neither inflating nor falsely depreciating that truth. It is spiritually obedient self-knowledge, maintained by the practice of regular self-examination in the light of a "clear beholding of Jesus in his Word." How then are we to obtain charitable love? Hilton's answer: "Be meek and lowly in spirit, and you shall have it. And what involves less effort than to be meek? Truly nothing." Authentic meekness is thus, on Hilton's definition, the necessary condition of self-transcending love, even as pride (in any form) is the hidden fount of self-serving cupidity.

At this point Hilton comes back to the problem of the perfidious "fellow Christian" against whom we may well harbor powerful resentments and concerning whom we may be stirred up by feelings of "self-pity, bitterness, or wicked will." When it seems that this person, despite all the layerings of grievous sin that hurt himself and others, must yet be regarded from our incomplete perspective as a "fellow Christian," then we owe that person (the sin notwithstanding) "perfect charity":

What it really comes to is this: if you are not stirred up against such a person in anger while faking an outward cheer, and have no secret hatred in your heart, despising him or judging him or considering him worthless; if the more shame and villainy he does to you in word or deed, the more pity and compassion you show toward him, almost as you would for someone who was emotionally or mentally distressed; and if you are so compelled by love that you actually cannot find it in your heart to hate him, but instead you pray for him, help him out, and desire his amending (not only with your mouth, as hypocrites do, but with a true feeling of love in your heart): *then* you will be in perfect charity toward your fellow Christian.

Loving the Sinner

Hilton's model for "perfect charity" is, unsurprisingly, the Lord Jesus. When most sorely oppressed by the injuries of a fellow Christian, says Hilton, we should consider

how Christ loved Judas, who was both his mortal enemy and a sinful dog. How good Christ was to him, how benign, how courteous, how humble toward him whom he knew to be damnable. He chose him for his apostle and sent him to preach with the other apostles. He gave him power to work miracles. He showed to him the same good cheer in word and deed. He shared with him his precious Body, and preached to him in the same manner as he did to the other apostles. He did not condemn him openly; nor did he abuse him or despise him, nor even speak evil of him (and yet even if he had done all of that, it would simply have been to tell the truth!). And above all, when Judas seized him, he kissed him and called him his friend.

All this charitable love Christ showed to Judas whom he knew to be damnable—without feigning or flattering, but in truthfulness of good love and pure charity. For though it might seem to us that Judas was unworthy to have any gift of God, or any token of love because of his wickedness, nevertheless in God's eyes it was worthy and reasonable that our Lord should show himself to him as he is.

Jesus' love for Judas was perfect charity, proceeding from perfect meekness. And this, reminds Hilton, is the standard of love to which Jesus calls his followers in the commandment that we love one another as he has loved us (Jn 13:34). This alone is evidence to the world of authentic discipleship—"for if you love as I have loved you, then are you my disciples." Authentic discipleship comes at a high cost, not the least of which, we might feel at times, is the cost of perfect charity toward our fellow Christians. Hilton agrees. That is why he concludes: "He that is truly meek, or would be meek, can love his fellow Christians. And nobody else can do so" (p. 92).

Now Hilton can come to the more visible problem of spiritual counterfeits, preachers and teachers who may not be, despite a multitude of deceptive appearances, merely sinful fellow Christians, but whose commitment to self-aggrandizement has grown so monstrous that deceiving and even destroying the flock are of scant concern next to their own quest for power or eminence. At this level, and given the context he has established, Hilton wants to "say something about how . . . a soul may recognize the light of truth when it shines from God, and distinguish it from that artificial light of the Enemy" (p. 113). His example is a distinction between the sun itself as source of light, and the effect dark clouds in a broken sky may have in making the sunlight seem to originate from another part of the sky. In some persons who pretend conversion, says Hilton, there is no transformation because "they will not recognize themselves for what they have been before [their conversion] through sin, nor acknowledge how they remain, in their own strength, nothing before God." They refuse the humility of self-examination, of exclusive focus upon Jesus, of silence and repentance. Rather, they arrogate to themselves unvalidated spiritual authority,

> supposing themselves possessed of great insight, which they feel is given to them suddenly without study beforehand, and also a great fervor of love, so it seems, to preach truth and righteousness to their fellow Christians. Therefore they count it a grace of God that he visits them with his blessed light "in preference" to other souls.
>
> Nevertheless, if such folk really look about themselves they will see that this light of insight and heat of passion that they feel comes not from the true sun, the Lord Jesus; rather, it comes from the Noonday Demon that feigns light and likens himself to the sun.
>
> This is the way that such counterfeiters shall be recognized. The light of knowledge of insight which is feigned by the fiend to a murky soul is always revealed between two black and stormy clouds. The over-cloud is presumption, the nether-cloud is the down-putting and undercutting of one's fellow Christians (p. 114).

The "light" such folk exhibit is accordingly not that of Jesus, but rather of what Hilton (like other medieval writers) calls the Noonday Demon, the bold-faced Lucifer who claims to be the Light, though he is in fact the Father of Lies and Prince of Darkness. How is the faithful Christian, consistently with meekness and charitable love, to distinguish those who serve this false light from those who serve the True Light "come into the world"? Well, by looking for these same two basic qualities of the Spirit of Christ—meekness and charitable love. When we do that, certain unmistakable evidences will emerge:

> Now whatever light of knowledge or experience of fervor shines upon a soul, when it is accompanied by presumption, self-promotion, and disdain of one's fellow Christians at the same time, it is not a light of grace granted by the Holy Spirit. This is so even when the knowledge in itself is of the truth. No, it is either of the devil if it comes suddenly, or of man's own wit if it comes by study. And it ought to be more widely recognized that this kind of feigned light is not the light of the true sun (pp. 114-115).

Such preachers "fancy that pursuit of their own willfulness is freedom of the Spirit." Moreover, they are "so blinded with a feigned light that they attribute their self-promotion and a lack of toleration to the laws of Holy church," and

> the words that they utter in their preaching begin to resound to back-biting, strife, discord, and the pronouncement of judgment on both communities and individuals. Yet they argue that all this is done in charity and a zeal for righteousness. It is not so, for as James the apostle says: "Where envying and strife is, there is confusion and every evil work" and "This wisdom descendeth not from above, but is earthly, sensual, devilish," whereas "the wisdom that is from above is first pure, then peaceable, gentle, and easy to be entreated, full of mercy and good fruits, without partiality, and without hypocrisy" (Jas 3:15-17). Wherever there is envy and contention, there is instability and all sorts of evil work. And therefore the cunning which brings forth such sins does not come from the Father of Light, our God, but it is earthly, beastly, even of the devil.
>
> By these tokens then—pride, presumption, intolerance, indignation, backbiting, and other such sins (for these soon follow after)—the counterfeit light can be distinguished from that which is true (p. 115).

The Acid Test: The Jesus Way

At this point we recognize what Walter Hilton is saying to us about proving—that is, demonstrating—the spirit of Christ. First, we cannot hope to "prove" anything unless we ourselves have first drawn close to our Lord, beholding him, meditating upon the light of his countenance, so that his perfect meekness and perfect charity are the normative temper of our discerning reflection. The acid test is whether we are sufficiently prepared to distinguish between the sin and the sinner, and it is provided by Jesus' treatment of Judas. When this modeling of perfect meekness and charitable love is grasped as displaying essential qualities of the True Light, then we can begin to see that false light is characterized by their opposites—pride and self-serving. Secure in the trustworthiness of this test, because it is nothing other than comparison with Jesus himself, we can see that our proper task is not to exclaim and declaim upon each sinful extravagance which understandably agonizes us inwardly for the wounds it creates in the body of Christ. Rather, it is to contemplate more closely the meekness and self-transcending love of our Lord Jesus himself, in which alone is our healing, and to encourage others to take up the same occupation. Hilton's pastoral counsel, apt for fourteenth-century England, is surely also suitable for us now. What it teaches is eternally true of the spirit of Christ in God's dealings with his people. It deepens our appreciation that our Lord does not force himself into a recalcitrant or preoccupied heart. And it offers us a pertinent, timely reminder that, as thankfully we may sing, "where meek souls will receive him, still the dear Christ enters in."

Notes

[1] The translation of *The Ladder of Perfection* (or *Speculum Perfeccion*) to which I refer throughout is that contained in *Toward a Perfect Love: The Spiritual Counsel of Walter Hilton*, which I had the honor of preparing for the Classics of Faith and Devotion Series (Portland, Ore.: Multnomah, 1988) under the direction of the General Editor of that series, Dr. James Houston. This volume contains also my translation of *Letter to a Layman* (or *Epistle on the Medled Life*).

[2] *The Epistle on the Medled (Mixed) Life* is directed to a deeply committed Christian lord, or as we might style him today, a "captain of commerce," persuading him to accept his lay work as a spiritual vocation in itself, and to offer it up as a sacrifice to God, so working toward the sanctification of ordinary life. *The Ladder of Perfection* is addressed to a young woman who has entered upon a formal religious vocation and taken vows. Another treatise, his *Epistola Aurea*, was written (successfully) to encourage Adam Horsley, then Chancellor of the Exchequer in England (1375), to leave the world of national politics for a full-time spiritual vocation.

[3] Augustine's "test of love," the assay of human intention by the litmus of charity/cupidity, is articulated in several places in his works, including his *Confessions* and *On the Freedom of the Will*. But his most influential passage on the subject throughout the Middle Ages was that found in his *On Christian Doctrine* (see esp. § 1.22.21-1.40.44; and §3.10.16).

14
Richard Baxter on Heaven, Hope, and Holiness

James I. Packer

ONE OF THE MANY PLEASURES OF BEING JIM HOUSTON'S COL-league at Regent College is team-teaching with him an annual seminar on Cistercian and Puritan spirituality, studied from original texts. Among the Puritans, Richard Baxter always figures large, as one whose writings and life express Puritan godliness at its noblest. Seminar members are invited to choose from three Baxter projects: an exploration of part one of *A Christian Directory,* where the basic principles of Puritan piety are brought together; a study of Baxter's view of what it means to be a minister, as focused in *The Reformed Pastor;* and an enquiry into the discipline of meditation on one's hope of glory, the subject of Baxter's sprawling masterpiece, *The Saints' Everlasting Rest.* Over the years, the third project has proved the hardest for students to do well, since they start so far away from Baxter's sense of reality. That, I hasten to say, is not a put-down for Regent students, many of whom are superb; it is, rather, a comment on the late-twentieth-century Christian culture of the West, which bequeaths to its children its own blind spots. The following pages attempt to bridge the gap between our mindset and Baxter's at this point, so that we may get close enough to him to learn from him on this momentous biblical theme. With my purpose, at least, I think Jim Houston will be pleased, whatever the quality of my attempt to carry it out.

In describing Baxter's theme as "momentous" and "biblical" I was already declaring an interest, about which I had better now come clean. I bring to this piece of writing three convictions. The first is that rejoicing in the "living hope" of "an inheritance that can never perish, spoil or fade—kept in heaven for you, who through faith are shielded by God's power" and "set[ting] your hope fully on the grace to be given you when Jesus Christ is revealed" (1Pe 1:4-5, 13) are integral elements in New Testament spirituality; and I see New Testament spirituality as the norm for all subsequent Christian devotion, just as New Testament doctrine is the norm for all subsequent Christian belief. My second conviction is that a good deal of what is involved in being "alive to God" in this or any age depends directly on having this "living hope" vivid in one's heart. I think here of the qualities of zeal, enterprise, energy, and persistence in well-doing for God; of loving, adoring worship as a daily habit; of meekness, sweetness, and selflessness under pain and disappointment; of a sense of proportion, a due appreciation of pleasure, and realism about death. My third conviction is that we Western Christians, by and large (Jim Houston being a shining exception), are to our shame a sluggish, earthbound lot compared with our Puritan predecessors, and that lack of long, strong thinking about our promised hope of glory is a major cause of our plodding, lack-luster lifestyle. A change for the better is needed at this point, and I believe Baxter can help us toward it; and that, I confess, is my main reason for choosing to write about him now.

Baxter the Puritan

Baxter claimed to be, and indeed was, a Puritan to his fingertips. The hindsight of history shows him to have been an outstanding example of that outstanding Anglo-Saxon type. Some, acknowledging his astonishing saintliness, reasonableness, breadth of ecumenical sympathy, and freedom from the bigotry and party spirit that besmirched so much seventeenth-century history, have thought of him as standing apart from the Puritan movement as a whole. But nobody in the seventeenth-century thought that, nor would any today, did they not picture Puritanism in terms learned from such as Macaulay, Hawthorne, Belloc, and Chesterton, as an essentially morbid movement, fed by a barbarous crypto-Manichaean theology that opposed grace to nature, revelation to rationality, godliness to good manners, and purity to pleasure—a movement, in short, that pitted Christianity against culture, and was shaped by a judgmental group mind that saw legalistic rigidity and pharisaic morality as marks of true religion. Certainly, Baxter was not like that!—but then, neither was the Puritanism of history, and it is high time that this venerable caricature, "distressingly and stridently recurrent" as it still is,[1] was finally laid to rest.

What, then, was the nature of historical Puritanism, the movement with which Baxter identified and that valued him as its best writer on the Christian life and, later, as the leading apologist for its ecclesiastical nonconformity?[2] The question is not too hard to answer. Puritanism according to Baxter, and as modern scholarship, correcting centuries of past misrepresentation, portrays it,[3] was a total view of Christianity, Bible-based, church-centered, God-honoring, Christ-exalting, Reformational, internationalist, literate, orthodox, and pastoral. It saw personal, domestic, professional, political, churchly, and economic existence as aspects of a single whole, namely society viewed as a *corpus Christianum*, and it taught everyone to order all departments and relationships of their life according to the Word of God, so that everything would be sanctified and become "holiness to the Lord." Puritanism's spearhead activity was pastoral evangelism and nurture through preaching, catechizing, and counselling (which Puritan pastors called "casuistry," the resolving of "cases of conscience"). Puritan pulpit instruction, which we can assess from the vast number of devotional books containing written-up sermons that were published by something like a hundred Puritan authors, highlighted the realities of a Reformed Augustinianism in the inner life—self-knowledge; self-humbling for sin, and repentance; faith in, and love for, Jesus Christ the Savior; the need for regeneration, and for sanctification (holy living, by God's power) as proof of its reality; the call to conscientious conformity to all God's laws, and to a disciplined use of the means of grace; and the blessedness of the assurance and joy from the Holy Spirit that all faithful believers under ordinary circumstances may know. Puritans saw themselves as God's pilgrims, travelling home through rough country; God's warriors, battling the world, the flesh, and the devil; and God's servants, under orders to worship, fellowship, and do all the good they could as they went along. Of this Christianity Baxter was a masterful teacher and shining example throughout the more than fifty years of his ministerial career. (Ordained in 1638, he died in 1691.)

Diligence in "duty" and wise use of time were basic Puritan virtues, and here Baxter was phenomenal. Though a sick man living in pain throughout his working life,[4] he was an omnivorous polymath, always studying, reading quickly and remembering well what he had read, and consistently thoughtful, knowledgeable, and judicious in the opinions he expressed on what the books had set before him. He was in fact the most voluminous English theologian of all time, who in addition to approximately 4 million words of pastoral, apologetic, devotional and homiletic writing reprinted in his *Practical Works*[5] produced some 6 million on aspects of the doctrine of grace and salvation, church unity and nonconformity, the sacraments, Roman Catholicism, antinomianism, millenarianism, Quakerism, politics and history, not to mention a massive autobiography and a systematic theology in Latin. And all these writings show the mature judgment of a clear, sharp, well-stocked mind, very honest and spiritually very alert. The mental and literary vigor of this chronic, often housebound invalid, like the evangelistic and pastoral vigor of his spectacular fifteen years in Kidderminster (1641-1642 and 1647-1661), during which most of the town came to faith, seems incredible: but Baxter's vigor is a matter of recorded fact.

Whence, we ask, came Baxter's energy? How did he manage it all? What kept him going? In an unfinished autobiographical poem he gives us part of the answer.

A life still near to Death, did me possess
With a deep sense of Time's great preciousness;
so that
I Preach'd, as never sure to Preach again,
And as a dying man to dying men.[6]

It is clear that, with one foot in the grave as he believed, Baxter enjoyed throughout his ministry that wonderful concentration of the mind that Dr. Samuel Johnson thought would flow from knowing one was going to be hanged in a fortnight. But it is also clear that the enhanced sense of urgency and responsibility and of the importance of the present moment that his expectations of death called forth was only half the story. Though Baxter worked up to the limit ("I doe [*sic*] as much as I can"[7]) and took no vacations, he was not tense and frantic, driven by guilt; rather, he was joyful and thankful, being drawn by love. The secret is not that he was a workaholic, but that he was, if I may coin a word, a praiseaholic. This is clear from what follows.

Death, Rest, Perfection

That death is for believers the gate of life; that our living in this world should be seen as preparation for dying out of it into a better one; and that wisdom says, in Alexander Whyte's phrase, "forefancy your deathbed" so as to retain a sense of reality were three Christian truths that Baxter understood very well, and as a man living at death's door he practiced assiduously two habits that these truths prompt.

The first habit was to estimate everything—values, priorities, possessions, relationships, claims, tasks—as these things will appear when one actually comes to die. This was Baxter's antidote to the creeping infection of worldly greed in its various forms.

The second habit was to dwell on the glory of the heavenly life to which one was going. This was Baxter's antidote to aimlessness, sluggishness, and drift.

During the winter of 1646, as he lay sick and lonely in a country house far from his Kidderminster home, broken in health and "sentenced to Death by the Physicians," Baxter the wordsmith and preacher started to write out homiletically "for my own use" his meditations on "the Everlasting rest which I apprehended my self to be just on the Borders of."[8] So he began his first and in some ways greatest book. Recovered, he saw what benefit his meditations had brought him, and made it a rule henceforth to meditate on heaven specifically for half an hour or more each day.[9] Also, it became a regular part of his ministry to encourage others to follow his example, as the fourth part of *The Saints' Everlasting Rest* most passionately does. In 1676 he wrote "one of the most beautiful of his books,"[10] a long admonitory address to himself that was printed in 1683 under the title *Mr. Baxter's Dying Thoughts upon Philippians 1:23.* The text is "For I am in a strait betwixt two, having a desire to depart, and to be with Christ; which is far better." Baxter's theme is, once again, the substance and ground of the Christian hope of glory, and the soliloquy centers this time on seeing the life to come not as rest from toilsome labor so much as the perfecting and fulfilling of human nature. At the end of his life he loved to meditate on the description of heavenly Jerusalem in Heb 12:22-24, a passage which, so he declared, "deserves a thousand thousand thoughts."[11] It was Baxter's habit of holding heaven at the forefront of his thoughts and desires that goes furthest to explain why, "when he spake of weighty Soul-concerns, you might find his very Spirit Drench'd therein,"[12] and whence over the years, pain-racked bag of bones that he was, he drew the motivation and mental energy that sustained his ministry. The hope of heaven brought him joy, and joy brought him strength, and so, like John Calvin before him and George Whitefield after him (two verifiable examples) and, it would seem, like the apostle Paul himself (see 1Co 15:10; 2Co 11:23-30; Col 1:29), he was astoundingly enabled to labor on, accomplishing more than would ever have seemed possible in a single lifetime.

Baxterian heavenly-mindedness is something that late-twentieth-century Christians find it extraordinarily hard to tune into, for several reasons over and above our low-level spirituality across the board. One reason is that our affluent culture is too comfortable and in the short term too gratifying. Life for English Christians, whatever their convictions, in the tortured and unhappy seventeenth century was harsh, full of pain, and in the end disappointing and indeed brutalizing, whereas modern Western culture conspires to massage everyone into feelings of dreamy contentment with things as they are, and has great and alarming success in so doing. Artificially induced inability to see this world as a wilderness drains away from us the joy and excitement about the hope of heaven's glory that marked New Testament Christians, patristic Christians, medieval Christians, Reformation and Puritan Christians, Wesleyan and Victorian Christians, and still marks Christians in black Africa. Indeed, our Western worldliness dulls our sense of God at every point, and where the sense of God is dim thoughts of heaven grow dim also.

A second reason is Western cultural prejudice against hopes of a better, celestial world as being escapist, and against the biblical imagery of heaven (robes, crowns, thrones, gold, jewels, and so on) as being jejune and repellent to civilized taste. Having shared these prejudices as an unconverted teenager, squirming when congregations sang "Jerusalem the golden / With milk and honey blest," I think I am now entitled to nail them as stupidities, the first a mental miasma spun off from Marxist materialism, the second a sign of the unbeliever's inability to "cash" pen-pictures of Near Eastern splendor in terms of the joyous fellowship with Christ for which they are metaphors and analogies. But the sad fact is that these prejudices are widespread, and the materialist, no-nonsense mindset of our technological Titanism reinforces them every day.

A third reason why heavenly-mindedness fails to register nowadays, even with Christians, might be labelled the misdirection of desire. As C. S. Lewis, expanding on Augustine, maintained, the pangs of Joy, in the special sense of sweet desire and longing, are universally felt, and are really a natural, built-in craving for God and heaven.[13] But because original sin has twisted all our desires in an egocentric direction, and because our technologically oriented culture shrinks our souls and erodes our capacity for moral and spiritual discernment, we imagine that the hunger of our hearts will be satisfied by sexual activity, aesthetic experience, making money, gaining and using power, or something similar, and we dismiss the idea that God and heaven are what our hearts seek as old-fashioned, unenlightened fantasy. Some Christians are only half-way to wisdom at this point, supposing that the God who satisfies and gives rest to the heart is One whom they can manage, deploy, and exploit in the interests of these secular objectives, rather than One whom they must worship, adore, trust, love, thank, and give themselves up to in radical self-denial: so far has original sin retained its corrupting influence in their lives. Misdirected, earthbound desire is so much part of life today that not even Christians are interested in heaven, and Baxter's statement, made a year before he died, "I live in almost continual thoughts of heaven,"[14] is likely to prompt no more than a yawn.

But it is worth learning to swim against the secularist stream (which nowadays often flows as strongly within as outside the churches) and to grasp Baxter's wisdom about heavenly mindedness as a basic dimension of being alive to God; so I proceed.

Heaven in the Head and the Heart

First question, then: Why should one meditate on heaven?

Baxter gives a series of reasons in *The Saints' Everlasting Rest*:

Consider, A heart set upon heaven will be one of the most unquestionable evidences of thy sincerity.... A heart in heaven is the highest excellency of your spirits here, and the noblest part of your Christian disposition.... A heavenly mind is a joyful mind; this is the nearest and truest way to live a life of comfort.... A heart in heaven will be a most excellent preservative against temptations, a powerful means to kill thy corruptions.... The diligent keeping of your hearts on heaven, will preserve the vigor of all your graces, and put life into all your duties .... The frequent believing views of glory are the most precious cordial in all afflictions.... It is he that hath his conversation in heaven, who is the profitable Christian to all about him.... There is no man so highly honoureth God, as he who has his conversation in heaven.... There is nothing else that is worth the setting our hearts on ... (4.3).

In short, the practice of meditation on the prospect of heaven will both honor God and do one good. As a cherishing of hope, it will reinforce the holiness of life whereby the hope is laid hold of; as a following of the Holy Spirit's lead, it will increase knowledge of the love of God, who has granted us heaven by his grace, and so increase our love for God in response. "We fall in with the heavenly Spirit in his own way, when we set ourselves to be most heavenly. Heavenly thoughts are the work which he would set you on; and the love of God is the thing which he works you to thereby."[15] Meditating on heaven is a head-clearing, heart-warming, invigorating discipline, hard work and ungratifying to the flesh, no doubt, but very enriching to the spirit. So Baxter had proved in his own life, and so he presented the matter to the Christian world.

Second question: How should one form ideas of heaven, to shape one's meditations?

One way is to analyze the idea of personal perfection. Basic to the Christian's self-knowledge, as God mediates it through the Scriptures, is the awareness of one's current imperfection, with which goes that other aspect of self-knowledge, awareness of one's desires that lack fulfillment at present. In *Dying Thoughts* particularly Baxter pursues this method of building up a notion of heaven. He describes heaven as a state in which every faculty is made faultless and is wholly occupied in knowing, adoring, loving and enjoying God. "What is heaven to me but God? God, who is light, and life, and love, communicating himself to blessed spirits, perfecting them in the reception, possession, and exercise of life, light, and love for ever.... God ... is heaven and all to me."[16] "It is the presence of God that maketh heaven to be heaven."[17] Heaven begins here: "the knowledge and love of God in Christ is the beginning or foretaste of heaven."[18] Full heavenly experience, however, remains future: "we ask for perfection, and we shall have it, but not here."[19] How, when, and where we shall enter heaven, how the soul will exist without the body in the intermediate state, what its experience will then be, and how soul and body will unite again, or the soul be freshly embodied, at the general resurrection if not in some way before, are matters completely opaque to us ("a hundred of these questions are better left.... Had all these been needful to us, they had been revealed"[20]). But revelation and reason unite to assure us of the certainty of that future fulfillment for which heaven is the God-given name.

Baxter spells this out in personal terms. The perfecting of his mind means that his omnivorous appetite for knowledge will be satiated at last. Understanding will be perfect. He will know everything, and know it thoroughly, by direct intuition, as God knows it. "I shall quickly, in heaven, be a perfect philosopher."[21] To arouse his eagerness, he reviews the celestial curriculum:

I. I shall know God better. II. I shall know the universe better. III. I shall know Christ better. IV. I shall know the church, his body, better, with the holy angels. V. I shall know better the methods and perfection of the Scripture.... VI. I shall know the methods and sense of disposing providence better. VII. I shall know the divine benefits, which are the fruits of love, better. VIII. I shall know myself better. IX. I shall better know every fellow-creature.... X. And I shall better know all that evil, sin, Satan, and misery, from which I am delivered.[22]

As one who aspired always to mental clarity on earth, Baxter rejoices to anticipate the full mental clarity of heaven.

Also, his will will be perfected. As external distractions from righteousness will be no more, so inner conflict will be over: "there will be nothing in me that is cross to itself; no more war or striving in me; not a law my mind, and a law in my members, that are contrary to each other ... all will be at unity and peace within."[23] Frustration will be a thing of the past: "I shall have all whatsoever I would have, and shall be and do whatsoever I would be and do."[24] Unimpeded and undistracted, the whole person will be joyfully devoted to the absorbing and joyous activity of loving the triune God. "Perfect, joyful complacency in God is the heaven which I desire and hope for";[25] "seeing and loving will be the heavenly life."[26] Baxter's capacity for action will be perfected too: "There are good works in heaven, and far more and better than on earth."[27] Perfect praise and perfect service, and both without end, are the realities in prospect. Much of this is necessarily wrapped in obscurity while we live on earth; the soul's "thoughts about its future state must be analogical and general, and partly strange."[28] Certainly, however, "in heaven we shall have not less, but ... more excellent sense and affections of love and joy, as well as more excellent intellection and volition; but such as we cannot now clearly conceive of."[29]

So far, Baxter has been forming his idea of heaven by extrapolating from the Christian's present relationship with God, other intelligent beings, and the world of things, and by eliminating from the scene pain, evil, and all frustration factors. The idea thus gained may now be amplified by introducing "analogical collections." In *The Saints' Everlasting Rest* Baxter gives the following rationale of this next move:

It is very considerable, how the Holy Ghost doth condescend in the phrase of Scripture, in bringing things down to the reach of sense; how he sets forth the excellences of spiritual things in words that are borrowed from the objects of sense ... doubtless if such expressions had not been best, and to us necessary, the Holy Ghost would not have so frequently used them; he that will speak to man's understanding, must speak in man's language, and speak that which he is capable to conceive....

But what is my scope in all this? ... that we make use of these phrases of the Spirit to quicken our apprehensions and affections ... and use these low notions as a glass, in which we must see the things themselves, though the representation be exceeding imperfect, till we come to an immediate perfect sight.[30]

The purpose of the biblical imagery is to make thoughts of heaven concrete, dramatic, and attractive, and the Christian's wisdom is to let his regenerate imagination feed on it accordingly, so that the significance of each pictorial item comes home to his heart.

So, in the first part of *The Saints' Everlasting Rest*, Baxter pictures Christ's return, the general resurrection, the final judgment, and the entry of God's people into the full glory of their promised inheritance; and he imagines the redeemed recalling their earthly pilgrimage.

To stand in heaven, and look back on earth ... how must it needs transport the soul and make it cry out.... Is this the end of believing? Is this the end of the Spirit's workings? Have the gales of grace blown

me into such a harbor? Is it hither that Christ hath enticed my soul?
. . . Is my mourning, my sad humblings, my heavenly walking,
groanings, complainings, come to this? . . . So will the memory of the
saints for ever promote their joys.[31]

He goes on to imagine the delights of fellowship with the universal
church, with Israelite saints and Christian saints, Fathers, Reformers,
and Puritans, in a passage so striking that it must be quoted at length.

It cannot choose but be comfortable to me to think of that day, when
I shall join with Moses in his song, with David in his psalms of praise,
and with all the redeemed in the song of the Lamb for ever; when we
shall see Enoch walking with God, Noah enjoying the end of his
singularity, Job of his patience, Hezekiah of his uprightness. . . . Will
it be nothing conducible to our comforts to live eternally with Peter,
Paul, Austin [Augustine], Chrysostom, Jerome, Wickliffe, Luther,
Zuinglius, Calvin, Beza, Bullinger, Zanchius, Paraeus, Piscator,
Camero[n]; with Hooper, Bradford, Latimer, Glover, Saunders, Philpot;
with Reighnolds [Rainolds], Whitaker, Cartwright, Brightman, Bayne,
Bradshaw, Bolton, Hall, Hildersham, Pemble, Twisse, Ames, Preston,
Sibbs?[32]

Baxter often refers to the communion of saints as a principal ingredient in heaven's joy. His bitter experience, as pastor and stateman, of the
pride and party spirit that sets Christians at each other's throats made
him long for the perfect peace and love of heaven. The triumph at the
Restoration of sectarianism over catholic principles in the restored
Church of England, from which two thousand Puritan pastors were
summarily ejected, was to him the greatest tragedy of his life, and as his
hopes for church peace in England grew fainter thereafter he dwelt more
and more on the truly catholic churchmanship that he would enjoy in
new Jerusalem. Though Puritanism has sometimes been represented as a
form of religious individualism, a cult of the isolated believer, and
though a highly developed individuality, such as we see in Baxter
himself, was certainly a mark of the movement, a passage like the just
quoted highlights that corporate and churchly frame within which this
individuality blossomed. The Puritan movement was in fact communal
and societal in its very essence, and we should not wonder that this
apotheosis of church fellowship should have bulked large in Baxter's
concept of heavenly glory.

The importance of clarity about what lies at the end of the Christian
pilgrimage seemed to Baxter incalculable. Human beings are rational
creatures, and rationality is a matter, among other things, of choosing
means to ends. The more strongly one desires an end, the more carefully

and diligently will one use the means to it. "The Love of the end is it that is the *poise* or spring, which setteth every Wheel a going."[33] But an unknown end will not be loved. "It is a known, and not merely an unknown God and happiness, that the soul doth joyfully desire."[34] Such desire will then give wings to the soul. "It is the heavenly Christian that is the lively Christian. It is strangeness to heaven that makes us so dull; it is the end that quickens to all the means; and the more frequently and clearly this end is beheld, the more vigorous will all our motion be. . . . We run so slowly, and strive so lazily, because we so little mind the prize."[35] So let Christians animate themselves daily to run the race set before them by practising heavenly meditation, "the delightfulest task to the spirit, and the most tedious to the flesh, that ever men on earth were employed in."[36]

This brings us to the third question: How are we to meditate on heaven? How, that is, are we to set about this task?

The Discipline of Heavenly Meditation

The first step, says Baxter, is to fix a time. In authentic Puritan fashion, he advocates an evangelical rule of life. "A Christian should have a set time for every ordinary duty, or else when he should practice it, it is ten to one but he will put it by. Stated time is a hedge to duty."[37] The time allotted must not be too short, for "as I cannot get me a heat without walking, no nor running neither . . . unless I *continue* some considerable time, no more can I in Prayer and Meditation."[38] Baxter's advice is to "set apart one hour or half hour every day."[39]

The task, as presented in part four of *The Saints' Everlasting Rest*, is a "set and solemn acting of all the powers of the soul upon this most perfect object, rest, by meditation."[40] This means that Christians are "to use your understandings for the warming of your affections, and to fire your hearts by the help of your heads"[41]—in other words, to turn their light into heat. "He is the best Christian who hath the readiest passage from the brain to the heart."[42] The procedure, modelled eclectically on the method set out by Joseph Hall in *The Arte of Divine Meditation* (1606), assumed, as we see, what Hall also affirmed, that the arousing of the affections is "the very soul of meditation whereto all that is past [i.e., all that precedes] serveth but as an instrument."[43] Meditation consists of consideration (discursive thought) followed by soliloquy (speaking to oneself in the presence of God). Baxter structures the exercise as follows.

Stage one, says Baxter, is to bring the truth about our promised rest before our minds as clearly and fully as possible and then to awaken ("act") the various affections—love, desire, hope, courage, and joy—in appropriate responses to this truth. When by this means our object of contemplation has become an object of love, desire, and delight, then is the time to enter upon the second stage, "pleading the case with our own souls.... Soliloquy is a preaching to oneself."[44] The aim of this is to move oneself to resolute Christian practice. Soliloquy thus corresponds to the "improvement" of "doctrine" by "uses" (applications) in a Puritan sermon. If heaven is so desirable, the Christian must say to himself, should I not be exerting myself much more to make sure of reaching it? The following passage shows what Baxter had in mind.

> In thy meditations upon all these incentives.... preach them over earnestly to thy heart, and expostulate and plead with it by way of soliloquy, till thou feel the fire begin to burn.... Dispute it out with thy conscience.... There is much more moving force in this earnest talking to ourselves, than in bare cognition, that breaks not out into mental words. Imitate the most powerful preacher that ever thou wast acquainted with.... There is more in this than most Christians are acquainted with, or use to practice. It is a great part of a Christian's skill and duty, to be a good preacher to himself.... Two or three sermons a week from others is a fair proportion; but two or three sermons a day from thyself, is ordinarily too little.[45]

Finally, believers should pass on "from this speaking to ourselves, to speak with God" in prayer; which is "the highest step that we can advance to in the work."[46] Earnest desire and hearty resolution, poured out in petition, will never lack God's blessing.

This habit of meditation, leading to prayer, will, says Baxter, be greatly promoted by hearing sermons about heaven ("happy the people that have a heavenly minister!"[47]), by talking to other believers about heaven, and by reading the books of creation and providence—another typical Puritan emphasis.

> Make an advantage of every object thou seest, and of every thing that befalls in thy labor and calling, to mind thy soul of its approaching rest. As all providence and creatures are means to our rest, so do they point us to that as their end. Every creature hath the name of God, and our final rest, written upon it.... O learn to open the creatures, and to open the several passages of providence, to read of God and glory there ... we might have a fuller taste of Christ and heaven in every bit of bread we eat, and in every draught of beer we drink, than most men have in the use of the sacrament.[48]

Such, then, in outline is heavenly meditation according to Richard Baxter: the mainstay, as he saw it, of Christian motivation, and the powerpoint of ongoing sanctification. Space forbids us to explore it further, but the essence of it is now clear, and anyone who wishes to follow up on Baxter's teaching can consult *The Saints' Everlasting Rest* directly. What has been reviewed, however, must leave us with some nagging questions. Could it be that here is a devotional secret we need to learn, and an inner discipline we need to recover? We have seen what Baxter believed that heavenly meditation did for him, and there can be no doubt as to his spiritual stature. Was he right to think it was heavenly meditation that made the difference? Would the practice benefit us as he claimed it benefited him? Does it bear at all on what is involved in being "alive to God" in these days? I leave my readers to face these questions as I close. What, I wonder, will Jim Houston have to say about them? I eagerly look forward, I confess, to finding out.

Notes

[1] N. H. Keeble, *Richard Baxter: Puritan Man of Letters* (Oxford: Clarendon, 1982) 104. Keeble illustrates from A. L. Rowse's *Milton the Puritan* (1977).

[2] See, for Baxter's role in Puritanism, Keeble, *Richard Baxter*; J. I. Packer, *A Man for All Ministries: Richard Baxter, 1615-1691* (London: St. Antholin's Lectureship, 1991); also in *Reformation and Revival* 1/1 (1992) 53-74; and *A Quest for Godliness: The Puritan Vision of the Christian Life* (Wheaton, Ill.: Crossway, 1990) 60-65, 302-308; Hugh Martin, *Puritanism and Richard Baxter* (London: SCM, 1954).

[3] See, for instance, William Haller, *The Rise of Puritanism* (New York: Columbia University Press, 1938); Perry Miller, *The New England Mind: I, The Seventeenth Century* (Cambridge, Mass.: Harvard University Press, 1939); M. M. Knappen, *Tudor Puritanism* (Chicago: Chicago University Press, 1939); and Martin, *Puritanism and Richard Baxter*.

[4] "Throughout his life he was subject to a bewildering variety of physical ailments, which he details in the *Reliquiae* and to which he refers in passing in many of his books. In one such passage, written in 1671, he recalled that 'since fourteen years of age I have not been a year without suffering, and since twenty two but few dayes, and since 1646 (which is about twenty five years), I have had but few dayes free from pain, (though through God's mercy not intolerable).' His memory seems not to have exaggerated his plight, for in a letter of 1650 he remarks that relief from pain comes 'perhaps once a moneth for a few hours unexpected'" (Keeble, *Richard Baxter*, 11; referring to *Reliquiae Baxterianae* [1696] 1.9-11, 80-83, 3.60ff., 173ff., 192, 198, and citing *A Second Admonition to Mr. Edward Bagshaw* [1671] 65).

[5] Richard Baxter, *Practical Works* (23 vol.; ed. W. Orme; 1830) —the edition I shall cite; first printed in four folios (1707), reprinted in four volumes in 1838 and currently available by mail order in four volumes from Ligonier: Soli Deo Gloria, 1990-1991. (Postal address: 213 West Vincent, Ligonier, PA 15658, USA).

[6] Baxter, *Poetical Fragments* (1681) 38, 40.

[7] Keeble, *Richard Baxter*, 6.

[8] *Reliquiae Baxterianae*, 1.108.

[9] "The Heavenly State cost him severe and daily thoughts, and Solemn Contemplations; for he set some time apart every day for that weighty work" (Matthew Sylvester, "Elisha's Cry After Elijah's God," memorial sermon for Baxter appended to *Reliquiae Baxterianae* [1696] 15).

[10] F. J. Powicke, *The Reverend Richard Baxter Under the Cross* (London: George Allen & Unwin, 1927) 97. Powicke mistakenly supposes it was written in 1683, but the 1676 date is proved by Baxter's statement on a letter to Sir Matthew Hale, dated May 5 of that year: "I am writing my own funeral sermon on Phil 1:23." He continues: "We never live like believers

indeed till the thoughts of heaven be sweeter to us than all our peace and hopes on earth, and till we truly believe that it is better to depart and be with Christ than to be here." The letter, first published in *John Rylands Library Bulletin* 24/1 (1940) 173ff., is printed almost in full in N. H. Keeble & Geoffrey F. Nuttall, *Calendar of the Correspondence of Richard Baxter* (Oxford: Clarendon, 1991) 2.186ff.

[11] William Bates, "A Sermon on the Death of Mr. Richard Baxter," *Works* (Harrisonburg: Sprinkle, 1990) 4.338ff.

[12] Sylvester, 14.

[13] See, in particular, *The Pilgrim's Regress* (London: Geoffrey Bles, 1933) and *Surprised by Joy* (London: Geoffrey Bles, 1955).

[14] N. H. Keeble, *"Loving and Free Converse": Richard Baxter in His Letters* (London: Dr. Williams's Trust, 1991) 3.

[15] Baxter, *Practical Works*, 12.222.

[16] Ibid., 18.426.

[17] Ibid., 12.122.

[18] Ibid., 7.576.

[19] Ibid., 18.369.

[20] Ibid., 18.259.

[21] Ibid., 18.359.

[22] Ibid., 18.356ff.

[23] Ibid., 18.368.

[24] Ibid., 18.369.

[25] Ibid., 18.371.

[26] Ibid., 18.389.

[27] Ibid.

[28] Ibid., 18.337.

[29] Ibid., 18.394.

[30] Ibid., 23.375ff.; see Keeble, *Richard Baxter*, 100-103.

[31] Ibid., 22.60f.

[32] Ibid., 22.122.

[33] *Reliquiae Baxterianae*, 1.129.

[34] Baxter, *Practical Works*, 18.295.

[35] Ibid., 23.237. When in 1670 Giles Firmin queried in print Baxter's insistence on sustained meditation, arguing that it made for imbalance and "melancholy" (depression), Baxter came back at him with the following rebuttal: "I find that whatever else I think of, of Christ, of Scripture, of Promises, of Threatenings, of sin, of Grace, &c. [*sic*] if I leave out *Heaven* and make it not the chief point of my Meditation, I leave out the sense of life of all. Thence must I fetch my Light, or I must be in Darkness; Thence must I fetch my Life, or I must be Dead, and my *Motives* or I must be Dull, or not sincere.... My hearing, Reading, and Studies grow to common things, if Heaven be not the principal part; My life groweth toward a common and a carnal life, when I begin to leave out Heaven: Death groweth terrible to my thoughts, and Eternity strange and dreadful to me, if I live not in such frequent and serious thoughts of the Heavenly Glory, as may render it familiar and grateful to my soul.... And I find myself unfit to Live or to Die, and that my soul is void of true Consolation ... when I grow a stranger to Heavenly Thoughts, and consequently to Heavenly Affections.... And that as nothing will serve turn instead of Heaven to be my happiness, so nothing will serve turn instead of Heaven to ... form my Heart and Life to Holiness. And therefore by experience I counsel all Christians that are able to perform it, especially ministers, and Learned men, to be much in the serious fore-thoughts of Heaven ..." (*The Duty of Heavenly Meditation Reviewed* [1671] 31ff.).

[36] Baxter, *Practical Works*, 23.175.

[37] Ibid., 23.318.

[38] Baxter, *Duty*, 19.

[39] Baxter, *Practical Works*, 23.406; "at least a quarter or 1/2 an hour, if not more, is best to

Edification.... I prove it from the Aptitude of the Means to its end" (*Duty*, 16ff.).

[40] Ibid., 23.310.

[41] Ibid., 23.338.

[42] Ibid., 23.340.

[43] Cited from John Booty's introduction to *John Donne* (Classics of Western Spirituality; New York: Paulist, 1990) 33.

[44] Baxter, *Practical Works*, 23.369.

[45] Ibid., 2.392.

[46] Ibid., 23.373.

[47] Ibid., 23.249.

[48] Ibid., 23.300.

15
On Spiritual Symmetry:
The Christian Devotion of
William Wilberforce

Murray A. Pura &
Donald M. Lewis

W ILLIAM WILBERFORCE (1759-1833) IS REMEMBERED AS A LEAD-
ing social reformer and as the most prominent evangelical of his day. He
did more than any other in his generation to secure the abolition of the
British slave trade (1807) and contributed much to the eventual elimination of the institution of slavery itself within the British empire (1833).
Although he was one of the leading political figures of his time, little
attention has been accorded him by academic historians. Sir Reginald
Coupland, sometime Professor of Colonial History at Oxford University, was the last professional scholar to write a biography of Wilberforce,
and his work appeared in 1923! Even at that, Coupland's biography is
directed at a popular audience, and Coupland, writing from the pontifical heights of his Oxford professorship, did not feel the need to footnote
his sources.

The purpose of this article is not to begin to address this deficiency.
Rather, its aim is to outline the contours of Wilberforce's religious
thought and his practice of Christian piety. In particular it seeks to
examine the key influences on him through a discussion of the writers
and personalities who influenced his growth in grace.[1] Such an examination is particularly needed in view of the fact that his two sons who
wrote his biography were High Anglicans and appear to have been

anxious to play down their father's evangelicalism.

Although throughout his adult life Wilberforce was a busy politician (entering Parliament at the age of twenty-one), following his conversion he read widely. While an undergraduate at Cambridge University he had learned Greek, which allowed him to study the New Testament in the original, and he systematically devoted large amounts of his time to reading both Scripture and devotional and doctrinal writers.

William Wilberforce's spirituality was one of balances struck. His entire life as a committed Christian, from his conversion in 1785 onwards, reflects this pattern of development. However prominent one aspect of his spirituality might be, there was always another side to it that kept him from taking it to extremes. The coin always had two different faces, yet these faces corresponded to each other and expressed a common theme.

An Anglican Puritan

Wilberforce was, overall, a Puritan in his theology and spirituality. Small wonder, since most of his favorite spiritual writers were seventeenth-century English Puritans or men profoundly influenced by them: Philip Doddridge (1702-1751), Richard Baxter (1615-1691), John Owen (1616-1683), John Flavel (d. 1691), John Howe (1630-1705), and Jonathan Edwards (1703-1758). He was also, to a large degree, a Calvinist, influenced in this regard by Owen, Howe, and Edwards, as well as by John Newton (1725-1807), John Witherspoon (1723-1794), Thomas Scott (1747-1821), and others. Puritanism stamped one side of his theological coin: it was soteriological;[2] it held to the authority of Scripture;[3] it held to the fallenness and depravity of humankind,[4] original sin,[5] Christ's substitutionary atonement,[6] justification by grace through faith in Christ alone,[7] regeneration,[8] providence and the sovereignty of God.[9]

Yet, on the other side of the coin, he held to unlimited atonement. Clearly he was not a thorough-going "five-point Calvinist." At the age of sixty-three he observed: "Every year that I live I become more impressed with the unscriptural character of the Calvinist system."[10] Despite all the Calvinist principles he adhered to, and all the Calvinistic Puritans who influenced him, he never personally considered himself to be a "systematic Calvinist." What seemed to offend him most was a cold and intellectual interpretation of God and his ways that appeared to leave no room for the mysteries of God and providence and the fallibility of human reason. After reading a piece by William Romaine (1714-1795), an Anglican evangelical minister in London with strong Calvinistic views, he observed: "Oh how unlike this is to the Scripture! He writes as if he had sat at the Council Board with the Almighty."[11] Wilberforce had imbibed the theological toleration which was developed among evangelicals by men such as Henry Venn (1724-1797), John Venn (1759-1813) and Charles Simeon (1759-1836)[12] following the Calvinist-Arminian controversy of the early 1770s. These Anglican evangelicals wanted to show the Anglican Church that their evangelicalism was based on Scripture, and confirmed by the Articles and Prayer Book of the Church of England, not by John Calvin's *Institutes*. But even though Wilberforce was not a strict Calvinist, the term "Puritan" is still appropriate for him if it is recalled that not all Puritans were necessarily strict Calvinists.[13]

Under this Puritan aegis, Wilberforce sought to be a faithful Anglican. The liturgy and the sacraments of Holy Communion and infant baptism were important to him. Yet, in balance to this, he believed there were other means of grace besides the discipline and sacraments of the Church of England—the Bible and preaching, to name two.[14] He was also adamant in declaring that a true Anglican faith had to be based on what he called "vital Christianity"[15]—i.e., evangelical doctrines. "This is the very Christianity on which our Establishment is founded; and that which her Articles, and Homilies, and Liturgy, teach throughout."[16]

Wilberforce was able to hold to Anglicanism on the one hand, and evangelicalism on the other, because he had fallen heir to a particular spiritual tradition. This was begun by those who, although influenced by the eighteenth-century evangelical revival, had chosen to remain within the Church of England. Anglican evangelicals tended to distance themselves from evangelical Dissenters—and indeed from the Methodism of John Wesley and George Whitefield, who were unhappy with the limitations of the parochial system of the Church of England.[17]

In this Wilberforce was particularly influenced by John Newton, the Anglican minister who had played a key role in his conversion and who had urged him to remain in politics. Newton himself had flirted with Dissent, but eventually resolved to devote himself to the discipline of the Church of England. Wilberforce himself wrote in 1789, four years after his conversion, that "the increase of dissenters, which always follows from the institution of unsteepled places of worship, is highly injurious to the interests of religion in the long run."[18] Yet Anglican evangelicals could not sever themselves completely from their Nonconformist brethren, for they themselves "firmly held that ultimate truth did not lie in one church order or another, but in the gospel itself."[19]

So Wilberforce played a major role in founding the British and Foreign Bible Society, one area of co-operation between the two evangelical groups.[20] He also had many Dissenting friends and benefited greatly from their conversation and writings. He remarked to William Jay, the Congregationalist pastor at Bath:

> Though I am an Episcopalian by education and conviction, I yet feel such a oneness and sympathy with the cause of God at large, that nothing would be more delightful than my communing, once every year, with every church that holds the Head, even Christ.[21]

In fact, though a staunch Anglican, Wilberforce took the sacrament of Eucharist at least twice in non-Anglican churches.[22] Although he found the Roman Catholicism of his day repugnant,[23] he favored the elimination of civil disabilities on Roman Catholics and even wrote about a Catholic whom he had met at Bath, stating that he had been "endeavouring to press on him the most important doctrines of true Christianity and of showing where the case is really so that he may embrace those doctrines and still continue a good Catholic."[24]   When his influential book *A Practical View* was published in 1797, it represented a watershed of his spiritual thought. It raised his stature in the Dissenting churches, strengthening a relationship which many Anglicans found hard to swallow: "They think I cannot be loyal to the Established Church because I love Dissenters."[25] In all this remarkable spiritual toleration and balance, Wilberforce was a Christian ecumenist ahead of his time.

Probably the greatest single influence in Wilberforce's spirituality and theology of balance and toleration was the English Congregationalist minister Philip Doddridge, who died in 1751, eight years before Wilberforce's birth. This influence was exerted through Doddridge's writings, principally his book *The Rise and Progress of Religion in the Soul,* which was published in 1745. The work was instrumental in Wilberforce's conversion, and its teachings became an integral part of his spirituality. When Wilberforce partook of Doddridge and his teachings he was imbibing Puritanism. "It is," states A. T. S. James, "the early Puritan mysticism, no doubt modified and reduced, but the same in its faith and its spiritual perceptiveness."[26] The volume encouraged Wilberforce in the most crucial elements of his spirituality: daily self-examination,[27] prayer,[28] the Eucharist,[29] continual communion with God,[30] morning devotions, the careful observation of providence, the importance of solitude,[31] evening devotions,[32] an expectancy of heaven,[33] benevolence to humankind and usefulness.[34] It also coaxed Wilberforce toward a position of religious toleration. "He was," says Geoffrey Nuttall of Doddridge, "desirous in principle not to exclude any whose theology might be mistaken but whose devotion to Jesus Christ, for all that, was unmistakeable."[35] Wilberforce, as in so many areas, followed Doddridge's example here.

Richard Baxter (1615-1691), the great Puritan writer and pastor, also profoundly moulded Wilberforce's spirituality and helped him achieve a refreshing balance. Baxter's particular brand of theology became known as Baxterianism, but his practical spirituality, like Wilberforce's, had no place for controversial or speculative theology. It was a spirituality which emphasized only the most crucial aspects of Christianity, the few fundamentals on which the variety of Christian denominations might be able to reach a consensus. The "mere Christian" was a person who would hold to the Decalogue, the Apostles' Creed, and the Lord's Prayer "by a faith that worketh by love."[36] "Provided there be this faith," Baxter said, "it matters not what opinions a man holds on any theological or ecclesiastical question, nor whether he be in error in these incidentals."[37] Horton Davies has called Baxter "the first exponent of Ecumenism in England."[38] Of him, Wilberforce wrote: "I must…express my unfeigned and high respect for this great man . . . his practical writings, in four great massy [sic] volumes, are a treasury of Christian wisdom."[39] These four folio volumes were constantly at Wilberforce's side, as much in 1814[40] as in his years of retirement.[41]

One of the strongest influences on the development of Wilberforce's spiritual balance was mentioned above: John Newton. He was the first evangelical Anglican preacher Wilberforce heard as an adult, and he was the man whose words of counsel were constantly able to comfort him during the difficult months following his conversion in his mid-twenties. Newton was a Calvinist, but as Ford K. Brown puts it, "the possibly unique Calvinist to whom it made no difference whether a man called himself a Calvinist or not provided he was manifestly making his way to the Cross."[42] He urged Wilberforce along the path of religious toleration and evangelical ecumenism. "I am sick of the spirit of party of all parties," Newton once wrote. "I wish to be able to throw some water upon the fires of contention."[43]

There was also the influence of John Venn, Rector of Clapham, and of the lay leaders in the "Clapham Sect." Venn went to Clapham in 1793 and became "the spiritual guide of the Clapham brotherhood,"[44] a group which met for mutual support in the Christian life as it related to public service. Most were Anglican evangelicals, but at least one was a Dissenter.[45] The members shared a common commitment to a "practical Christianity" which worked itself out in the areas of philanthropy, education, and moral and social reform. The group remained an important influence on Wilberforce from 1792 through to its breakup in 1815. Its spirit was one of tolerance, and Venn himself, whom Wilberforce greatly admired, served as the group's mentor, in matters including religious toleration.[46]   In Wilberforce's view Venn was "heavenly-minded, bent on his Master's work, affectionate to all around him, and above all to Christ's people."[47]

The people who contributed to Wilberforce's spiritual balance—whether through their writings, sermons or personal friendships—reflect the spiritual symmetry which was a hallmark of his Christian faith. He could benefit from the Congregationalist Philip Doddridge, as well as from the Anglican John Venn, from the Jansenist Blaise Pascal, whose *Pensées* he found "highly valuable,"[48] from the Calvinist John Newton, or the Catholic mystics Cardinal Fénelon and Madame Guyon.[49] How could Wilberforce, no mystic himself, benefit from such widely divergent teachers in his spiritual growth and development? Wilberforce had a simplicity of faith: wherever he could find God and Christ, wherever he could find help in seeing and serving God and Christ, there Wilberforce went. His spiritual tastes ran along the same lines as his spiritual service, namely that which honored God and that which was eminently practical, not speculative. Early influences like Doddridge, Newton, and Baxter had taught him to despise no believer. As a result, he read so broadly that inevitably each teacher was balanced by another. Although a committed evangelical, he was not a dogmatist, and even as a politician he retained his independence, sometimes siding with the Tories, sometimes voting along independent lines. He was a staunch Anglican, but he admitted to other means of grace and took the Eucharist in non-Anglican churches. He was an Anglican evangelical, but he worked alongside, loved, and learned from Dissenters. He was a Puritan, but he delved into the French Catholic mystics. He was adamant about not being a "Calvinist," yet he held to the general Calvinist outline of belief, and was influenced more by Calvinists than by any other single group of Christians. Such was his breadth. Such was one of the most potent and vital aspects of the legacy he bequeathed to the evangelical movement:

> God knows . . . that it has been . . . and shall be more and more my endeavour to promote the cordial and vigorous and systematical exertions of all the friends of the essentials of Christianity, softening prejudices, healing divisions and striving to substitute a rational and an honest zeal for fundamentals, in place of a hot party spirit.[50]

In Private and in Public

Nor was his merely a balance that manifested itself theologically, in terms of a broad understanding of God's Spirit working variously in and through all sorts and groups of Christians and their teachers. Spiritual symmetry exhibited itself in all his daily routines. The balance was there when he rose for his daily devotions in the morning, and it ran through his entire day, manifesting itself in his final devotions before retiring.

When he was confessing and mortifying his personal sins, he could be very hard on himself. It is easy to make the same mistake in reading Wilberforce's journals and diaries that others have made in reading the private papers of the Puritans, and that is to construe the dark self-scrutiny found there in an exclusive sense as somehow indicative of the whole of the man. But the keeping of a personal journal, a habit the Methodists and Anglican evangelicals inherited from the Puritans of the sixteenth and seventeenth centuries, was meant to give them a place to talk especially about their sins in order to learn to see them better and in so doing be able to overcome them. Michael Hennell states that this written self-examination was "the evangelical equivalent to the confessional."[51] There was another side to Wilberforce which was not hinted at in his confessions. "None of the playfulness of his letter writing obtruded into the diary," observes John Pollock, "nor the exuberance and joyousness which delighted his friends."[52]

Of course; it was not meant to. That was not the diary's or the journal's purpose. Few who read his diary would think that this is the man of whom Madame de Staël, a leading French socialite, commented: "Mr. Wilberforce is the best converser I have met with in this country. I have always heard that he was the most religious, but I now find that he is the wittiest man in England."[53] It is clear that away from the spiritual discipline of the journal Wilberforce was a man of optimistic temperament, an individual whose company was relished by all sorts of people because of his charm, intelligence, and good humor. "Interior severity," comments Pollock, "helped create the joy which he considered a mark of genuine Christianity."[54] Joy was crucial to Wilberforce's spirituality. "Religion," he complained in a letter to a friend, "is made to wear a forbidding and gloomy air and not one of peace and hope and joy."[55] He sought, in his words, "to preserve a constant and sober mind with a gay exterior."[56] His joy balanced the darkness of the journal-confessional, but this exuberance was in its turn placed in perspective. His bright and outgoing personality and spirituality were always tempered with an understanding that life was serious business, a spiritual warfare, as the Puritans had taught him. "Let neither his joys intoxicate," Wilberforce wrote of the Christian, "nor his sorrows too much depress him."[57]

Prayer and meditation were critical to Wilberforce. He tried to achieve an attitude of constant prayer "without interruption to his labours," interposing "occasional thoughts of things unseen."[58] He hated it when prayer was neglected: "There is nothing which makes God more certainly withdraw his grace."[59] Yet, crucial as prayer was, it had to be balanced with deeds that glorified God. A Christian's life must be useful in terms of benefiting humankind spiritually. "Let him still remember," he said of the Christian, "that his chief business, while on earth, is not to meditate, but to act."[60] Wilberforce did act, with great intensity, and involved himself in a broad range of causes in Christ's name. Prayer energized him. Sir Reginald Coupland comments that it was his faith that was "the secret of Wilberforce's indomitable perseverance," bracing him "for the business of the active world outside."[61] But frequently he could not take time for prayer and Scripture reading because he was overworked.[62] He often sought a counterbalance by taking days of solitude in the country: "Through nature I look up to nature's God."[63] He deemed these excursions critical to his spiritual and emotional health. "I wish," he said, "I could sentence some of my friends to a little solitary imprisonment. They might then see things in their true dimensions."[64]

Besides these trips into isolated regions of England, Sundays were preserved as days of holiness, spiritual refreshment and rest from the week's labors. His sabbath observance sustained him when his daily devotions had faltered. When retired he observed: "Often on my visits to Holwood [the country residence of his close friend William Pitt, the Prime Minister], when I heard one or another speak of this man's place or that man's peerage [elevation to the House of Lords], I felt a rising inclination to pursue the same objects, but a Sunday in solitude never failed to restore me to myself."[65]

Like his spiritual forebears, the Puritans, Wilberforce considered that the keeping of the Lord's Day was the factor "on which the very existence of religion depended in England."[66] So he helped found the Society for the Better Observance of Sunday in 1800. He and Lord Belgrave promoted an unsuccessful bill to suppress Sunday newspapers. Nevertheless, Wilberforce balanced this ideal of a Lord's Day with a moderate Sunday observance rather than a rigid one. In 1821 he wrote in a letter:

> Often good people have been led by the terms of the Fourth Commandment to lay more stress on the strictness of the Sunday than on its spirituality.[67]

As the Puritans did, Wilberforce also looked to see God's providence working itself out on a national scale, within a framework of divine blessings and curses. He believed strongly in the concept of a "Christian nation." If a people responded in obedience to God's demands upon them, they would be blessed. If they persisted as a people in resisting God's purposes for them, they would be judged, in history, by God. Thus Napoleon and his army became, in his mind, God's tool of judgment on the sins of England and other European countries.[68] But when Britain ended its involvement in the slave trade in 1807, Wilberforce was sure that God would smile on her. "God will bless this country," he said immediately following the passage of the bill. "The first authentic account of the defeat of the French has come today."[69] Wilberforce was a patriot and he wanted to see his nation prosper. But he did not see every military victory as a sign of God's approval. Britain did not have a divine right to wage wars or to seize territory. Since God's claims came before the claims of any country, it was conceivable that the two sets of claims might as easily be mutually exclusive as providentially bound together:

> If by patriotism is meant that mischievous and domineering quality which renders men ardent to promote ... the aggrandizement of their own country, by the oppression and conquest of every other—to such patriotism ... that religion must indeed be an enemy whose foundation is justice, and whose compendious character is "peace" and good-will towards men.[70]

It was only natural that Wilberforce, as an Anglican Evangelical, should see the spiritual and the eternal as more important than the material and the temporal. This world was not the only existence, nor was it the existence which would endure. His first duty was to make sure that not only he himself but all those he could influence were fit for heaven. "O remember, that the salvation of one soul is of more worth than the mere temporal happiness of thousands or even millions."[71] So he supported both home and world missions. He helped to found the Church Missionary Society and the British and Foreign Bible Society so that the gospel message and the Scriptures could be taken throughout the world. He wrote *A Practical View,* which became the most widely read religious work of his day, a best-seller which promoted evangelical Christianity and took it into the homes of England's middle and upper classes.

Souls and Bodies

No discussion of Wilberforce's spirituality would be complete, however, without mentioning his concern with his own personal evangelistic responsibilities. After all, he was "the evangelical of the evangelicals." Wilberforce knew well that many of his peers had effectively been inoculated against any living personal faith by their exposure to the formalities of the Church of England in British boarding schools. He felt that it was his personal duty to attempt to persuade his friends and acquaintances of their need for a personal conversion, a commitment to trust in Christ's atonement and to live their lives under his lordship. He apparently kept a list of friends whom he had been speaking with in order that he might keep track of his efforts. The following are some excerpts from the list:

S...and Mrs. What books reading? To give them good ones—Walker's Sermons. Call on Mrs. S. and talk a little. Lend her Venn's last Sermon. Education of their children, to inquire about. Prayer, etc. Their coming some Sunday to Battersea Rise to hear Venn. Call often, and be kind.

Lady A ... and Sir R. Has he read Doddridge? Be open to her, etc.

Lady E ... Speak pretty openly, yet tenderly.[72]

He would often spend an hour following dinner thinking out how he might develop "launchers"—openings in conversation with friends so as to launch into a talk of religion. Cynical eighteenth-century aristocrats took it from Wilberforce. As Coupland comments: "if they smiled at 'the saint' they never derided him, nor ever voted him a bore. When the little man came in late to a dinner-party, bristling, maybe, with 'launchers,' every face, says a contemporary, 'lighted up with pleasure at his entry.'"[73] Wilberforce himself told a story against himself in this regard. Once, after talking for some time to an ill friend, "Lord N...," Wilberforce was aware that he had not broached the issue of religion. Another friend came in and asked the invalid how he was. Lord N ... replied: "As well as I can be, with Wilberforce sitting here and telling me I am going to hell."[74]

Wilberforce, however, could set aside his evangelistic concerns and the copious volumes of spiritual reading to enjoy Shakespeare, the adventure novels of Sir Walter Scott, James Boswell's *Life of Johnson,* and the Greek and Latin classics. He liked domestic dancing. He was a good friend of the poet William Wordsworth. He loved his excursions to the Lake District. But these material enjoyments could never become ends in themselves. For the Puritans, innocent pleasures were "necessary in moderation to refresh the body."[75] Thus, Wilberforce, heir of the Puritans, and of evangelicalism as well, tended to depreciate the pleasure found in material objects because such pleasure had to be subordinated to higher spiritual goals. "Now and then," he said to one of his children while in the Lake District, "when we need rest from severe labours, it may be permitted us to luxuriate in such lonely spots, but it is to fit us for a return to duty."[76] Relaxation was balanced with duties to be performed, and these duties were in their turn balanced with spiritual and material refreshment.

But many have criticized Wilberforce precisely on this point, claiming that he had no real intrinsic concern for the African slaves or for England's poor except in terms of spiritual conversion. Some have gone as far as to accuse Wilberforce of having no concern at all for the victims of England's Industrial Revolution. As for England's poor, the facts speak for themselves. He supported Elizabeth Fry and Samuel Romilly in their efforts for penal reform and contributed to efforts to humanize the English criminal code. Medical aid for the poor was important to him. Twice he supported Sir Robert Peel's factory acts, in 1802 and 1812. The Society for Bettering the Condition of the Poor was founded in Wilberforce's home. It "called for definite legislation to limit the hours worked by children in the cotton mills, to regulate the age and conditions of apprenticeship and to provide for regular inspection."[77] He founded the Climbing Boys Society to help the children employed as chimney sweeps. He championed popular education, especially education of the poor and deaf, at a time when even political radicals scorned the concept. He kept several schools for the poor operating at his own expense. He and Arthur Young, the eminent English agriculturalist, worked on several methods by which to come up with better and cheaper food for Britain's poor. This did not result in all of those Wilberforce helped becoming Christians. But he did it because it mattered to him. Temporal suffering was not ignored due to spiritual expediency. In the case of the African slaves, Wilberforce spoke of "the habitual immorality and degradation and often grinding sufferings of the poor victims of this wicked system."[78] Their misery upset him so much that in April of 1793, soon after Louis XVI's execution in France under the blade of a guillotine, with fears of a bloody revolution in England racing through London's streets, Wilberforce wrote to a friend: "If I thought the immediate Abolition of the Slave Trade would cause an insurrection in our islands, I should not for an instant remit my most strenuous endeavours."[79] Wilberforce and the evangelicals fought the slave trade because, as Ian Bradley asserts, "they were profoundly moved by human want and suffering."[80] This was the other side of the coin. Wilberforce cared enormously for the human soul, yes. But he also cared enormously for human beings themselves.

Struggles Within Symmetry
Wilberforce was not perfect in achieving an optimal balance for his spirituality. Even with his recognition of his need for solitude and rest, he often overexerted himself. His frequent fasting throughout his life

hurt his health.[81] At times his habit of rising early for personal devotions wore him down physically.[82] He cried during his meditations, straining and damaging his weak and delicate eyes.[83] He could pierce himself with guilt, believing once that God had struck his wife with a terrible illness in order to punish Wilberforce for a feeling of exultation in which he had indulged.[84]

On top of this, he struggled all his life with poor health. He almost lost his life in 1788 to what was probably ulcerative colitis. In order to treat this, for the rest of his life he daily took a small dose of the aspirin of the day: opium. Its long-term side effects were depression and indolence, both of which he fought against mightily. His body itself was frail: for his last fifteen to eighteen years he had to wear a metal frame to support his arms and upper torso. During his lifetime, he grieved for the loss of his sister and his two daughters and many friends. During the long-drawn-out conflict over abolition, on several occasions he agonized over the apparent absence of God.[85]

Yet he persevered, and so did the symmetry of his spirituality. Indeed, it was the beauty, the balance, and the strength of his evangelical faith as he worked it out in terms of his own personality and frailty that enabled him to be the man he was and to accomplish the deeds God placed in his hand. This spirituality was the backbone of his life and vocation, the point and counterpoint of his Christianity.

Notes

[1] Much of the research for this paper is based on Murray Andrew Pura, "Vital Christianity: A Study of the Religious Thought of William Wilberforce" (M.Th. thesis, Regent College, 1987).

[2] Doreen Rosman, *Evangelicals and Culture* (London: Croom Helm, 1984) 10-12.

[3] William Wilberforce, *A Practical View of the Prevailing Religious System of Professed Christians, in the Higher and Middle Classes in this Country, Contrasted with Real Christianity* (Edinburgh: Johnstone & Hunter, n.d.) iv.

[4] Ibid., 22, 23, 32.

[5] Ibid., 31, 32, 339.

[6] Ibid., 50-51.

[7] Ibid., 256-257.

[8] Ibid., 50.

[9] Wilberforce, quoted in Robert Isaac Wilberforce & Samuel Wilberforce, *The Life of William Wilberforce* (5 vol.; London: John Murray, 1838) 4.242. Regrettably, this biography written by two of Wilberforce's sons tends to play down his evangelicalism.

[10] Wilberforce, quoted in Wilberforce & Wilberforce, *Life*, 5.162; Wilberforce, *A Practical View*, 47; Wilberforce, British Museum Add MSS 38191.280, Liverpool Papers, letter to Lord Liverpool, 30 Sept. 1821, cited by John Pollock, *Wilberforce* (London: Constable, 1977) 153.

[11] Wilberforce, Diary, 17 Sept., 1830, cited by Robin Furneaux, *William Wilberforce* (London: Hamish Hamilton, 1974) 278.

[12] W. J. Clyde Ervine, "Doctrine and Diplomacy: Some Aspects of the Life and Thought of the Anglican Evangelical Clergy, 1797-1837" (Ph.D. thesis, University of Cambridge, 1979) 32-35.

[13] *The Westminster Dictionary of Christian Spirituality,* 1983 ed., s.v. "Puritan Spirituality," by N. H. Keeble.

[14] Rosman, *Evangelicals and Cultures,* 13.

[15] Wilberforce, *A Practical View,* 315.

[16] Ibid., 317.

[17] G. R. Balleine, *A History of the Evangelical Party in the Church of England* (London: Longmans, Green, 1911) 37. Many of the early Anglican evangelical clergy were indebted for their conversions not to contacts with Methodists but to their own reading. The distance between the Established Church and Dissent was widened in the early 1790s when some Dissenters expressed sympathy with the early path of the French Revolution. See: D. M. Lewis, *Lighten Their Darkness* (Westport, Conn.: Greenwood, 1986) 11-17.

[18] Wilberforce, quoted in Wilberforce & Wilberforce, *Life,* 1.248.

[19] Ervine, 29.

[20] Ibid., 30.

[21] Wilberforce, quoted in William Jay, *The Autobiography of William Jay* (ed. George Redford & John Angell James, 1854; repr., Edinburgh: The Banner of Truth Trust, 1974) 298-299.

[22] Ibid., 298.

[23] Ibid., 305.

[24] Wilberforce, Private Papers, 275-276, cited by Furneaux, *William Wilberforce,* 321.

[25] Wilberforce, Hull MSS, Diary, n.d., cited by Pollock, 153.

[26] A. T. S. James, "Doddridge: His Influence," *Philip Doddridge* (ed. Geoffrey F. Nuttall; London: Independent Press, 1951) 37.

[27] Philip Doddridge, *The Rise and Progress of Religion in the Soul* (1745; repr., Glasgow: Chalmers & Collins, 1825) 280, 316.

[28] Ibid., 284.

[29] Ibid., 308.

[30] Ibid., 316.

[31] Ibid.

[32] Ibid., 326.

[33] Ibid., 328.

[34] Ibid., 417.

[35] Geoffrey Nuttall, *Richard Baxter and Philip Doddridge* (London: Oxford University Press, 1951) 15.

[36] Richard Baxter, *Naked Popery* (London, 1677) 7; *The True Catholick and Catholick Church Described* (London, 1660) 10, 16-7, 19; *Universal Concord* (London, 1660) 33; cited by N. H. Keeble, *Richard Baxter* (Oxford: Clarendon, 1982) 24.

[37] Baxter, cited by Keeble, *Baxter,* 24.

[38] Horton Davies, *The English Free Churches* (London: Home University Library, n.d.) 79.

[39] Wilberforce, *A Practical View,* 295.

[40] Wilberforce & Wilberforce, *Life,* 4.163.

[41] Ibid., 5.249.

[42] Ford K. Brown, *Father of the Victorians* (Cambridge, U.K.: Cambridge University Press, 1951) 172.

[43] John Newton, Olney MSS, cited by John Pollock, *Amazing Grace* (San Francisco: Harper & Row, 1981) 161.

[44] Ernest M. Howse, *Saints in Politics* (Toronto: University of Toronto Press, 1952) 16.

[45] Elie Halevy, *A History of the English People in 1815* (New York: Harcourt, Brace, 1924) 381.

[46] See Donald Bloesch, *Essentials of Evangelical Theology* (2 vol.; San Francisco: Harper & Row, 1978-1979) 2.265.

[47] Wilberforce, quoted in Wilberforce & Wilberforce, *Life,* 2.32.

[48] Wilberforce, *A Practical View,* 264, 375.

[49] *WDCS,* 1983 ed., s.v. "Jeanne-Marie Bouvier de la Motte Guyon" by Michael Richards.

[50] Wilberforce, Sidmouth MSS, letter to Henry Addington, 9 Nov. 1799, cited by Pollock,

Wilberforce, 153.

[51] *WDCS*, 1983 ed., s.v. "Evangelical Spirituality" by Michael Hennell.

[52] Pollock, *Wilberforce*, 45.

[53] Quoted in Coupland, *Wilberforce*, 286.

[54] Ibid., 66.

[55] Wilberforce, Lincolnshire Papers, letter to Lord Carrington, 17 Aug. 1829, cited by Pollock, *Wilberforce*, 46.

[56] Wilberforce, quoted in Wilberforce & Wilberforce, *Life*, 1.317.

[57] Wilberforce, *A Practical View*, 267.

[58] Ibid., 268.

[59] Wilberforce, quoted in Wilberforce & Wilberforce, *Life*, 1.317.

[60] Wilberforce, *A Practical View*, 267.

[61] Reginald Coupland, *Wilberforce* (London: Collins, 1923) 190.

[62] Wilberforce & Wilberforce, *Life*, 1.207.

[63] Ibid., 3.157.

[64] Ibid., 1.337-338.

[65] Quoted in Coupland, *Wilberforce*, 187.

[66] Ibid., 3.266.

[67] Ibid., 2.451-452.

[68] Ibid., 3.357, 4.246.

[69] Ibid., 3.303.

[70] Wilberforce, *A Practical View*, 307.

[71] Wilberforce, quoted in Wilberforce & Wilberforce, *Life*, 4.206.

[72] Quoted in Coupland, *Wilberforce*, 191.

[73] Ibid., 192.

[74] Ibid.

[75] M. M. Knappen, ed., *Two Elizabethan Puritan Diaries* (Chicago: Society of Church History, 1933) 6.

[76] Wilberforce, quoted in Wilberforce & Wilberforce, *Life*, 4.389-90.

[77] Garth Lean, *God's Politician* (London: Darton, Longman & Todd, 1980) 144.

[78] Wilberforce, Roberts MSS, letter to S. Roberts, 31 October 1827, cited by Pollock, *Wilberforce*, 288.

[79] See Pollock, *Wilberforce*, 123.

[80] Ian Bradley, *The Call to Seriousness* (New York: Macmillan, 1976) 119.

[81] Wilberforce & Wilberforce, *Life*, 2.351.

[82] Ibid., 2.23.

[83] Ibid., 4.364.

[84] Ibid., 2.294.

[85] Ibid., 5.171.

16
Aspects of Christian Brethren Spirituality

Ian S. Rennie

THE FOUNDERS OF THE CHRISTIAN BRETHREN WERE PART OF A protest movement that emerged within evangelical Anglicanism in the 1820s and 1830s.[1] They were not only displeased with general aspects of what was then known as the United Church of England and Ireland, but they were also unhappy about certain tendencies within its evangelical section to which they adhered.[2]

The New Evangelicals
The leaders of the new Evangelicals,[3] as we may call them, represented an area of relatively new societal penetration for evangelical Anglicanism. They were converts from the upper class: from the aristocracy, the landed gentry and military officers, the most conservative sectors of society. They were used to exercising power, and it could be expected that their influence would be felt in any movement or institution with which they aligned themselves. While those who would become the founders of the Brethren represented only a small fraction of the new Evangelicals, almost all of them well represented its social ethos.

These young, well-bred, well-educated and well-traveled new Evangelicals were inevitably exposed to current movements of deep-level cultural change, but without in any way changing their conservative social orientation. In fact, they would use the new culture to buttress their traditional commitments. Under the influence of Romanticism, the new Evangelicals recoiled from the culture of the Enlightenment, often referred to as the Augustan Age, with its scientific models, its individualism, its activism and its optimism. They were particularly distressed by its popular expression in bourgeois entrepreneurialism, to which so much of evangelical Anglicanism, let alone Nonconformist evangelicalism, seemed wedded.[4] The new Evangelicalism, under the impact of Romanticism, had a deep sense of history, which caused it often to look for guidance on the questions of the present and future to the answers of the past. Its adherents longed for the organic and the corporate, amid what to them was the wilderness created by Enlightenment thought and action. They anticipated radical divine inbreaking, in the human spirit, in the church, in the nation and in the world. They showed an intensity of spirit which almost inevitably produced polarity. Not all evangelical Anglicans by any means would share this outlook, but where it was embraced it made a very decided difference.

The new Evangelicals were filled with fear.[5] They dreaded the social consequences of liberal thought. Tampering with what they conceived to be the God-given order of society, it would undermine the foundations of Britain's Constitution, the ideal of Protestant Christendom, and their own privileged position. They were also afraid of its theological and spiritual outcome. It was natural for them, as members of their social class, to tour Europe, particularly after the cessation of hostilities in 1815. What they saw of liberal continental Protestantism, with its rationalistic biblical criticism and theological ambiguity, frequently appalled them.[6] They became aware that such views would soon enter the United Kingdom, if they had not already begun to do so. While older evangelicals, in their uninformed optimism, fostered by the exuberantly business-like reports of such voluntary mission agencies as the British and Foreign Bible Society, looked for the imminent triumph of the gospel everywhere, including the world of educated European Protestantism, the new Evangelicals were not so sanguine. Above all, they were terrified by events in Ireland, where a large number of the new Evangelicals, including many of the future Brethren, had the closest of links with the Protestant, Anglo-Irish, land-owning aristocracy. A rejuvenated Roman Catholic peasantry was rousing itself against ancient injustices,[7] aided and abetted by political liberalism. To the new Evangelicals this scenario could only be comprehended in apocalyptic terms.

The new Evangelicals were also fearful of certain developments within evangelical Anglicanism. In order to expedite the evangelical take-over of the Church of England, which the older evangelical Anglican leadership fully anticipated and worked toward, a judicious policy was developed. Everything possible was removed which could give offense to the "powers that be" in church and state. Gentility was emphasized, good relations with the rich and fashionable which might be useful were encouraged,[8] Puritanism with its threat of revolution was no longer seen as an important part of the evangelical heritage, systematic Calvinism was allowed to lapse, and hyper-Calvinism, with its supposed threat of antinomianism, was attacked.[9] The problem was two-fold. The new Evangelicals, who were already part of the rich and fashionable world, in some ways despised it after their conversions, and naturally did not esteem evangelical truckling to it. But they were also committed Calvinists, with some of them verging on hyper-Calvinism. The reason seems to be that they were not converted in areas of evangelical Anglican power, namely London, the Home Counties, Cambridge and Yorkshire. They came to faith in Christ in areas such as the West Country of England, where evangelicalism was not so strong, the new policies were not so inculcated, and older forms of evangelical Calvinism remained;[10] and in southern Ireland, where evangelicalism did not penetrate Anglicanism to any great extent until the second decade of the nineteenth century, and then with an intensity which found Calvinism congenial.[11] It was prized not simply because it was viewed as a true exegesis of the Bible, and because it explained their "darkness to light" conversions, but because it "offered a stern, rich spiritual culture . . . more passionate in tone than the elder evangelicalism,"[12] and one which well suited their Romantic taste.

Finally, the new Evangelicals were afraid that the evangelical leaders were buying into liberalism. In order to facilitate the spread of the Bible on the Continent, both Roman Catholics and rationalistic Protestants were regarded as colleagues, and when the implications of this were pressed, the new Evangelicals were greeted with an obfuscation hardly designed to encourage confidence among the critical.[13] Then, outstanding evangelical leaders such as the Clapham Sect, the Rev. Daniel Wilson of Islington, and Bishop C. R. Sumner of Winchester, also supported full civil liberties for Nonconformists in 1828 and Roman Catholics in 1829.[14] For those who highly valued classical Christendom, with its faithful Protestant national church within a godly state, this dismantling of Christendom in favor of a more secular concept of the state was felt as fraught with terrible danger for the unity of the church and the survival of the nation. For the new Evangelicals, attuned to the Puritan understanding of providence, the riots and cholera epidemic which accompanied the decade of the 1830s were signs of God's displeasure. In such a setting it was natural that they should seek to develop a new form of evangelical Anglicanism, which would lead some, such as the Brethren,[15] out of the Church of England altogether. And as the new Evangelicals discerningly saw evidence that the great Second Evangelical Awakening (ca. 1785-1825) was coming to an end, they were convinced that some fresh, radical approaches were necessary.

In this setting the new Evangelicals turned to various sources for help. While they were undoubtedly looking to God for assistance and direction, they believed that God directed them to individuals and groups where they heard the voice of God interpreting the Bible. In this process they acquired certain distinctive emphases, almost all of which had a lengthy historical pedigree and provided answers for their fears.

The purpose of this paper is to examine some of those ideas which all new Evangelicals held in common, some of those shared only by the seceders from the Church of England, and some of those enunciated only by the Brethren. Then the Brethren spirituality which grew out of this seed-bed will be examined.

This study deals with Brethrenism as it existed from its inception until World War II. During this period of over a century, in spite of numerous divisions among the Exclusive Brethren and tensions among the Open Brethren sufficiently strong to be regarded as quasi-divisions, there was a large measure of ideological and spiritual continuity within the movement. This should not be considered strange, since both sections were part of the same intimate fellowship for almost two decades prior to 1848, and their unique distinctives were hammered out in that early period. There is, however, a difference in ecclesiology, which has a bearing on spirituality, and this must be noted.

The Bible
The first aspect of new Evangelical thought to be considered dealt with the inspiration of the Bible. This was received from the Scotsman Robert Haldane, who, although a generation older than most of the new Evangelicals, had certain particular affinities with them. A lay evangelist, together with his brother James Alexander, he was a scion of an ancient landed Scottish family. A man of monumental energy and enthusiasms, he resigned his naval commission after his conversion, and planned to sell his estate and go to India as a missionary. When that was not possible, he gave himself to an indefatigable evangelistic ministry in Scotland, and then further afield.[16] As a peripatetic layman, often the first herald of the Evangelical Awakenings in many a Scottish parish, and without any ecclesiastical permission, he soon found himself outside the Church of Scotland, although greatly respected by many within it. He enjoyed the fellowship of the far greater number of evangelicals

of his social class in the Church of England, and visited there frequently. But his staunch Calvinism, his inability to be temporizing about anything, and his well-developed sense of Scottish superiority all made him hesitant about the recognized evangelical leadership in the Church of England.

One of the key events in Haldane's life was his visit to Geneva in 1816. Here he came across a Reformed state-church which was at the opposite end of the theological and spiritual spectrum from himself. He led a number of theological students to personal faith in Christ, providing one of the main sources of the renewal movement in the Francophone world, Le Réveil as it was called. As he examined the causes of the deterioration of Genevan Calvinism, he came to the conclusion that it depended on an inadequate view of biblical inspiration. So he wrote *The Evidence and Authority of Divine Revelation*, which in 1829, in much fuller fashion, would be published as *The Books of the Old and New Testaments Proved to Be Canonical, and Their Verbal Inspiration Maintained and Established.* He insisted on verbal inspiration, rather than the plenary view, which had been held by almost all involved in the preceding Evangelical Awakenings. The plenary theory was an author-oriented view, which taught a graduated scale of divine superintendence, and emphasized that only sufficient divine energy was expended to ensure that the message of each part of the Bible was truthful. Haldane, instead, affirmed a text-oriented theory, which stated that God had inspired all the words of the original documents of Scripture with the same completeness, a view which had been held particularly in post-Reformation Lutheranism.[17]

The new Evangelicals enthusiastically welcomed Haldane's verbal theory and supported his attack upon the traditional evangelicals and the plenary view. He had particularly close ties with the new Evangelicals in Ireland. Lord Roden of Dundalk was the most prominent layman in what came to be known as the Second Reformation, and he was a close friend of Haldane, who visited him frequently after 1822.[18] Through this friendship Haldane was introduced to the Irish evangelical aristocratic connection. While he met the Jocelyns, the Pennefathers, the Howards, the Synges, the Lefroys, the Trenches, the Shaws and many others, it is also important to notice that he was warmly welcomed by such proto-Brethren relatives as Theodosia, Lady Powerscourt, Lord Congleton and John Nelson Darby.[19] They appreciated his Calvinistic theology, evangelistic zeal, hatred of Roman Catholicism and liberalism in all its forms, and his social status. He bequeathed much to this eager group of young people, including his view of the Bible.

Alexander Haldane, who from 1830 for over half a century would be the proprietor of the powerful new Evangelical newspaper, the *Record*, represented his uncle's views in London from 1822. As a young lawyer of good family, who had received much of his education at an English school conducted by an evangelical clergyman, he was readily welcomed in evangelical Anglican circles. He first made his name, however, through his leadership in what was known as the Apocrypha Controversy in the British and Foreign Bible Society.[20] Robert Haldane discovered that the Bible Society was allowing the Apocrypha to be included in versions for the Continental market. Scottish Calvinism had historically been the section of magisterial Protestantism most opposed to the use of the Apocrypha, and to this was added Haldane's suspicions about some of the policies of both evangelical Anglican and Nonconformist leadership. When they professed to be unable to see the point of his protest when an increased number of Bibles were being disseminated, he again became convinced that the basic problem lay in an inadequate view of the Bible. Alexander potently represented verbal inspiration, and by his action helped to persuade others that there were weaknesses in evangelical Anglicanism, that a new evangelicalism was needed, and that verbal inspiration was an essential component.[21] All the Brethren accepted verbal inspiration, and in 1903 William Kelly, the most learned and able of all their theological writers, gave classic expression to this Brethren doctrine of Scripture in *God's Inspiration of the Scriptures*, which in a uniquely Brethren way took detailed evidence from every book of the Bible.

In a special way the Brethren view of the Bible tended to produce among them an exclusively Bible-oriented spirituality. All thoughtful evangelical Christians, and certainly the new Evangelicals, read the Bible regularly and copiously. The Brethren, however, when adding to verbal inspiration other distinctives, often appeared to read little else. In fact Neatby insists that their favorite form of recreation was the Bible Reading.[22] Viewed from this viewpoint, Brethren spirituality appears restricted, cerebral, and serious. But undoubtedly, in good Puritan fashion, the answer would be that through a singular concentration on the Bible we are liberated into fellowship with God in his immensity and incomprehensibility, that the truth of God must be addressed first to the mind, and that solemn expectancy must be the attitude of those who live *sub specie aeternitatis*, awaiting the Bridegroom's voice.

The literal interpretation of the Bible tended to be a correlate of verbal inspiration, and the Brethren made themselves singular champions of this hermeneutic, which is sometimes described as biblicism. And it also had an influence on their spirituality. There was no place for cultural contextualization. The meaning and application were clear, and universally so. This biblicism may not have expressed the rugged confidence of the self-made person of the American frontier expounded at exactly the same time in Alexander Campbell's Restoration movement, but at least, on the intellectual side, it carried a similarly breath-taking sense of dogmatic certainty. There were no problems or questions once the purportedly literal meaning had been divined.

Verbal inspiration also gave rise to a distinctive form of Brethren teaching, known as the Bible Reading, which in many ways is the precursor of the modern genre of expository preaching. Christian preaching from the point of view of plenary inspiration was primarily textual or topical, stressing one basic theme. Many who shifted from plenary to verbal inspiration did not accordingly alter their preaching style. But the Brethren were nothing if not consistent. Thus those engaged in biblical teaching would dig into a section of Scripture at a time, perhaps a paragraph, starting with the words and then the phrases and sentences. From this detailed approach many themes emerged. If one has only known Brethren preaching as monotonously evangelistic, typologically bizarre or excessively boring, then one has no idea what a wonderful new world of rich biblical fare many Christians were brought into through the teaching of the ablest of the Brethren. And in sequence this teaching would go on every day for weeks on end. The Brethren were thus people who knew their Bibles both particularly and thematically. This gave a special character to their spirituality, and probably did more than anything to make rationalistic biblical criticism unpalatable to the Brethren. Through their teaching the Brethren knew that the Bible was the living and powerful Word of God.

Premillennialism and Apostasy
In what they believed to be Britain's and Europe's extremity, the new Evangelicals turned for guidance to another Scot, Edward Irving. Or perhaps it should be said that they were swept along by his vision, his passion and his erratic Romantic genius. Irving was a minister of the Church of Scotland who had pastored an expatriate Presbyterian congregation in London since 1822. With his eloquence and intelligence he quickly became one of the best-known preachers in London. He believed that he was a prophet sent from God, and the new Evangelicals, at least for a time, gave every evidence that they too believed this. They shared Irving's antipathy for liberalism in all its forms, and for a bustling, pragmatic evangelicalism. They yearned with him for a godly national

church living in the power of the Spirit, and set within a godly nation ruled by the Word of God, even if only for a brief "latter rain" of glory before the second coming of Jesus Christ.[23]

The first major article on Irving's agenda for the renewal of Christianity was premillennialism, and although there were new Evangelicals who did not welcome this emphasis, most did, and none more than those who would lead the Brethren.[24] In fact, the Brethren would add a few eschatological refinements of their own. Irving, in good Romantic style, was reaching back into history. He was finding his inspiration in this case, as in others, in seventeenth-century Puritanism, for in their comprehensive vision for church and nation, the Puritans had included a number of premillennialists.

Premillennialism affirmed the basic Christian conviction of the victory of Jesus, but limited much of its application to a future millennial age, which Jesus would soon personally inaugurate. Evangelicals heretofore had largely been postmillennialists, who shared an optimistic philosophy of history which envisioned the preaching of the gospel and the work of the Spirit producing an almost millennial state on earth, a virtually converted world thus fittingly prepared for Christ's eternal reign. Now, however, the tables were turned. Society and the church were on the downgrade until the parousia, although this might be interrupted by a brief "latter rain" of the Spirit's power. But only the personal presence of Jesus Christ would permanently rectify the world's ills.

Irving began to stress premillennialism in his public ministry in 1827, and soon after, the future Brethren among the new Evangelicals were immersed in the subject. J. G. Bellett of Dublin returned home overwhelmed by the teaching he had received on a visit to Irving's Regent Square Church in 1828.[25] Darby was devouring Irving's writings,[26] Lord Congleton attended one of the conferences led by Irving on this theme at Albury in Surrey,[27] and it was reported that Lady Powerscourt made an appearance at at least one of these gatherings.[28] A group of new Evangelicals at Oxford, with close ties to Plymouth, who would soon be of singular importance to Brethrenism, and whose leader was the brilliant and extremely young B. W. Newton, were deeply impressed with the subject.[29] George Muller, who would soon dominate the West Country Brethren center of Bristol, arrived in England from Germany in 1829 to be enrolled in the training school of the Evangelical Anglican London Society for Promoting Christianity Amongst the Jews, where there was a strong new Evangelical input. Although the Society was never officially identified with the new Evangelicals, the two lecturers in the training school would certainly have propelled students in that direction.[30]

Eschatology, with its attendant philosophy of history, inevitably has a bearing upon spirituality. To a spirituality which was Puritan in its seriousness and Bible-centeredness, premillennialism added a note of profound pessimism concerning the fortunes of Christianity in this age of the church and society. The hope of world-wide awakening and revival was lost. "The calling out of a people for his name" was not held in tension with "discipling the nations." In fact, the great Second Evangelical Awakening, out of which the new Evangelicals had come, was downplayed and even denied.[31] Amid such pessimism it was impossible for the future Brethren to acknowledge and weigh the fact that most of them came from areas where evangelical Anglicanism was particularly weak, and that their class-consciousness was keeping most of them from having any sympathetic knowledge of Nonconformity. And it was even more impossible for them to realize that in other parts of the country the denominations had seldom if ever been in such a healthy state. Thus it was all too easy for them to dismiss reality, and when in that state, with a very human intellectual consistency, to interpret their own movement as an expression of spiritual renewal, rather than as a movement of defense, as it most definitely was in most of its aspects. In such a setting, even if the Brethren movement was regarded as a sign of hope amid the darkness, it was a hope that was greatly scaled down from worldwide awakening.

But Irvingite premillennialism went further, making use of the theme of the Gentile Apostasy as far as the denominations were concerned,[32] and producing at least among the Brethren a theology and spirituality of sectarianism. The early evangelicals, both inside and outside the Church of England, thought little of apostasy, however deplorable was the condition of the churches. They were renewal people, who had all the positive expectation in the world. But when the situation appeared impropitious, apostasy was revived as an element of premillennialism. The new Evangelicals all agreed that Roman Catholicism was apostate. In fact it was viewed as Satan's great counterfeit, at every point duplicating truth with falsity. This gave a new rigor to traditional Anglo-Saxon "No Popery."[33] The new Evangelicals also agreed that wherever Protestant liberalism held sway, as in much of Continental Protestantism, especially embodied in Geneva, it too was apostate in its ecclesiastical expression. The Lutheran and Reformed bodies were not true churches and were heading for judgment. So far, they were of one mind. But there was a question that would in due course split the new Evangelicals, and this concerned the Church of England. Most new Evangelicals, even with catholicizing Tractarianism staring them in the face after 1833, affirmed that the foundations of the Church of England were solidly Protestant. The Brethren, on the other hand, had a different evaluation.

Almost all the early Brethren were raised within the Church of England. Some loved it deeply, and, of course, when they felt forced to leave it, saw its apostasy in particularly somber hues. Early in 1831 Darby and Newton decided to put the Church of England to the test. Working with their close friend H. B. Bulteel, a Plymouth man who was curate of St. Ebbe's, Oxford, they agreed that when he next preached before the university he would call the Church of England back to its Calvinistic formularies and to a non-erastian union with the state. This he did with great zeal, but the Bishop of Oxford replied with an attack on Calvinism.[34] This confirmed their fears, and from then on the Brethren, with slightly different pacing, were on their way out of the apostate Church of England. Since evangelical Nonconformists also seemed to be departing from their Calvinistic heritage, they were readily dismissed as apostate as well.

Belief in the apostasy of the rest of the church was fortified by Darby's development of futurist premillennialism. The new Evangelicals had been historicist premillenarians, but Darby saw the difficulty of stretching the apocalyptic depictions of Daniel and Revelation over an ever-expanding historical continuum. As a result, changing the meaning of apocalyptic days from years to literal days, he laid great stress upon a seven-year tribulation, to be followed by the millennium in connection with the second advent. Moreover, it was literal Israel and not the church which was the major subject of biblical prophecy.[35] From this point on it is observable that while historicist new Evangelicals tended to remain in the Church of England, futurists like Darby tended to leave.

It is quite true that Darby and the Exclusive Brethren on one hand and A. N. Groves, Muller and the Open Brethren on the other approached aspects of the subject of the church from a slightly different point of view. But, however they worked out the details, both sides believed in the Gentile Apostasy, and that it applied to all denominations except their own. Darby, with a strong sense of the unity of the church and strict logic, assumed that true Christians in the apostate denominations would join the Brethren. The Opens, on the other hand, allowed for a modicum of ecclesiastical non-absolutism, perhaps because they were slightly less aristocratic, and thus more flexible and individualistic. As a result they were prepared to have fellowship with those they conceived to be true Christians and even true congregations that were still functioning amid the apostate mass of Christendom.[36] But there was no recognition of any spiritual validity for the denominations of which these people were a part. While Open Brethren had fellowship with evangelical Christians in other denominations, the thought of working with conventional denominational structures, and leaders in their official capacity, even if evangelical, was abhorrent. As a result Brethren spirituality was wedded to a narrow conception of the church, and one in which it was difficult to retain both personal vision and personal humility.

Separation from Society

Premillennialism also taught that society was sliding into the same ruin as the denominations, prior to the appearing of Jesus Christ. For people coming from the very conservative social network of the early Brethren, the political and social scene pointed clearly in this direction. The removal of civil disabilities from Nonconformists in 1828 and Roman Catholics in 1829 suggested blatant apostasy, while the conjunction of cholera and the Great Reform Bill of 1832 suggested God's displeasure with England and Ireland. The plans afoot to remove some of the privileges of Irish Anglicanism, and to provide a modicum of education to Roman Catholic children on a non-Protestant basis, was the last straw.[37] This was also an eschatological sign, for the preponderance of Roman Catholicism in Ireland led to the belief that the stirrings there were merely an indication of the upheavals that would accompany increasing national apostasy. A journalist, knowing the reputation of the Brethren for Puritanism, but indicating how the Brethren went beyond Puritanism, stated that "Mr. Newton strongly objects to constitutional monarchy, and 'goes in' for the 'right divine of kings' in a way that would have delighted a Stuart."[38] What the Brethren actually did, of course, was to separate themselves from apostate society. So the Brethren movement, numbering many cultured people, withdrew from politics, community life, and culture in general, to await the return of Christ.

At the same time, some at least of the Brethren had hearts full of Christian compassion for the needy of society. So while they sedulously avoided the paraphernalia which the voluntary societies had bequeathed to organized philanthropy, they were famous for orphanages, that most ancient and Christ-like form of Christian social service. Names such as Barnardo, Muller and Fegan come readily to mind in this connection.

Thus we meet the strange situation of a Christian body that withdrew from a state church and from its attendant society, not as most Nonconformists have done, because the situation was unjust, but because church and state did not retain the historic inequities of Christendom. When such people retired from social involvement, one would expect them to retain conservative social attitudes, and this they did. Their social pessimism was so strong that when the Third Evangelical Awakening swept a great number of working people into the Brethren assemblies after 1859, the social tones from Birmingham, Manchester, Glasgow, the Moray Firth and Belfast were as negative as those from the upperclass Brethren of the Dublin-Plymouth-Oxford axis. Newton expressed the spirituality of social withdrawal when speaking about the factory children: "Therefore they must suffer and die. The foundations of everything are out of course and no man can rectify them. But we wait for God's Son from heaven."[39]

Charismatic Spirituality

Another distinctive mark in Brethren spirituality was the charismatic activity of the Holy Spirit in the church. Although the imminent return of Jesus Christ was the ultimate answer to all evil, the proximate answer was the direct activity of Jesus Christ by the Holy Spirit.[40] Once again, Edward Irving was the progenitor of this approach, being among the first Protestants to seek to undo the Protestant ban upon the miraculous gifts of the Spirit.[41] He taught that amid the world's darkening, there would be a brief "latter rain" of the Spirit, characterized by the charismatic gifts. Not all the new Evangelicals were prepared to follow Irving at this point, but those soon to move out of the Church of England were most interested.

Word of speaking in tongues arrived in London in the early spring of 1830 from Port Glasgow on the Clyde, and Darby was one of the first to make the pilgrimage. Staying for several weeks, he came reluctantly to the conclusion that the effusions of a fifteen-year-old girl, and interpretations which quoted the Authorized Version inaccurately, were not worthy of the Spirit.[42] In spite, however, of one example of false fire, he and his friends were by no means prepared to jettison the whole idea. Healings began to occur in circles associated with the L.S.P.C.J., with which a number of future Brethren were involved,[43] and then prophetic utterances in tongues appeared in Irving's congregation. The early Brethren pulled back at the exercise of the gift of prophecy, but there were ample indications that among the Brethren a laundered charismaticism was operative.[44] So Brethren spirituality also had a freeing, joyful, egalitarian charismatic element.

Anyone who has ever attended a breaking of bread service does not need much convincing that this is a charismatic gathering, once accretions of custom have been penetrated. Ministry is predicated on gift, not on education or ordination. There is, at its best, the quiet, tense, expectant waiting for the Spirit to call into operation the gift appropriate for the occasion. Another example of dependence on the direct activity of the Holy Spirit is the pervasive aversion to organization. Human planning must be kept to a minimum so that the Spirit may minister unhindered. And all Christians, at least theoretically, are gifted for some form of ministry.

Brethren missionary work also evidences a singularly charismatic spirituality, and once again the input of Irving was seminal. Irving groaned within himself when he saw the highly organized and confident missionary societies of his day. Thus he took the first opportunity to share his missionary vision when invited to speak at the annual meeting of the London Missionary Society in 1824. He poured out his soul on the theme of Apostolic Missions for four hours.[45] Actually, many of his ideas had come from reading the reports of the converted Jew Joseph Wolff, who during his Roman Catholic phase had studied at the Propaganda in Rome and made Francis Xavier his life-long hero. Now in his Protestant period, this Romantic of the Romantics was a new evangelical, working among the Jewish people of the Middle East for the L.S.P.C.J. Generously funded by the aristocratic and inordinately wealthy banker Henry Drummond, who was becoming one of Irving's closest friends, Wolff was largely free of institutional responsibilities and direction. Wolff's missionary journeys among Jews and Gentiles possess an almost legendary quality. The miraculous intervention of the Spirit was experienced all the time. And it was this ideal that Irving enunciated.[46]

This approach to missions was followed by the Brethren, and was embodied in the large "faith mission" movement. Groves followed this model overseas, as did Muller at home, and subsequent Brethren missionaries wherever they went. All was under the direct leading of the Spirit. There were no titled patrons, no committees and no fund-raising schemes. Prayer was made, direction was given, finances were supplied, protection was afforded and workers were raised up. Hudson Taylor, through his contact with the Brethren, transferred this plan of operation to the China Inland Mission and a host of other "faith" organizations. But it all came from the Brethren, for whom God was indeed Jehovah-Jireh, the Lord who will provide, so that "God's work, done in God's way, will never lack God's supply." And the Brethren received it from Wolff, and Wolff from the Jesuit Xavier.

Hyper-Calvinism

Finally, at least so far as this essay is concerned, Brethren spirituality exhibits a strong strain of hyper-Calvinism.[47] This extreme emphasis on divine sovereignty, linked with other highly distinctive characteristics, had emerged in late Puritanism, influencing many Baptists and some Congregationalists. When the First Evangelical Awakening began, most of the evangelical Anglicans adopted the theological position known as Moderate Calvinism, which was well suited to ardent evangelistic activity. A small number, however, opted for hyper-Calvinism. The outstanding Anglican exemplar of this position was Augustus Montague Toplady, the hymnwriter. In subsequent years the Anglicans who held this viewpoint tended to reside in the West Country, and the *Gospel Magazine* was their periodical.

Hyper-Calvinism was not shared by many other new Evangelicals; it was something of a Brethren specialty. The key connection between hyper-Calvinism and the Brethren was Robert Hawker, vicar of Charles Church, Plymouth, for almost half a century before his death in 1827, and the most prominent hyper-Calvinist in the Church of England.[48] Groves, who had close links with Plymouth, greatly valued Hawker,[49] while Bulteel was one of Hawker's converts, and emphasized his mentor's distinctives through his ministry. At Oxford Bulteel led Newton, another Plymouth man, to faith in Christ, and made sure that he was introduced to Hawker's views.[50] Darby also had great appreciation for Bulteel. Other early Brethren from the Plymouth area, such as Captain W. C. Rhind, had been part of Hawker's congregation.[51] The rapid growth of the Brethren assembly at Plymouth is most easily explained by the fact that many of Hawker's congregation were at loose ends after his death, the type of ministry to which they were accustomed not continuing at Charles. It is also suggestive, as well as symbolic, that Ebrington Street, where the assembly met, is only a stone's throw from Charles Church, if you leave by the back door and angle to the left. Thus the ecclesiastical title Plymouth Brethren was more than simply the name of the most prominent early assembly. It expressed the source of some of the hallmarks of Brethrenism.

Although Plymouth was the major source of Brethren hyper-Calvinism, there were other points of contact. Half a dozen or so young, West Country, hyper-Calvinistic clergy, from socially prominent families, left the Church of England in 1815-1816 to become hyper-Calvinistic Baptist pastors in a movement known as the Western Schism. And there was some measure of contact between them and the Brethren. Bethesda Chapel, Bristol, ever associated with Muller, had previously been the place of ministry of one of the members of the Western Schism, an Irishman named T. D. Cowan.[52] Since Muller secured the use of Bethesda when Cowan was returning to the Church of England, it would be quite natural for some of his erstwhile Baptist followers to throw in their lot with the new order of things.[53] James Harington Evans was another Western Schism man, who became pastor of John St. Baptist Chapel in London, from whence would come the saintly Robert Chapman of Barnstaple. Drummond the banker, although he left the new Evangelicals with a number of others to join Irving's Catholic Apostolic Church rather than the Brethren, had shared much with the founders of the Brethren in their new evangelical days. He was converted through another Western Schism man, T. C. Snow,[54] and then funded the building of the London Chapel for his relative Evans.[55] Drummond arrived in Geneva soon after his conversion, where he sought to carry on the work of Haldane. There he injected his hyper-Calvinism, adding an element which made Le Réveil a speckled and somewhat puzzling bird among nineteenth-century Calvinistic renewal movements.[56] This input into Switzerland also helps to account for the ready reception which Darby received in various quarters in that country. Brethren hymnbooks also reveal this connection, with *Hymns for the Little Flock*, for example, having five selections from Hawker.

The Brethren did not accept all of hyper-Calvinism, but they chose enough to add singular elements to their spirituality. All of Calvinism stressed the objective accomplishments of God in Christ, and, as might be expected, hyper-Calvinism understood this matter more extensively than heretofore. When dealing with the great theme of union with Christ, traditional Calvinism had always taught that there was growth within this foundational aspect of sanctification. Hyper-Calvinism, on the other hand, emphasized an eternal and complete union.[57] Brethren hymns are full of this theme, particularly in its corporate aspect. J.G. Deck expressed it: "In Thee the Father sees us, Accepted and complete," while Chapman wrote: "Perfect in comeliness art thou, in Christ, the risen Lord."

Another aspect of the stress on divine sovereignty in hyper-Calvinism dealt with the use of means. It was felt that human planning and organization were contrary to God's will in Christian service. God was to be allowed to operate in his own time and way. He did call and send people, but in such a way that all the initiative and accomplishment were seen to belong to God, and thus to him went all the glory. As a result, Brethren spirituality has frequently evinced the paradox of people of remarkable competence being diffident about any form of organized activity.[58]

Hyper-Calvinism also gained for Brethrenism the epithet of antinomianism.[59] Some might have thus accused them because of their strongly Calvinistic concept of grace in every aspect of the Christian life. Others would undoubtedly have felt that their hesitancy to confess sin because of complete positional sanctification pointed in this direction. But the hyper-Calvinistic inheritance was particularly seen in their attitude to perseverance and the Old Testament moral law. In the first case the eternal security of the believer was sometimes stressed by insisting that one of the elect, dying in gross sin, could never be lost. This sundering of grace and responsible holiness called forth attack. So did the hyper-Calvinistic slogan that "the Old Testament law was not a law for a New Testament people." This statement, while intending to stress that gratitude rather than duty was the major motivation in the Christian life, expressed it in such a way that outsiders were upset. Not only did Arminians make the charge, but fellow Calvinists, who believed strongly that the moral law was the pattern of the Christian life, viewed the hyper-Calvinistic effort as tragic. While from another vantage-point hyper-Calvinistic piety might be described as excessively introspective, moralistic, and even legalistic, from the viewpoint of this paragraph, it gave to the Brethren in some aspects a freer concept of the Christian life, more akin to Lutheranism.

In dealing with the influences of hyper-Calvinism, a word should be said about the subject of assurance. For the magisterial Reformers this was not particularly a matter of concern, since in a day of awakening assurance is a natural reflex of the gospel. The Puritans, however, particularly aware of the danger of self-delusion in the Christian life, insisted that there must be the evidence of moral life to substantiate the assumption, and this view became widespread among Anglo-Saxon Protestants. Early hyper-Calvinists, however, developed a different approach. Perhaps drawing on the understanding of some Puritans that assurance was derived from an experience known as the sealing of the Spirit, they sought for assurance in occasional visits of Christ to the soul by the Spirit. While the Brethren did not adopt this approach, it at least suggested to them that there were alternatives to evidentialism. Thus the Brethren opted for an assurance based on the promise of the gospel, with an almost syllogistic certainty, which has sometimes been paraphrased and parodied as "God says it; I believe it; that settles it; I'm saved."[60] Assurance was an essential aspect of the Christian life, and in this biblicistic form it gave an uncanny sense of confidence to Brethren spirituality.

Conservative and Progressive Radicalism

In conclusion, it should be noted that Brethren spirituality expressed distinctives that were fairly radical and extreme. This was quite natural for a spirituality spawned in young Romantics amid a context of fear. While in most instances it was a conservative radicalism, at certain points it could only be called a progressive radicalism. The former description fits its view of the Bible and premillennialism, while the latter would apply to its charismatic emphasis and the place of the law in Christian experience. It was in the creative tension between these two forms of radicalism that Brethren spirituality emerged.

Brethren theology and spirituality had a remarkable influence on evangelical Protestantism during the century or so here under consideration. In fact, the emergence in the later nineteenth and early twentieth centuries of a self-conscious conservative evangelism owed a considerable debt to the Brethren, while the form of conservative evangelicalism known as American Fundamentalism might be described as the Brethrenization of evangelicalism, so wholesale was the transposition. Actually, the influence of the Brethren became much greater in America than in Britain. In America, however, the conservative radicalism of the Brethren was greatly preferred, with the progressive elements played down. Thus if Brethren spirituality is to be fully appreciated, it must be seen in its British milieu between Waterloo and World War II.

Notes

[1] The standard histories of the Brethren are H. H. Rowdon, *The Origins of the Brethren 1825-1850* (London: Pickering & Inglis, 1967), and H. R. Coad, *A History of the Brethren Movement: Its Origins, Its Worldwide Development and Its Significance for the Present Day* (London: Paternoster, 1968). The difficulty is that the former, though excellent as far as it goes, is largely factual, not dealing to any great extent with ideas and attitudes, while the latter suffers from the bane of old-fashioned church history, which tended to use history to demonstrate that one's own group was correct, in this case the Open Brethren in distinction from the Exclusives. As a result there is still immense value in W. B. Neatby, *A History of the Plymouth Brethren* (London: Hodder & Stoughton, 1901).

[2] D. W. Bebbington, *Evangelicalism in Modern Britain: A History from the 1730s to the 1980s* (London: Unwin Hyman, 1989), chap. 3, "A Troubling of the Water: Developments in the Early Nineteenth Century," 75-104.

[3] There has been no specific study of this important group of evangelical Anglicans, but their presence has been recognized. In the nineteenth century they were commonly referred to as Recordites, after the extensively circulated newspaper directed by Alexander Haldane for half a century. In the article by W. J. Conybeare, "Church Parties," in his *Essays Ecclesiastical and Social* (London, 1855), it was estimated that about 40% of evangelical Anglicans belonged to this discernible tradition. In more recent days they have been called "Peculiars," David Newsome, *The Parting of Friends: A Study of the Wilberforces and Henry Manning* (London: Murray, 1966); "Radicals," Timothy Stunt, "John Henry Newman and the Evangelicals," *Journal of Ecclesiastical History* 21 (1970) 65-74; Evangelicals "shifting into a lower key," G. Best, "Evangelicalism and the Victorians," *The Victorian Crisis of Faith* (ed.

A. Symondsen; London: SPCK, 1970) 37-56; and "Ultras," W. J. C. Ervine, "Doctrine and Diplomacy: Some Aspects of the Life and Thought of the Anglican Evangelical Clergy" (Ph.D. thesis, Cambridge, 1979) 251-307.

[4] This popular, Enlightenment-oriented evangelical culture is the object of sustained derision by F. K. Brown, *Fathers of the Victorians: The Age of Wilberforce* (Cambridge, U.K.: Cambridge University Press, 1961). The new Evangelicals would have agreed with a good deal of his analysis.

[5] The fear, and the extreme reaction which it produced, can well be seen in *Dialogues on Prophecy* (3 vol.; ed. H. Drummond; London, 1827, 1828, 1829), which were a stylized account of the discussions at Henry Drummond's home, Albury Park, Surrey, attended by prominent new Evangelicals, and directed by Edward Irving; and in the pages of Irving's mouthpiece, *The Morning Watch.*

[6] R. Haldane, *Review of the Conduct of the Directors of the British and Foreign Bible Society, Relative to the Apocrypha and to Their Administration on the Continent* (Edinburgh, 1825); *Second Review of the Conduct of the British and Foreign Bible Society, Containing an Account of the Religious State of the Continent* (Edinburgh, 1826).

[7] D. Bowen, *The Protestant Crusade in Ireland* (Dublin: Gill & Macmillan, 1978) 1-26.

[8] Cf. Brown, *Fathers.*

[9] *Christian Observer* (1817) 413, 577, 727, 802; (1818) 81, 86, 296, 382.

[10] L. P. Fox, "The Work of the Rev. Thomas Tregenna Biddulph with Special Reference to His Influence on the Evangelical Movement in the West of England" (Ph.D. thesis, Cambridge, 1953).

[11] A. R. Acheson, "The Evangelicals in the Church of Ireland, 1784-1859" (Ph.D. thesis, Queen's University, Belfast, 1967).

[12] H. Willmer, "Evangelicalism, 1735 to 1835" (Hulsean Prize Essay, Cambridge, 1962) 33.

[13] *Christian Observer* (1827) 499-502; R. Haldane, *The Authenticity and Inspiration of the Holy Scriptures Considered; in Opposition to the Erroneous Opinions That Are Circulated on the Subject* (Edinburgh, 1827) 3-4.

[14] *Christian Observer* (1829) 190-196; G. H. Sumner, *Life of Charles Richard Sumner* (London, 1876) 160-161.

[15] The other significant seceding body at this time was the Catholic Apostolic Church.

[16] A. Haldane, *The Lives of Robert Haldane of Airthrey and His Brother James Alexander Haldane* (Edinburgh, 1855).

[17] R. Preus, *The Theology of Post-Reformation Lutheranism* (St. Louis: Concordia, 1970) 254-403.

[18] Haldane Papers, Gleneagles House, Gleneagles, Perthshire, Scotland; when consulted these papers were uncatalogued, but they have since been acquired by Edinburgh University.

[19] Cf. Acheson, "Evangelicals."

[20] A. Haldane, *Lives,* 468ff.

[21] W. G. Turner, *John Nelson Darby: A Biography* (London: C. A. Hammond, 1926) 46-47.

[22] Neatby, *History,* 278.

[23] E. Irving, "Preliminary Discourse," in J. J. Ben Ezra, *Coming of Messiah in Power and Glory* (London, 1827). This discourse is a fine example of Irving's theological ability, without the bitterness and extreme judgmentalism which quickly developed when he sensed that his self-styled prophetic ministry was not widely recognized.

[24] E. R. Sandeen, *The Roots of Fundamentalism: British and American Millenarianism 1800-1930* (Chicago: University of Chicago Press, 1970). J. Ward, "The Eschatology of John Nelson Darby" (Ph.D. thesis, University of London, 1976), argues that the philosophy of history of dispensationalism was more important than eschatological premillennialism, which seems something of a distinction without a difference. D. L. Embley, "The Origins and Early Development of the Plymouth Brethren" (Ph.D., Cambridge, 1967), in contending against eschatology as basic, insists that the key is found in practical ecclesiastical issues such as the indiscriminate use of the burial service, baptismal regeneration, and wholesale

admission to communion. Although these were important early factors, Brethrenism would never have taken the course it did without premillennialism.

[25] Rowdon, *Origins,* 50.

[26] *The Collected Works of J. N. Darby* (ed. W. Kelly; London, 1877) 2.1-47.

[27] *Record* (11 April, 1860).

[28] Ward, "Eschatology," 21.

[29] Rowdon, *Origins,* 63.

[30] R. Steer, *George Muller: Delighted in God* (Wheaton, Ill.: Harold Shaw, 1975) 36. The lecturers were Thomas Boys and Algernon Sydney Thelwall, *Christian Observer* (1831) 573.

[31] *Dialogues* (Drummond, ed.) 2.708.

[32] H. McNeile, *The Abominations of Babylon: A Sermon Preached in Behalf of the Continental Society* (London, 1826); E. Irving, *The Last Days: A Discourse on the Evil Character of These Our Times, Proving Them to Be the "Perilous Times" of the "Last Days"* (London, 1828).

[33] An example of this genre is still offered by the Brethren publisher Loizeaux, or has been until recently, A. Hislop, *The Two Babylons, or Papal Worship Proved to Be the Worship of Nimrod and His Wife* (Neptune, N.J.: Loizeaux Brothers, 1959).

[34] Kelly, *Works,* 3.6-7.

[35] O. T. Allis, *Prophecy and the Church: An Examination of the Claim of Dispensationalists That the Christian Church Is a Mystery Parenthesis Which Interrupts the Fulfilment to Israel of the Kingdom Prophecies of the Old Testament* (Philadelphia: Presbyterian & Reformed, 1945).

[36] This is the position of A. N. Groves; cf. Mrs. Groves, *Memoir of the Late Anthony Norris Groves, Containing Extracts from His Letters and Journals* (London, 1857). In the present reconstruction of their history, many very open Brethren have sought to portray Groves as so charitable in relations with other evangelicals that he was something of an ecumenical evangelical. This interpretation fails to hold in tension his love for all in whom he believed that he discerned the life of Christ, and his eschatological beliefs, with their corresponding ecclesiastical rigor when it came to assessing institutional Christianity.

[37] Kelly, *Works,* 32.426-490.

[38] *Christian Brethren Research Fellowship Broadsheet* 8 (April, 1973) 6.

[39] B. W. Newton, *Thoughts on the Apocalypse* (London, 1844) 293.

[40] Kelly, *Works,* 32.281-322, 333-336.

[41] Ibid., 1.54-102.

[42] Ibid., 6.450.

[43] *Christian Observer* (1830) 708ff.; J. Hill, Diary (8 March, 1831) MSS St. Edmund Hall, 67/8, Bodleian Library, Oxford; *Monthly Intelligence of the Proceedings of the London Society for Promoting Christianity Amongst the Jews* (January, 1831) 15; (April, 1831) 63.

[44] Kelly, *Works,* 1.103-121.

[45] E. Irving, *For Missionaries After the Apostolic School, a Series of Orations* (London, 1824).

[46] J. Wolff, *Missionary Journal and Memoir* (3 vol.; London, 1824); *Travels and Adventures* (London, 1868); H. P. Palmer, *Joseph Wolff: His Romantic Life and Travels* (London: Heath Cranton, 1935).

[47] P. Toon, *The Emergence of Hyper-Calvinism in English Nonconformity 1689-1765* (London: Olive Tree, 1967).

[48] J. Williams, ed., *The Works of the Rev. Robert Hawker D.D.* (10 vol.; London, 1831); Embley, "Origins," 75.

[49] Groves, *Memoir,* 100.

[50] Rowdon, *Origins,* 61.

[51] J. B. I. (sbell), *Faithful unto Death: A Memoir of William Graeme Rhind, R.N.* (London, 1863).

[52] H. H. Rowdon, "Secession from the Established Church in the Early Nineteenth Century," *Vox Evangelica* 3 (1964) 76-88. Unfortunately the common hyper-Calvinism of the seceders is not emphasized.

[53] Fox, "Work," 108ff.; J. Kennedy, *The Torch of the Testimony* (Bombay: Gospel Literature

Service, 1965) 211, states that those who formed the original Bristol assembly had heretofore been baptized as believers. Unless he was simply assuming this as standard practice, the comment would seem to indicate, contra Coad, *History of the Brethren*, 41-42, that in Bristol the Baptist strand was very important, and given the nature of the situation, they would likely be hyper-Calvinists.

[54] (H. Drummond), *Narrative of the Circumstances Which Led to the Setting Up of the Church of Christ at Albury* (London, 1834) 6-7.

[55] J. Grant, *Metropolitan Pulpit* (London, 1839) 2.305-337.

[56] T. Stunt, "Geneva and British Evangelicals in the Early Nineteenth Century," *Journal of Ecclesiastical History* 32/1 (1981) 35-46. Stunt traces the origin of the separatist emphasis in Le Réveil to Moravianism, but given the impact of Drummond's hyper-Calvinism, it is likely that his call for separation amid what he conceived to be the apostasy of the Genevan Church would not be without influence.

[57] Williams, *Works*, 1.144, 211f.

[58] Willmer, "Evangelicalism," 100-109.

[59] Williams, *Works*, 1.99, 215; D. Steele, *Antinomianism Revived; or, the Theology of the So-Called Plymouth Brethren Examined and Refuted* (Boston, 1887).

[60] P.D. Airhart, "'What Must I Do to Be Saved?' Two Paths to Evangelical Conversion in Late Victorian Canada," *Church History* 59/3 (1990) 372-385. The objective character of the Brethren view of assurance is reminiscent of Sandemanianism; see Rowdon, "Secession," *Vox Evangelica* 3 (1964) 76-88, although the historian of Brethrenism does not examine the possible link.

Part IV
Integrative & Interdisciplinary

17
The Worries of This Life, the Deceitfulness of Wealth, and Secularization in Modern Society

Craig M. Gay

T HE ASSUMPTION THAT "NEWER IS BETTER" IS WEARING A LITTLE thin these days in spite of our continuing commitment to "progress." The irony in this is evident in so-called postmodern suggestions that we now need to "progress" beyond progress. Although it remains unclear just exactly what these "postmodern" suggestions mean, at the very least they seem to mean that it will be worth taking another look at a number of things we thought we had progressed beyond. For evangelical Christians, this often means taking another look at what happened in the church between roughly the fifth and the sixteenth centuries; for it turns out that many of our ancestors in faith had some very insightful things to say. It is precisely along this line that Jim Houston has been so helpful to many of us. Jim is a man of many talents, not the least of which is his ability to shed "old" light on new circumstances, that is, his ability to render traditional and biblical concepts relevant to the sorts of problems we face today. For the most part this has meant moving back and forth between the traditional idioms of the Bible and church theology and of modern psychology. And yet Jim has always been an astute observer and critic of contemporary society and culture as well, and he has managed to go some distance toward integrating traditional theological insights with an historical and sociological imagination. The following essay reveals my debt to Jim Houston along this latter line; for it represents an attempt to render a curious yet characteristic feature of modern society—namely, its tendency toward secularity—intelligible in terms of several basic biblical insights. As the title of the essay suggests, I will argue that the process of secularization is described and diagnosed quite accurately using the two categories found in Jesus' parable of the sower: "the worries of this life" and "the deceitfulness of wealth."

In this parable (Mt 13:1-9; Mk 4:1-9; Lk 8:4-8) Jesus likens different responses to his message to the ability of different kinds of soil to support and nurture plant growth. Some soil, of course, is rich and deep and yields an abundant harvest; and other soil is either so hard or so rocky that the seed scattered there cannot germinate or, even if it does, it cannot properly develop root and so becomes subject to drought and disease. Falling intriguingly in between the good and the bad soils, however, there is also another kind of soil that might be good were it not for the fact that it is infested with the seeds of thistles and weeds. Indeed, the problem with this soil is not that it will not support plant growth, but that it supports the growth of too many of the wrong kinds of plants. In his interpretation Jesus tells his disciples that this weed-infested soil signifies those who, while perhaps understanding and believing the gospel message, become so preoccupied with what he terms "the worries of this life and the deceitfulness of wealth" that the gospel is rendered "unfruitful" in them. These are people who have been deceived, either by the sheer number of their concerns or by the lure of wealth, into locating their hopes and aspirations in the wrong places, that is, in the temporal and passing rather than in the eternal and lasting. These are people who are so busy managing and controlling their own lives that the seed of the gospel—which requires a measure of peace and quietness—is prevented from producing its fruit in them. It is to this last kind of soil—or at least the kind of person it is meant to represent—and specifically to "the worries of this life and the deceitfulness of wealth" that I would like to draw attention. The contemporary church, it seems, is full of such people these days (I count myself among them); and, at least in part, this is because the process of secularization in modern societies has led us to focus a great deal of energy on "the worries of this life" and has thus rendered us uniquely susceptible to being deceived in the manner that Jesus suggests. Put differently, the challenge of secularization in contemporary society may not lie so much in the direct threat that secularity poses to religious faith as in the subtle and indirect distraction and diversion of religious faith toward things that ultimately do not matter very much. Thus while the temptation to locate our hopes and aspirations in the wrong places is not new, the process of secularization provides exceptionally strong socio-structural support for focusing our spiritual energies on *temporal* rather than *eternal* matters. To see why this is the case, however, it may be necessary to modify our understanding of just what secularization is.

Secularization

The word "secularization" comes from the Latin *saeculum*, which meant "century" and connoted the temporal over against the eternal. The term "secularization" was apparently first used in negotiating the Peace of Westphalia in the mid-seventeenth century and denoted the transfer of properties from ecclesiastical to "secular" authorities. The word has subsequently been used in Roman Catholic canon law to describe the return to the "world" of a person formerly in clerical orders.[1] In a sociological sense, however, "secularization" does not refer to the explicit promotion of secularity so much as it refers to a process in which religion—at least as it has traditionally been understood—forfeits its place in society, a process in which religious ideas, values, and institutions lose their public status and influence. One author has defined secularization, for example, as "a process through which, starting from the center and moving outward, successive sectors of society and culture have been freed from the decisive influence of religious ideas and institutions."[2] And another author has noted:

> Secularization sums up a strikingly significant aspect of modern life. Unlike previous times, and unlike many non-advanced societies, the warp and woof of social life contains little explicit reference to religion (at least as conventionally defined), and is held together only by rational contract and bureaucratic rules. Christianity, which was in several important respects the midwife of modernity, is forsaken or simply forgotten. The cultural capital it once provided has been squandered and allowed to dwindle into insignificance.[3]

Yet beyond referring to something that happens to religion *from without*, as it were, secularization must also be understood as something that happens to religion *from within*, that is, it must be understood in terms of a subtle shift of emphasis on the part of religious believers themselves away from traditionally "religious" concerns and toward other, largely "secular" matters. In the case of Christians, evidence of this shift of emphasis is given in the fact that the traditional concern for "eternal life" and for salvation *from* this world have given way to the purportedly more relevant concerns *of* "this world." This shift has occurred on a number of levels. At the level of theological reflection, this shift has entailed a more-or-less concerted effort to eliminate traditional notions of transcendence from theology altogether,[4] something evangelical philosopher Bernard Zylstra (following social historian Eric Voegelin) termed "immanentization." Zylstra defined "immanentization" as a kind of absorption of the God of the Bible into the realm of human culture.[5] Within the realm of human culture, then, human creativity and "this-worldly" projects eventually elicit the devotion once reserved only for God and for the coming of his kingdom. At the level of the average believer, on the other hand, the secularization of religion from within may simply involve the seemingly innocent reconceptualization of Christian faith so that it is seen as something to be put to use in the service of "this-worldly" goals like individual success, personal fulfillment, and/or psychological well-being. At either level, this subtle shift of emphasis has the effect of reducing religion to a more-or-less exclusively human affair, and hence it is not difficult to see why such a shift might contribute to the kind of spiritual malaise and fruitlessness mentioned in Jesus' parable of the sower. Indeed, one might even go so far as to say that one of the principal effects of the process of secularization is to insure that the "worries of this life" will be pursued with something approaching religious intensity. And yet this happens in such a way that we hardly even notice it. We hardly even realize how thoroughly our spiritual energies have at first been distracted and then finally co-opted by "this world." The reasons for this have to do with the degree of power and control over our lives that modernity has afforded us, power and control that may be described in terms of a kind of "technological affluence."

Of course, most of us would not characterize ourselves as affluent, and for the most part we assume that the "affluent" and the "wealthy" are a relatively small and privileged elite far removed from our modest and largely middle-class existence. And thus we make the tacit assumption that because we are not "affluent" in this relative sense, we must be immune to the kind of deceit mentioned in Jesus' parable. But such assumptions cannot bear the weight of even a moment's reflection. After all, what is affluence but the ability to control the environment and to realize our projects and aspirations in the face of various kinds of impediments to them? Along this line, we would do well to recall that even the lowliest member of the middle class today possesses a greater ability to control critical elements of his or her own environment than the wealthiest of citizens in Jesus' day. Think, for example, of the availability of modern medical knowledge and technology and the ways in which we have been freed from all manner of diseases and infirmities; or think of our access to modern transportation systems and the ways in which it is now possible for us to traverse the entire planet relatively cheaply and easily; or think of the simple availability of food in modern society, food which has been produced and distributed in such a way as to free most of us from the concerns of subsistence entirely and so has enabled us to focus our energies and talents on innumerable other pursuits. This list could obviously be expanded; but the point to make here is simply that we should not underestimate the degree of material and technological affluence that modernity has afforded us and, more importantly, that we should not underestimate the control over our environment that we have been able to purchase with this affluence. Of course, a number of interesting temptations have come in conjunction with this control, temptations which have a lot to do with the secularization of modern societies.

Tempted Through Technology
One of the temptations that has tended to accompany technological affluence is the simple denial of finitude, a denial which at its extreme finds expression in a kind of tacit denial of the reality of death.[6] Of course, few of us would actually deny the eventuality of our death, but the quality of modern health care tempts us to put off the consideration of this eventuality indefinitely. Dr. Johnson is reported to have said that the prospect of death "wonderfully concentrates the mind." If so, we have become expert in avoiding this sort of mental concentration. To the extent that the consideration of death inevitably moves one to ask religious questions, furthermore, this tacit denial of death is probably also linked to a kind of unconscious avoidance of religion and religious questioning. Time enough, we say, to deal with these questions after our retirement or after we reach seventy, or eighty, etc. In truth, many of us will probably never be old enough to candidly contemplate the significance of the limits that death sets to our earthly existence.

Another temptation that has tended to accompany technological affluence has been that of assuming that all human problems must lend themselves, at least in principle, to humanly calculated solutions. As Peter Berger has observed describing our modern technological outlook:
What previously was experienced as fate now becomes an arena of choices. In principle, there is the assumption that all human problems can be converted into technical problems, and if the techniques to solve certain problems do not as yet exist, then they will have to be invented.

The world becomes ever more "makeable." This view of the world is essentially that of the engineer. First expressed in engineering proper, in the systematic manipulation of nature and of machines, it is carried over into multiple forms of social engineering (including politics), and finally into engineering approaches to the most intimate areas of interpersonal experience (including psychology, qua the engineering of the self).[7]

As Berger's comments indicate, modern technological affluence has had the effect of vastly expanding the range of matters for which we now feel responsible. Even in the context of recent "postmodern" criticism of scientific and technological optimism, the critics themselves still assume *a priori* that the human condition is a problem that it is up to human beings to solve. Indeed, to this end not a few scholars are now proposing that we "engineer" a new religious outlook which will enable us to cope with our universal responsibilities more effectively than did traditional religion. As the authors of the first *Whole Earth Catalogue* put it a number of years ago: "Now that we know we are gods, we might as well get good at it." And so in the language of the parable of the sower, the list of "the worries of this life" has grown quite long for modern people, and it seems to grow longer with each passing day. To suggest that there may actually be limits to what we are capable of accomplishing in this world, however, is to be guilty of "copping out" of our responsibility for solving the pressing problems of human existence; never mind that many of the most pressing of these problems are those we have created while trying to solve other problems. Again, in the language of Jesus' parable of the sower, the thorns have grown particularly thick in modern technological society.

Along similar lines, modern technological affluence has required us to participate in an increasingly complex social order by way of a multiplicity of roles and relationships. As such, we are forced to spend a great deal of time and energy changing roles and moving back and forth between widely discrepant "life-worlds." Researching the effects of modernization on small Middle Eastern villages, Daniel Lerner coined the term "psychic mobility" to describe the mental consequences of this constant change. "Whereas the isolated communities of traditional society functioned well on the basis of a highly constrictive personality," Lerner observed,

the interdependent sectors of modern society require widespread participation. This in turn requires an expansive and adaptive self-system, ready to incorporate new roles and to identify personal values with public issues. This is why modernization of any society has involved the great characterological transformation we call psychic mobility.... The expansion of psychic mobility means that more people now command greater skill in imagining themselves as strange persons in strange situations, places and times than did people in any previous historical epoch. In our time, indeed, the spread of empathy around the world is accelerating. The earlier increase of physical experience through transportation has been multiplied by the spread of *mediated* experience through mass communication.... Radio, film and television climax the evolution set into motion by Gutenberg. The mass media opened to the large masses of mankind the infinite *vicarious* universe.[8]

Of course, it is not difficult to see that the "infinite vicarious universe" of modernity is nothing if it is not distracting. And so our list of "the worries of this life" must also include the construction of our own identities. Given our tacit denial of death, however, this construction need not be concerned—at least not *yet*—with identity in any ultimate sense; and so the construction of self takes on something of a game-like quality in which we try on various identities "for size," as it were, certain that there will always be more time to arrive at who we "really" are.

Now, although there is obviously much more that could be said about the temptations that accompany technological affluence, suffice it here to say that there are a number of peculiar features of modern technological society which make it increasingly plausible for us to locate *all* of our hopes and aspirations in "this world" as opposed to "the world to come"; and that the mental impact of these peculiar features of modernity have had a lot to do with the process of secularization in modern societies. Put differently, while the temptation to "worldliness" is certainly not new, it is provided with an unusually strong socio-structural basis in modern societies. Only the affluent, after all, can "afford" to locate all of their aspirations in "this world." In the context of the tremendous material transformations recent centuries have witnessed, furthermore, it is not terribly surprising that we have been tempted to ascribe a kind of religious legitimacy to our material and technological projects. The net effect of this ascription, however, has been to distract our attention away from traditional religious concerns. Instead of imagining ourselves as pilgrims on a brief sojourn through this "vale of tears," we have grown accustomed to thinking that we are already in possession of God's kingdom and that we are waiting only for a few relatively minor adjustments to be revealed in the *eschaton.*

Yet if the thorny problem of secularization is, in the final analysis, simply a matter of our having been distracted by "the worries of this life" and of our having been deceived by technological affluence, then a number of solutions to this problem begin to suggest themselves fairly readily, solutions which largely have to do with trying to avoid the peculiar distractions of modern life. Along this line we have noted that one of the critical temptations that has accompanied technological affluence has been that of assuming that we are responsible for and capable of solving all of the problems of material existence by means of rational procedures and techniques. But, of course, technologically driven economic growth and the rationalization of human existence have become, just as Max Weber suggested, something of an "iron cage" for us. While we have reaped previously unimaginable material rewards from our engineering of this world, one sometimes wonders if we are not like the rich fool in Jesus' parable (Lk 12:13-21), unaware that "this world" in general and our lives in particular are rapidly passing away. In this context it has become imperative that we rediscover and reassert limits to our responsibilities and projects. Happily, these sorts of limits are actually celebrated in the Scriptures, particularly in the commandment to observe the sabbath.

Sabbath

While it would be naive and perhaps even theologically mistaken to suggest that the simple observance of the sabbath day would solve the problem of secularization, our attempts to work toward a solution to this problem would be aided by what might be called a sabbath *attitude*. This is because a sabbath attitude would enable us to put our problems and our responsibilities in perspective by relativizing them over against God's purposes for us and for his creation. A sabbath attitude, for example, would flatly reject the notion that we create ourselves through our own labor or that we are somehow responsible for inaugurating the kingdom of God by means of our own conscious calculated effort. The sabbath attitude would also flatly reject our preoccupation with the pursuit of *temporary life* at the expense of any consideration of *eternal life*.[9] Instead, such an attitude would affirm the goodness of creatureliness as such, and, by encouraging us to rest in God's provision for us, it would transcend the "iron cage" of rationalized material progress, which, although it is of some instrumental value, cannot ultimately satisfy us. In sum, the sabbath attitude is one that celebrates the notion of limit and the fact that certain boundaries are part and parcel of the created order and so are beyond the scope of our control. As Abraham Joshua Heschel has commented, "The Sabbath is the day on which we learn the art of surpassing civilization."[10] Indeed it appears that our rediscovery of the sabbath and of a sabbath attitude may be the only way of preventing our civilization from surpassing us.

Yet in addition to calling a halt to the seemingly inexorable expansion of the realm of human responsibility, we need to stress that there is one thing for which we probably need to take much more responsibility. As ironic as it sounds, we need to take more responsibility for our *selves*. This point was made quite perceptively by Søren Kierkegaard over a century ago. The "secular mentality," Kierkegaard observed, consisted in attributing infinite worth to objects unworthy of it, and in attributing finite worth to truly infinite objects. With respect to the development of self, Kierkegaard noticed that secular society tempts us to focus a great deal of our time and energy on matters which are merely accidental to our true selves, and to neglect that which is essential to ourselves and our characters. "Surrounded by hordes of men," Kierkegaard wrote,

> absorbed in all sorts of secular matters, more and more shrewd about the ways of the world—such a person forgets himself, forgets his name divinely understood, does not dare to believe in himself, finds it too hazardous to believe in himself and far easier and safer to be like the others, to become a copy, a number, a mass man . . . . In fact, what is called the secular mentality consists simply of such men who, so to speak, mortgage themselves to the world. They use their capacities, amass money, carry on secular enterprises, calculate shrewdly, etc., perhaps make a name in history, but themselves they are not; spiritually speaking, they have no self, no self for whose sake they could venture everything, no self before God—however self-seeking they are otherwise.[11]

Thus in addition to stressing the limits of our responsibilities for the world as such, we may also need to stress, somewhat paradoxically, that we need to take much more responsibility for ourselves individually; for the deceit of worldliness lies precisely in the neglect of matters of infinite importance in favor of those which are finite and rapidly passing away. True spirituality, after all, begins with the recognition of the infinitude of the individual human spirit.

Simplicity

Perhaps most obviously, however, the battle against the "worries of this life and the deceitfulness of wealth" probably needs to be waged by trying to eliminate the number of things we are distracted by in our technologically affluent context. We may, in other words, need to simplify our lives. Of course, along this line we have a lot to learn from our ancestors in faith and particularly from those who have lived in the various traditions of Christian asceticism. The following comments, for example, are attributed to Anthony the Great (d. 356) and appear in the *Philokalia* under the heading "On the Character of Men and On the Virtuous Life":

> Men who are forced by need or circumstance to swim across a great river emerge safely if they are sober and watchful; and even if there are violent currents and they are briefly submerged, they save themselves by grasping the vegetation that grows on the banks. But if they happen to be drunk, then however well trained they may be as swimmers they are overcome by the wine; the current sucks them under and they lose their life. In the same way the soul, finding herself dragged down by the currents of worldly distractions, needs to regain sobriety, awakening from sinful materiality. She should come to know herself: that, though she is divine and immortal, yet to test her God has joined her to a body, shortlived, mortal and subject to many passions. If, drunken with ignorance, indifferent to her true self, not understanding what she is, she lets herself be dragged down by sensual pleasures, she perishes and loses her salvation. For, like the current of a river, the body often drags us down into shameful pleasures.[12]

And so we are reminded that successfully negotiating our way through this life requires a kind of "spiritual sobriety" that is alert to the many dangers and temptations that threaten to submerge our souls in "the currents of worldly distractions." Now, granted that serious questions do need to be raised about Anthony's denigration of materiality as such, it is undoubtedly true that the kind of spiritual sobriety he describes is threatened by material*ism*, or by the preoccupation with purely material matters. This is simply because the logic of desire for material things, at least beyond certain limits, is such that it can never be satisfied. Another one of the Desert Fathers, Neilos the Ascetic (d. 430), is said to have advised his disciples as follows:

> We should remain, then, within the limits imposed by our basic needs and strive with all our power not to exceed them. For once we are carried a little beyond these limits in our desires for the pleasures of this life, there is no criterion by which to check our onward movement, since no bounds can be set to that which exceeds the necessary. Pointless effort and endless labor wasted on what is unnecessary serves only to increase our longing for it, adding more fuel to the flames.[13]

Neilos went on to outline the sorts of absurdities that inevitably result from the attempt to satisfy purely material desires beyond the reasonable limits of need, and in so doing he describes something very much like late-twentieth-century consumer society. And it is certainly true that a good part of our modern industrial economy is based upon the simple insight that human desire for comfort and pleasure has no limit and hence that the market for comfort and pleasure has no limit either. Indeed, our desires are ruthlessly insatiable unless they are directed toward those things for which they were created. Ultimately, of course, this means that we must direct ourselves and our desires toward God in love and trust. As Augustine (d. 430) observed so insightfully, all things "can be occasions of sin because, good though they are, they are of the lowest order of good, and if we are too much tempted by them we abandon those higher and better things, your truth, your law, and you yourself, O Lord our God. For these earthly things, too, can give joy, though not such joy as my God, who made them all, can give."[14] The "worries of this life and the deceitfulness of wealth," in other words, really are like so many thorns and thistles in our lives preventing us, not simply from being fruitful, but also from enjoying fruitfulness.

To reiterate, it appears that the real challenge of secularization in modern society does not lie so much in the direct threat that secularity poses to religious faith as in the indirect distraction and diversion of essentially religious aspirations toward all sorts of things that ultimately do not merit them and cannot satisfy them. The process of secularization makes it increasingly plausible, in other words, for us to focus our faith and hope entirely in "this world" instead of "the world to come," in *temporal* instead of *eternal* existence. The reasons for this, furthermore, are not particularly mysterious, but appear to have to do with the fact that we have been tempted by "technological affluence" to deny our own finitude as well as to exaggerate our own ability to unravel the mysteries of the human condition. By way of attempting to resist becoming further distracted by "worries of this life" and further deceived by wealth, then, I have suggested rediscovering three things: first, a sabbath "attitude" that relativizes our own projects over and against God's salvation project for us; second, a responsibility for ourselves before God that precludes allowing ourselves to be absorbed in purely secular matters; and last, a kind of ascetic discipline of simplicity that will hopefully enable us to avoid wasting valuable time and effort trying to sate the insatiable. These sorts of rediscoveries, then, together form a kind of spiritual equivalent to weeding our gardens, which is something we simply have to do if we want anything worthwhile to grow in them. It is also helpful to recall what Jesus said to his disciples after his encounter with the rich young man (Mt 19:16-26; Mk 10:17-27; Lk 18:18-27). Astonished at Jesus' assertion that it is very hard for the affluent to enter the kingdom of God, his disciples asked him: "Who then can be saved?"

"With man this is impossible," Jesus responded, "but with God all things are possible." I for one am very thankful for this.

Notes

[1]   See Peter L. Berger, *The Sacred Canopy: Elements of a Sociological Theory of Religion* (Garden City, N.Y.: Anchor, 1967) 106ff.

[2]   Os Guinness, *The Gravedigger File: Papers on the Subversion of the Modern Church* (Downers Grove, Ill.: InterVarsity, 1983) 51.

[3]   David Lyon, *The Steeple's Shadow: On the Myths and Realities of Secularization* (Grand Rapids: Eerdmans, 1985) 2.

[4]   "The death of God," Thomas J. J. Altizer wrote, for example, describing the movement of "secular theology" in *The Gospel of Christian Atheism* (Philadelphia: Westminster, 1966) 154, "abolishes transcendence, thereby making possible a new and absolute immanence, an immanence freed from every sign of transcendence."

[5]   Bernard Zylstra, "Marxism and Education: Some Observations," in *The Challenge of Marxist and Neo-Marxist Ideologies for Christian Scholarship* (ed. John C. Vander Stelt; Sioux Center, Iowa: Dordt College Press, 1982) 246.

[6]   See Ernest Becker, *The Denial of Death* (New York: Free Press, 1973).

[7]   Peter L. Berger, *Pyramids of Sacrifice: Political Ethics and Social Change* (Garden City, N.Y.: Anchor, 1976) 20.

[8]   David Lerner, *The Passing of Traditional Society: Modernizing the Middle East* (New York: Free Press, 1958) 51-53.

[9]   Abraham Joshua Heschel, *The Earth Is the Lord's: The Sabbath* (New York: Harper & Row, 1966) 45.

[10] Ibid., 27.

[11] Søren Kierkegaard, *The Sickness unto Death: A Christian Psychological Exposition for Upbuilding and Awakening* (Princeton, N.J.: Princeton University Press, 1980) 33-34, 35.

[12] Nikodimos of the Holy Mountain & Makarios of Corinth (compilers), *The Philokalia: The Complete Text* (trans. and ed. G. E. H. Palmer, Philip Sherrard, & Kallistos Ware; Boston: Faber & Faber, 1979) 350-351.

[13] Ibid., 246.

[14] Augustine, *Confessions*, 2.5 (New York: Penguin, 1961) 48.

18
Constructing a Legitimate Natural Theology

Walter R. Thorson

I PROPOSE TO ARGUE THAT PROPER NATURAL THEOLOGY AND NATural science are distinct activities with a mutual coherence and interdependence. Sound natural theology sustains and informs natural science through influence on scientific presuppositions and motivation; in turn it is educated by scientific understanding toward a deeper appreciation of the rationality and wisdom of God's intentions in creation. The abandonment of natural theology in Christian thought reflects tragic misunderstanding about the needs of natural science as an activity which ultimately *requires* spiritual integrity to remain creative or even truthful. Modern developments in science require a deeper insight into science's own meaning which materialist dogmas hinder, and which Christian faith may liberate—if we know what we are doing.

Natural Theology and Natural Science
Natural theology concerns understanding about God learned from creation—as distinct from God's personal revelation. Its status is ambiguous because the Scriptures consistently teach that true knowledge of God comes by hearing God's Word and responding to it in faith. Yet there are definite assertions in Scripture that understanding *about God* is found in creation,[1] and they deserve thoughtful consideration. They are given deeper meaning by modern scientific discoveries. Natural theology is *not* the same thing as natural science, but a mutual coherence should be recognized between them. Grasping creation's deeper meaning liberates scientific thinking; sound appreciation of scientific truth reveals the depth and rationality of spiritual questions. Both natural science and

natural theology can then have *spiritual integrity.*

Natural theology and *natural science* are not the same thing. The decline of natural theology since 1700 is mostly the result of confusing the two. The confusion arises from medieval misconceptions of natural theology and its purpose, which unfortunately are still quite common. In defense of a literalist interpretation of biblical creation accounts, proponents of "creation science" deny the competence even of astronomy, physics or chemistry to say anything valid about the world's history or development. They claim the Bible makes specific *scientific* statements about the history and nature of the physical world, *and that unbiased scientific study supports these claims.* In the resulting warfare, such "science" has definitely had the worst of it—and truth has been the main casualty on *both* sides.

But today many Christians believe that modern science is legitimate and that many of its findings about the world are true. As a result, they interpret the biblical accounts of creation in other than strictly literalist terms. I believe this approach is valid and consistent with genuine faith, though difficulties remain. I have a close acquaintance with scientific truth. Like Luther, I have a captive conscience—it is obligated to the Word of God, and also to truth about God's creation. Today every one of us—scientist or not—has too much experience of the authority of scientific truth not to let it shape our understanding of reality to some extent. Integrity about this gives God a *proper honor.*

However, people who take this view have often abandoned any notion of natural theology. Biblical teaching about creation's witness to God tends to be read in purely subjective terms—as pointing to an inner experience *based on our faith,* rather than an objective reality manifest in *creation itself.* Logically, this means that creation "speaks" only to the converted, and therefore a *natural* theology is strictly impossible. It means, for example, that Psalm 19 only describes an *existential* response to an interior witness from God's Spirit, one the writer believes human beings everywhere can have. But surely this falls short of what the Scripture is actually saying. Paul affirms that in creation there is a rational witness to God so powerful and direct it requires deliberate suppression to ignore.[2]

A genuine natural theology grows out of genuine natural science. The Scriptures teach that intelligent appreciation of creation *does* yield a witness to God. Of course, it does not require scientific knowledge to be effective. I recall my five-year-old son's reaction to the stars one clear night in the mountains, and have no doubt of the objectivity of that witness to his unfolding mind. But deeper, more rational appreciation of creation should enhance that witness, and there is ample evidence it does. Natural theology will grow as an educated response to scientific understanding, provided we are not led astray by idolatry. Spiritual meaning need not be *imposed* on nature; it has a logic fully compatible with what nature *is*.

Modern science began in this attitude.[35] An understanding that the world's order is rational but contingent is crucial to natural science. Certain misconceptions in medieval thought about God's relation to creation were really vestiges of pagan culture: (1) the assumption of a necessary connection between nature's order and the mind of God, which fosters belief that this order must be explained in theological terms; (2) the assumption that human reason is a direct manifestation of the divine image, rather than a creaturely gift, which encourages belief that knowledge of creation can be given *a priori* by reason. These ideas, which found full expression in medieval rationalism, really came from the Greek pagan philosophers, not from biblical habits of mind. Platonism is an epistemological myth regarding the divinity of human reason; in all Greek philosophy, the world's nature is necessarily linked, *sui generis*, to the divine. The doctrine of God's transcendence, so essential to the meaning of the Incarnation, is foolishness from this viewpoint. Greek church fathers, who understood that Plato and Aristotle were pagans, insisted in the creeds that Jesus Christ is *begotten* of the Father, but that the worlds were *made*; it is a vital distinction, theologically and scientifically.

As long as medieval thinking about nature was controlled by these pagan ideas, it tended to hinder a scientific appreciation of creation. The idea that creation's order is contingent originated as a biblical criticism of medieval rationalism: reason cannot limit the sovereignty and freedom of God in creation. Implications of contingency for the empirical study of nature were more fully grasped after the Reformation. Calvin's understanding that God's relation to man and creation is based on God's grace rather than on rational necessity influenced both the theology of the Reformation and its natural philosophy. Torrance[4] has pointed out that this perspective created greater liberty in explaining natural phenomena and favored a dynamic rather than a static picture of the world's order and forms. Seen as creaturely rather than divine, nature became a legitimate realm for human inquiry. While this "dis-godding of nature" has had its less happy results in a sinful world, it remains a biblical insight. Creation is *authentic*, yet not *autonomous*; it has its own contingent being, yet is a coherent expression of divine intentions. In this understanding lay the seeds of modern science.

The Contribution of Robert Boyle

Robert Boyle understood the aims of natural science more clearly than most of his seventeenth-century contemporaries—and also its limits in relation to a sovereign Creator.[5] In his famous analogy with the Strasbourg clock, he argued that viewing the world as a machine for scientific purposes is really more compatible with a biblical view of God's relation to the world than the organistic concept of nature which it superseded. First, it establishes a transcendent distancing of God from the order of creation, as a maker, in contrast to the immanent generation implied in an organistic model. This distance liberates scientific inquiry; medieval conceptions hindered it by partly deifying nature. Second, analogy with a clock implies inherent limitation in a mechanical description of nature. Boyle's view does not share the denial of intent in nature's order which underlies Ionian atomism and modern materialism. What a clock is cannot be understood from its mechanical structure only, but requires reference to the reasons of its design and purpose; what creation *is* cannot be understood without reference to objective reasons transcending the description of it given by physical science. This is very different from the materialism of Hobbes, who argued the adequacy of mechanical description as giving a complete account of each reality. Boyle did not share Newton's naive theological view that gaps in the physical description of the universe would reveal the *necessary* place for God behind it; he left that as an open question.

We shall see later that Boyle's analogy with the clock offers even more insight regarding natural science and its relation to natural theology—insight Boyle could not himself have shared because science was still in its infancy. But a better grasp of the main points Boyle did make could have avoided most of the destructive warfare between science and a false natural theology which has occurred since. Atheist materialism is a simple fraud. As Hobbes did, it combines Newtonian physics with Ionian atomism and its denial of intention in the world. But a major point of Boyle's analogy is that such a combination is patently unwarranted for a machine; as a creature of our making, a machine is known to have reasons as well as causes. If the fraudulent combination is accepted, "natural theology" has to refute atheism by refuting the adequacy or even the validity of physical science as an account of causal structure, and we get God-of-the-gaps arguments or medievally conceived attempts at "creation science." A second error is to confuse reasons and causes, instead of grasping their coinherence in the real world as Boyle's analogy requires. Much of the bad "natural theology" which blocked early development of biology and geology involved this confusion.[6] There is nothing objectively wrong with interpreting the complex functional design of the eye as an expression of divine intentions, but that does not constitute biological explanation. Yet Darwinism makes the same confusion in reverse, since it assumes without real evidence that mechanical causes somehow create sufficient reasons (the fashionable buzzword for this is now "emergence"). The only physical systems for which we know that causes offer a complete explanation are not machines in the sense intended by Boyle's analogy,[7] which presupposes that the universe is not fully determined by mechanical causation.

We have seen how mistaken notions of natural theology originated in medieval and even pagan ideas, and how Boyle's analogy makes room for natural science and natural theology as distinct activities. But is natural theology needed? To deny its relevance to science implies a split between spiritual and material realities. By abandoning natural theology, we imply that there can be an understanding of creation which needs no spiritual insight to sustain it, that it does not matter what the presuppositions for science are—or even perhaps that these presuppositions must exclude the possibility of transcendence, a priori. The disturbing decay and blindness apparent in the intellectual life of Western culture is a symptom of the wider effects of such belief.[8] Moreover, science itself is a powerful historical testimony to the need for spiritual presuppositions in an intellectual enterprise.

Presuppositions for Science

A poster in my office shows the open ocean and a pair of sea birds flying out toward it. It is titled "The pursuit of truth will set you free even if you never catch up with it." As I take it, this almost-biblical truth applies well to the scientific enterprise, and those who have loved science will understand it. Because they were aware of the spiritual basis for science, Boyle and others like him saw the work of science as an expression of godliness. But we seem to have lost this. Reductionism's claim that the mechanical description of the world is the only reality has not led us to reject scientific truth, but may have shaken our confidence that it needs a basis in deeper spiritual truths. Science is an expression of human creativity, but its focus is what the Lord has made, not our own making, and its aim is true "under-standing." Hence there must be harmony between the hand and the eye, metaphorically speaking—between the doing of an enterprise and the subsidiary contextual field which guides it, oversees it, and gives it meaning. The presuppositions of science are tacit beliefs which form its working context: they indirectly define its methods and its proper subject matter, and provide motivation to sustain it. Not to realize that these presuppositions exist, and that science is both limited and sustained by them, is a serious error which could cause the enterprise to founder in the long run. A sound natural theology sustains scientific creativity by its tacit influence on presuppositions.

The character and development of scientific paradigms depends on the adequacy of the supporting presuppositions. A less appreciated negative consequence of the Enlightenment's worship of a mechanist worldview is the extent to which the Newtonian model became axiomatic to the nature of scientific explanation in the century after. I cannot tell the detailed story here, but the fundamental discoveries of Michael Faraday about electromagnetic fields and their theoretical formulation by James Clerk Maxwell in the famous equations named after him involved a rejection of the entire Newtonian paradigm.[9] As Einstein pointed out later, Maxwell's work contains the essential conceptual change needed for the theory of relativity—and also for the modern paradigms of theoretical physics, based on sophisticated mathematical invariances. Yet Maxwell's colleague William Thomson (later Lord Kelvin) accused him of "mysticism" because he had abandoned the Newtonian model, and Maxwell himself was deeply troubled at first by its irrelevance for the new theory. Maxwell left us some clues about his freedom in theoretical innovation. His remarks reveal both the effect of presuppositions in science and the direct influence of his sincere Christian faith: *the forms which physical theory may take are open to great novelty since their only obligation is to conform to the reality and inner coherence of what God has freely created.* The Creator's sovereignty implies contingency in nature, and hence the models used to describe it may depend on a much broader context of presuppositions than those provided by current scientific knowledge itself.

God and Transcendence

Is there an objective witness to God in creation? Recent developments in physics have led to a remarkably coherent "unification" of fundamental physical laws, and to some surprising conclusions concerning the physical universe.[10] A consistent interpretation of many bits of accumulated evidence about the history of the universe is emerging, and it is a disturbing one for old-time materialist religion. The universe seems to have originated in a singularity involving an enormous outburst of light. While a possible relation of the "Big Bang" picture to the opening words of Genesis should be taken seriously, we should not let the apparent congruence become axiomatic to our thinking about creation—any more than the Newtonian world-model should have become axiomatic in earlier times. What is relevant to natural theology is the intense speculation generated by this cosmological picture. A great flux of books by physicists and astronomers about it has appeared in the past decade.[11] Apparently, something needs explanation; somehow, people did not expect this odd outcome from the program of Newton and Boyle! My point is simple: current fascination with cosmology is the evidence of an objective witness in the physical facts to a transcendent meaning. "There is no speech or language where their voice is not heard"; how people *interpret* what they hear depends on their spiritual state.[12]

This fascination is, however, in one way misguided. Why do people think that a search for tokens of the Creator must focus on cosmology, as if that is where God's interest and intentions should be expressed? Biblical perspective is different: he made the stars also. These remote things in all their strangeness are yet not the most interesting in creation, and they have less to do with the glory of God than the simplest flower. Biblical language is carefully measured on this subject: The heavens declare the glory of God, the firmament shows his handiwork—but God's glory is not found in the heavens. I suggest that the use of the auditory metaphor for this most visual of all experiences is deliberately intended to play down its importance as communication about God. Psalm 19 begins by affirming an objective witness to God in the cosmological frame, but deliberately moves away from it to a different focus—the nearness of God to the human condition. The focus of the Bible is not scientific; but if we have a scientific interest, and if questions of natural theology are prompted by it, then the Scriptures direct our thinking away from an undue fascination with cosmology. The strong-est evidences to God are not found there, but closer to home.

Psalm 8 takes the next step:

O LORD, our Lord, how majestic is your name in all the earth! You have set your glory above the heavens. From the lips of children and infants you have ordained praise.... When I consider your heavens, the work of your fingers, the moon and the stars, which you have set in place, what is man that you are mindful of him, or the son of man that you care for him?

What is communicated here? (1) God's glory is *above*, or *beyond*, the heavens, a common Old Testament usage denoting God's transcendence; (2) divine excellence is *evidenced* on earth; (3) humanity is not insignifi-cant, but precisely the opposite—the contact with transcendence centers in human beings, since God is concerned with them. I propose we take this seriously, as a program for natural theology.

Four centuries of physical science began with the study of the heavens, and modern cosmology seems to be a kind of culmination of this study. The belief that the starry heavens above are no more divine than the earth beneath our feet was important to the development of physics; the same contingent order rules both. Physical science made progress when men stopped believing that the celestial spheres are the locus of transcendence in our universe. Boyle recognized that transcendence has a different relation to us. He shifted the boundary of the transcendent from the physical world to the limits of a discourse. He argued that creation's witness to transcendence comes from the context of meaning that surrounds and sustains scientific knowledge. There is nothing wrong with Boyle's view. Its power is evidenced by the fuss over the implications of cosmological theory in the past decade. However, its logic can be developed further. Reductionism is the *denial* of transcendence; if this is wrong, then we should ask where stronger objective evidence for a transcendent reality is to be found, so that reductionism would be shown to be the absurdity it is. I suggest the search must focus on the study of life, and of the human being—and in particular, on the logic of the discourse we must use to make these realities intelligible. As we try to study life and then consciousness and intelligence *scientifically*, would it really be surprising to find that changes in the nature and presuppositions of such science must also occur, and that these changes raise the questions of natural theology even more powerfully?

Scientific Explanation

The kind of natural science established by Boyle's "mechanical philosophy" has been immensely successful. While we must leave the question open, just as Boyle did, there seems little reason so far to expect that we will turn up gaps in the machine picture as evidence of transcendence.[13] Within the limits of measurement, each physical description is a physical description, and seems to obey the laws of physics, so far as we can test them critically. The mechanical model *works*, in ways unanticipated by its pioneers, right down to the delicate chemistry of living things, so that we know with increasing detail what the complex structure of even the human brain and body are like, and in some cases can directly link diseases to the molecular species that cause them or are produced by them. However, the critical question is whether such description adequately *explains* the objective realities manifested in life and intelligent behavior. There are organizing principles which control the function of living things, and these can be studied at a molecular level; but it is quite another question whether we understand them logically.

Obviously, the laws of physics form a necessary structural base for the operation of such functional principles; but are they sufficient to account for them? Reductionism requires a positive answer to this question. Its basic thesis is simple: *Physics + time + chance = life.* As a scientist, I prefer to remain agnostic about this thesis. What we do know, more or less, is that life on this planet has emerged in some unfolding process, and, structurally at least, there is a good deal of evidence for the idea that different kinds of living things are related to each other in that unfolding. But we have almost no idea what made the unfolding occur, or precisely how the innovative aspects which appear so suddenly in successive orders of living things were created. The hypothesis of evolution has proved helpful to biology because it raised in at least a primitive form the legitimate *scientific* problem posed by evidence of a process in life's unfolding. What is not helpful is to ignore or deny the possibility that solution of the problem may involve new concepts. Darwinism's insistence that the process is adequately explained by mechanics plus chance variation is just a religious belief—and a rather unconvincing one, if one looks at the evidence available. In the thesis of reductionism, *time* and *chance* are mere speculation. Scientifically they constitute an admission of gross ignorance, and philosophically an unedifying display of unwarrantable dogmatic belief.

What are the alternatives? We cannot solve the scientific problem of evolution by saying "God did it"—that's theology. In fact, to offer this answer to the scientific question is to accept a reductionist definition of science as correct—and abandon the goal of scientific explanation. This is not the choice of spiritual integrity; creation's secrets are there for us to study. The proper answer is to recognize as Maxwell did that the presuppositions of science are responsible to the coherence and order manifested by the contingent reality of creation, and not to dogmas based on past scientific presuppositions.

Functional Logic
There are unmistakable developments in modern science indicating that we are going to have to shift Boyle's boundary between the transcendent and the non-transcendent again; and Boyle's clock indicates the sort of shift we must make. To understand any machine as a machine, we must grasp not merely the structural principles which it employs, but the functional principles which it embodies. These belong logically to a different sort of discourse than the structural principles do. Although structural principles form a substratum upon which functional logic relies, that logic is neither generated from nor completely determined by them. Its criteria of meaning are derived from the achievement of a

certain goal, not from the statement of necessary relations; and the notion of a successful achievement implies the existence of rules of rightness by which success or failure are judged. In his analogy with the clock, Boyle was content to leave issues of functional logic in the domain where transcendence is acknowledged, and outside the domain of natural science. He had no need to do otherwise. For the purposes of physics, such issues are irrelevant, since physical science is *par excellence* the science of structure and causal relation; hence the idea of shifting functional logic to the domain of non-transcendence never occurred to Boyle.

But today we have scientific reasons to do this. We have isolated the structural units at the heart of the self-reproductive capability of living things, and we cannot make them intelligible without appealing to functional logic. In the thirty years since DNA/RNA base-pair sequencing and its relation to genetic information and biological development was discovered, I have never heard a talk or read an article which did not explain it by analogy with the communication of sequenced information in a digital computer. But a digital computer is a machine embodying functional logic toward achievement of certain logical tasks; and the meaning to which such analogy refers is not the structure which such a machine employs, but the logic of information processing it performs. Manipulation of genetic material in research is guided not merely by the necessary understanding of its structure, but by the belief that strands of material with sufficient complexity retain functional integrity—and understanding that function is the object of such research. Functional logic is alive and well and living quietly in molecular biology! I believe it is an open scientific question whether we might learn at a logical level what the internal "rules of rightness" governing biological systems are, and how these rules are embodied in the physical structure. It is also an open question whether this logic "emerges" from physics, and if so, how. I am agnostic about it, but tend to favor the view that physical structure will *not* account for the functional rules in the long run. To introduce reductionist dogma into the problem now is simply repressive. Yet that is precisely what most evolutionists insist on doing with the origin of life. They have not been very successful with it so far.

Functional logic is more openly recognized in current developments in the field of intelligence simulation, or "cognitive science."[14] The presuppositions of work in this field are more open because the functions to be explained (and perhaps simulated by a machine) are the workings of our own intelligence. At present the primary impetus in the field is technological: can we design mechanical systems which perform the same feats we do? Perhaps the most interesting problem is under-standing the remarkable ability of human intelligence to transcend a problem's structural context in assessing its functional meaning. Com-puter simulations have to represent functional elements as symbols and manipulate them structurally; it is not clear whether the brain does the same. It is now widely recognized that both functional and structural logic are necessary elements in any intelligence simulation program, even at very primitive levels. Notions of achievement and problem solution in terms of ends (rather than of means only) play a healthy part in the conceptualization of research. Even more interesting from a philosophical standpoint are studies of computer systems which selec-tively alter algorithms performing certain tasks by regard to their success (measured by standards of speed, absence of error, etc.). In this way a concept like natural selection can be explored functionally. However, I am not interested in whether the analogy to living systems is fully valid or not; I am very interested in the fact that it appears to be regarded as legitimate scientific thinking.

Natural Theology Reappears

One of the hazards of making such a transition in the presuppositions of science is the tendency to misunderstanding it involves. We saw that even the sort of paradigm shift involved in Maxwell's electromagnetic theory brought forth the accusation of "mysticism." When physics began, many people stuck dogmatically to the older view that somehow it interferes with the prerogatives of God regarding the heavens to account for their motion with mechanics; it took a long while to understand that a discourse making no reference to God directly can be both useful and true, and that it does not threaten God's sovereignty as Creator. In the same way, many people today cannot discuss functional logic without slipping into metaphysical language. Some do so because they are not interested in the scientific problems such logic addresses, but in its underlying presuppositions—i.e., they confuse science with natural theology. However, reductionists have the same sort of problem, since their religious dogmas are also threatened by such a science. This is inevitable as long as one insists on defining science as truth derivable from physics alone. Accusations of vitalism or mysticism may be ex-pected. Only after the achievements of a new science have become more fully manifest does diehard opposition to it cease.

However, we must also understand Boyle's insight that shifting the boundary between the non-transcendent and the transcendent does not eliminate transcendence. The questions of natural theology can only intensify, because the presuppositions of a science based on functional logic have to be more open to theological options than those needed to support physics. If such a change in science does develop and prosper, the claim that life is "the result of blind chance" will become a great deal less credible than people now find it. That nature's order is in some way intended (or "programmed") could become more acceptable as a worldview, though not necessarily a biblical one. Evolutionism can still preserve its mindset and program by going pantheist; it is in the process of doing so already. It is my own belief that the closer we get to a genuine scientific study of humans as intelligent, conscious beings, the more open our categories of intelligibility and explanation will necessarily become to biblical habits of mind. In that sense, natural theology not only flourishes in the soil of scientific work, but *sustains* science and ultimately gives it meaning as a rational appreciation of God's creative intentions. The only other meanings we seem able to give science so far have all turned out to be idolatrous.

In this essay I have tried to sketch how a legitimate natural theology can be properly related to a legitimate natural science in a positive relationship. Such an ideal picture takes no account of the problem of sin in human history, and it must be seriously questioned whether our present culture is up to the spiritual challenge of handling truth with the integrity required—especially in view of what is now happening to spiritual, moral and intellectual life. But this does not change our calling. Christians of all people have the best reason to toil and strive for truth, because "we have put our hope in the living God, who is the Savior of all men, and especially of those who believe" (1Ti 4:10).

Notes

1 Useful lessons about natural theology (good and bad) may be seen in its interaction with natural science. Citations below are a sample:
(a) Ian Barbour, *Issues in Science and Religion* (New York: Prentice-Hall, 1966; paperback ed., New York: Harper Torchbook, 1971) esp. chap. 2-5, 8.
(b) Colin Russell, *Cross-currents: Interactions Between Science and Faith* (Leicester, U.K.: Inter-Varsity, 1985) esp. chap. 4-8.
(c) H. Nebelsick, *Circles of God: Theology and Science from the Greeks to Copernicus* (Edinburgh: Scottish Academic Press, 1985).
2 Ro 1:18-23.
3 R. Hooykaas, *Religion and the Rise of Modern Science* (Edinburgh: Scottish Academic Press, 1972); see also ref. 1(b).
4 T. F. Torrance, *Theology in Reconstruction* (London: SCM, 1965; repr. in paperback ed., Grand Rapids: Eerdmans, 1975) esp. chap. 2-5.
5 Insight into Boyle's thinking and citations of his works are given by Eugene M. Klaaren, *Religious Origins of Modern Science* (Grand Rapids: Eerdmans, 1977) chap. 4 & 5; see also Hooykaas [ref. 3] and Russell [ref. 1(b)].
6 Some appreciation of the negative influence of "natural theology" on biology/geology

can be found in Barbour [ref. 1(a)] and Russell [ref. 1(b)]; but see also Peter J. Bowler, *Evolution: The History of an Idea* (Berkeley: University of California Press, 1984).

[7] Two simple examples of systems where we know causes offer complete explanation are (a) order in a crystalline structure, which can be deduced as the necessary consequence of minimizing the total energy of the aggregate system; (b) equilibrium thermodynamic properties of a gas, which can be fully derived using statistical analysis of the physical interactions. These are quite obviously *not* machines. More moot examples are the complex self-ordering behavior of systems far from equilibrium, now being studied by nonlinear dynamics; in these cases, though behavior is extremely complex and even chaotic in a technical sense, it is explained fully by the laws of mechanics. A revealing name for such systems is "dissipative structures," which indicates a function (dissipation of energy or other physical properties along a gradient); in what sense is such a system a machine? Some scientists propose that these systems are prototypes of life, since they arise spontaneously and are self-sustaining given boundary conditions establishing relevant physical gradients; but this is only conjecture. Boyle's choice of the clock as the paradigm of a machine shows that the idea of functions not fully determined by causal relations is an essential point in his analogy.

[8] A distorted view of science as an impersonal, autonomous knowledge has been projected by positivist tradition. It has powerfully eroded all sense of values, purpose or meaning in Western culture and fosters attitudes inimical to freedom at every level. Michael Polanyi's efforts to develop an epistemology of personal knowledge were motivated by his recognition of this spiritual disaster. See Michael Polanyi, *Personal Knowledge: Towards a Post-Critical Philosophy* (London: Routledge & Kegan Paul, 1958; paperback ed., New York: Harper Torchbooks, 1975). A superbly readable book for non-scientists, explaining the relevance of Polanyi's epistemological ideas to our cultural crisis, is Drusilla Scott's *Everyman Revived: The Common Sense of Michael Polanyi* (Lewes, U.K.: Book Guild, 1985).

[9] For an appreciation of Maxwell's work from a philosophical standpoint, see James Clerk Maxwell, *A Dynamical Theory of the Electromagnetic Field* (ed. T. F. Torrance; Edinburgh: Scottish Academic Press, 1982). This work includes a reprint of Einstein's tribute to Maxwell's work, and an introduction by Professor Torrance commenting on the relation of Maxwell's work to the history of science. See also the essay "Christian Faith and Physical Science in the Thought of James Clerk Maxwell" in T. F. Torrance, *Transformation and Convergence in the Frame of Knowledge* (Belfast: Christian Journals, 1984).

[10] Though the conclusions of cosmological studies are undoubtedly more speculative than those tested routinely in laboratory experiments, the subject matter and goals of the observational sciences such as astronomy, geology and paleontology are clearly scientific. It is a mistake—and encourages regression to the medieval view of natural theology and natural science—to adopt the notion of a radical *category* difference between "operation science" and "origin science" as proposed for example by Norman L. Geisler and J. Kerby Anderson, *Origin Science* (Grand Rapids: Baker, 1987).

[11] The following brief list of citations is only representative:

(a) Robert Jastrow, *God and the Astronomers* (New York: W. W. Norton, 1978).

(b) P. C. W. Davies, *God and the New Physics* (New York: Simon & Schuster/Touchstone, 1984); see also *The Cosmic Blueprint* (New York: Simon & Schuster/Touchstone, 1988).

(c) Steven Weinberg, *The First Three Minutes* (New York: Basic Books, 1977).

(d) Stephen Hawking, *A Brief History of Time: From the Big Bang to Black Holes* (New York: Bantam, 1988).

(e) J. D. Barrow & F. J. Tipler, *The Anthropic Cosmological Principle* (Oxford: Oxford University Press, 1986).

[12] Jn 12:27-30.

[13] A possible qualification of this view lies in the problems raised by the interpretation of quantum mechanics. Physics has always assumed that an isolated chunk of material reality has a perfectly definite state of being and that such a state can be characterized by assignable and definite "measurables." Quantum mechanics, while not interfering with

the more mundane and classical consequences of this notion on a large scale, has forced us to recognize that such ideas have limits; these limits are essentially epistemological since they deal primarily with what we can know about the world through physical observations, rather than with what the world actually is.

[14] Three works I have found stimulating and helpful in giving a general view of this field are the following:

(a) Joseph Weizenbaum, *Computer Power and Human Reason: From Judgment to Calculation* (San Francisco: W. H. Freeman, 1976).

(b) David E. Goldberg, *Genetic Algorithms in Search, Optimization and Machine Learning* (Reading, Mass.: Addison-Wesley, 1989).

(c) Hubert L. Dreyfus, *What Computers Can't Do: A Critique of Artificial Reason* (New York: Harper & Row, 1972).

19
Spiritual Formation and Theological Education

Walter L. Liefeld &
Linda M. Cannell

IS IT MERELY AN ABERRATION FOR MATURE STUDENTS TO FEEL THAT they do not need God in seminary? Is it strange to hear students commenting on how dry their spiritual lives have become while in seminary? Is it surprising that one professor responded to a proposal to introduce a course on spiritual formation into the curriculum with the question, "But how can we grade prayer?" Even with a charitable allowance for humor, that remark can serve as a reminder of the frustrations that may accompany attempts to include spiritual formation in the curriculum of theological education.

Educating Pastors
In the early centuries of the Christian church, the primary focus of the education of the priest or pastor was on spiritual or character formation. Carl Volz observed that this emphasis is hardly surprising, since the Christian church, even today, values the ideals of spirituality. However: "What appears unique to the earlier times of the church ... is the high valuation placed upon the character, rather than the skills, of the pastor."[1] Chrysostom warned against using the spiritual disciplines as a pious escape from the duties of the pastoral office; but the warnings, given as a corrective, did not obscure the fact that the early church fathers and mothers were concerned that persons not assume the clerical office if they "lacked the necessary spiritual maturity, even though they may possess knowledge and skills. On balance the primary qualification

for ordination in antiquity was to possess the desire for God."[2]

The dominant structure of many seminaries today, however, tends to favor academic instruction, tolerate the practical, and compartmentalize the spiritual. For many years, some administrators and faculty have been searching for ways to integrate the theoretical and practical disciplines. In recent years, the question of how to include spiritual formation has been brought into the discussion. However, effective integration of the three aspects has seldom been achieved in the evangelical Protestant seminary. The common academic pattern, drawn from the university model, continues to be departmentalization with further specialization within those departments.

The reasons for the fragmentation and isolation of the disciplines have been a subject of concern in the literature for several years. Leclercq expressed his concerns about spirituality in his comparison of the scholastic method and monastic spirituality.[3] Though Leclercq's purpose was to compare monastic and scholastic methodology, it was not his intention to discredit the scholastic method. He does, however, distinguish between the scholastic method (which is oriented primarily toward learning) and the monastic method (which is oriented primarily toward spirituality).[4] Both orientations are legitimate. However, there is increasing concern that the scholastic method, further shaped by the Enlightenment, and influenced by American educational systems, has become dominant in the theological school; and that the study of theology has become a science supporting the profession of the ministry.

Farley[5] attributed this situation to the fragmentation of a formerly unified view of theology. He described the shifts in theological education which have led to the present situation where theology (or *theologia*, sapiential knowledge) as a unitary discipline is largely absent. Theology has diversified into practical ministry skills and an aggregate of disciplines which tends to emphasize the cognitive over the spiritual.

Whatever the causes of the current situation, and however we might assess it, we are left with some basic questions about spirituality itself. What is spirituality? What is the relation of spirituality to spiritual growth, to doctrinal maturity, to daily obedience? Why do so many students feel they "lost their spirituality" in seminary? Why do some students claim that even the biblical and theological courses had a negative effect on their spiritual vitality? If these feelings are valid, where does the responsibility lie for such failure? There are, at least, five possibilities: (1) The teaching faculty may have failed to integrate the subject matter with spiritual instruction and encouragement. (2) The administration and faculty may have failed to provide a healthy environment and comprehensive instruction in spirituality. (3) The student may have failed to use the opportunities offered him or her. (4) The church may have failed to supplement the student's academic experience with a healthy environment of worship and spiritual teaching. (5) Those who had nurtured the student spiritually prior to her or his entrance into seminary may have failed to continue their support in prayer.

What Is Spirituality?

If spirituality is to be fostered, it would seem that we need first to agree on a basic definition of spirituality. But, like gossamer, the meaning of this word is fragile and dissolves in our hands even as we grasp for it. As Tilden Edwards reminds us, "No dimension of theological education is more frustrating to define intellectually than the spiritual."[6] However, if an academic faculty is to provide those aspects of biblical and doctrinal knowledge, along with an environment and modelling that will facilitate spirituality, some understanding of the meaning of spirituality is necessary and the reasons for any definition must be clear. The following is offered *toward* a definition of spirituality.

(1) Any definition of spirituality must begin with the vertical axis of our relationship with God. This needs to be highlighted. Much of the literature seems to assume it tacitly or buries it within a complex of many spiritual ideals. Much of the present "spiritual" tide in North America, especially that which majors on self-actualization, leaves the concept of the divine undefined. Even where God is identified, some of the biblical requirements for a relationship are left unspecified. Can a biblical definition of spirituality omit such elements as personal holiness, trust, obedience, and growth in the knowledge of God? It is especially imperative in a school of divinity that one's concept of spirituality be integrated with *theology*, though it must be understood that right theology does not equal spirituality.

(2) There is a tendency to bring our own preferred spiritual ideals and disciplines into our assumptions about the meaning of spirituality. Thus we may confuse mere tranquillity on the one hand, or a practice like meditation on the other, with spirituality itself. Spirituality is indeed a matter of the spirit, but not all peace or inward reflection is biblical spirituality, nor is all asceticism. But at the same time, such aspiration and discipline is not contrary to true spirituality as has sometimes been thought. The typical Protestant uneasiness with medieval asceticism and spiritual disciplines should not be allowed to rule out helpful spiritual practices.

Lovelace observed that Luther and Calvin reacted against Western

Catholic spirituality because Catholics believed they were being justified only as they were being sanctified.[7] This led to a spirituality which
required a progression to perfection through spiritual exercises. Because
of this reaction, Luther and Calvin may have gone to an extreme in
avoiding the use of spiritual exercises for spiritual growth. Lovelace
believes that "the new interest in spiritual disciplines shows that we are
trying to recover balance."[8] While a definition of spirituality need not
include the means toward that end, neither should it exclude spiritual
disciplines if means are included. Above all, prayer must not be excluded,
for in its true use, prayer is not mere exercise but is communion with
God, and is right at the heart of spirituality.

(3) In many quarters, the idea popular some decades ago that the truly
spiritual person avoided certain activities (e.g., dancing and movie-
going) has been replaced with a more healthy perspective. It is increasingly recognized that mature exercise of freedom is itself a mark of
spiritual maturity. Still, a person who desires intensely to be spiritual can
all too easily transform ideals into rules, so any definition of spirituality
should be cautious about specifying behavioral requirements.

(4) Although we may think of spirituality as ethereal, it does not exist
in the realm of pure spirit. We do not hold the negative pagan Hellenistic
view of the body. Therefore, spirituality must be truly incarnational and
involve the presentation of our bodies to God (Ro 12:1). One cannot
object to the "mortification of the flesh," if we understand that to mean
the crucifixion of sinful desires. But the body that God created is not
to be regarded as irrelevant or detrimental to the life of the spirit; rather,
spirituality must be exercised *in* the body; it must be "incarnational."
Jesus did this, and those who practice the "imitation of Christ" do so in
a body like his. Likewise, students of theology must realize that using
our minds to discern God's will is an appropriate expression of
incarnational spirituality, as the second verse in Romans 12 makes clear.

(5) While spirituality is based on a loving relationship with God, the
first great commandment about that love is immediately followed by
the second commandment about loving one's neighbor. Unless one is in
forced isolation, one's spirituality will be expressed in social relationships and, we might suppose, also in social justice. Can an explanation of
spirituality that is to be relevant to those who serve God in this world
overlook this factor?

(6) The very term "spirituality" implies some connection with the
Holy Spirit. Lewis S. Chafer wrote his book *He That Is Spiritual*[9] on that
premise. Can a proper definition of spirituality be offered without
taking Paul's injunction in Ephesians 5 to "be filled with the Spirit" into

account? Surely not.

(7) Scripture must be the basis for spirituality. We cannot let extraneous unbiblical ideas control or modify our understanding of spiritual life. At the same time, though, we must not imagine that spirituality is mere knowledge of Scripture.

By now it is apparent that a "definition" that is at once concise and comprehensive is virtually impossible. *Understanding* what constitutes spirituality is a more attainable goal than *defining* it. The fact that spirituality is a complex matter should also alert theological educators to the fact that a "spiritual life week," morning prayers, Compline at evening, daily chapel, retreats, disciplines, prayer before class and so forth do not in themselves guarantee spiritual formation in students (or faculty, for that matter).

This complexity in understanding and in seeking a definition is not unique to the contemporary situation. The term "spirituality" and its equivalents have been used in different ways over time. Following the New Testament use of "spiritual," from the patristic period to the eleventh century, the focus in spirituality-talk was on life in the Spirit. From the twelfth to the sixteenth centuries, the meaning shifted to designate that which was ecclesiastical as opposed to "worldly." The focus of the idea on the interior life re-surfaced in the seventeenth century, leading to debates into the eighteenth century as to whether or not all Christians could experience the mystical life.[10] The Puritans and Pietists added the requirement of works to spirituality in order to avoid "cheap grace." The leaders of the First and Second Great Awakenings conceived of a spirituality that "involved waiting on God in corporate prayer for Pentecostal outpourings of the Holy Spirit to energize the church and form it into troop movements assaulting the kingdom of darkness."[11] Spirituality, as it developed through this period, had a distinct social conscience. The nineteenth century emphasis broadened to include the experiential or practical dimensions, and in the early twentieth century the Pentecostal movement added the conviction that every believer can possess supernatural gifts.

Through the twentieth century, spirituality has come to be understood as "the integration of all aspects of human life and experience,"[12] a much broader understanding than that of the earlier "spiritual theology" which focussed on the interior, holy life.

Based on all the above suggestions and observations, we propose the following as a definition constructed especially with the goal of spiritual formation in a theological institution in mind:

Spirituality is a growing desire to know, love and please God that is being actively fostered in the power of the Holy Spirit through prayer and other appropriate disciplines and is actualized in an obedient life that expresses the love of God to others in their own spiritual and social needs.

The Study of Spirituality
Through the early 1970s and into the 1980s, various conferences were convened to study spiritual formation.

The Executive Committee of the Association of Theological Schools appointed and funded a Task Force to prepare a report on Spiritual Development to be presented to the 1972 biennial meeting.[13] Subsequent to this work, the A.T.S. was given funding to begin a two-year project (1979-1980) to prepare faculty, clergy and lay leaders as spiritual mentors and to study the issue of spiritual formation.[14] Questionnaires sent to faculty participants in advance of the conferences[15] revealed two major areas of concern: (1) how can they develop, model and guide others in the spiritual life, and (2) how can they initiate a process of spiritual formation. Most faculty indicated that their seminary had not developed a clear set of practices and assumptions in this area. Several observed that many students are still in the process of working out their religious commitment and are coming to the seminary with little faith formation.[16]

One of the outcomes of this project was a sense of what was stimulating the need for spiritual formation in the seminary: (1) there is a lack of spiritual formation in the backgrounds of entering students; (2) students are searching for guidance to help them discern how the Spirit is working in their situation; (3) greater contact with other religious traditions has created a sharper awareness of spirituality; (4) there has been a re-discovery of the Christian contemplative tradition; (5) the experiential component in American Christian church history increases concern for spiritual formation; (6) the presence of women in formerly all-male student bodies and faculty has added a new spirit to the theological school—one that is arguably more conducive to spiritual formation; (7) social and political crisis has motivated concern for the spiritual; and (8) increasing concern is felt over a fragmented curriculum with no integrating center. Spiritual formation, it is felt, could provide that center.[17]

In 1987, the Programme of Theological Education sponsored yet another conference on spiritual formation involving twenty-one persons (students, teachers, pastors and administrators). Samuel Amirtham, the director of the Programme, prepared a report of their discussions and extended an invitation to participate in the ongoing dialogue.[18] The report repeats the theme that spirituality is looked upon with suspicion in the academic community, questions whether teachers of theology are able to promote spiritual formation and asks, if not, what kinds of training for faculty will be required.[19]

The interest expressed through the conferences suggests that spiritual formation is a matter of increasing concern in theological schools. Among these, the seminaries of the Catholic Church have a tradition of spiritual formation and include spiritual formation as part of seminary education.[20] The Mundelein Seminary (Mundelein, Illinois) is concerned with the task of developing priests who will "live and work and pray with and among the people in parish ministry."[21] Because of the demands of this ministry, the Spiritual Formation Program is an integral part of the curriculum and is designed to address the seminarians at several levels.

The seminary is convinced that spiritual formation needs to be organized. However, it recognizes that "organized programs of spiritual formation do not equal spiritual formation . . . the process of spiritual formation is not contained in a particular program structure . . . . The Spirit gives growth and increase."[22]

Programs of spiritual formation are not as common in Protestant seminaries. The evangelical Protestant seminary does not welcome easily an emphasis on spiritual formation, nor, by and large, has it ever done so. Perhaps a reason for this can be traced to a belief that the church is the proper environment for spiritual formation. Cognitive instruction is thought of as the province of the seminary, with spiritual formation happening implicitly and informally.

In the fall of 1983, Perkins School of Theology (United Methodist) incorporated spiritual formation as a curricular requirement. The pattern of John Wesley's "class meeting" was used as the model for the program. The review of this program in *The Christian Century*[23] recorded that (1) some faculty and students expressed strong misgivings about the program in an academic community; (2) others objected that the format was too rudimentary for a graduate school of theology; (3) some felt that the need to involve a large number of the campus community was burdensome and inefficient. Encouragement to continue the program came, however, from several leaders and students. The "rudimentary exercises" brought a freshness to faith; the dynamics of the small groups provided a supportive environment for students during their first year; the sense of shared pilgrimage was felt to be valuable for future ministry.

Spiritual formation is still part of the curriculum at the school and is required of all M.Div., M.R.E. and M.S.M. students. The current coordinator indicates that now there is more variety in the program and the format is more flexible than was the original Wesley-style format.

In 1991, one faculty member from each of nine different seminaries in the Chicago area was interviewed to determine the issues and problems involved in the development of spiritual formation.[24] Six Protestant seminaries were involved in this study.

All the Protestant seminaries offered elective courses in spirituality. Nearby Catholic resources were used for several of the electives.[25] Only one Protestant seminary required participation in a small group experience. Two other Protestant seminaries had optional groups for this purpose.[26] Three Protestant seminaries encouraged spiritual direction. One of the three used spiritual directors from a nearby Catholic seminary. Several seminaries in the area, including Catholic, Anglican, liberal Protestant and evangelical Protestant, have offered a joint, annual spiritual life course. Two Protestant seminaries scheduled important retreat times for the purpose of spiritual formation. Only one of these seminaries required attendance. Instruction in spirituality was limited in the Protestant seminaries; all of it was optional.

This limited study seems to support an impression that spiritual formation at Protestant seminaries is generally *ad hoc,* and is introduced only when one or two interested faculty members begin to offer elective courses and encourage optional group experiences. Resistance to spiritual formation centers around the concerns that the church is the proper environment for spiritual formation, that legalism will eventually characterize programs of spiritual formation, and that the spiritual environment of the seminary is healthy enough without such programs.

Eugene Peterson, speaking at a seminary faculty retreat, has observed that a separate program of spiritual formation may not be as appropriate as an understanding that all faculty are to act as "spiritual directors." We easily abandon the personal responsibility we all have as models and "pastors" to our own students when spiritual formation is structured and assigned to some professional. This only confirms in the student's mind an elitist view of ministry and reduces the faculty member to the confined role of academic specialist. Perhaps if we can conceive of spiritual formation as a concern *every* maturing Christian should have for others, we will see the community and growth environment of a theological school as an ideal supplement to the church rather than quibbling as to whether the church alone should do it. "Therefore, a foundational purpose for the formation of Christians must be to help each one be a healthy, helping, receptive, and maturing member in the body of Christ. Involvement in local communities of believers is the place for this to be worked out, and the seminary must build community within itself and link seminarians to other communities as necessary."[27] Amirtham echoes Bramer's concern and emphasizes the importance of the integration of the various communities for the development of spirituality. "Where there is a gulf between the theological school and the congregation or where students and staff are segregated and do not share some common life together it is difficult to have the appropriate basis for a process of spiritual learning."[28]

What Is the Seminary to Do?

In an earlier day, the typical student of divinity could be expected to have received a certain measure of spiritual formation in the church, not to mention the family. The divinity college could attend to the academic side of theological education with at least some confidence that the church was doing its part. Not all modern theological students, however, have strong church links, and it is also true (this has been observed especially by missions executives) that a large percentage of people going into Christian work today come from dysfunctional families.

The theological school, therefore, cannot dismiss its responsibility for spiritual formation by claiming that this has traditionally been the role of church rather than seminary. Many students now come from secular university backgrounds, and some have expressed their concern that the divinity school fosters their spiritual life less adequately than the Christian groups that helped them survive on the secular campus.

It would be tragic if the members of a theological faculty who have been immersed in Bible and theology, informed by church history, trained in the mysteries of the mind and spirit and experienced in pastoral ministries and cross-cultural encounters could not together guide the students for whom they are responsible through a holistic process of spiritual formation.

Closely allied with the question of whether church or theological school is the ideal location for spiritual formation is that of whether clergy need a different level of spirituality from that of laity.

Is an extra measure of formation needed because the pastor or missionary will meet more serious problems, be under heavier spiritual attack and be subject to more complex personal demands than are experienced by lay people? This question deserves attention, especially with the whole question of the clergy/laity distinction now under serious discussion. If an intensification of spiritual formation is desirable for some, this must be done with care because as George Lindbeck warns, "it carries with it the peril of increasing the gap between clergy and laity."[29] Lindbeck goes so far as to say that "special ministerial spiritual formation should be avoided wherever possible because of the dangers of clerical elitism."[30] The danger *is* real, and his caution should be applied to the entire enterprise of theological education. Christopher Armstrong makes the provocative comment that "the learning ministerial community is both a peril and an opportunity."[31] But wherever and however development for ministry takes place, there should be agreement that theology and spirituality must never be separated.

Possible Approaches to Spiritual Formation

We have not yet asked what verb should precede the term spirituality. Do we (1) *achieve* it, (2) *experience* it, or (3) *practice* it? If (1), then it is a goal or objective and seminaries that consider it their responsibility should provide all the necessary information and encouragement toward its fulfillment. If it is (2), it is a state or circumstance, perhaps an event. In this case seminaries should provide the environment and atmosphere that will allow it to be felt or to take place. If it is (3), then it is something one does, and seminaries ought to provide the tools, the equipment, the coaching, and the opportunities to effect or perform it. Probably most of those who have been writing in the area would say that it is more a matter of growth than (1) assumes, less subjective than (2) implies, and not as mechanical as is assumed in (3). Even the word "formation," so often used today, may be overly programmatic. Do we "form" spirituality? Is it like extruded aluminum? Perhaps "develop" would be a more appropriate verb, but in any case administrators and faculty would do well to engage in this kind of discussion about goals before the planning stage begins.

It appears that some Protestant seminaries are tending to borrow heavily from Catholic models when they design programs of spiritual formation. Some excellent models are available, but is the program itself what is most needed? Should not each seminary work out its own rationale and determine the best way to proceed in its own setting? There is also a tendency to equate "mentoring" or "discipling" with spiritual formation. As Eugene Peterson observed, these terms, in Christian settings, suggest the downloading of information (something faculty members are far too ready to do anyway) or counselling. They present images of a type of direction that is not always appropriate for spiritual formation. Peterson feels that the relationship between the spiritual director and the student need not be as intensive as in, say, the counselling relationship. The student and spiritual director may meet only once every few weeks or months. What students may need most out of a program (small groups, retreats, etc.) is the opportunity to witness what God is already doing in their lives and in the lives of others, rather than just sitting under still more teaching. The biblical material will become necessary—but not as the first item on the agenda. Student and spiritual director (or companion) need to walk together for a time until it is determined just what content or teaching is needed.

Programs in themselves, therefore, do not generate spirituality. Yet some deliberate planning is needed. In view of this, the following proposals are offered as *approaches*, rather than as a *program*.

(1) Determine the *existing need* from three perspectives: (a) The *biblical teachings* about spirituality. (b) A *realistic assessment* of the spiritual maturity of incoming students. A possible strategy would be to repeat this once every student generation. (c) The *outcomes expected* from a theological education. This is an opportunity for faculty and students to discuss together what the *church* expects of a seminary graduate and Christian leader. It should be noted that an increasing number of churches are becoming disappointed at the inability of seminary graduates to function well spiritually and pastorally.

(2) Distill from the above what *kinds* of spiritual formation can best be included in a student's experience during his or her theological education.

(3) Construct both a *map* and an *itinerary*, the map to visualize the kinds of learning and experience that will facilitate spiritual growth, the itinerary to chart possible routes to that end. For example, it may be decided that students should read some of the devotional classics, participate in corporate prayer, meditate on certain passages of Scripture, and receive direct spiritual guidance. This constitutes the map. It may further be decided that as far as is practicable, and with flexibility, the student should begin with the Scriptures, move to the corporate experience, receive personal spiritual direction and then study the devotional classics. This is the itinerary. Decisions such as these should be made by representatives of students, faculty and administration working together.

(4) A *spiritual orientation* might be planned for incoming students. This could provide a corporate devotional experience and an explanation of expectations and description of the "map" and "itinerary" just mentioned.

(5) The faculty could analyze their respective *courses* to determine what subjects could be most fruitful for stressing the spiritual dimension. Even courses in pastoral theology can miss opportunities. One graduate said that in seminary he learned pastoral *duties* but not pastoral *caring*. No wonder Eugene Peterson finds so many pastors who are not truly pastoring.[32]

(6) Some *integration* between "academic" and "practical" perspectives

can be achieved by team teaching. Instructors from various disciplines could be joined by visiting ministers and lay persons.

(7) Faculty and others could discuss together the implications of their being *models* of spiritual maturity. This introduces the subject of qualifications for faculty appointment. While a seminary should appoint the best-qualified person in each field, those qualifications should include the spiritual as well as the academic.

(8) It may be appropriate to appoint a *Director of Spiritual Formation* or equivalent person. This person would bear the basic responsibility of seeing that resources and direction are provided to help the students mature spiritually. Such an appointment can provide a needed unifying direction, but must not allow others to relinquish their own responsibilities for offering spiritual guidance.

(9) On every appropriate occasion, whether in the classroom, chapel or informal dialogue, spiritual formation should be linked with *ethical behavior* and *social responsibility.* (The danger, of course, is the tendency to identify one's own choice of ethical response as *the* spiritual option.)

(10) One of the most frequent criticisms of seminary graduates is an inability to relate well to others. No doubt several factors contribute to this, but surely relational skills are associated with spiritual development through *corporate experiences.* Spiritual sharing can have the side effect of developing social ability.

Last Thoughts
This chapter has ranged from need to concept to history to program. Underlying all has been the conviction that theology and spiritual formation belong together and inform each other.

> Bruce Demarest and Charles Raup of Denver Seminary observed:
> Protestantism suffers from the scourge of *intellectualism* [emphasis theirs] when it believes that deepest human needs can be satisfied by right thinking about God. Some evangelicals identify Christianity with a formally correct theology or coherent world-view.[33]

George Lindbeck is careful to show both that theological skill is often positively influenced by spiritual practice and that theology helps shape the community's awareness of "who are and are not spiritually mature."[34]

Tilden Edwards' A.T.S. report included a pertinent observation that makes a fitting conclusion to this chapter. During the discussions one participant stated, "We undertake our spiritual life primarily for the praise of God, not for the instrumentality of being better ministers." Edwards commented, "This is difficult to remember in the functional atmosphere of many schools."[35] This brings the whole issue down to two crucial factors. It is not so much the formal program as the heart of the school's mission that determines the outcome, and the outcome itself should always be viewed as the praise of God.[36]

Notes

[1] Carl Volz, "Seminaries: The Love of Learning or the Desire for God?" *Dialog* 28/2 (Spring, 1989) 104.

[2] Ibid., 105.

[3] Jean Leclercq, *The Love of Learning and the Desire for God* (trans. Catherine Misrahi; New York: Fordham University, 1982).

[4] Ibid., 4-7, 217-225.

[5] Edward Farley, *Theologia: The Fragmentation and Unity of Theological Education* (Philadelphia: Fortress, 1983).

[6] Tilden Edwards, "Spiritual Formation in Theological Schools: Ferment and Challenge," *Theological Education* 17/1 (1980) 9.

[7] Richard Lovelace, "Evangelicalism: Recovering a Tradition of Spiritual Depth," *The Reformed Journal* 40/7 (1990) 20.

[8] Ibid., 25.

[9] Lewis Sperry Chafer, *He That Is Spiritual* (Grand Rapids: Zondervan, 1965).

[10] Sandra M. Schneiders, "Theology and Spirituality: Strangers, Rivals, or Partners," *Horizons* 13/2 (1986) 258ff. See her article for a more complete treatment of the history of spirituality.

[11] Lovelace, "Evangelicalism," 22.

[12] Schneiders, "Theology," 65.

[13] David E. Babin et al., *Voyage, Vision, Venture: A Report* (Dayton, Ohio: American Association of Theological Schools, 1972).

[14] See reports of conferences in Edwards, "Spiritual Formation," 7-52.

[15] Less than half of the questionnaires were returned.

[16] A recent *Atlantic Monthly* article described today's seminarian as older, experienced, married, separated or divorced. Many come to seminary from a career and are studying for the ministry as a second career. Many come, not because they have found God, but because they are searching for him. Spiritual formation in the theological school, therefore, has to address two populations: those who are searching for God and those who come with a clear sense of vocation. See Paul Wilkes, "The Hands That Would Shape Our Souls," *The Atlantic Monthly* 266/6 (1990) 59-88.

[17] Edwards, "Spiritual Formation," 21-23.

[18] Samuel Amirtham, "Spiritual Formation in Theological Education: An Invitation to Participate," Programme on Theological Education, World Council of Churches, Report and Study Paper, Geneva, 1987.

[19] Ibid., 6.

[20] Tilden Edwards' report of the 1979-1980 conferences indicated that a number of the faculty in Catholic schools see their involvement in spiritual formation primarily on the academic level, and notes that this is a source of tension and debate in these schools. See Edwards, "Spiritual Formation," 24.

[21] Mundelein Seminary, *Formation Program 1990-1991* (Mundelein, Ill.: Mundelein Seminary, 1990-1991) 1.

[22] Ibid., 12.

[23] David Lowes Watson, "Spiritual Formation in Ministry Training," *The Christian Century* 101/5 (6-13 February 1985) 122-124.

[24] David J. Seiver, "Spiritual Formation in Christian Seminaries: A Study of Nine Programs," unpublished paper, Trinity Evangelical Divinity School, April 1991.

[25] Ibid., 15.

[26] Specific details not in the paper were clarified through a verbal interview with Seiver.

[27] Paul Bramer, "A Model of Seminary Education for Spiritual Development," unpublished doctoral paper, Trinity Evangelical Divinity School, 1991, p. 8.

[28] Amirtham, "Spiritual Formation," 6.

[29] George Lindbeck, "Spiritual Formation and Theological Education," *Theological Education* 24, Supplement I (1988) 18.

[30] Ibid., 30.

[31] Christopher Armstrong, "Person and Institution: Spirituality in Ordination Training," *Can Spirituality Be Taught* (ed. Jill Robson & David Lonsdale; London: Way Publications, Association of Centres of Adult Theological Education and British Council of Churches, 1988) 37.

[32] See, for example, the introduction to his *Working the Angles: The Shape of Pastoral Integrity* (Grand Rapids: Eerdmans, 1987).

[33] Bruce Demarest and Charles Raup, "Recovering the Heart of Christian Spirituality," *Criswell Theological Review* 2 (1989) 322.

[34] Lindbeck, "Spiritual Formation," 19-20.

[35] Edwards, "Spiritual Formation," 30.

[36] The authors express their gratitude to Paul Bramer and David Seiver, students in the Ed.D. program at Trinity Evangelical Divinity School, for sharing with us the results of their own research and thinking about spiritual formation and theological education.

20
The Earthy Spirituality
of Gerard Manley Hopkins

Loren Wilkinson

Ａt Oxford, James Houston taught geography; at Regent, he teaches spiritual theology. In that first career he was concerned with the relationship of people to the earth; in the second, with their relationship to God. His treatment of creation spirituality in his book *I Believe in the Creator* happily unites the two concerns.

The Alleged Unearthliness of Christian Faith

To many Christians, the tension between the two concerns is extreme (if not unreconcilable), for by a long tradition, the things of earth and the things of heaven are thought to be opposed. That apparent opposition appears frequently in our hymnody. For example, the second line of the wonderful fifth-century Greek hymn "Let All Mortal Flesh keep Silence" is commonly translated, "Ponder nothing earthly-minded . . . ." And in a more recent hymn we sing:

Turn your eyes upon Jesus
Look full in his wonderful face
And the things of earth will grow strangely dim
In the light of his glory and grace.

There may be valid theological reasons for such language, but at best the shunning of earth is a minor Christian theme, which should be understood only within the full biblical doctrine of creation and redemption. That fuller Christian picture is caught well in the words of another hymn:

Joy to the world, the Savior reigns
Let earth receive her king;

Let every heart prepare him room
And heaven and nature sing.

Unfortunately, the conviction that Christian theology turns one away from the earth is widespread. Indeed, the opposition of Christendom and the earth is almost an axiom in a growing religious movement which attempts to bring together earth and spirituality. So it is appropriate in a book honoring James Houston to reflect on the connections between God and earth.

This I propose to do by looking at the poetry and prose of another Oxonian whose work reflects both an appreciation of the earth and a deep Christian spirituality: that is the Jesuit priest Gerard Manley Hopkins.

But before turning to a consideration of Hopkins' eloquent retrieval of basic Christian truths, it will be helpful to look a little more closely at the unfortunate but widespread contemporary opinion that Christians worship a God aloofly transcendent from creation, and thus should themselves "ponder nothing earthly."

That opposition is usually assumed rather than argued, but if the case were made explicitly it would go something like this:

• The patriarchal religions, of which the chief offender is Christianity, worship a transcendent Creator God who is utterly detached from his creation.

• As the creation was brought into being by the will of God, so it will be destroyed by the will of God.

• The only thing in creation with ultimate value is humanity, made "in God's image" for an eternal, personal relationship with the Creator.

• Ultimate human salvation is not experienced in the body, in the earth, in creation: rather, these created things are backdrop for a spiritual drama whose culmination is in an un-earthly heaven.

• Given this scale of values, Christendom sees the earth not as divine, sacred, or even intrinsically valuable, but rather as raw material; "natural resources" for the playing out of the human drama.

This is a harsh picture, a barely recognizable caricature of biblical faith. But harsh as it is, it nevertheless forms part of the mental landscape of a great many of our contemporaries. Here, for example, is novelist Ursula LeGuin's picture of the patriarchal worshippers of one God (called "One") in her recent Utopian novel *Always Coming Home:*

One made everything out of nothing. One is a person, immortal. He is all-powerful. Human men are imitations of him. One is not the universe; he made it and gives it orders. Things are not part of him nor is he part of them, so you must not praise things, but only One.... They say that as there was a time when One made everything, there will be a time when everything will stop being, when One will unmake everything. Then will begin the Time Outside of Time. He will throw away everything except [those] who obeyed him in every way and were his slaves. They will become part of One then, and be forever. I am sure that there is some sense to be made of this, but I cannot make it.[1]

The passage reflects a deep repugnance at what is perceived to be a belief that God cares only for (some) humans, and will "throw away" the non-human. The same sort of horror at God's alleged unearthliness is evident in a remark of Susan Griffin in an anthology of "ecofeminist" literature. She calls the idea of

the divine as immanent . . . a concept foreign to those raised in Judeo-Christianity. The view that we've grown up with is that the divine and matter are separate and that matter is really dangerous. The material world belongs to the devil. What's under your feet is closer to hell . . . .[2]

Nor is this criticism of a transcendent God limited to non-Christians. Here is Matthew Fox, a Dominican scholar, criticizing what he takes to be the prevailing theistic understanding:

Over the years I have met many serious spiritual seekers who called themselves atheist. Yet I have come to realize that most atheism is a rejection of theism . . . I do believe that if the only option I was given by which to envision creation's relationship to divinity was theism that I would be an atheist too.[3]

Clearly, the offending element in Christian theism as it is perceived by these critics is the notion of divine detachment from creation, a detachment which, presumably, we are supposed to share, and which thus is perceived to provide justification for harsh human treatment of the earth. Rightly or wrongly, these critics say that our mis-use of the earth is rooted in Christian spirituality, a spirituality in which, necessarily, "the things of earth grow strangely dim."

It has thus become a matter of some urgency to many people to develop a "new spirituality," one which does not distance the object of prayer and worship from the earth. Matthew Fox calls this a "creation spirituality." Others, suspicious of the concept of "creation," refer simply to "earth spirituality."

A recent anthology in this "new spirituality" is called *Earth Prayers*. It is a rich and eloquent assembly of words for the earth drawn from major religions, native religious traditions, and contemporary poets. Many Christians are included as well. But the excerpts are introduced by the anthologists in words which make clear that ultimately their goal is the recapture of divine immanence, and the rejection of any notion of the separateness of Creator from creation:

The voices in this book address the "Lord," the "Great Spirit," "Wakan Tanka," "Goddess"—each acknowledging the spiritual precedents of their culture. *Underlying these differences in salutation is the recognition that the transcendent is not separate from creation.*[4]

Thus the exclusive emphasis on divine transcendence—a kind of deism into which certain types of Christian piety are all too prone to deteriorate—is being challenged today by a rejection of any transcendence at all. The "spirituality" which results is a kind of pantheism in which the earth is regarded as the sole authoritative sign or sacrament of the divine. Thus the editors of *Earth Prayers* affirm confidently: "The Earth itself *is* Christos, *is* Buddha, *is* Allah, *is* Gaia."[5] To such a pantheistic understanding the Christian "scandal of particularity" is scandalous indeed.

Christians have no choice but to reject this kind of "earth spirituality." But at the same time we need to be able to hear and respond to the truth which it represents: that surrounding and nourishing the human world—from which it increasingly seems determined to eliminate any awareness of God—is the *created* earth, which does not fail to speak of the Creator. In Hopkins' best-known line, "The world is charged with the grandeur of God."[6]

Indeed generations "have trod, have trod, have trod" on both Creator and creation, and earth indeed is

... seared with trade; bleared, smeared with toil
And wears man's smudge and shares man's smell.

But

... for all this, nature is never spent;
There lives the dearest freshness deep down things ....

Christians affirm, as did Hopkins, that it is through the work of the triune God that "nature is never spent," and that "the Holy Ghost over the bent world broods." Many in our time are open to see God moving in creation—but are closed to his moving in their own heart. Hopkins' thought can perhaps help those of us who know the Creator in Christ to extend that fuller knowledge of him to those who know him dimly through creation.

Though none of Hopkins' poetry was published in his lifetime (indeed, not till 1918, 30 years after his death in 1888) Hopkins has gradually come to be recognized as one of the greatest—though one of the most idiosyncratic—of English poets. Much of his strength lies in his very idiosyncrasy. His single-minded pursuit of words back to their Celtic or Germanic roots, his dramatic compressions of syntax, his Welsh "vowel-music" and Old English "sprung rhythm" all combine to give his best poems a communicative power which is both archaic and new, and which has made him stylistically one of the strongest influences on twentieth-century English poetry.

Thus the vivid vehicle of Hopkins' verse conveys a fresh awareness of God's presence to his creation, and of our much more ambiguous presence in it. Many of these poems have become very well known. Not as well known, but crucial to an understanding of the poetry, is the profound theological understanding that informs them. I would like to consider then several of the main points of Hopkins' grasp of the three-fold relationship between God, earth and human beings—as expressed in his poetry, and amplified in his various prose writings. Both poetry and prose, as we shall see, retrieve for our day crucial truths basic to a much needed and genuinely Christian "spirituality"—which is a spirituality of earth because it is a spirituality of the Maker and Redeemer of earth.

Hopkins' Understanding of God's Immediacy to Creation

Hopkins had a deep sense of the presence of God to creation. His greatest poems celebrate this closeness. We have already quoted the opening line from one of his best-known poems: "The world is charged with the grandeur of God." It is significant to note, however, in this and in Hopkins' other great nature poems, that he never confuses God and creation. The world is not simply the grandeur of God, for the world *is not* God, or any part of him. Rather it is "charged" with God's grandeur. "Charged" is a rich word, for it suggests both an electrical current (which will "flame out" in lightning) and the delegated duty of being placed "in charge" of something. But in both meanings the source, the head, is elsewhere: it is not the world itself. Likewise, when Hopkins speaks later in the poem of "the dearest freshness deep down things" he is not implying (as many wish to today) that when one penetrates to the center of anything one finds God; rather, that the deep things of creation are nurtured by "the Holy Ghost [who] over the bent world broods." Again the picture is one of intimacy, but not identity.

Most of Hopkins' nature poems express, in different ways, this closeness of the Creator to a creation from which he nevertheless remains separate. Often Hopkins is troubled by the discrepancy between the overwhelming loveliness of the created world and our response, which is to ignore it or (worse) to destroy it. His distress at human deafness to the Creator is evident in these concluding lines from a sonnet on Wales, "The Valley of the Elwy":

Lovely the woods, waters, meadows, combes, vales,
All the air things wear that build this world of Wales;
    Only the inmate does not correspond:

The created loveliness is everywhere, but we who live in it "do not correspond." Here Hopkins touches on a crucial notion: the complementary nourishing relationship which ought to exist between creation and the human heart.

In another sonnet, written also in the autumn of Hopkins' "great year," 1877, we find this three-fold relationship of creation, Creator, and responsive human heart spelled out much more precisely. "Hurrahing in Harvest" ought to be better known, and I quote it in full:

Summer ends now; now barbarous in beauty, the stooks rise
Around; up above, what wind-walks! what lovely behaviour
O silk-sack clouds! has wilder, wilful-wavier
Meal-drift moulded ever and melted across skies?

I walk, I lift up, I lift up heart, eyes,
Down all that glory in the heavens to glean our Saviour;
And, eyes, heart, what looks, what lips yet gave you a
Rapturous love's greeting of realer, of rounder replies?

And the azurous hung hills are his world-wielding shoulder
Majestic—as a stallion stalwart, very violet-sweet!—
These things, these things were here and but the beholder
Wanting; which two when they once meet,
The heart hurls wings bold and bolder
And hurls for him, O half hurls earth for him off under his
    feet.[7]

The poem begins in the first quatrain with an exclamation over the beauty of the fields and skies of autumn. The description is eloquent, but the sentiment fairly conventional. The next quatrain, however, takes a striking turn: the poet
                    lift[s] up heart, eyes,
Down all that glory in the heavens to glean our Saviour.
The imagery of gleaning—collecting the leavings from a crop—is appropriate for autumn. But the object of the gleaning—"our Saviour"—is startling. How can our Savior be gleaned from a fine fall day? But this perception of Christ in the heavens is not a mere subjective whim: for the Savior gives a "rapturous love's greeting" of replies "realer" and "rounder"

than that received from any person.

Yet Hopkins is not just "seeing God in nature." God is still transcendent, a "glory in the heavens" (and "heavens" here keeps its ancient double meaning of both "sky" and "God's place"). What the "beholder" sees is, literally, a perfect fit between God and nature. The image which opens the sestet is confusing at first: "The azurous hung hills are his world-wielding shoulder" initially appears to be a conventional association of God with the curved hills, which supposedly support the sky upon them. This would be the sort of association of God with the earth—usually some form of Gaia, a feminine goddess—which is conventional in mythology and common today. But once again Hopkins is not associating God and earth. These are "hung hills" and they support not the sky, but the world. What he is describing is the horizon line, above which is the azure sky, an outline-image of the Creator's "world-wielding shoulder." Hopkins' inspired perception turns the world upside-down—back to its proper place—in which the earth is upheld by God. It is no wonder that such a seeing hurls the beholder, "O half hurls earth for him off under his feet."

In such poems, Hopkins is pressing as close as he possibly can the connection between Creator and creation, but maintaining the distinction: God is always the transcendent Creator, graciously inclining towards his creation. In the last lines of "Pied Beauty," which describes the dappled, "pied," ever-changing world, he makes plain that all that "fickle, freckled" beauty comes from God:

He fathers forth whose beauty is past change
    Praise him.[8]

Nature is always changing ("a Heraclitean fire," Hopkins puts it in a much later poem), but God, the source of beauty and object of praise, is changeless. The phrase "fathering-forth" is significant, for it answers, without apology, the common ecofeminist objection that the idea of the *fatherhood* of God reflects an unacceptable distance and detachment of the Creator, whereas the *motherhood* of God would suggest better God's womb-like nurturing of the earth. Though Hopkins occasionally uses feminine metaphors to express the Creator's relationship to the earth (as in, for example, the Holy Ghost's "brooding" in "God's Grandeur"), he is insistent on the distance implied by fatherhood, and often uses "fathering" as a verb, as if to underline that the life the earth brings forth is not its own.

In one of Hopkins' theological essays, written as an introduction to a meditation on the *Spiritual Exercises* of Ignatius Loyola, he puts in arrestingly precise if paradoxical fashion the closeness of God and earth which he has suggested so richly in his poems:

> God is so deeply present to everything ... that it would be impossible
> for him but for his infinity not to be identified with them, or, from
> the other side, impossible but for his infinity so to be present to them.
> This is oddly expressed, I see; I mean, a being so intimately present as
> God is to other things would be identified with them were it not for
> God's infinity or were it not for God's infinity he could not be so
> intimately present to things.[9]

It is, in other words, the very greatness of God which allows him to be
so close to his creatures; if he were any less than infinite, he would be one
with his creation. In his infinity he can lavish himself upon creation and
yet remain wholly other and undiminished. In the same essay Hopkins
puts the point in a different way, playing on the description of Christ as
Word (elsewhere, in a poetic fragment, Hopkins speaks of the Trinity as
"Immortals of the eternal ring / The Utterer, Uttered, Uttering"[10]):

> God's utterance in himself is God the Word, outside himself is this
> world. This world then is word, expression, news of God. Therefore
> its end, its purpose, its purport, its meaning, is God, and its life or work
> to name and praise him.[11]

In speaking thus of the closeness of Creator to creation Hopkins is
drawing on a medieval theologian whom he admired greatly, Duns
Scotus. One of the ideas for which Scotus is particularly remembered is
his assertion (in contradistinction to Thomas Aquinas) that the Incarnation was not occasioned by human sin, but rather that it was in the divine
purpose from the beginning. The idea makes a subtle but important
difference in the way we view the earth. As James Cotter explains (in a
profound study of Hopkins' Christology, *Inscape*), this discussion was
"not a purely abstract debate about possible acts of God if human history
had not taken the course it did." Rather, Scotus

> hoped by establishing the purpose of God's creative act as genesis in
> Christ, to show the unity and perfection of the divine concern for
> creatures. This unity is the Father's love for man made manifest in the
> likeness of his Son. The natural order is existentially oriented toward
> Christ who is its masterpiece and culmination. Christ's priority of
> nature ... places him first in the order of causality, which is counter-
> pointed in the order of time ... the Lamb is slain from the beginning.
> The act by which the Father sums up all the *pleroma* in his crucified
> Son, this is the one creative act of love from and to which all being
> flows. Creation and atonement, two decrees from man's temporal
> points of view, are actually simultaneous in God.... Nature exists from
> the start in a supernatural order, creation in Christ, and waits patiently

for the deliverance of man and his passing over into completion in his Lord. Only the redeemed man is one with the cosmos, for he has answered the call that brought him into existence. Only he is truly one with nature. [12]

Such a Christology is not beyond dispute. Some would say it confuses "the order of creation" and "the order of salvation." But perhaps we have exaggerated that distinction, and we need to rethink it today in response to a world insistent that the church has effectively denied the value of creation. A linking of Christ and creation is by no means a modern innovation. It has for long been a part of Eastern Orthodox thought, as is evident in these words of twentieth-century Orthodox theologian Vladimir Lossky:

It was the divinely appointed function of the first man . . . to unite in himself the whole of created being, and at the same time to reach his perfect union with God and thus grant the state of deification to the whole creation . . . . Since this task was not fulfilled by Adam, it is in the work of Christ, the second Adam, that we can see what it was meant to be.[13]

Such an understanding reflects the biblical tradition of Christ as "second Adam," in which redemption is seen to be the setting right of what God has made. This was the Christology of many of the church fathers. Thus in the fourth century Athanasius says in *On the Incarnation:*

For this purpose then the incorporeal and incorruptible and immaterial Word of God entered our world. In one sense indeed, He was not far from it before, for no part of creation had ever been without Him Who, while ever abiding in union with the Father, yet fills all things that are. But now He entered the world in a new way.[14]

It is this uttered Word, "never far from" creation, which the poet gleans in "Hurrahing in Harvest" and from whom (because the Word has entered the world "in a new way") he can receive a "rapturous love's greeting of realer, of rounder replies."

Hopkins' understanding of the presence of God to creation reflects as well the second-century Irenaeus' understanding. Irenaeus wrote,

For the Creator of the world is truly the Word of God: and this is our Lord, who in the last times was made man, existing in this world, and who in an invisible manner contains all things created, and is inherent in the entire creation, since the word of God governs and arranges all things; and therefore He came to His own in a visible manner, and was made flesh, and hung upon the tree, that He might sum up all things in Himself.[15]

Thus when Hopkins says, "The world is charged with the grandeur of God," he is expressing in poetic form a christological understanding that is as ancient as the church: for we can go further back than Irenaeus to find the same idea. It is in the New Testament in such passages as Col 1:16b-17: "All things were created by him and for him. He is before all things, and in him all things hold together."

The Christian in Creation: "Selving" the Earth

Such a picture of the presence of God to creation sets right the current common misunderstandings about Christian belief and teaching. But what does it imply for Christian practice? Here again Hopkins is a rich resource for all those seeking a *Christian* spirituality which does not leave creation behind.

Hopkins had a deep sense of the uniqueness of each created thing. He coined the term "inscape" to describe that created distinctness, and again found Duns Scotus' ideas of *haecceitas*, "thisness," to be useful. His thinking on this point was already well formed by the time he discovered Scotus, but the confirmation of the "subtle doctor's" dissent from Aquinas on this point was a comfort in the heavily Thomist Jesuit environment. In the Scotist understanding, things are intelligible not because of their participation in a species; rather, each thing is uniquely itself. Cotter thus describes the Scotist position to which Hopkins had come:

> The...Scotist concept of *haecceitas* defines the thisness that constitutes an existent, that makes this being *be*.... For Scotus, as for Parmenides, being is univocal, unique, not a sharing in other being or an analogous reflection, but its self, one in the One, word of the Word.[16]

Hopkins' journals—especially in the long years of his novitiate, after he had resolved not to write poetry—are filled with wonderfully detailed attempts to catch these creaturely selves in the net of words. Here is a sample of the richness of those journals.

> 1870, Mar. 12: The next morning a heavy fall of snow. It tufted and toed the firs and yews and went on to load them till they were taxed beyond their spring. The limes, elms, and Turkey-oaks it crisped beautifully as with young leaf. Looking at the elms from underneath you saw every wave in every twig (become by this the wire-like stem to a finger of snow) and to the hangers and flying sprays it restored, to the eye, the inscapes they had lost. They were beautifully brought out against the sky, which was on one side dead blue, on the other washed with gold.[17]

For the most part this is simply precisely observed, well-described detail. Yet always Hopkins is questing for "inscape," for the individuating center of uniqueness. Sometimes Hopkins suggests that such a center, if it could be found and "worded," is itself the Word in whom all things consist, which at the same time gives each thing its uniqueness. Consider his oft-quoted description of the bluebells:

> 1870, May 18: ... I do not think I have ever seen anything more beautiful than the bluebell I have been looking at. I know the beauty of our Lord by it. Its inscape is mixed of strength and grace, like an ash tree. The head is strongly drawn over backwards and arched down like a cutwater drawing itself back from the line of the keel. The lines of the bells strike and overlie this, rayed but not symmetrically, some lie parallel. They look steely against the paper, the shades lying between the bells and behind the cockled petal-ends and nursing up the precision of their distinctness .... [18]

The description continues in even greater detail. But the profound point for us is in Hopkins' recognition that in the very "precision of their distinctness" is that which conveys "the beauty of our Lord." Poetically, this doctrine of each thing's created inscape is best put in the opening lines of one of Hopkins' sonnets:

> As kingfishers catch fire, dragonflies draw flame;
> As tumbled over rim in roundy wells
> Stones ring; like each tucked string tells, each hung bell's
> Bow swung finds tongue to fling out broad its name;
> Each mortal thing does one thing and the same:
> Deals out that being indoors each one dwells;
> Selves—goes itself—*myself* it speaks and spells,
> Crying *What I do is me: for that I came.* [19]

The picture is of a self-declaring world in which "each mortal thing" "finds tongue to fling out broad its name."

Yet, paradoxically, these self-declaring things are mute without humans. They do what they do without choice or freedom. As Hopkins put it in a meditation:

> "The heavens declare the glory of God." They glorify God. *But they do not know it.* The birds sing to him, the thunder speaks of his terror, the lion is like his strength, the sea is like his greatness, the honey like his sweetness... but they do not know they do, they do not know him, they never can .... This then is poor praise, faint reverence, slight service, dull glory. Nevertheless, what they can do *they always do.* [2]

Human beings, though, are different: they have a choice: they can praise God with their God-given selves—or choose not to. "Man was made to give, and meant to give, God glory." He has a choice about remaining silent—or uttering the praises that lie latent but mute in creation itself.

In "Ribblesdale," for example, Hopkins describes the burdened earth of
a mis-used valley, appealing to heaven but

with no tongue to plead, no heart to feel;
That canst but only be . . . .

Yet the "plea" of the earth to man and God alike—wordlessly repeated all
over the earth in the painful century since Hopkins wrote—is real. It
depends, however, on human perception, response and articulation. As
Hopkins puts it in the same sonnet:

And what is Earth's eye, tongue, or heart else, where
Else but in dear and dogged man?[21]

Hopkins was all too aware that the human relationship to the created
earth is not usually one of respectful watching and utterance, but of
heavy-handed use. Thus an observation like this one:

April 8, 1873: The ashtree growing in the corner of the garden was
felled. It was lopped first: I heard the sound and looking out and seeing
it maimed there came at that moment a great pang and I wished to die
and not see the inscapes of the world destroyed any more.[22]

In another intensely elegiac poem, called "Binsey Poplars, Felled, 1879,"
Hopkins laments another needless logging:

My aspens dear, whose airy cages quelled,
Quelled or quenched in leaves the leaping sun,
All felled, felled, are all felled.[23]

He follows this personal grief with a shrewdly observed insight which
sounds very much like twentieth-century ecological wisdom:

O if we but knew what we do
    When we delve or hew—
Hack and rack the growing green!
    Since country is so tender
To touch, her being so slender,
That, like this sleek and seeing ball
But a prick will make no eye at all,
Where we, even when we mean
    To mean we end her.

Thus Hopkins recognizes the fragility of ecological balance, and the
danger of even our well-meaning mendings or "improvements" of
creation. But unlike many today who advocate what seems like a human
withdrawal from the earth, Hopkins had a profound sense of our role
as voices, tongues for creation. In this poem, and elsewhere, he uses the
word "selve" as a verb:

After-comers cannot guess the beauty been.
    Ten or twelve, only ten or twelve

> Strokes of havoc unselve
> The sweet especial seen.

If we can "unselve," we can "selve"—that is, give utterance to—a mute and groaning creation. Here Hopkins seems to be drawing on the implications of Paul's rich but cryptic words in Romans 8 about a creation "groaning as in the pains of childbirth" and "wait[ing] in eager expectation for the sons of God to be revealed."

Again, Hopkins restores an insight from the fathers which has been kept vital in the Eastern Church. Irenaeus spoke of the unfallen Adam's task as the completion, with God, of creation. Something like this is surely implied in the biblical understanding of *naming* in Genesis 2. Thus, as Kallistos Ware puts it in a common Orthodox understanding:

> It is his [humankind's] God-given task to reconcile and harmonize the noetic and the material realms, to bring them to unity, to spiritualize the material, and to render manifest all the latent capacities of the created order.[24]

Conclusions

We have only sampled the richness of Hopkins' poetry, and the theological understanding which lies behind it. But in a period when it has become commonplace to speak of the destructive unearthliness of the Christian and the God whom Christians worship, that Hopkins' poetry and thought introduce us to a way of following Christ which makes plain that there is no tension between knowing God and knowing the earth. It is appropriate, then, to recall the achievement of Gerard Manley Hopkins in honoring the achievement of Dr. James Houston. For both have helped us see that when we know God in Christ, we are not turned away from the earth, but released to care for it: to be, in Hopkins' words, its "eye, tongue . . . heart." For as we have been given back our selves by God in Christ, we can, by God's grace, give utterance to the mute selves of God's earth.

Notes

[1] Ursula K. LeGuin, *Always Coming Home* (New York: Harper & Row, 1985) 200.
[2] Susan Griffin, "Curves Along the Road," in *Reweaving the World: The Emergence of Ecofeminism* (ed. Irene Diamond & Gloria Orenstein; San Francisco: Sierra Club, 1990) 87.
[3] Matthew Fox, *The Coming of the Cosmic Christ* (New York: Harper & Row, 1988) 57.
[4] Elizabeth Roberts & Elias Amidon, ed. *Earth Prayers* (San Francisco: Harper, 1991) xxiv. Emphasis added.
[5] Ibid., xxi.
[6] These and the following lines are from Hopkins' sonnet "God's Grandeur," in *The Poems of Gerard Manley Hopkins* (ed. W. H. Gardner & N. H. MacKenzie; London: Oxford University Press, 1967) 66.
[7] Ibid., 70.

[8] Ibid.

[9] Gerard Manley Hopkins, *The Sermons and Devotional Writings of Gerard Manley Hopkins* (ed. Christopher Devlin, S.J.; London: Oxford University Press, 1959) 128.

[10] Hopkins, "Margaret Clitheroe," in *Poems*, 182.

[11] Hopkins, *Sermons*, 129.

[12] James Finn Cotter, *Inscape: The Christology and Poetry of Gerard Manley Hopkins* (Pittsburgh: University of Pittsburgh Press, 1972) 122-123.

[13] Vladimir Lossky, *The Mystical Theology of the Eastern Church* (trans. members of the Fellowship of St. Alban & St. Sergius; London: James Clarke, 1957) III.

[14] Athanasius, *On the Incarnation* (trans. & ed. a Religious of C.M.V.; Crestwood, N.Y.: St. Vladimir's Orthodox Theological Seminary, 1953) 33-34.

[15] Irenaeus, *Against Heresies, The Ante-Nicene Fathers* (vol. I, The Apostolic Fathers: Justin Martyr, Irenaeus), *Translations of the Writings of the Fathers down to AD 325* (ed. Alexander Roberts & James Donaldson; Grand Rapids: Eerdmans, 1978), 5.18.3, 546-547.

[16] Cotter, *Inscape*, 126.

[17] *The Journals and Papers of Gerard Manley Hopkins* (ed. Humphrey House; London: Oxford University Press, 1959) 196.

[18] Ibid., 199.

[19] Hopkins, "As Kingfishers Catch Fire," *Poems*, 90.

[20] Hopkins, *Sermons*, 239.

[21] Hopkins, *Poems*, 90.

[22] *Journals*, 230.

[23] Hopkins, *Poems*, 78.

[24] Kallistos Ware, *The Orthodox Way* (Crestwood, N.Y.: St. Vladimir's Press, 1990) 63.

Womb... Wing... Wind. Poems of the Spirit: A Hexagonal Cycle

Luci N. Shaw

1 * WOMB
Virgin

As if until that moment
  nothing real
  had happened since Creation

As if outside the world were empty
  so that he and she were all
  there was—he mover, she moved upon

As if her submission were the most
  dynamic of all works; as if
  no one had ever said Yes like that

As if that day the sun had no place
  in all the universe to pour its gold
  but her small room

Diamonds that leap

When the leaf fell and brushed my hand
I began to reverse the world. I asked:
What if this warped willow leaf, yellow,

scaled with age, could
smooth to a green blade and flicker
into the knot of a spring twig, like
a serpent's tail disappearing
into his home? That was one question.
It was a whirlpool, pulling in

others: What about a river?
Might its waters rush up
the hills and split to a scatter

of diamonds that leap to their rain
clouds like homing salmon? Can a love
shrink back and back to like,

and the crack of a small, investigative
smile? Would God ever suck away creation
into his mouth, like a word regretted,

and start us over? And this: Can a man
be born when he is old? Can he
enter again into his mother's womb ...?

2 * WING
Careless flying
Luke 12:24-26
I

I have been considering
the ravens, who live
without worrying
and have no bins or barns

And have no reaping machines.
Yet they are fed well—their bodies
sleek, gloved in black silk.
With what a minor tempest

They startle and settle,
yet they are the poets of motion.
Like folk songs their wings wheel
and hover, carcless

As falcons. I am their
anxious scribe, listening myself
into their coarse
cries, storing the separate

Notes in small black spaces
at the back of my skull.
God, if I were a bird I think
I would stop worrying:

Enough to wear, to eat. And one
more hour of life is, you say,
not worth the care. So, I'm
a bird. Nested in down,

I think I will float in a
dream of flight all night,
waking at the gold call of the sun
from the world's lip.

II

St. Francis could name me
his small sister.
He wasn't a bird either
but he would know how to fold

His hands around my minor
warmth, then toss me, his arms
splayed, and let the air
catch me easy as feathers.

Watching ravens rise to God,
black steps moving on gold
ladders, gave him enough wonder
it took all his life

To exult in. His praise
escaped often to heaven, his eyes
following. Eventually he himself
learned to fly, lifted by birds.

A bird in the church
Oxford, July, 1991

    The black bird, not harbored like us at
one lowly level, has entered this stone cage
with its fluidities of enclosed light.
Between crossbeam and cornice, wide

and high and low and up again, through the sun's
transfixing shafts, her wings open and
close on a bewilderment of interior air,
until, as though coming home, she settles

on the arm of the crucifix. Having found
a nesting tree, she lodges at last
where vertex and horizon meet, resting
in the steady pain of Christ's left eye.

3 * WIND
Ghostly

    I think often about the invisible
God—doubly covert. I mean, now and again
Father and Son made their appearances,
speaking bold in thunder, blood,
or salvation. But the third
Person is like a ghost. Sometimes
he silvers for a moment, a moon sliver
between moving leaves. We aren't sure.

What to make of this ... How
are we meant to see him? As energy
hovering, birdlike, over chaos,
breeding it into ferns and whales?
Blessing the scalps of the righteous
with a pungency of oil? Bleeding the hard
edge of warning into all those
prophet voices? Etching
Ezekiel's view with oddities—
eyes in wheels spinning like astrolabes?
Crowding Mary's womb to seed its dark
clay? Wising up fools to improbable truth?
Filling us like wine bottles? Bursting

from our mouths in champagne gasps
of surprise? This for sure—he finds
enough masks to keep us guessing:
Is it really you? Is this you also?

It's a cracked, crossover world, waiting
for bridges. He chooses a shape—fire, dove,
wind, water, oil (notice—in him
oil and water mix), closes the breach
in figures that flicker within
the closed eye, tongue the brain, sting
and tutor the soul. Once incarnate
in Judaea, now he is present
(in us in the present
tense), occupying our bodies—
shapes to be reshaped—houses
for this holy ghost. In our special flesh
he thrives into something
too frequent to deny, too real to see.

Stigmata

The tree, a beech, casts
its melancholy of shadow on
the road, bears the weight of sky
on the tips of its branches.
The smooth trunk invites me
to finger five bruise-dark holes
where death was cut away. Years
have pursed the thickened
skin around the scars into
mouths that sigh, "Wounded.

Wounded." As the hurt begins to
feel me out wind possesses the tree
and a hush comes overhead; not that
all sounds die, but half a million
beech leaves rub together in the air,

washing out bird calls, footsteps,
filling my ears with old pain
and the new song of cells swelling.
"Hush," they say
with their green lips. "Hush."

22

Christian Faith and the Social Sciences in a Postmodern Age

David Ley

BEFORE JIM HOUSTON WAS A THEOLOGIAN, HE WAS A GEOGRApher, and an eminent one at that. As undergraduates at Oxford in the mid-1960s, we attended his lectures with respect, and were careful readers of his books, notably *A Social Geography of Europe* and, for specialists, the 800-page opus *The Western European World.* Not that Jim ever detached his faith from his social science. Years later, I was told a characteristic story by a fellow lecturer at Oxford, who had also left the town with the dreaming spires for a distant corner of the world. During the 1950s they had driven to London together on a motorcycle to attend professional meetings at the Royal Geographical Society. As they careered along the A40 with the wind rushing past their faces, Jim had engaged his fellow traveler in a spirited apologetic for the Christian faith. Like every university lecturer, he knew a captive audience when he saw one! But unlike many other lecturers, Jim Houston had a message that was not easily forgotten, so that thirty years later it was this incident from their early years at Oxford which flooded into the mind of his secular colleague.

The blending of difference into a higher unity, the integration of our fragmented life, the declaration that God is the Lord of all creation, these were the articles of faith that brought Regent College and Jim Houston together in the late 1960s. The early years of building that temple of learning were also spent teaching in the Department of Geography at the University of British Columbia. Here was a practical outworking of the truth that knows no boundaries. There was never a question, either, that the place of Regent College was in the forum of scholarly exchange, so that its location had to be on the campus of a secular university.

The Need for Integration

This essay is similarly concerned with the challenge of integration, a challenge both intellectual and existential. Its starting point is the separation and alienation, the cleavage perceived and real, today as in the past, between religious belief and the social sciences. It is a gulf of both ignorance and prejudice, and it extends in both directions. It stands revealed both in careful pronouncements and in spontaneous small exchanges. On the part of the church we know that in some quarters there is a perception of the social sciences as the prisoners of secular humanism, while at the same time the same voices parade their own cultural captivity by their remarkably uncritical views of the workings of society. Yet distortions flow equally from the social sciences in their ignorance of religious belief. I recall a psychologist a few years ago who evinced genuine surprise that I attended a Presbyterian church, since he thought Presbyterianism had disappeared in the early years of Canadian confederation. Another colleague confided that I was the first religious person he had ever met. And, besides ignorance, one does not have to look hard for prejudice. Consider the following, written by a graduate student in a recent course of mine: "a project to reaffirm religion and tradition would reintroduce the pollution of the cultural sphere that was prevalent before the rise of modernity." But this Enlightenment war-cry is itself strangely dated in our postmodern age which has lost the former supreme confidence in human reason. Today such a bald assertion would be seen for what it is, a declaration of faith rather than a reasoned statement—but we will get to that later.

It is my contention that the gap which separates religious belief and the social sciences is *mutually prejudicial*. The church unnecessarily limits the effectiveness of its ministry to the world by avoiding the insights of social science which aid an understanding of that world. And interestingly, signs of a similar realization have entered influential segments of the world of the social sciences in recent years, a sense that its comprehension of society is incomplete without some knowledge of areas which have been the historic purview of theology. But before reaching this more hopeful conjuncture, it is worth examining the origins of this damaging division that we have inherited.

By Sight, Not by Faith

In 1865, an unknown young Irishman, William Lecky, published his

History of the Rise and Influence of the Spirit of Rationalism in Europe.
During the following half century it was reprinted more than twenty
times. Lecky's thesis, which so captured the mood of the times, was that
from the seventeenth century an irreversible sentiment of rationalism
had pervaded European culture, expelling an earlier theocentric
worldview. It was a compelling thesis for it had a contemporary ring,
being part of a second great outpouring of rationalist thought in the
period from 1855 to 1870. In 1859 Darwin's astonishing essay *The Origin of
Species* had appeared, extending scientific discourse to a realm which had
always been the monopoly of religion. Two years later J. S. Mill's
Utilitarianism pressed positivist method into the realm of ethics, while
in 1867 the first volume of Marx's *Capital* brought to bear on human
societies the same scientific naturalism that Darwin had applied in
biology.

For Lecky, intellectual progress is marked by the decay of a theocentric
worldview and its replacement by scientific rationalism. In this crucible
of debate the stakes could not have been higher. Consider its effect upon
John Ruskin, a famous Oxford art historian of the period. Brought up
in an evangelical home, in the 1830s he was extolling natural theology and
espousing the view that geology was a science of "sermons in stones."[1]
This position deeply influenced his theory of art. In the 1850s he railed
against contemporary shifts in intellectual life because of their fabrica-
tion, at every turn, of a denial of Christ. But the floodtide of skepticism
could not be held back, and in 1858 he announced his own lamented loss
of faith. "It is so new to me," he wrote that year, "to do everything
expecting only death."

By the 1870s Ruskin had returned to Christianity, but others did not.
One of the most piquant examples is Friedrich Engels, collaborator and
often financial supporter of Karl Marx. Engels grew up in a middle-class
German home, deeply impregnated by a pious Protestant faith. At the
same time the elder Engels was an industrialist and millowner, who had
a business interest in Manchester. Thither he sent his young son in the
early 1840s to learn the factory system as it had been "perfected" in the
cotton industry of Lancashire. But while there Engels began an apprenticeship his father could not have imagined. As he looked at the
tormented lives of the millworkers and the desolate environment of the
city, he pieced together the fragments of an altogether different
worldview.[2] His parents' piety now seemed to him the mark of an
outrageous hypocrisy, blind to the most rudimentary justice.[3] If religion
was the source of that blindness, then science would expose that
ideology as a deceptive opiate, which led people away from their true

destiny.

It was in this intellectual climate that Nietzsche declared the death of God, although unlike others, he was not above hinting at some of the consequences:

> What are we doing when we unchain this earth from its sun? Whither is it moving now? Whither are we moving? Away from all suns? Are we not plunging continually? Backward, sideward, forward in all directions? Is there still any up or down? Are we not straying as through an infinite nothing? Do we not feel the breath of empty space?[4]

Nietzsche thought that in an era when Western humankind was coming of age, this would be an uncomfortable, but only temporary disorientation. In fact, his powerful imagery would resonate with many descriptions today of the postmodern condition, a condition in which *all* intellectual foundations, *all* metanarratives, are treated skeptically.[5] Solid ground, a privileged and protected vantage-point, seems quite inaccessible.

Not surprisingly, a central project for a number of the nineteenth-century founders of the social sciences was the replacement of religion by a normative science of "man." This was the objective of Auguste Comte, who proposed a new "positive science," the science of society, which would become the new secular religion, provide a rational basis to social life, and replace discredited traditional religions. For Marx, "the criticism of religion is the premise of all criticism," and was a task he felt was accomplished and completed in his early work, leaving his mature intellect free to engage in more demanding material issues.[6] Similarly, the seminal French sociologist Émile Durkheim considered that the great religions "are mistaken in regard to the real nature of things: science has proved it." Like Comte, Durkheim conceived of sociology as the rational replacement of historic religion, for "the old gods are growing old or already dead, and others are not yet born."[7] Little wonder that by the time of Max Weber, the spread of rationalism and materialism seemed irreversible, and the progressive disenchantment of the world seemed an accomplished fact. But already, by the early years of the twentieth century, some uncertainty existed for Weber about the shape of this future brave new world of social engineering. Instead of offering emancipation from the old tyrannies, might it not usher in a new slavery of behavioral conditioning, an existential iron cage, in which all lived, straitjacketed? Well might Weber ask that question.

A Postmodern Reassessment

So in reviewing the positions of the pioneers of the modern social sciences, we see nothing less than the vanguard battalion in the movement toward secularization. And so it has remained through much of the twentieth century. Indeed, had this paper been written twenty years ago there would not be much left to say. Some nuances, some qualifiers, certainly might have been added, but the basic profile would remain unchanged, with the foundations established in the nineteenth century continuing as the established wisdom. An objective science of society in a world where people were come of age had replaced the subjective hopes of historic religion. Yet quite unexpected historical events will not permit such a conclusion today: the emergence of the church as a bulwark of democratic movements in Eastern Europe, liberation theology and its profound effect in Latin America and elsewhere, the explosive occurrence of the Iranian Revolution and the export of militant Islam, the emergence of the Moral Majority as a significant force in American politics in the 1980s—all of these unanticipated events testify that religious belief is as active as ever, indeed perhaps more active as a force in the public arena. At the same time some of the certainties of a received secular tradition have passed rapidly from the scene, along with, most notably and at astonishing speed, the Communist empire of Eastern Europe, Christianity's most violent, though not most effective, adversary.

In the social sciences and humanities as well, there are profound rumblings against the established orthodoxy, not yet a new consensus, but most certainly an influential criticism of received views which is breaking out all over, and creating some significant possibilities for dialogue with theology. These are most interesting times. I will touch on just two of these areas where fruitful engagement across the chasm of separation is possible, namely the debates surrounding postmodernism and post-empiricism. The prefix "post" immediately alerts us to the reality of reaction against the entrenched positions of the past.

Postmodernism is a complex and controversial movement which has swept over the arts and social sciences. It does not signify quite the same thing in any two fields, but this much is consistent: a skepticism toward the absolute claims of received wisdom, particularly the tight rational model of modernism, originating from the Enlightenment but systematized, and with its residual deism finally expelled, in the nineteenth and early twentieth centuries. There are troubling and unresolved issues in the stances adopted by postmodern authors, but here I will confine myself to what appear to be important insights and promising directions for a re-admission of theology as a credible discourse partner in the realm of social science and the humanities.

Remember Nietzsche's depiction of "an infinite nothing," "the breath of empty space." Nietzsche, we said, felt that this would be a temporary disorientation. But as Weber observed the disenchantment of the world, he was, as we have noted, far less certain:

> With the progress of science and technology, man has stopped believing in magic powers, in spirits and demons; he has lost his sense of prophecy and, above all, his sense of the sacred. Reality has become dreary, flat and utilitarian, leaving a great void in the souls of men which they seek to fill by furious activity and through various devices and substitutes.[8]

The language of the void provides a remarkably consistent set of images in the discourse of modernity,[9] and one task tackled by certain postmodernists has become the virtual re-enchantment of the world, a sometimes painstaking attempt to infuse fresh symbolism and meaning into the human realm. The sense of what has been lost has some intriguing dimensions to it. Consider these two observations, the first by a British art critic, the second by an architectural critic, neither of whom professes religious belief. For Peter Fuller, a most pressing concern is "the desultory sense of spiritual vacuity" in contemporary art objects that is the direct inheritance of the modern era.[10] Fuller turns ultimately, though with less than complete conviction, to nature as a cosmological hearth, but the space he has opened allows entry for other persuasions also. Christopher Jencks reveals the same terms of reference in a quite remarkable passage which would have formed high treason for the rational purists of the modern movement in architecture:

> Surely the ultimate paradox and strength of post-modernism is its adamant refusal to give up the imperatives of the spirit at a time when all systems of spiritual expression have been cast into doubt.[11]

Elsewhere, Jencks assures us that he writes as an agnostic, and frankly acknowledges that this viewpoint provides little help in the critical search for legitimate meaning in architecture.

The argument expressed by such authors calls for a fuller model of human nature and culture than the stripped-down model of the human animal inherited from the nineteenth century. There is a hope for "a clearing ahead of us"[12] out of the thicket of modernism, and in this opening the voice of religious belief is surely a legitimate participant, in a conversation where all the speakers acknowledge that much is now tentative and uncertain. There are some informative lessons for such a dialogue in the reaction to the positivism of Comte and J. S. Mill in the human sciences by American Reformed theologians in the late nineteenth century. Scholars like James McCosh, President of Princeton Theological Seminary, saw acutely the dangerous line being trodden by the positivist social sciences. They assailed positivism's materialism, its rejection of the metaphysical and spiritual, and its incomplete model of human nature which left the human individual no better than "a refined animal."[13] Moreover, such epistemological closure was inconsistent, for had not Comte entitled his ambitious philosophy the Religion of Humanity, and was not its claim to the stature of objective science concealing a most unbending set of foundational values and presuppositions?

The criticism of McCosh and others was of a truly prophetic nature, for it prefigured the second contemporary development in the social sciences on which I wish to comment, the post-empiricist attack on positivism. Max Weber, like the positivists and many other social scientists, had urged that social science should be value-free, that is, that there should be a clear separation between objective facts and subjective values. But this imperative assumed that such a separation was possible, that facts were indeed innocent and, like a bed of fossils, were lying there waiting to be uncovered by the gaze of the observer. But there are many today who would claim that such a separation is inherently unattainable, that fact and value cannot be prized apart by epistemological decree. Scientific research is shot through with fundamental commitments and basic beliefs, both implicit and explicit. Usually such valuing is not deliberate or pernicious, but is an expression of our humanity, of our God-given ability to recognize and apply values. But it makes "facts" far more duplicitous than they may seem to an uncritical eye, and so a full empiricist position which urges the objectivity, indeed, the scientific objectivity, of facts is not attainable. Facts are unconditionally stained by values.

Consider the recent statement of one of my colleagues on campus that regulatory controls preventing the demolition of affordable rental housing in the city of Vancouver will aggravate the housing crisis for lower-income families, because like any controls they will discourage new development. This judgment is informed by a theory of the urban land market that makes certain choices and rejects other perspectives. It is a viewpoint that ultimately *believes* in the adequacy of the private market, and contemplates public sector regulation as muddying the waters. Because of its value commitment, certain facts are overlooked: first, that demolition controls do preserve affordable units and, second, that new replacement units are not affordable. "Valuing unavoidably enters the process of concept formation."[14] Good social science requires a full recognition of the value-ladenness of both concepts and facts.

This realization has some important ramifications. The fundamental beliefs of positivist social science have been identified as prediction and control, but what if one were to begin with quite different normative values? This is clearly the position of Marxist social science, which certainly in its activist form has well-defined guiding beliefs and value commitments. Could not Christian guiding beliefs also generate a particular perspective in concept formation and selection of relevant facts? Ruskin, for example, considered that all true science "begins in the love, not the dissection of your fellow-creatures; and it ends in the love, not the analysis of God."[15] Would it not be possible for guiding beliefs such as neighborliness, justice, obligation and rights to provide the foundations of concept formation? Might we not, like the American Reformed theologians of the last century, interrogate theoretical positions for their consistency with a Christian view of human nature? If so, what might we make, for example, of the thoroughgoing egoism that Adam Smith observed as a fundamental trait that was concretized in the market system? But the central point to stress here is that post-empiricist criticism, in laying bare the value-basis of propositions, has shown positivist assertions of rationality to be only one of a varied set of foundational value commitments. As such, neither positivism nor for that matter Marxism has any basis for claiming a privileged status, and in this new position of epistemological democracy (some would see it as anarchy) it is sheer prejudice that would forbid utterance to religious worldviews.

Toward an Advantageous Partnership

The current emphasis on values and valuing has been accompanied by a new and deep interest in ethics across the social sciences and humanities. For the alliance of the market system, positivist science and a technological society produced a tight cultural hegemony, where questions of ethics were defined and resolved at the pre-conscious level. As William Blaikie observed so wisely in the late nineteenth century (1887): "It is very seldom that the individual conscience, even in the case of the best men, becomes sensible at once of the vices of its age. How many good men in this country, in the early part of this century, were zealous defenders of slavery, and in America down to a much later time!"[16] But if slavery had been abolished in Blaikie's time, colonialism had not, and many issues bound up with an abusive cultural politics practiced by European nations were not treated as ethically problematic. This is not written, it should be added, from any sense of a superior historic vantage-point, for

I have no doubt that succeeding generations will detect the mote in our eyes as well—though possibly not the beam in their own!

But I digress. The point is that in a postmodern era where positivist epistemology is seriously questioned, so too the ethics incorporated in the positivist project become problematic. In many fields there is an urgent search for a normative base, for an ethics which satisfies an increasingly complex and plural society. I have before me an announcement for a new book on the topic of evaluation methodologies. It includes a pivotal chapter, "Ethics and Politics: The Twin Failures of Positivist Science."[17] New journals abound on the search for a new ethics. The Social Sciences and Humanities Research Council in Canada has identified applied ethics as one of a small number of topics targeted in its strategic grants program. Philosophy departments across the country are experiencing a reversal of declining student numbers as they add new courses in various fields of ethics. One of the leading Western sociologists of the left calls for the rediscovery of ethics as a central category of life; a second, on the right, posits the urgent need for a deeply rooted moral belief system.[18] There is surely an accumulated wisdom that Christian theology may offer as balm to soothe this frenzy. Others certainly think so: "The moral values which religion generated and embodied for centuries can help in the work of renewal in our country, too. In fact this is already happening" (Mikhail Gorbachev).[19]

So there are legitimate, indeed compelling, points at which the divide between Christian belief and the social sciences may be bridged, to the benefit of the social sciences. But if theology has an opening for a thoughtful presence in contemporary debate, why should it bother to take advantage of it? There are two significant reasons I would like to reflect on briefly. First, the engagement with the social sciences will help the church to understand, and thus serve, society more effectively. Second, the church will also then better understand itself in relation to society. Let me fill these points out more fully.

In the quest to understand society, things are not always as they appear; causes and consequences may be concealed, subtle explanations may on the surface seem implausible. A recent personal example makes the point. I met a former mayor of Toronto in the course of my inner city research, a civic leader knowledgeable on housing matters. I mentioned that some analysis had shown that the best predictor of gentrification (social upgrading) in the inner city housing market was the amount of office space built in each metropolitan area. To my surprise, the well-informed mayor had not made this connection in his own mind between housing markets and labor markets. For him the cause was concealed from the consequence.

But there are other, equally troubling, connections which have not been made closer to home. Each month our church, like many others, includes a bulletin insert in the order of service, a news sheet distributed by Tyndale House Publishers entitled "The Church Around the World." The news vignettes are often stimulating, but they sometimes show a lack of understanding in their approach to society. Consider three juxtaposed stories in the issue for December 1989. The first announced an American poll with the finding that "84 percent of the population firmly believe in Jesus Christ." A second story stated that one in every 500 Americans is in prison, and urges the need for "full-time, Bible believing prison chaplains." A third announced that there were 3 million homeless people in the United States and that a World Vision program involving 400 churches had resettled 145 families. These vignettes give considerable pause for thought. First, what about the unarticulated connections between the three stories? Is it not incongruous, to say the very least, that a nation with the highest level of belief in the person of Jesus should also have the third highest rate of incarceration in the world and 3 million homeless people? Just what does such widespread personal belief mean if it is associated so powerfully with poverty and disorder?

Second, what about the palliative measures? More chaplains, more support for World Vision. Yes, of course, these are responses of godly obedience, but are they enough? Are more chaplains an adequate response to the epidemic of crime and its associated misery for the families of victim and aggressor? Are we satisfied that 145 families (or even 145,000 families!) are resettled, when so many more face the depredations of the streets? There can be no doubt that love for the stranger is a profound expression of Christian charity, but in a complex society it is not enough. When the Republican Party appealed to the voluntary sector to take up the slack from social programs that were terminated in the early 1980s, they were asking the churches (in particular) to assume the impossible role of caregiver for programs that had cost $128 billion in 1980. The job, understandably, was not done.

Third, to address the injustices of crime and homelessness we have to account for them as more than individual misfortunes, or individual guilt, and thereby as requiring more than individual solutions. While care for the homeless and the prisoner is necessary, so is attention to the structures that in most instances have led to their misfortunes. Any explanation offered by the social sciences would include both individual circumstances and systemic pressures, what some theologians might call sinful structures, including high unemployment, inadequate social programs and institutional racism. To attack these systemic pressures would be to engage in a strategy of prevention, which might lighten the load for the hard-pressed caring agencies who see the victimized too often when it is already too late.

There is a good deal here for the church to ponder. Particularly in conservative evangelical circles we tend to limit our attention to the individual, and lose sight of the broader context which bounds and often limits individual freedom. We forget, too, that we are social creations and that we have social obligations. Too often our model is that of the rugged individualist, not unlike the model of Christian in *Pilgrim's Progress.* Christian exudes virtues of obedience and determination which have rightly inspired believers down the centuries. But such individualism is less than the whole truth, both in explanation and in ethics. In my mind I have a picture from near the beginning of that odyssey, when Christian abandons his wife and children, even as they beg him to return. What happened to them besides their grief? Abandoned, they eventually decided to take up the same pilgrimage. In the meanwhile, did they become destitute? With time might they have joined the ranks of the homeless, his sons forced to steal to survive?[20]

Beyond Cultural Captivity

There is one further point to make in my case for a bridging of the division between religious belief and the social sciences. In engaging the social sciences, the church may not only receive a fuller understanding of society, but also gain a richer appreciation of its own positioning in society. To what extent is the church a counter-culture, salt and light to a world in need? To what extent has immersion in that world and its ends meant that the church takes on the character of a world it has been instructed to transform? That of course was the serious failing of the church at Corinth, which had become polluted by the sophistry and sensuousness of the society of its day.

Often our cultural captivity is of such a magnitude that we are unaware of it (as William Blaikie noted). The various practices of ideology critique as taught in the social sciences encourage a state of mind which is self-conscious about its own values and ideological commitments, and may give account of them. For example, to what extent may we connect the individualism which is an emphasis of our theology with the unrecognized individualism of the market place around us? Why is it that in his book *Fragmented Gods* Reginald Bibby finds the supermarket metaphor so powerful, depicting us as religious consumers who pick and choose our commitments, ever alert to the special offer, without taking up the cost of discipleship?[21]

In *Less Than Conquerors,* Doug Frank considers the conservative church as it entered the twentieth century.[22] He notes the harsh criticism uttered by Billy Sunday against consumerism, but observes that as an appeal to individual action alone, it was only ever a partial and ineffectual critique. It failed, writes Frank, because it did not deal with the systemic nature of the problem, the power of social structures. That same consumerism, he adds ominously, continues not only to infiltrate but indeed to define the church. He would appear to be correct. A survey commissioned by the Christian Advertising Forum in 1982 could not find a distinctive pattern of consumer behavior among Christians. The devastating conclusion of the poll was that "scriptural exhortations to lead a Christ-like, Bible-based lifestyle are consistently ignored. American Christians have been captivated by secular opportunities and possessions."[23] The cultural captivity of the church is a matter of the utmost seriousness. I am suggesting that the tools of social science (they are no more than that) can aid us to be more self-conscious, and thus more faithful in making not only the right connections, but also the right separations.

And so I conclude facing the narrow path which Jim Houston has so faithfully trod, a path not defined by the false integration of compromise, for that surely is the broad avenue with another destination, but a path defined by both integration and distinction, gloriously in the world yet gloriously apart from it. For over twenty years as a Christian social scientist I have been challenged, inspired, and all too frequently chastised by these words: "Do not be conformed to this world, but be transformed by the renewing of your mind" (Ro 12:2). For the secret of finding and following the narrow path lies precisely here.

Notes

[1] Peter Fuller, *Theoria: Art and the Absence of Grace* (London: Chatto & Windus, 1988) 35.
[2] Friedrich Engels, *The Condition of the Working Class in England* (ed. W. O. Henderson & W. H. Chaloner; Oxford: Basil Blackwell, 1958).
[3] Steven Marcus, *Engels, Manchester and the Working Class* (New York: Random House, 1974).
[4] Quoted in Stephen Kern, *The Culture of Time and Space: 1880-1920* (Cambridge, Mass.: Harvard University Press, 1983) 178-179.
[5] Jean-Francois Lyotard, *The Postmodern Condition* (Manchester: Manchester University Press, 1984).
[6] Cited in R. O'Toole, *Religion: Classic Sociological Approaches* (Toronto: McGraw Hill Ryerson, 1984) 65.
[7] E. Durkheim, *The Elementary Forms of the Religious Life* (New York: Collier, 1961) 83, 474-475. I am grateful to Bruce Martin for these citations: B. Martin, "Faith without Focus: Neighbourhood Transition and Religious Change in Inner City Vancouver" (M.A. thesis, University of British Columbia, 1989).

⁸ Quoted in Daniel Bell, "The Return of the Sacred? The Argument on the Future of Religion," in *The Winding Passage* (New York: Basic Books, 1980) 324-354.

⁹ See Kern, *Culture of Time*, and D. Ley, "Modernism, Postmodernism and the Struggle for Place," in *The Power of Place* (ed. John Agnew & James Duncan; London: Unwin Hyman 1989) 44-65.

¹⁰ Peter Fuller, "Towards a New Nature for the Gothic," *Art and Design* 3/3-4 (1987) 5-10.

¹¹ Charles Jencks & William Chaitkin, *Architecture Today* (New York : Abrams, 1982) 217.

¹² Bell, "Return," 353.

¹³ Charles Cashdollar, "Auguste Comte and the American Reformed Theologians," *Journal of the History of Ideas* 34 (1978) 61-79.

¹⁴ David Lyon, "Valuing in Social Theory: Postempiricism and Christian Responses," *Christian Scholars' Review* 12 (1983) 324-338.

¹⁵ Fuller, "Towards," 165.

¹⁶ William Blaikie, *The First Book of Samuel* (repr., Minneapolis, Minn.: Klock and Klock, 1978) 400.

¹⁷ Egon Guba & Yvonna Lincoln, *Fourth Generation Evaluation* (Newbury Park, Calif.: Sage, 1989) chap. 4.

¹⁸ Jürgen Habermas, *Toward a Rational Society* (London: Heinemann, 1971); Daniel Bell, *The Cultural Contradictions of Capitalism* (New York: Basic Books, 1976).

¹⁹ Reported in *Maclean's* (11 December 1989) 32.

²⁰ Dominique Lapierre's remarkable account of poverty in Calcutta in *The City of Joy* (Garden City, N.Y.: Doubleday, 1985) describes poignantly and repeatedly the dissolution of moral standards before the immanent catastrophe of starvation.

²¹ Reginald Bibby, *Fragmented Gods: The Poverty and Potential of Religion in Canada* (Toronto: Irwin, 1987).

²² Doug Frank, *Less Than Conquerors* (Grand Rapids: Eerdmans, 1986).

²³ Quoted by Peter Williamson, "The Loss of a Christian Way of Life," in *Summons to Faith and Renewal* (ed. P. Williamson & Kevin Perrotta; Ann Arbor, Mich.: Servant, 1983) 68.

23
The Community of Faith as the Locus of Faith-Learning Integration

Kenneth R. Badley

Educators have now voiced their concern for *EDUCAtional integration* and *curriculum integration* for all of a century. For almost half that century, *the integration of faith and learning* has been the goal of men and women of faith who have aimed to express what shape education should take when informed by supernaturalist convictions. Yet one wants to know what *the integration of faith and learning* means. Precisely what do those who popularize this phrase envision for education? What will happen in classrooms? What will transpire in students' minds? What will take place in the church?

Despite achieving popularity as a slogan, "integration" still lacks precision in at least four ways. First, the term can denote fusion, incorporation, dialogue and transformation: four different things. Second, integration could be a process or a product. Will we always find ourselves called to *integrate faith and learning,* or can we hope to finish at some time and then embody our findings in a canon? Third, we need someone to clarify how integration connects to psychological adjustment and personal life, even to sanctification. Finally, debate continues as to where the integration of faith and learning occurs. Does this integration happen in a student's consciousness? Or does it embed itself in curriculum designs as a consequence of the careful discussions of those who plan the substance and sequence of courses?

In what follows, I will respond to the questions about the locus of integration. To do so, I will trace and then try to wed two discrete lines of reflection: Christian thought regarding education and educators' thought regarding integration. In weaving these two lines of thought together, I will contend that the community of faith is the optimum context for integrating faith and learning.

The Church and Education

To begin, what has the church ever done about education? The short reply, of course, is "almost everything." People of Christian faith have always cherished a special interest in education. We may grant the truism that Greek thought shaped learning in Western culture. We should note promptly, however, that Christian effort spread that learning. To be fair, we should look at the Christian attitudes at the time of declining Roman power. Some held that Christianity should have nothing to do with its surrounding culture. Tertullian clearly expresses this outlook in his paraphrase of 2Co 6:14:

> What is there in common between Athens and Jerusalem? between the Academy and the Church? ... away with all projects for a "Stoic," a "Platonic" or a "Dialectic Christianity." ... The Son of God was born, I am not ashamed of it because it is shameful; the Son of God died, it is credible for the very reason that it is silly; and, having been buried, He rose again, it is certain because it is impossible.[1]

Jerome also alludes to Paul by inquiring, "How can Horace go with the psalter, Virgil with the Gospels, Cicero with the apostle?"[2] Comparable interpretations did not die with Tertullian and Jerome, with Alcuin centuries later, or even with some fundamentalists in our century. Throughout church history there have always been some Christians who have persistently viewed separation from culture as essential to correct expression of biblical faith.[3] The conviction that education cannot befriend faith usually figures as part of the separation stance.

Not all patristic or medieval Christians agreed with Tertullian and Jerome, however. As early as the second and third centuries Clement of Alexandria and Origen endeavored to reconcile Christianity with classical philosophy. They articulated what in effect was an early form of scholasticism and fashioned the base for the Christian philosophizing which reached its zenith in Thomas Aquinas' attempt to recover Aristotle and make Greek philosophy more palatable to late medieval Christians. The goal of Thomas, and Thomism after him, was nothing less ambitious than the synthesis of theology with all knowledge.[4]

Contemporary with the success of this monumental synthesis of theology and learning, the universities of Europe came to life. The church found itself comfortably ensconced in power politically, and, in the curriculum, theology reigned as the "queen of the sciences." As it had done for several rather bleak centuries, the church sponsored schools at all educational levels, and should take credit for fostering much of what literacy and learning remained in Europe at the time.

However, the scientific spirit of Renaissance learning and exploration appeared in this milieu and, eventually, forced the church to adapt and retreat. Church dogma faced increasing difficulty making its tradition- ally dominant contribution to the organization of knowledge, perhaps because it had completed its job of articulating the grand vision based on theology. Medieval speculations and synthesis proved inadequate to the new task of discovering the world. As a result, for some five or six centuries, thinkers saw it as their role to expand the stock of knowledge through science and exploration. Observation and reason, rather than authority, became the final measures of epistemological matters. Chris- tendom stared its own dismantling in the face, a dismantling nowhere more evident than in académe. Simultaneously, the influence of the church upon everyday public life declined. To a greater degree than it had done for centuries, the future life people expected in heaven shrank in importance relative to present life on earth.

By the eighteenth and nineteenth centuries, another new breeze began to blow in the universities. The spirit and the fruit of the Enlighten- ment manifested themselves in a shift toward the natural sciences and the professions. This shift came accompanied, especially in America, by a corresponding loss of interest in training ministers. Puritans, for example, established Harvard and Princeton. But those universities shifted in the nineteenth century to regard the whole realm of knowl- edge as their proper domain. The universities allowed the sciences and philosophy to dislodge theology from its standing as chief. Scholarship required objectivity. Higher education could make no more room for dogma and indoctrination, the ostensible hallmarks of education in- formed by faith. On another front, the elective system replaced the fixed curriculum. Yale, Michigan, and Virginia led the way toward offering a new type of higher education where student choice determined the course of study.

The twentieth century completed the secularizing process in all levels of public education. It also watched many more confessional colleges become universities with divinity schools attached. Some went further, creating departments of religious studies in which students studied Christianity alongside other major religions. Repeating the steps taken a century earlier, teaching and learning were to be freed from the doctrinaire style that allegedly characterized church-sponsored education. The liberal-conservative controversies at the beginning of this century created a special problem for people of evangelical conviction, especially in North America. Evangelicals lost control over the prominent seminaries and found themselves exiled to the margins of higher education. The ecclesiastical monopoly on education was broken. Academic Christendom ended. Viewed from the other side, that which had consistently furnished the "uni-" in university was banished. But, having shaken off its confessional past, higher education now confronted a new demand: it had to procure alternative ways to craft a cosmos from the dozens of competing disciplines, worldviews, and values that, lacking any organizing hub or principle, produced only competition, dissonance, atomization, and chaos. We have followed educational developments into our own century. The chaotic state we find there leads us now to turn our attention to integration.

Educators, Integration, and the Locus of Integration

What have educators had to say about integration? Again, the short reply is "almost everything." A brisk survey of the territory educators have claimed for integration in the last hundred years reveals abundant optimism and zeal. They have maintained that integration in or of the curriculum relates to curriculum sequencing, choice of subject matter, teaching methodologies, and, according to some, even mental health. The first expressions of concern for integration began to appear in the 1890s. Without attributing causality prematurely, one can recognize that following closely on the eclipse of supernaturalist epistemologies, Thomistic and otherwise, interest in educational integration began to increase. This is not to argue that educators of the nineteenth century saw around them disintegration. Nonetheless, by the century's end, interest in educational integration had put down roots and was growing. In the present century, this regard for integration flourished three times. *The integration of faith and learning* made its appearance as part of the second of those flourishes, in the 1950s.

Why do educators keep calling for educational integration and, inside the kingdom, for integrating faith with learning? One can accept or reject the argument that a Christocentric worldview had previously provided the coherence in education. Regardless of the church's part in educational history, a survey of the educational landscape now will uncover deep concern about educational disintegration. Education faces charges of fragmenting, pigeonholing, compartmentalizing, splintering; of haphazardly adding without connecting, and of becoming trivial and isolated.[5] This unhappy state of affairs has elicited hundreds of calls for integration and thousands of separate efforts to forge integration. In the midst of this clamor, the locus of integration persists as one of the controversial questions surrounding integration. Yet no one has ever explicated the concept adequately. The parallel question of where faith and learning should or will be integrated has likewise gone unanswered.

Educators have proffered three different answers to the locus question. Two of the answers approximate the opposing sentiments in the debate often labelled "the logical versus the psychological." A third approach considers both elements as necessary for integration to occur.

Some educators look at integration, and, by implication, faith-learning integration, as a process that happens within the consciousness of students. On this account, integration is the fruit of several psychological or pedagogical processes. One can distinguish two lines of thought within this view. One line emphasizes personality adjustment. It focuses on the student's construction of a coherent and worthwhile cognitive whole from the various elements of the curriculum. Some Christians explicitly view faith-learning integration in this way. They have been quick to appreciate the explanatory value of the concept of *worldview* or *Weltanschauung* in trying to articulate their conception of faith and learning integration. "Worldviewish integration," by which one sees the connections among the various disciplines of thought and between thought and daily life, makes intuitive sense to some students. The Christian student who sees his or her own mind reconstructed in God's hands (Ro 12:1-2) often gains an insight into the meaning of education to which other students are not privy. The kind of perspectival transformation or *integration* spoken of in Romans 12 fits, albeit roughly, into the "student-as-locus" answer to the question at hand.

Others give a quite different answer. Rooted in a logical or epistemological frame of reference, they view the curriculum as the primary locus of integration. When one emphasizes the logical aspects of integration, the planning and sequence of the curriculum contents become paramount. Designed right, the curriculum will foster integration. Designed wrong, the curriculum anneals the compartmentalization and splintering that already bedevil the modern university and mind. A typical expression of the notion that integration occurs in curricula or in knowledge appears in Webster's Dictionary. Webster's definition of integration reads: "The organization of teaching matter to interrelate or unify subjects usually taught in separate academic courses or departments." One finds many other definitions of "integration" within educational literature affirming that the curriculum is the locus of integration. Additionally, much of the criticism of curriculum focuses, for example, on curricular or institutional departmentalization as the opposite of integration, and calls for specialists to draw together so the relationships between their specialties can become apparent. In these accounts, the curriculum, not the student's consciousness, explicitly functions as the locus of educational integration. Outside specifically educational thought, one finds a long line of thinkers attempting to unify knowledge by classifying the fields of knowledge in various arrangements. A brief review of intellectual history brings to mind the major attempts of Aquinas, Dewey, Plato, Bacon and Hegel, along with the lesser known attempts of Wundt, Comte and Bentham. In most of these schemata where knowledge requires no knowers, the person seems to slip from the picture.

A third group of thinkers envisions twin loci: the student and the curriculum. Careful curriculum planning and student effort figure as necessary conditions (or at least as typical conditions) for educational integration to occur. In these accounts, it is individual students who do or do not achieve integration. Integration is dependent on the learners themselves successfully grasping the relationships between disciplines, and between curricular contents and daily life. This requirement recalls the description of the "psychological" answer to the locus question. Educators cannot produce integration for learners or hand it to them somehow ready-made. However, they are actively to foster integration by the thoughtful way in which they arrange and offer content. This requirement recalls the "logical" answer to the locus question. It also recalls the attacks against subject-based curricula: unsuitable curricular arrangements hinder students from seeing the relationships that exist between the areas of knowledge. Put negatively, we see that the interactive answer to the locus question is this: integration is not only a curricular affair to be planned by committees, deans, curriculum designers and professors. Nor is it a strictly internal matter, a project best left to students themselves. Curricular and institutional arrangements do matter. But students must assemble a cognitive cosmos for themselves. Neither condition is sufficient. Both are necessary.

What should one make of this three-sided debate? Classroom experience points to the efficacy of the more demanding, interactive view. While bad pedagogy can hinder integration, good pedagogy will not ensure it. And although good pedagogy will not ensure integration, we do not want to discourage it. Conceivably, a student might emerge from the most chaotic curriculum with an education we could accurately label *integrated*. This possibility shows the importance of the student's mindset and worldview to the integration of faith and learning. We are compelled to admit that regardless of what happens in curriculum, if integration ever happens anywhere it happens in the consciousness of students.

The Community of Faith and the Integration of Faith and Learning

Educational thinkers have carried on the locus discussion largely without reference to faith. Yet the answer we accept to the general locus question directly affects our understanding of how students will integrate faith and learning. If integration in general cannot be guaranteed by logical curriculum design, then neither can the integration of faith and learning. The corollary to that statement, of course, serves as a charter for any Christian in higher education: if the student's consciousness is the locus of integration, then those of us wanting students to "take captive every thought to make it obedient to Christ" (2Co 10:5) ought to attend as carefully to what goes on in their thinking and in their development and understanding of their theistic worldview as we do to our course syllabi and class preparation.

In the divine economy of higher education today, four distinct kinds of institutions have found a part: the public university, the Christian liberal arts college, the Bible college and the seminary. We do not expect to find hostility to faith in the last three institutions named. Thus, their students should find it simpler to reconcile their faith with their course contents. But in the public university, we expect that course contents will not be pre-interpreted by people sympathetic to Christian faith. Professors will not teach in such a way as to reconcile the course contents with Christian theology or convictions. No one will point out in advance for the student the points of agreement, disagreement, and connection or common interest between a given topic and Christian thought. The course contents, where they are hostile to faith, will come to the student in their harshest forms, unmediated with any eye to maintaining faith or enhancing understanding from a Christian perspective. Whatever we may think about integration in general, we thus grasp that the curriculum, in the public university at least, is clearly not the locus of faith-learning integration.

If I have described this particular educational milieu accurately, students in it live in a vulnerable position. They must face the challenges of the world of thought while assuming no conflict exists between the truth therein and the truth of Scripture. Presumably they do so with God's help, but, as I have described it, they will do so without any supporting social structure. In such circumstances, many students will become discouraged, lose faith altogether, or maintain faith only by lapsing into religious schizophrenia. In view of these possibilities, the whole church must consider its part in the process of integrating faith and learning.

We all maintain our beliefs—of any kind—in the face of others' questions and sometimes our own doubts. And we find our beliefs easier to maintain when some around us believe as we do. We might call this the "social component of belief." Periodically, we may also remember the minority status of the Christian at university. Typically, these young Christians find Christian belief challenged in their first weeks of university. They face questions—almost daily—not only about the tenets of their faith, but about their epistemology, their views of marriage, family and culture, and their convictions about the final source of meaning. Under this questioning, students come to feel keenly and existentially that they are in a cognitive minority. Further, they sometimes feel the creeping doubt that they are wrong after all, and the majority right about which worldview makes the most sense of life.

As we come to appreciate these aspects of belief, especially the cognitive status of the Christian in university, we might respond by asking how we can aid students in keeping faith while facing the daily onslaught of analysis and critique. We can aid our students by coming alongside them in the midst of their tensions. When we do, we shift the locus of integration by implicitly inviting them to continue their struggles, not alone, but within the relative safety of the faith community. Integration finally happens within the consciousness of the student, but the student can approach the task in a far better frame of mind if he or she sees that others have pulled alongside.

What qualities does the community of faith possess that make it the superior context in which to integrate faith and learning? Part of the answer lies in exploring *community.* Perhaps the best-known analysis of community was that offered by Ferdinand Tonnies a hundred years ago in *Gemeinschaft and Gesellschaft.* In this book, translated as *Community and Society,* Tonnies portrays community in opposition to society.[6] Industrial society severs natural affiliations in its pragmatic, impersonal, rational concern with production and efficient organization of life. People still need *Gemeinschaft*-type connections, however, and they will seek those connections in family, friendships, other voluntary relationships, village and church. From Tonnies' splitting of community and society, we now derive the not-always-negative sense that community implies a polarity of *us* and *them.*

Who are the "us" in Tonnies' picture? All communities ask this question, but especially when we speak of the community of faith, we want and need to understand if we are merely an aggregation of separate individuals or if something larger bonds us together. We shall see ourselves as sharing some of the characteristics of a federation, an association, a fraternity, a company, a lodge, a caste, a union, an order, a group of settlers, a consort, a guild, a troupe or a troop. Regardless of which comparisons strike us as most truly apropos, we shall realize that we have no reason to revert to the separationist stance of Tertullian or Jerome with regard to faith and learning. Rather, we can embrace the reality of Christ's work in us and in our behalf, a reality that makes us different from other communities. And we can embrace the admission that our common sympathies engender trust. The safety that the group perspective provides for its individuals implies that those individuals support each other and stand with each other, burying smaller disagreements in favor of larger common commitments. In this kind of context, we shall be able to support those who struggle to reconcile their faith and learning. When they face opposition, students can take reassurance from the fact that others believe as they do. They are therefore safe. Although physically alone, students can stand knowing the church stands with them. But they cannot take such reassurance unless we have given them warrant to do so by our actions.

Baldly, the church does not integrate faith and learning. The persons doing the learning will be doing the integrating. But the church can help. In my own attempts to help, I meet different university students for coffee from time to time. At some point in the conversation I ask, "How is it going?" or even, "Well, are you still a Christian?" These simple questions often lead quickly to the student's recounting to me the questions that Blake's poetry or Skinner's psychology have raised for Christian faith. Three threads seem woven into the experience of most Christian university students. These threads repeatedly appear in my conversations with students. First, they want to keep their faith. Second, they want to participate fully in their classes and, more broadly, in the intellectual life of the whole university. Third, they feel that their congregation does not understand their existential discord.

In attempting to reconcile these desires and perceptions, these young adults face two problems. They need to persevere through their own periods of doubt. And they desperately desire some word about resolution: where will they find it, can anyone help them, and how long it will take? For these Christians, *the integration of faith and learning* clearly connects to what they see as the very survival of their faith. Curriculum design is the furthest thing from their minds. But older Christian adults can move into students' situations at the very point of these tensions. Face to face with the students we know, we should underline that we think tough questions about faith are justified; anyone in their circumstances would undergo the same doubts. If the assessment that integration occurs inside the student is even half right, then one task of the community of faith is to remind our students day after day that we do share in community. We should remind them that, in the midst of their struggle to reconcile their faith commitments with what they are learning, we love them. We should show them that they are among us and not outside us during their university years. We should remind them that God loves them, that we can survive their period of doubt, that they can survive their period of doubt, that fine Christian people at all times have contemplated the perplexities of existence, meaning, evil, and identity, and that one is neither silly nor ungrateful for asking these questions. We share their doubts and their joys. Their intellectual burdens may be theirs. But we have made their burdens ours as well; we want to help carry those burdens. Our students may be able to reconcile—integrate—their beliefs with their learning alone. But they are more to likely to succeed in that integration as we invite and draw them, their efforts, and all their tensions into the community of faith.

Notes:

[1] From chap. 7 of "The Prescription Against Heretics," cited in J. V. Langmead Casserly, *The Christian in Philosophy* (London: Faber & Faber, 1949) 21-22.

[2] Letters, xxii, 29, cited in Leland Ryken, *Triumphs of the Imagination* (Downers Grove, Ill.: InterVarsity, 1979) 13.

[3] See Lev Shestov, *Athens and Jerusalem* (trans. Bernard Martin; Athens, Ohio: Ohio University Press, 1966), and H. Richard Niebuhr, *Christ and Culture* (New York: Harper & Row, 1951) 45-82.

[4] See Étienne Gilson, *The Spirit of Medieval Philosophy* (New York: Scribners, 1940).

[5] See Philip H. Phenix, *Realms of Meaning* (New York: McGraw-Hill, 1964) 36-37; Harry S. Broudy, Joe R. Burnett, & B. Othaniel Smith, *Democracy and Excellence in American Secondary Education* (Chicago: Rand-McNally, 1963) 11; and Richard Pring, "Curriculum Integration," *The Philosophy of Education* (ed. R. S. Peters; London: Oxford University Press, 1973) 123-126.

[6] *Community and Society* (trans. and ed. C. Loomis; New York: Harper & Row, 1963).

24
Prophetic Spirituality: Markings for the Journey

Ron Dart

THE SHOPPING MALL OF POSTMODERN THOUGHT[1] HAS MANY kinds of stores in it; a few of these shops specialize in spirituality. We are immediately confronted with many options when we enter these attractive stores. If we meditatively read through some of the books, dialogue with people in the shops or look at any of the posters (advertising all sorts of retreats and workshops), we soon come to see that spirituality can and does mean many things. Does this mean, then, that all options are equally valid? Is it possible to discover an authentic Christian spirituality in the marketplace of competing religious traditions? This short essay will offer a few suggestions to help us on our journey.

Markings: A Metaphor for the Journey
We live in an age in which the old paths have been overgrown, the ancient springs have been deserted and the golden string seems lost. There is a fervent religious longing in our time, but the longing, although intense and real, often lacks depth and direction. The tension that exists between religious desire as such and how that desire should be shaped, formed and educated is the challenge of authentic Christian spirituality. The classical past can teach us a great deal about the nature of desires, and the need to order and organize them towards a certain end. If we are willing to trek to these ancient springs, we might just find the water we need to nourish us on our own hike through time.

Dag Hammarskjöld's book *Markings*[2] has been a faithful companion on my pilgrimage since it was given to me as a gift twenty years ago. The metaphor of markings can assist us on our journey into the authentic sources of Christian spirituality. Markings are important for hikers; without them it is easy to become disoriented in the high regions. If we pay due attention to the metaphor of markings, we might find the path we need, a path that will guide us to the still point of Love that is the source and center of all things.[3]

There are three markings I have spent, perhaps, too much time at in this paper: spirituality and tradition, spirituality and experience and spirituality and political justice. I have also spent time, although much less, at two other markings: spirituality and the church and the relationship of Christian spirituality to the spirituality of other religious traditions. There are, obviously, many other markings on the journey, but a paper of this brevity can only deal with a few. Our desires will take on a new depth and focus as we heed these markings, and as our desires are rightly ordered towards their true end, we will move ever closer to an authentic Christian spirituality.

Spirituality and Tradition
We hear a great deal these days about the clear-cutting of our forests, and the impact such brutal treatment of the trees has on our environment, but we should also be aware how our tradition has been clear-cut. A few stumps remain to remind us that once a great forest of wisdom, goodness, and beauty stood high; now there is little but thin soil, bushes and weeds. It is ironic that many who claim to be Christian, embracing a faith firmly rooted in the thick soil of time and history, are often a-historical. Many well-meaning Christians go blank when a serious discussion of tradition is offered as a guide for us.[4] It is the communal memory of tradition that informs and teaches us how the cloud of witnesses have interpreted the Bible and made sense of their faith in different times and places.

Those who long to move forward on the journey without taking the time to look back often head down dubious and questionable trails. Tradition offers us insight and wisdom if we are open to receive it. This does not mean, though, that tradition is an end in itself or that all the answers we seek can be found within the memory of the community. Tradition is thick with diverse and conflicting traditions; hence tradition is incapable by itself of offering comprehensive guidance. Everything hinges on how tradition is interpreted, and the interpretive eyeglasses that are chosen inevitably involve presuppositions that constantly need to be reassessed and evaluated. Gadamer's *Truth and Method* highlights, in a sensitive way, the importance of tradition; he also demonstrates that the method we use to interpret tradition will predetermine the insights we find. But, if we think and live from tradition, we are less likely to be beguiled by many of the modern gurus who peddle cheapjack spiritual wares. Tradition, at its best, protects us from various forms of myopic reductionism, and it does this by offering serious alternatives to the moment we live in. The alternatives we pick from tradition will determine how we face the challenge of the postmodern world.

The Christian heritage is a blend of three traditions: Orthodox, Roman Catholic and Protestant. Protestant spirituality is the youngest child in the family. Orthodoxy and Roman Catholicism are much older, and there is a stone-quarried wisdom in these traditions that is often lacking in Protestant spirituality. Western spirituality is indebted to Roman Catholic and Protestant thought and the tensions, inhibitions and theological struggles between these two constituencies.

Contemporary writers on Orthodox spirituality, like George Maloney[5] and Paulos Mar Gregorios,[6] point the way to all sorts of concealed vistas of insight. They offer an open hand, and if we take it, they will lead us along paths that reveal many forgotten places. As we pass through the doors that Maloney and Mar Gregorios open up to us, we will discover a world, like Hagia Sophia itself, rich with beauty, fragrance and wisdom. As we enter this splendid cathedral, all sorts of new possibilities will light up our soul. The Orthodox understanding of icons,[7] their spirituality,[8] their generous natural theology, their understanding of deification and union in Christ and their conciliar view of the church,[9] can renew a weary Western Christianity that has lost the ability to soar like the eagle.

The light of Orthodoxy had an important impact on Celtic Christianity, and, I suspect, as we seek out the lost places of Celtic Christianity, we will uncover a hidden treasure.[10] Orthodoxy and Celtic Christianity never participated in modernity, unlike Protestantism and Roman Catholicism, so they have insights to offer that can take us into the postmodern world in a creative and illuminating way. Orthodoxy and Celtic spirituality should not be idealized or romanticized, but, if we hope to find the authentic wells of Christian spirituality, we must be willing to trek to these places and lower our buckets.

Classical Christian spirituality has also dealt with issues like feminism,[11] environmental concerns,[12] and God-language[13] in ways that can teach us a great deal. If we are willing to bend our ear to the past, we might just hear a voice that will speak the word that will lead us through some of the brambles and thickets we are caught in to an open clearing. Tradition will not provide all the answers we need, but without the marking of tradition, it is much easier to lose our way on the journey.

Spirituality and Experience

I deliberately began this paper on spirituality with tradition, because tradition encourages us to exercise rather than exorcise our communal memory. Human experience that banishes memory trivializes spirituality and reduces the significance of religious experience to the very smallest circle turns.

Spirituality can be defined as our experience of union with God.[14] This is what makes spiritual theology different from dogmatic, biblical, or systematic theology. Spirituality begins with experience and reflection on experience. Since all religious experience must be interpreted, Christian spirituality attempts to deal with the meaning of our experience as we, by grace, grow in union with God. Memory plays an important role in how we experience God and how we interpret how we experience God. Those who reduce the meaning of spirituality to a few intense and concentrated events, like a Damascus or Sinai experience, a rapturous moment of inexpressible union with the divine, an overwhelming sense of the holy[15] or a merging with the One,[16] highlight an important feature of spirituality, but there is more to mature Christian spirituality than a few intense experiences. Those who are too eager for these types of things or who use ascetic techniques to induce them[17] usually do damage to themselves.

Union with God is much more demanding, elusive and subtle than many gurus make it out to be. If we are going to have an adequately broad understanding of spirituality and experience, we must be willing to live with uncertainty, have a vision of what it means to be fully human and be ever open to the tug of the divine Lover.

I have mentioned that memory plays an essential role in our experience of God; so do our affections and intellect.[18] Any kind of Christian spirituality that does not hold together memory, affections and intellect enters a forest with little light and few paths out; this trinity of the soul is the mirror and gateway into the Holy Trinity. Many Christians who hunger for a deeper experience of God often come from a tradition that subordinates the intellect and elevates the affections, or pampers the intellect and represses the affections. Unfortunately, much discussion of Christian experience by pietists never gets far beyond reacting to rationalism. The pietism, for example, of *Pia Desideria*[19] is a reaction to an arid Lutheran orthodoxy just as *Pilgrim's Progress, The Imitation of Christ* and *Practising the Presence of God* are, in their different ways, reactions to the dry scholasticism of the late medieval period. Pietists are on the right track when they insist on the importance of experience; they go wrong when they identify their shallow level of experience with the depths of authentic spirituality. Books like Augustine's *Of True Religion,* Dionysius the Areopagite's *Mystical Theology,* Gregory of Nyssa's *Life of Moses,* John Scotus Erigena's *The Voice of the Eagle* or Bonaventura's *The Mind's Road to God* are excellent correctives to the inadequate religiosity of pietism and the charismatic movement.[20]

Whenever the intellect and affections are separated and memory is nudged out of the house of the soul, we tend to get a dysfunctional spirituality. When this occurs, sentimentality rules the day, all sorts of silly emotional experiences are equated with authentic spirituality, and God's name is taken in vain. This, I fear, is the lot of much modern Christianity.

Augustine's *Confessions* and Rousseau's *Confessions* highlight what occurs when our desires are ordered by love (*ordo amoris*) and what happens when human experience turns in on itself in search of itself. Augustine's soul, like Chartres cathedral, is open and spacious, whereas Rousseau is trapped in the maze of his ego. Augustine argued that when our intellect is illuminated by the divine order and our memory is stirred to constantly remember the highest, our affections (desires) will naturally move towards their proper place as a homing pigeon instinctively flies homeward.

Authentic Christian spirituality never ignores the hard fact that death is the door into life. The cheap grace that dominates much populist religion refuses to face the uncomfortable notion that we are called to die, to take up our cross, to challenge the pretensions and imperialism of our ego. Kierkegaard once said, "God made all things out of nothing, and everything he wishes to use, he first reduces to nothing." John of the Cross often spoke of the need to face the nothingness (*nada*) that we often identify as the I; it is as we are willing to move into this dark night of death that the fullness (*todo*) of the new self comes into being.[21] Real death means letting go, detaching ourselves or moving away from the district of addictions, dependencies and fictions regarding ourselves and God that we have created;[22] it also means being open to allow our intellect, memory and affections to be purged of impurities. There is a Zen story of a professor who went to visit a Zen master. The roshi poured tea into the professor's cup and kept pouring until the tea spilled onto the professor's lap. The professor jumped up and began to vigorously protest; the Zen master calmly said, "You are like this cup. You are so full of your opinions, nothing can enter."[23] Meister Eckhart spoke about the tendency we have to equate the nothingness of the ego with the I. It is only as we realize the ego is empty that we are in a position to be filled with the divine life. John of Climacus dealt with this when he observed how we can be a success, mastering the ocean in the sense of gratifying the many wants of the ego, but when we are called to turn inward, to return to port and home, we often ignore the invitation. It is when we return to harbor that we realize the ship of the ego needs an overhauling; it is at port that this takes place. But, as John suggested, it is a pitiable sight to see those who have mastered the ocean of the outer life lose their bearings and shipwreck in the harbor of the inner life. It is only as we are willing to be stripped and refitted that we will be able to slip by the Sirens that lure on all sides.

The spiritual tradition in Christianity uses different images to point to this latent new self in all of us. Some authors talk about the seed of the word (*logos spermatikos*) while others speak about the spark of the soul (*scintilla animae, Seelen fünklein*). But the tradition agrees that in the depths or the ground of the soul the potential exists for a reborn life. The new life we are offered is a gift, a birth and an awakening. The *Brautmystik* or bride-bridegroom tradition of spirituality that we see so beautifully written about by Origen, Bernard of Clairvaux and Teresa of Avila as they interpret the Song of Songs, and the *Wesenmystik* tradition of spirituality that we see so exquisitely described by Evagrius, John Erigena and the Rhineland mystics converge in the God of Love who is pure Being. This new life in God is outlined in Paulos Mar Gregorios's *Cosmic Man*. The new being we are called to live forth must shed the cocoon of the ego, be illuminated by the divine light and grow into an existential understanding of union with God; this is the aim and purpose of the spiritual life, and Jesus the Christ is the gateway to this new reality.

The new life in Christ will mean, naturally, different things to different people. Each person has a unique disposition and is at a different stage or passage of life, and authentic Christian spirituality must take these variables into consideration in the area of spiritual direction.[24] Each person has a God-given destiny (fate), and the task of life is to be open to the unfolding process of God's calling, and to love it (*amor fati*). It is as a person awakens to the new self that the deeper meaning of fate, vocation or calling is revealed, but openness to the pressure of the Being of God is essential throughout. Blake wisely realized that individual calling is like a golden string, and as each of us follows the lead of the string we are offered, we will be led to the gates of the new Jerusalem, a city that is being built in time but will not be completed till the curtains of history are closed.[25]

Our calling is both individual and corporate, in time yet beyond time, immanent yet transcendent. Union with God, if it is legitimate union, must lead us to share God's love for the world, a world God created, sustains and continues to love. Any form of spirituality that merely turns inward but does not turn outward is not authentic spirituality. Unfortunately, some of the finest writers on spirituality never moved outward in a serious and substantial way; they were so concerned about essential and spiritual integrity, that they turned their backs on time and history. A graphic and telling example of this is the lapsed Roman Catholic Martin Heidegger.[26] He was so concerned with challenging the pretensions of modernity and thinking through the meaning of being in time that he was oblivious to how many people were being mistreated in Nazi Germany in his time. Heidegger is a perfect example of thought and spirit detached from time and history. Although many writers on spirituality do not go to this extreme, there is a dangerous tendency to reduce spirituality to aesthetic, liturgical, cultic and inner experiences that are not connected with the world of matter, society and politics.

Spirituality and Political Justice

Classical Greek and Jewish thought affirmed that to be human was to be social and political; those who turned away from responsibilities to the city were viewed as less than human. In fact, classical philosophers assumed it was impossible for persons to completely realize or actualize their unique potential if they refused to struggle for justice in the city. This means that, to be fully human, a person must participate in the political process, and this participation must be informed by the desire to create a just city. When injustice reigns, the prophetic voice of justice must be heard. Plato, Aristotle and the Jewish prophets never separated the inner quest for wisdom from the passion for justice in the political sphere; this separation is a problem of modernity. As we move beyond modernity, we must step beyond this fragmented way of looking at reality. When Christians reduce their faith to the private/church/sacred, and refuse to move into the realm of the public/state/secular, they prove how trapped they are within the cage of modernity.

Many writers realize we need to harmonize the inner-outer in a much deeper way, but at the present time, there are few who are actually doing this.[27] There are some, of course, who are trying to understand how a prophetic spirituality can come to be, but those who assume they have synthesized the two often lack depth and breadth in both the spiritual and the prophetic. Blake, as I mentioned above, realized that we are called to move towards the New Jerusalem, but he also realized the New Jerusalem was in seed form, in time and history. In this sense, he echoes the *Pater Noster* (thy kingdom come, thy will be done on earth as it is in heaven). The move from spirituality to political justice raises all sorts of dilemmas, but unless the move is made we will create a new gnosticism, though unlike the asçetic gnosticism of the past, it will be a bourgeois gnosticism. Bourgeois gnosticism turns inward in search of religious fulfillment while turning a blind eye to those who are suffering in time. Those who refuse to face the brutality of the world we live in while enjoying a life of inflated material advantage lack credibility when they talk about spirituality. The time is past when we can safely keep spirituality and political justice in two mutually exclusive spheres.

Simone Weil, a tough writer on spirituality, never separated spirituality from political justice. She wrote *Gateway to God* and *Waiting on God*, but she also wrote such political classics as *The Need for Roots* and *Oppression and Liberty*. She was a person who criticized Marxism and capitalism and pointed the way to a much older conservative political tradition, a tradition I might add that has little or nothing to do with the Neoconservatism (which is really Neoliberalism) of our time. Simone de Beauvoir said of Simone Weil, "Her heart would miss a beat for something that happened at the other end of the earth," and inscribed on her tombstone are these words: "My solitude held in its grasp the grief of others till my death." Simone Weil, like Dorothy Day,[28] was a woman deeply immersed in the Being of God, and both knew the price of holding in their grasp the grief of others. An authentic Christian spirituality must be willing to face the grief of others, be there to comfort those who mourn and ask serious questions about the causes of such grief.

The feudal world we live in is thick with inequalities. Let me cite a few statistics:

• 20% of the world's population (First World states) manage 65% of the world's income, while 70% of the world's population (Third World states) manage 17% of the world's income.[29]

• Two out of three people in the world are ruled by governments that torture and kill their citizens, and political opponents are held prisoner in more than half the countries in the world.[30]

• Fourteen million children under five die each year from hunger-related causes (40,000 a day).[31]

• 1.2 billion people (more than 20% of the world's population) live in a state of absolute poverty.[32]

• The money required to provide adequate food, water, education, health care and housing for each individual on earth would be about US$21 million a year. This is as much as the world spends on arms every two weeks.[33]

• There are 16 million refugees in the world today (2.3 million refugees

are Palestinians). Most of the refugees are women and children.[34]
· There are an estimated 16 million children working as "child slaves."
· The U.S. and Canada are moving further, in their aid and development programs, away from the 0.7% of GNP set by the UN. The U.S. is the lowest of the Western states at 0.24% of its GNP, while Canada has dipped under 0.43%. Most of their major recipients of aid are leading human rights violators, but because trade is lucrative, the human rights record of the recipient country is ignored.

The immediate response to such obvious inequalities is philanthropy, works of mercy and works of charity. We must never denigrate these important activities, but we must question whether aid and development organizations seriously address the structural inequities in our global village.[35] The social inequalities of our world order are inextricably related to the power interests of competing states and empires. Dom Helder Camera said, "When I feed the poor I am called a saint; when I ask why the poor are poor I am called a communist." Camera's statement can open an important door for us into the meaning of political justice.[36]

There are those who never get beyond works of mercy, but for those who keenly realize that this never deals with the deeper problems of structural injustice, the question of why the poor are poor must be asked. Shaw's *Major Barbara* pointed out a glaring flaw in the works of mercy approach. Dom Helder Camera's question opens up the issue of structural injustice. Unfortunately, those who criticize international capitalism or the Liberal International Economic Order (LIEO) are often called communists. This, of course, is a silly reaction, but we hear it all the time. Capitalism and communism, as ideologies, are equally brutal, although they are brutal in different ways. Those who wave the flag of either approach demonstrate how trapped they are within a modern paradigm of what constitutes the common good. Such people on both sides would do well to heed the insights of Simone Weil, Dorothy Day, Dag Hammarskjöld or the universal ethics of international law.[37] International law, at its finest, sets a universal standard for justice, and states can be judged on how they conform to such standards. When states sacrifice international law on the altar of security interests, they slip into a dangerous tribalism that usually crushes justice under the boot of militarism.

Augustine, in chapter four of book four of *The City of God*, said:
Remove justice, and what are kingdoms but gangs of criminals on a large scale? ... It was a witty and a truthful rejoinder which was given by a captured pirate to Alexander the Great. The king asked the fellow, "What is your idea, in infesting the sea?" And the pirate answered with

uninhibited insolence, "The same as yours, in infesting the earth! But because I do it with a tiny craft, I am called a pirate; because you have a mighty navy, you're called an emperor."

Augustine raises, in principle, the question of empires or states as authentic agents of justice, but in practice, Augustine was a firm and ready advocate of civil religion.[38] In this sense, Augustine stood outside the prophetic approach that is at the heart of Jewish religion, and he stands in striking contrast to John Chrysostom. It is somewhat amusing the way Augustine attempts to reconcile, in *The City of God*, the aims of the Roman empire with the Christian church. The fact that the Roman empire crucified his Lord, most of the early disciples, and many early Christians, never seems to have entered deeply into Augustine's Constantinian perspective. Yet in principle, Augustine is prepared to equate empires with gangs of criminals. Chrysostom saw much deeper into this issue, and he paid the prophetic price for linking principle and practice.

The search for justice in the political realm will take us to the center of state and empire power and the nature of national security. The prophetic attitude toward the state that we find in Daniel 7 and Revelation 13[39] will inevitably collide with the civil religion of modern bourgeois liberalism that walks uncloaked, so freely, within the house of Western Christianity. Modern Christianity participates so deeply in the liberal project that it is virtually impossible to distinguish between liberals, evangelicals, and fundamentalists on deeper and essential issues.[40] This social and political reality highlights how religious faith is shaped by the ethos it inhabits.

There is little question in our time that the American empire still sits on the throne, although Japan and the European community are mounting some of the marble steps. But, when the security interests of Western alliance states are threatened, ranks are closed and Third World states are kept in place; this is the lesson of the Middle East War of 1991.[41] The UN Charter, the Universal Declaration of Human Rights and the International Bill of Human Rights are soon dismissed when *Realpolitik* takes front stage. Unfortunately, most Christians either uncritically support the empire or state they are raised in, on substantial issues, or they react so strongly to civil religion that they slip into political ideology (which they confuse with prophetic religion).[42] All empires, states and liberation movements must be judged by divine standards; when this task is ignored, ruling elites of whatever ilk confirm Augustine's insights about kingdoms being gangs of criminals on a large scale.

I am always surprised by the violent reactions many people have to

Noam Chomsky.[43] I have read plenty of silly caricatures offered as serious criticisms of him, but I have yet to read a serious critique of his criticism of the American empire. Chomsky stands within the prophetic tradition in his view of the state, or in his case the empire, although his excessive attention to the horizontal forces him into a reductionistic and materialistic corner.

There is a danger, of course, when we deal with time and history, that we become confined to the horizontal, falsely assuming that politics and an altering of national and international structures will create a new and better world. The Social Gospel of the turn of the century and various forms of liberation and political theology share in this temptation, but the temptation of equating liberal bourgeois values with the kingdom of God is equally a problem. Bourgeois Christianity clings desperately to personal peace, security, property, possessions, and it is willing to sell its soul to the state to maintain the status quo of a feudal world order. It is too easy to criticize political positions that do not directly affect us. The beam in the eye of Western Christianity is a liberal bourgeois one, and until we are prepared to realize this and go to the divine physician to have it removed, we should be hesitant about taking the mote out of the eye of those we differ with.

Martin Luther King Jr. once said, "We shall have to repent in this generation, not so much for the evil deeds of the wicked people, but the appalling silence of the good people." The split that has played such a damaging role in the West in the last 500 years between public-private, state-church is being healed, but as the public square is being filled again by concerned religious people, many of these "good people" are quite silent on major issues of injustice, and they are apologists for civil religion. Kierkegaard's image of the wild goose settling into the barnyard, being fattened by all the delicious food of the farmer, speaks a haunting message if we remember that the wild goose is the symbol of the Holy Spirit in Celtic Christianity.

It is "the appalling silence of the good people" that is most frightening. Reports from groups like Freedom House, Human Rights Watch, Amnesty International and the UN development program go beyond the limited means of measuring a state's health by the GNP and the PQLI index. But, in our interdependent world, the connections that exist between states, and the means one state uses to support human rights violations within another state, need to be dealt with. The appalling silence of good people on the domestic and international scene needs to be faced.

We are in desperate need of a prophetic spirituality that is rooted in biblical thought and tradition. This prophetic spirituality must have an international and national focus, and it must be willing to criticize ideologies of the left, right and middle. A prophetic spirituality must stand on the boundary and speak the word of justice to all groups; it cannot be taken in by liberation, political or liberal bourgeois attempts to reduce the depth, breadth and height of the kingdom of God to some project or agenda. As we follow the wild goose, we will rise and fly, and in the process offer a new direction to those in the barnyard of the modern bureaucratic state.

Spirituality and the Church

Spirituality and the prophetic must meet again; as these two embrace and kiss, the church will be born anew. The church should always be in the process of reforming itself (*ecclesia semper reformanda*), and when it does this, mystics and prophets will find their place again in the body of Christ rather than being forced to the periphery of the church.[44] Authentic Christian spirituality must grow into a deeper understanding of the inner-outer life and the mystical union between Christ and the church and discern how these tensions are to make sense in the world of time, history, society, politics and our international global community.[45]

The marks of the church (*notae ecclesae*) must always be used as a plumb line to measure the authenticity of reform. When mystics, prophets, revivalists or renewalists minimize or ignore any of the marks of the church (one, holy, catholic and apostolic), we can be sure the unity Christ so longed for will be violated. Augustine, in his day, bemoaned the tragic fact that many loved to embrace the head of the church (Christ), but they drove daggers and knives into the vulnerable flesh of Christ's body (the church). A genuine prophetic spirituality will remind and recall the church to its markings. The markings of the church point the way, ultimately, to the mystical union between Christ and the church that Gregory of Nyssa described so compellingly in his sermons in *The Song of Songs*. When Christology is separated from ecclesiology, or when an ecclesiology ignores the marks of the church (*notae ecclesae*), we should feel a certain uneasiness.

A serious ecclesiology must also take into consideration the issues of church-kingdom of God, institutional church-mystical church, the church denominational-church local and the way the institutional church often marginalizes its contemplatives and prophets. I think it would be fair to say that a prophetic spirituality that dismisses the institutional church as irrelevant lacks depth, credibility, and authenticity. In sum, the tension that exists between prophetic spirituality and the institutional church must be struggled through in each generation, but there are markings by which the depth of that struggle can be measured and evaluated.

Spirituality and Jesus the Christ

Jesus the Christ, for the most part, has been tamed and domesticated in modern versions of Christianity. The Jesus who had no place to lay his head stands in stark contrast to his modern followers who have large houses, water beds, plump pillows and a couple of cars (the modern equivalent of horses and chariots). The Jesus who had few clothes is quite different from his modern devotees who have closets full of them. The Jesus who challenged the religious establishment of his day, an establishment that had a good working relationship with the Roman empire, has been converted in our day into a faithful friend of the G-7 nations. The cycle is complete; the Master has been mastered. Our seminaries are doing their best to outdo universities in their Faustian quest for knowledge; Jesus spent little time in such places in his day, and when he did he usually questioned much of the enterprise. Christian professors whose shelves are lined with books could learn much from the one who had few, but whom many books are written about. Modern Christians who proudly stand on the prow of Trident submarines and bless Stealth bombers don't seem to notice the inconsistency. Can we imagine Jesus on the prow of a Roman war galley?

J. Pelikan, in his classic book *Jesus Through the Centuries*, pointed out how the image of Jesus is shaped by time and history. Once we realize that our understanding of who Jesus is is shaped by the ethos we live in, we are less likely to be too confident of a simplistic interpretation of him. This means we should be cautious about using the name of Jesus too glibly. The Jesus that we meet in Scripture certainly lived a very different kind of life from most of his followers today. The cross that many wear around their necks was not a pleasant symbol in Jesus' day; a comparable symbol in our own day would be the hangman's noose or the electric chair. But the cross, like the one who was hung on it, has become a safe cultural symbol; the meaning it has today is almost opposite to what it once meant.

There are those in our pluralistic age who talk much about a Copernican revolution in religious thought. This, in interpretation, means Jesus is reduced to the level of great religious leaders like Moses, Muhammad, Siddhartha or an avatar in Hinduism. Such a position fails to take into account that when Jesus the Christ came into history, the Roman empire was pluralistic. Pluralism is not a new thing, and those who use it to relativize the claims of Jesus the Christ demonstrate how they have turned their backs on history. As we thread together a Christology that is indebted to the patristic formulations of Antioch, Rome and Alexandria, we will be in a position to meet the questions of our pluralistic global village. The tough historicism of Antioch, the mystical approach of Alexandria and the legal approach of Rome, when synthesized in a coherent way, can form a solid perspective.

If we claim that Jesus is Lord, we must be careful what we mean when we say this. The language of Christianity has been emptied of its substantive content, and the vessel has been filled with the thin waters of secularism. So, although the time-honored language is still used, it means something quite different today from what it once did. If we are going to proclaim that Jesus the Christ is Lord, we might just find ourselves challenging those who use the same language but mean something different by it. In short, the church needs to be converted, just as much as the world it is trying to convert. An authentic Christian spirituality must take up this daunting task of speaking to the church and the world; this can only be done when a prophetic spirituality defines the meaning of Christian spirituality.

Conclusion: Christian Spirituality Equals Prophetic Spirituality

Authentic Christian spirituality must face the imposing challenges of Nietzsche, Freud, Marx and Locke. The intellectual rigor of Nietzsche, the probing demands of psychoanalysis, the social vision of Marx and the soothing rationalizations of Locke have each, in their different ways, delegitimated Christianity as it has taken shape in the post-Reformation world.

Pietism falls to pieces when it is confronted by the tough questions and demands of some of the most thoughtful men and women of the modern world. But spirituality goes deeper, reaches higher and stretches broader than pietism. Authentic Christian spirituality takes us through the challenges of modernity rather than turning its back on them and walking away.

Authentic Christian spirituality is prophetic spirituality, and this type of spirituality, as it takes its bearings from the markings on all sides, will deftly avoid the temptations of asceticism and pietism.[46] Prophetic spirituality takes us ever inward, into greater and greater depths, and it moves us outward, to speak in an ever bolder way the message of the kingdom of God, a message that will confront the pretensions of all empires, states and liberation groups.

Authentic Christian spirituality is centered in our experience of union with the risen Christ, but the Christ of authentic Christian spirituality is quite different from the domestic Christ who is safely confined and enshrined in our churches and seminaries. The demands of Jesus the Christ will shake the foundations of Christianity, other religions and our larger society and world order. Our union in Christ will move us to love this world as Christ loves it, and this will mean comforting the afflicted and afflicting the comfortable.

New Age religion, which seems to challenge Christianity and other classical religions, should not be taken seriously; it is intellectually shallow and politically naive and it appeals to those who want the fruit of religion but do not want to be rooted in the soil that produces the fruit.

I have spent time at a few markings in this paper. There is, obviously, much more that needs to be said, but if the markings I have mentioned are heeded, the journey into authentic Christian spirituality will, I think, be more direct, because better directed. But the essential thing is not to linger at the markings; it is to get on with the pilgrimage. The markings merely point the way and confirm to us we are on the narrow path; they are not the destination.

Notes

[1] Huston Smith, *Beyond the Postmodern Mind* (London: Theosophical Publishing House, 1989); Alasdair MacIntyre, *After Virtue* (Notre Dame, Ind.: University of Notre Dame Press, 1984); Albert Borgamann, *Crossing the Post-Modern Divide* (Chicago: University of Chicago Press, 1992); Barry Cooper, *The Restoration of Political Science and the Crisis of Modernity* (Lewiston, N.Y.: Edwin Mellon, 1989); Pauline Marie Rosenau, *Post-Modernism and the Social Sciences: Insights, Inroads, and Intrusions* (Princeton, N.J.: Princeton University Press, 1992); Thomas Oden, *Agenda for Theology: After Modernity What?* (Grand Rapids: Zondervan, 1992).

[2] See Sven Stolpe, *Dag Hammarskjöld: A Spiritual Portrait* (New York: Charles Scribners, 1966).

[3] Lanza Del Vasto, *Return to the Source* (New York: Schocken, 1972). Bede Griffiths, *Return to the Centre* (London: Fount Paperbacks, 1978).

[4] Jaroslav Pelikan, *The Vindication of Tradition* (London: Yale University Press, 1984). There is an important sense in which tradition and modernity must be juxtaposed, but we must remember that tradition is not a monolithic block; tradition is thick with diverse and conflicting perspectives, and we can find almost anything somewhere in tradition. There is, of course, establishment tradition, but there is no reason that traditions that have been on the fringe or peripheral might not be more authentic. In short, when we go to tradition we need more than tradition to determine what has the most integrity within tradition; those who assert that tradition is the redemptive key beg all sorts of important questions.

[5] George Maloney, *Uncreated Energy: A Journey into the Authentic Sources of Christian Faith* (New York: Amity House, 1987).

[6] Paulos Mar Gregorios, *The Human Presence: Ecological Spirituality and the Age of the Spirit* (New York: Amity House, 1987).

[7] Anthony Ugolnik, *The Illuminating Icon* (Grand Rapids: Eerdmans, 1988).

[8] Vladimir Lossky, *In the Image and Likeness of God* (New York: St. Vladimir's Seminary

Press, 1974).

9 John Meyendorff, *The Orthodox Church* (New York: St. Vladimir's Seminary Press, 1981).

10 T. G. Wallace, *Our Debt to the Celtic Church* (London, Ontario: Sutherland Press, 1954). Christian Bamford and Will Marsh, *Celtic Christianity: Ecology and Holiness* (New York: Lindisfarne, 1986). Ron Ferguson, *Chasing the Wild Goose: The Iona Community* (London: Fount Paperbacks, 1988).

11 Women have played an essential role in the history of Christian spirituality from the beginning. The Mary-Martha paradigm, the role of Mary (Jesus' mother), of Monica (Augustine's mother) and of Macrina (Gregory of Nyssa and Basil's mother) are just a few examples of women determining the direction of Christian spirituality. Wisdom is, also, one of the highest virtues in spirituality, and this is seen as a feminine attribute. Women mystics have offered the Christian tradition rich insights: Hildegaard of Bingen, Julian of Norwich, Teresa of Avila, Mechthild of Magdeburg and Catherine of Genoa are just a few women who have played a pivotal role in forming the history of Christian spirituality. Those who insist that the Christian tradition is patriarchal do not know the tradition in much depth or breadth.

12 The classical notion of natural law and nature (*physis, natura*) takes into sacred consideration the issue of the environment. The environment is so essential in classical Christian thought that most theologians and contemplatives insisted that it is a mirror of God, and we can know something about God through the creation. Humans are a blend of *imago Dei* and *imago mundi*, and the fact that we are a part of the earth means when we damage it, we damage ourselves. Most contemplatives, beginning with Anthony and culminating in Francis, had a keen sense of affinity with nature. Those who argue that Christianity gave rise to a view of nature that reduces it to a thing or It to be manipulated and exploited do not realize that the West has not been Christian in any serious sense for the last 500 years. Christianity in the last few hundred years has become so secularized it has virtually nothing to do with its classical source. In short, Christian language is still used, but the substance is gone and all the meanings have changed to adapt to the expectations of modernity.

13 God, in any serious theological language, is viewed as Being itself (*ipsum esse*). Gender language, like animate and inanimate language, when applied to God, is metaphorical and must always be viewed as such or we reduce God to a human creation; this is the heresy of anthropomorphism that the early church criticized and people like Marx, Nietzsche and Freud have played an important role in pointing out. The Christian tradition of spirituality speaks about the affirmative way (*via positiva, cataphatic*) but it always checks and balances this tradition by the negative way (*via negativa, apophatic*). Those who do not understand the language of theology-spirituality usually end up saying rather foolish things and reacting in silly ways. Much of the modern debate about the Father-Mother nature of God fails to take into consideration that God is neither yet both; those who absolutize any metaphor or even try to balance metaphors inevitably create idols of one linguistic shape or another.

14 There is a danger of defining spirituality as a pure experience, detached from socialization, ethical concern or social-political responsibility. This reductionistic approach to spirituality must be firmly resisted. See A. C. Danto, *Mysticism and Morality: Oriental Thought and Moral Philosophy* (New York: Harper & Row, 1972); James Horne, *The Moral Mystic* (Waterloo, Ontario: Wilfred Laurier University Press, 1983).

15 Rudolf Otto, *The Idea of the Holy* (London: Oxford University Press, 1923).

16 R. C. Zaehner, *Concordant Discord: The Interdependence of Faiths* (Oxford: Clarendon, 1970); Frederick Copleston, *Religion and the ONE* (New York: Crossroad, 1982). Zaehner and Copleston have honestly and faithfully faced the issue of the relationship of Christian spirituality and the spirituality of other religions. They have pointed out in a consistent and convincing way why Christian spirituality is superior, but they have recognized truth, and important rays of truth, in other traditions of spirituality. The real challenge to authentic Christian spirituality does not come from New Age spirituality with its shallow

and simplistic perspective, but from Neotraditionalists such as Guenon, Schuon, Lings and Nasr. See Seyyed Hossein Nasr, *Knowledge and the Sacred* (New York: Crossroad, 1981).

[17] The ascetic techniques that were supposed to create the conditions for the perfect life in classical spirituality involved great effort and struggle, and they often created a dangerous form of praxis legalism that reduced the spiritual quest to a formulaic technique. The quest for certainty is always a seductive Siren in spirituality as in many other areas of life.

[18] See Bonaventura's *The Mind's Road to God*, chap. 3.

[19] Ron Dart, "Bonaventura and Spener: Two Notions of Renewal" (unpublished paper).

[20] The charismatic movement merely adds a few extra rooms to the house of pietism. Serious Christian renewal will only begin when the house of pietism is razed, and new foundation stones are put in place. Prophetic spirituality is the key to serious renewal; it will be resisted by the revivalists of the pietist-charismatic ilk, but this is to be expected.

[21] Richard Hardy, *Search for Nothing: The Life of John of the Cross* (New York: Crossroad, 1982).

[22] Nietzsche, Freud and Marx have done a superb job for Christianity; they have pointed out how our understanding of God is, for the most part, a projection of socialized desires. Any form of Christianity that has not faced the serious challenges of Nietzsche, Freud and Marx will be trivial, inadequate and probably idolatrous. When we make images of God that have little to do with God, we worship an idol; when we destroy and bury these images (anthropomorphisms) we will be in a position to be indwelt by the God of all creation.

[23] Paul Reps, ed., *Zen Flesh, Zen Bones: A Collection of Zen and Pre-Zen Writings* (New York: Anchor, 1930) 5.

[24] Benedict Groeschel, *Spiritual Passages: The Psychology of Spiritual Development* (New York: Crossroad, 1986). E. Erikson, A. Maslow and L. Kohlberg are also important people to consult in this area.

[25] The Christian view of history is not cyclical, evolutionary, revolutionary or romantic. We live east of Eden, and we are moving towards the New Jerusalem. We are called to proclaim and live kingdom values. This yet-not yet tension is historical yet points beyond history.

[26] Martin Heidegger and Hannah Arendt are examples of the polarization between the inner and outer. Arendt studied with Heidegger, but when he aligned himself with the Nazis, she saw, quite clearly, the failure of any philosophy or religion that was not in touch with history. She did her doctoral thesis with Karl Jaspers on Augustine and his view of love. Arendt came to see that Augustine, like Heidegger, lacked a keen sense of time and history, and this meant that both of them legitimated civil religion and became lapdogs of the ruling elite. Arendt, unfortunately, turned more and more to the political, to time and history rather than exploring how eternity and time and the transcendent and the horizontal interpenetrate. Elizabeth Young-Bruehl, *Hannah Arendt: For Love of the World* (London: Yale University Press, 1982).

[27] Thomas Merton's *Contemplation and Action*, Jim Douglass's *Contemplation and Resistance*, Elizabeth O'Connor's *Journey Inward Journey Outward*, Robert McAfee Brown's *Spirituality and Liberation* and Matthew Fox's *Creation Spirituality* are each in their own fashion trying to deal with this issue, but I do not think any of these attempts are successful in a meaningful or substantial way.

[28] Mel Piehl, *Breaking Bread: The Catholic Worker and the Origin of Catholic Radicalism in America* (Philadelphia: Temple University Press, 1982).

[29] Andrew Webster, *Introduction to the Sociology of Development* (London: MacMillan Education, 1990).

[30] Amnesty International Press Release, 28 May 1991.

[31] Douglas Roche, "After the Cold War: A New Approach to Global Security" (unpublished paper) 3.

[32] Ibid., 3.

[33] Jon Bennet, *The Hunger Machine* (Toronto: CBC Enterprises, 1987) 25.

[34] David Matas, *Closing the Doors: The Failure of Refugee Protection* (Toronto: Summerhill, 1989) 13.